HISTORY SAFARI™

by
Burt Cutler
&
Craig Strasshofer

published by

Educational Insights®

19560 South Rancho Way, Dominguez Hills, California 90220

Book Design:
Rick Irons

Contributing Authors:
Ellen Bradford
Robert Brennan Sr.
Andrea Cooper
Burt Cutler
Marie Kilbane
Henry Steddom
Craig Strasshofer
Willard Williams

Maps and Cartography:
Magellan Geographix (SM),
Santa Barbara, California

Illustrators:
Jeanni Brunnick
Dennis Carmichael
Gerald Fried
Shannon Hogan
Linda Ingber
Mandy Meng
Ivan Pavlovits
Leonid Rabinovich
Tim Scoggins
Craig Stephens
Lionel Talaro
C. Winston Taylor
Belgin Wedman
David Wenzel
Guiwei Zhao
Svetlana Zubelevitsky

Please retain this information.

EI-8510

PREFACE

The book you are holding is an unusual introduction to the study of world history. Its objective is to give you a broad understanding of some of the awesome events that have taken place and of the amazing people who have lived and died since humankind first appeared on the world stage.

It has been said that "those who do not study history are doomed to repeat it." Clearly, an understanding of the past is an important element in helping us evaluate people, ideas, and events as we plan our future. But most people are not historians, so how can we make history understandable and interesting? One feature of this book is a wealth of illustrations that encourage you to visualize history. As you read, look closely at the pictures. You'll find that sometimes a picture truly is worth a thousand words. As the chapters of history unfold, colorful maps provide a clear understanding of where the events took place, and timelines provide a picture of the interrelationships of events at different places and times. Finally, to add an element of serious fun, we've included a unique electronic quizzer that will help you remember what you read as you test yourself and measure your knowledge.

The most difficult aspect of writing this book has been in deciding what and what not to include. If it appears that we've placed less emphasis on the cultures of Asia or Africa than those of Europe and the Western world, it is not because the former are any less impressive or significant. Rather, it is in acceptance of the fact that the authors and most readers of this book are living in a Western culture. We hope that the historical overview presented here will encourage readers to learn more about the history of the non-western world by investigating the many books available on the subject.

This book is not intended to give a detailed analysis of any particular place or period of time. Nor does it present any new information or theories regarding the study of history. The writing of history has been going on for several thousand years. In fact it's very likely that your local library has on its shelves a copy of the world's first great history book, written by Herodotus more than two thousand years ago! And considering that literally thousands of books have been written about just one historical figure, Napoleon, it would be less than realistic to expect a single volume to provide a complete understanding of humankind's place in the world. But it is hoped that these pages will show how fascinating history can be and whet your appetite for more. Perhaps reading about history will become a regular and enjoyable part of your life. One day you may even decide to go to the library to check out the astounding things that Herodotus had to say!

TABLE OF CONTENTS

Chapter 1
Our Place in the Universe

Where do we earthlings fit in the universe?
Is there life elsewhere? How and when did it all begin? How many stars lie beyond the stars we can see in the night sky? In the last half of the twentieth century, scientists have amassed substantial proof that our universe began with a "Big Bang."

According to the Big Bang theory, fifteen billion years ago there were no stars or planets—no universe as we know it today. All matter and energy was tightly compressed into one chunk of hot gases. Then came the "Big Bang." The gases erupted in an indescribably massive explosion. In the first thirty minutes of time, all the original hydrogen and helium in the universe were formed and started moving outward in all directions at an incredible rate of speed. After about 100 million years some of the expanding gases began to cool, coalesce, and form clusters of stars.

When a star begins to form, gravity pulls the gases toward the star's center. As the gases are pulled inward, they pick up speed and their energy and temperature increase. After this goes on for twenty million years (!), the temperature becomes incredibly hot—enough to produce monstrous nuclear reactions. These nuclear reactions produce all the chemical elements, such as carbon, oxygen, iron, gold, and silver, along with tremendous bursts of light. All the light from every star, including our own sun, comes from nonstop nuclear activity!

The process of new stars being born (and very old stars dying) occurs continuously throughout the universe. That's how our own sun was formed over 4.5 billion years ago at the edge of a galaxy, or cluster of stars, that we call the Milky Way. Then the young sun spun off a blazing trail of cosmic gases and particles, which eventually formed nine planets, including Earth, orbiting around the parent star.

Our solar system, which includes the planet Earth, is part of an almost unimaginably huge universe. When we look up at the night sky we see hundreds of stars. Scientists have calculated that the mass of our galaxy, the Milky Way, is about 200 billion times that of an average star. That's how they conclude that there are about 200 billion stars in the Milky Way. And spread throughout the universe there are about ten billion galaxies! So how many stars are there in the universe? Only about 2,000,000,000,000,000,000,000!!! Incredible, isn't it? It's such a mind-boggling number that even most astronomers find it impossible to comprehend.

How do we know? Astronomy, the science that studies the stars, has made phenomenal discoveries since Galileo devised the world's first astronomical telescope almost four hundred years ago. Today astronomers use sophisticated instruments to measure not only the locations, but the relative motion of stars. They have found that all galaxies are moving away from one another. Using a wide array of scientific weapons—complicated computer programs, information gathered by satellites—they have established that these motions stem from the original Big Bang.

Galileo invented the world's first astronomical telescope over 400 years ago. With it, he saw four of Jupiter's moons.

We can't see them, but scientists are certain that many stars have their own planetary systems. In our solar system only one of the nine planets, our own Earth, has the right conditions to sustain life. It is the right distance from the sun (not too hot, not too cold, but just right!). It also has a protective atmosphere and the right combination of chemical components.

Is it possible that, with the many billions of trillions of stars in the universe, there's intelligent life in some other solar systems? Most scientists believe that it is not only possible but very likely. But the stars are so far away that it's doubtful whether we'll ever know for sure. For these authors that's most fortunate. Can you imagine what a job it would be to write the histories of *all* the many worlds?!

Earth went through many cataclysms during its first several billion years. Imagine the volcanic activity, the torrents of rain, the lightning and thunder, hurricanes, and earthquakes, as the molten ball of the new planet cooled and began taking shape, and its outer crust began to form.

The earth's crust is not a solid shell. It's actually divided into plates that move away from and toward one another. We know that during the past 600 million years there have been tremendous movements of continents, and new continents have been formed. This process continues even today. For instance, North America is moving away from Europe at a rate of 0.8 inches (2 cm) per year. The Himalaya Mountains were formed during the Cenozoic Era, as the subcontinent of India slowly smashed its way into southern Asia.

As these immense changes in landmass occurred, the seas rose and fell, shifting their locations many times. Mountainous areas were submerged and sea floors were pushed up and exposed. That's why fossils of sea creatures are often found in today's inland areas or on top of present-day mountains. And that's why fossils of tropical plants are often found in cold areas, or even under water, giving us a permanent record in rock of how the weather has been altered by the forces of change that still affect the earth.

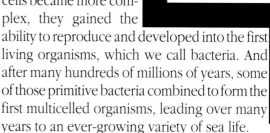

Trilobites have been on Earth for 600 million years. Their fossils are everywhere.

More than three billion years ago, conditions became just right to sustain *life*. The first simple molecules combined to form larger, more complex molecules. Eventually the first primitive cells were formed in the sea. As the cells became more complex, they gained the ability to reproduce and developed into the first living organisms, which we call bacteria. And after many hundreds of millions of years, some of those primitive bacteria combined to form the first multicelled organisms, leading over many years to an ever-growing variety of sea life.

A characteristic of living things—even the most elemental single-celled bacteria—is that they release oxygen into the space surrounding them. As the oxygen level built up high in the upper atmosphere, some of the oxygen turned into a special form of oxygen called ozone. Ozone prevents the sun's harmful ultraviolet rays from reaching the earth's surface. So about 350 million years ago, when a substantial ozone layer had been formed, living things could safely emerge from the oceans and begin to inhabit dry land. Primitive land plants produced even more oxygen, and the atmosphere became richer.

This was the beginning of the process that ultimately resulted in today's world. And it's still going on. Old species of animals and plants are dying out every year, and new species are coming into existence. There are actually many millions more species that have died off than there are species alive today. In fact, the animals that live on Earth today represent only 1 percent of the total number that have ever existed.

306 million years ago: Land masses formed one huge continent called Pangaea. Then they began to move apart.

160 million years ago: Pangaea split apart to form Laurasia and Gondwanaland.

20 million years ago: As the earth's crust kept shifting, the continents as we know them today were formed.

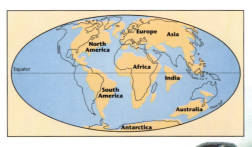

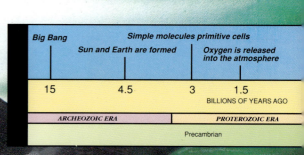

Big Bang	Simple molecules primitive cells	
	Sun and Earth are formed	Oxygen is released into the atmosphere
15	4.5	3	1.5

BILLIONS OF YEARS AGO

ARCHEOZOIC ERA	PROTEROZOIC ERA

Precambrian

8

The Early Paleozoic seas teemed with life.

During the Late Paleozoic Era, giant sea scorpions roamed the oceans, and the first land plants appeared.

During the Mesozoic Era, sharks appeared in the watery depths...

...and dinosaurs ruled the earth.

Trilobites	First fish (vertebrates)	Primitive plants inhabit dry land	First sharks	Giant ferns	Land masses form one huge continent Pangaea		Dinosaurs					
							Pangaea splits apart to form Laurasia and Gondwanaland	First birds	Grasslands		Continents as we know them are formed	

600   470   408   400   380   306   230   160   150   120   70   20

MILLIONS OF YEARS AGO

TODAY

EARLY PALEOZOIC				LATE PALEOZOIC		MESOZOIC ERA			CENOZOIC ERA	
Cambrian	Ordovician	Silurian	Devonian	Carboniferous	Permian	Triassic	Jurassic	Cretaceous	Tertiary	Miocene

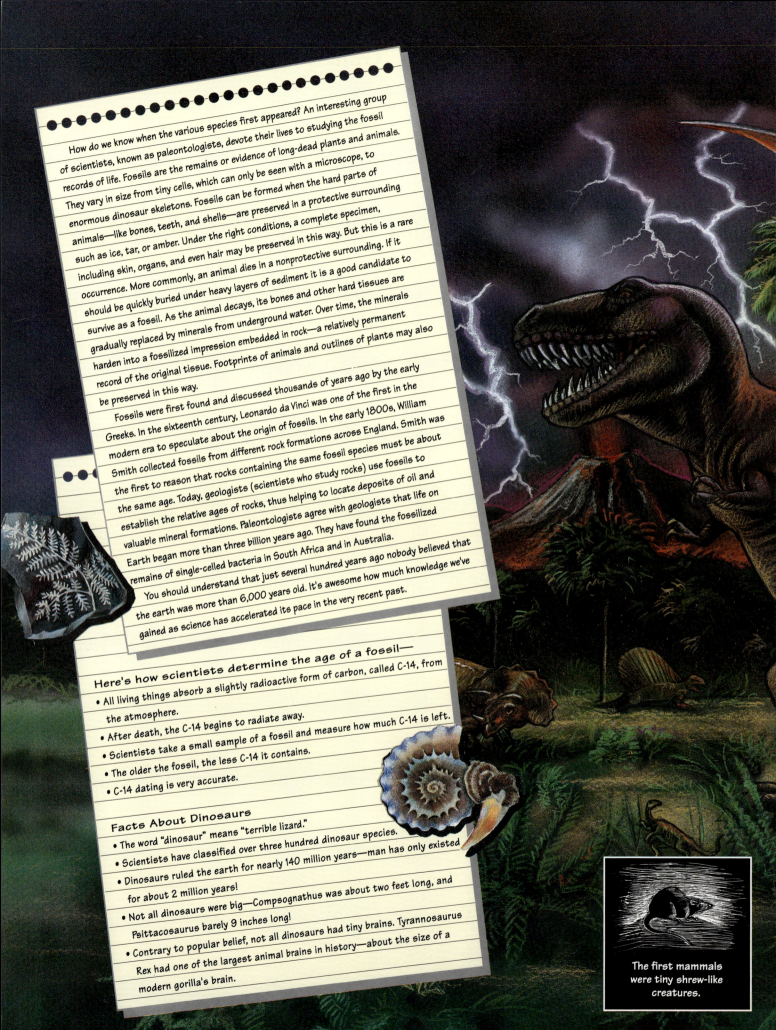

How do we know when the various species first appeared? An interesting group of scientists, known as paleontologists, devote their lives to studying the fossil records of life. Fossils are the remains or evidence of long-dead plants and animals. They vary in size from tiny cells, which can only be seen with a microscope, to enormous dinosaur skeletons. Fossils can be formed when the hard parts of animals—like bones, teeth, and shells—are preserved in a protective surrounding such as ice, tar, or amber. Under the right conditions, a complete specimen, including skin, organs, and even hair may be preserved in this way. But this is a rare occurrence. More commonly, an animal dies in a nonprotective surrounding. If it should be quickly buried under heavy layers of sediment it is a good candidate to survive as a fossil. As the animal decays, its bones and other hard tissues are gradually replaced by minerals from underground water. Over time, the minerals harden into a fossilized impression embedded in rock—a relatively permanent record of the original tissue. Footprints of animals and outlines of plants may also be preserved in this way.

Fossils were first found and discussed thousands of years ago by the early Greeks. In the sixteenth century, Leonardo da Vinci was one of the first in the modern era to speculate about the origin of fossils. In the early 1800s, William Smith collected fossils from different rock formations across England. Smith was the first to reason that rocks containing the same fossil species must be about the same age. Today, geologists (scientists who study rocks) use fossils to establish the relative ages of rocks, thus helping to locate deposits of oil and valuable mineral formations. Paleontologists agree with geologists that life on Earth began more than three billion years ago. They have found the fossilized remains of single-celled bacteria in South Africa and in Australia.

You should understand that just several hundred years ago nobody believed that the earth was more than 6,000 years old. It's awesome how much knowledge we've gained as science has accelerated its pace in the very recent past.

Here's how scientists determine the age of a fossil—

- All living things absorb a slightly radioactive form of carbon, called C-14, from the atmosphere.
- After death, the C-14 begins to radiate away.
- Scientists take a small sample of a fossil and measure how much C-14 is left.
- The older the fossil, the less C-14 it contains.
- C-14 dating is very accurate.

Facts About Dinosaurs

- The word "dinosaur" means "terrible lizard."
- Scientists have classified over three hundred dinosaur species.
- Dinosaurs ruled the earth for nearly 140 million years—man has only existed for about 2 million years!
- Not all dinosaurs were big—Compsognathus was about two feet long, and Psittacosaurus barely 9 inches long!
- Contrary to popular belief, not all dinosaurs had tiny brains. Tyrannosaurus Rex had one of the largest animal brains in history—about the size of a modern gorilla's brain.

The first mammals were tiny shrew-like creatures.

Quiz

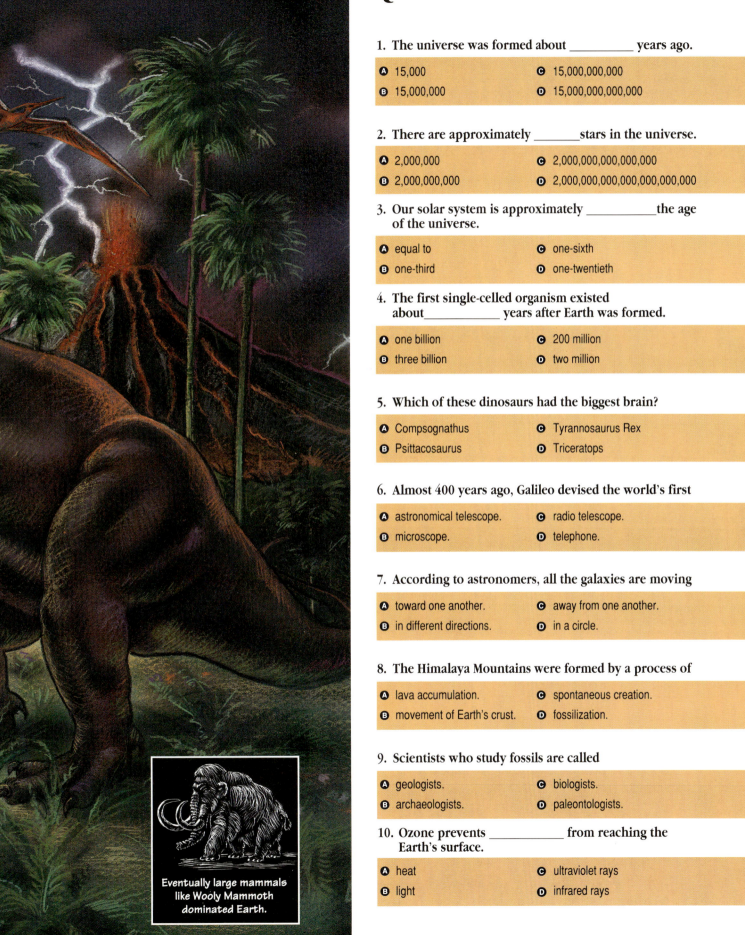

Eventually large mammals like Wooly Mammoth dominated Earth.

1. The universe was formed about _____ years ago.

Ⓐ 15,000
Ⓒ 15,000,000,000
Ⓑ 15,000,000
Ⓓ 15,000,000,000,000

2. There are approximately _____ stars in the universe.

Ⓐ 2,000,000
Ⓒ 2,000,000,000,000,000
Ⓑ 2,000,000,000
Ⓓ 2,000,000,000,000,000,000,000

3. Our solar system is approximately _____ the age of the universe.

Ⓐ equal to
Ⓒ one-sixth
Ⓑ one-third
Ⓓ one-twentieth

4. The first single-celled organism existed about_____ years after Earth was formed.

Ⓐ one billion
Ⓒ 200 million
Ⓑ three billion
Ⓓ two million

5. Which of these dinosaurs had the biggest brain?

Ⓐ Compsognathus
Ⓒ Tyrannosaurus Rex
Ⓑ Psittacosaurus
Ⓓ Triceratops

6. Almost 400 years ago, Galileo devised the world's first

Ⓐ astronomical telescope.
Ⓒ radio telescope.
Ⓑ microscope.
Ⓓ telephone.

7. According to astronomers, all the galaxies are moving

Ⓐ toward one another.
Ⓒ away from one another.
Ⓑ in different directions.
Ⓓ in a circle.

8. The Himalaya Mountains were formed by a process of

Ⓐ lava accumulation.
Ⓒ spontaneous creation.
Ⓑ movement of Earth's crust.
Ⓓ fossilization.

9. Scientists who study fossils are called

Ⓐ geologists.
Ⓒ biologists.
Ⓑ archaeologists.
Ⓓ paleontologists.

10. Ozone prevents _____ from reaching the Earth's surface.

Ⓐ heat
Ⓒ ultraviolet rays
Ⓑ light
Ⓓ infrared rays

Early hominids learned to cooperate and to make tools!

Chapter 2
Early Man

Paleontologists and anthropologists (scientists who study the origins, customs, and beliefs of humankind) have been working with increasing intensity over the past century to establish the origins of humanity. It is a fascinating field of study that is constantly evaluating new information. In the 1980s a new group of scientists, the microbiologists (scientists who study microscopic organisms), joined the quest. They believe that in a few short years they will be able to accurately date and place the origin of the very first human beings.

From the fossil record, scientists have established the following timeline. The first upright-walking creature to be classified as a "hominid" (member of the human family) was given the name *Australopithecus.* (*Austro* is Latin for "southern," and *pithecus* is Latin for "ape.") These characters roamed the earth about 3.75 million years ago. The first fossils of early man were discovered in the nineteenth century. They were dubbed *Homo erectus* (erect or upright man). In the twentieth century, fossils were found that were clearly predecessors of *Homo erectus.* Because some simple tools were found nearby, and because the designation *erectus* had already been used, this species was named *Homo habilis* (tool-making man). *Homo erectus* was followed in turn by *Homo sapiens* (wise man). The earliest version of *Homo sapiens,* *Homo sapiens neanderthalensis,* first appeared about 200,000 years ago. About 30,000 years ago, the first version of modern man, *Homo sapiens sapiens,* appeared. We know that *Homo sapiens neanderthalensis* vanished from the world stage at about the same time, but scientists are still speculating why that occurred.

To get a good picture of where and when humans appeared in the world, look at the map on this page. Early man, *Homo habilis,* first appeared in southern Africa (1) about two million years ago. Over a million years

ago, a more advanced species, *Homo erectus,* began to move out of that region. Fossilized remains of *Homo erectus* have been found in the Middle East (2), in Java (3), in Asia (4), and in Europe (5). The first *Homo sapiens* species, *Homo sapiens neanderthalensis,* was found only in Europe and the Middle East. *Neanderthalensis* dates to about 200,000 years ago. About 20,000 years ago, modern humans crossed over the then-existing ice connection between Asia and America to populate North (6) and South (7) America.

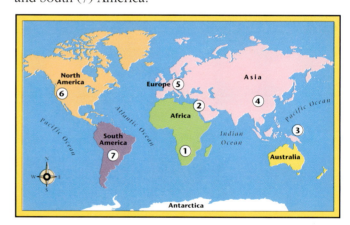

We know that *Homo sapiens* developed all over the world from *Homo erectus* predecessors. However, we do not know how *Homo sapiens* came to be differentiated into the wide divergence of physical and cultural types that we see in the world today. It is likely that adaptation to climatic differences and geographic location over long periods of time caused different groups of people to develop along slightly different lines. What we do know is that variations in physical characteristics or cultural behavior do not indicate any significant differences between the people of the world. It is pointless to think in terms of "inferior" or "superior" human groups, when history clearly shows us that mighty civilizations have appeared all over the world, and great things have been accomplished by every race of humankind.

Cranial Capacity in cubic inches (in³) and in cubic centimeters (cm³)

Chimpanzee
24 in³
(400 cm³)

Gorilla
30 in³
(500 cm³)

Homo habilis
45 in³
(750 cm³)

Homo erectus
(Peking man)
64 in³
(1,075 cm³)

Homo sapiens sapiens
81 in³
(1,350 cm³)

The shape of the human brain also differs from that of an ape. Sections of the brain affecting memory and information processing are much more developed in humans.

Today, even the term "race" is quickly losing its meaning as scientists learn that there are far more similarities among people than differences between them. Rigid division of humanity into groups with names like "Caucasoid," "Negroid," or "Mongoloid," based upon such superficial qualities as skin color or physical appearance, are now seen as having little or no value as we research our past and try to predict our future.

By about 10,000 years ago, early humans had wandered all the way to the tip of South America.

During the last ice age, primitive humans migrated all over the world.

THE AGRICULTURAL REVOLUTION

Four times during the past several million years the earth has witnessed "ice ages," periods of severe cold that turned vast areas of the planet into glacier-covered wasteland—forbidding, barren, and devoid of life. The most recent ice age began about 75,000 years ago. Much of Europe and Asia was freezing cold. As water froze, sea levels dropped, exposing land previously covered by water. These temporary land bridges allowed primitive peoples to migrate all over the world—from Korea to Japan, from mainland Europe to England, from Asia to North America. We know that by about 8000 B.C.E.* the descendants of the original Asians who crossed into North America had wandered all the way to Tierra del Fuego, the southernmost tip of South America.

Sometime between 10,000 and 12,000 years ago Earth started to warm up again. As the temperature increased, the great glaciers retreated toward the poles and the seas rose, covering the land bridges once again. Slowly, meadows and forests grew and animals returned to the once-desolate lands. The primitive peoples fol-

*Western cultures refer to the time before the birth of Christ as B.C. and the time after the birth of Christ as A.D. But since most of today's world is non-Christian, it is appropriate to find a universally acceptable alternative to this system. A growing trend replaces the designation B.C. with B.C.E. (Before the Common Era) and A.D. with C.E. (Common Era).

14

lowed, hunting the animals for their meat and skins, and gathering fruits, nuts, and berries from the bushes and trees. Thus we call these early people "hunter-gatherers." The temperate climate and plentiful supply of food allowed them not only to survive but to thrive—and to multiply. From an estimated world population at that time of five million people—despite the ravages of war, disease, and natural catastrophe—the human population has increased by a thousand fold. Today we number more than five *billion*!

What ignited this population explosion was the Agricultural Revolution—the earthshaking discovery of techniques for the planting and harvesting of grains. The first large farming communities developed about 8000 B.C.E. in the submountain areas between the Caspian Sea and the Persian Gulf, in an area called Asia Minor. Here wheat and barley grew wild, the seeds scattered by the winds. By observing the cycles of nature over long periods of time, the people

Early farmers probably made baskets of woven grass.

came to realize that they could control the food supply by gathering seeds and sowing them where and when they wanted. Eventually they learned to develop bigger and better crops by carefully selecting seeds that came from plants with the characteristics they found most de-

Paintings on rocks and in caves show that even the first humans were accomplished artists!

He may not look like a revolutionary, but this early farmer tending his crops is helping to change the world.

Storytellers passed knowledge from generation to generation.

The first tools were made from bone and stone.

sirable. In China the favored crop was rice. In Mexico it was maize, from which corn is derived. But everywhere the process was the same, as were the results.

Having tied themselves to the land and their crops, the people found it inconvenient to travel great distances on hunting expeditions. So in time they learned to domesticate certain animals. Now they had milk, meat, and wool to supplement the cereals they were growing. They were wanderers no more. Now they were farmers, and for the first time they understood what it meant to have permanent homes.

The Agricultural Revolution was certainly a revolution in terms of the enormous impact it had on the development of humanity. But it didn't happen overnight. Agriculture spread through Europe at an average rate of only one mile per year! It didn't reach England until about 4000 B.C.E. Ever so slowly this new way of life moved down from the mountains to the plains and the nearby major river systems. In Mesopotamia people learned to make trenches and ditches to divert water to their fields. Later, in Egypt and China, the problem was how to retain water during the dry season. The people overcame this challenge by learning how to build dams.

Pottery was molded by hand from coils of clay.

None of this was easily done. People found that they had better results when they worked together. Communities became larger, and the need for organization and leadership led to the development of rudimentary forms of government. Soon the settled villagers found themselves falling prey to the attacks of jealous outsiders. Clamoring voices cried out for protection and walls were built around the towns.

Larger communities and increasing levels of organization led to specialization of labor. Now, instead of every individual or family being entirely self-sufficient—doing everything by themselves—different people did different things. Initially, each person tended toward the type of work he or she was best at. The potter made pottery, the basketmaker wove baskets, and the toolmaker fashioned tools. Where more goods or crops were available than were required to meet the immediate needs of the community, the surplus became the basis for trade with neighboring settlements.

Hunters worked together to hunt large animals.

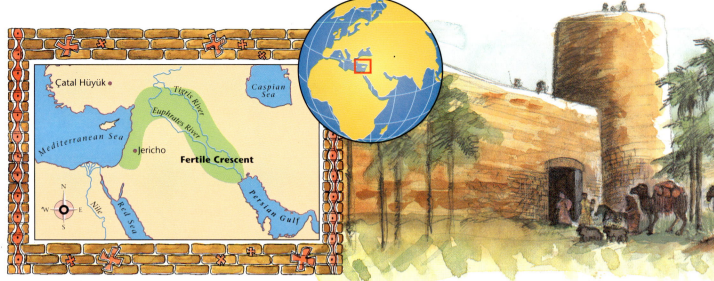

Around 8000 B.C.E., two of the earliest large towns were developed at Çatal Hüyük in Anatolia (present-day Turkey), and at Jericho near the eastern end of the Mediterranean Sea. *Archaeologists* (scientists who excavate and study the remains of early human cultures) have unearthed the remains of these towns. Thus we know that the inhabitants of Jericho built round houses of mud bricks. We know that they buried their dead under their houses. Thus we can conclude that the culture had risen to a relatively sophisticated level of religious or spiritual thought. Jericho grew larger as more people came to farm the fertile land. Many other people were envious of the wealth and stability of the town, and the danger from marauding nomads was ever-present. So Jericho surrounded itself with a great stone wall.

Never in all of history has a successful wall been built. Eventually the walls of Jericho came tumbling down, and the town was overtaken by invaders. After that the houses were built with square corners. Perhaps the new residents brought this new style of architecture with them, or perhaps the new way would have developed in spite of the invaders. Archaeologists and historians can only guess at questions like this. What do you think?

The people of Çatal Hüyük responded to the need for defense in a different way. They elevated their houses on stilts and platforms and used ladders to climb in and out through the roofs. Once safely inside, they could pull the ladders up behind them, keeping intruders out.

Jericho and Çatal Hüyük achieved a certain level of development and then progressed no further. Why didn't they go on to become the world's first great civilizations? It would seem that conditions favorable for limited grain production are not, in and of themselves, sufficient to support a society consisting of tens of thousands of individuals. More optimum conditions were to be found in

In Çatal Hüyük, the people climbed in and out of their houses through holes in the roofs!

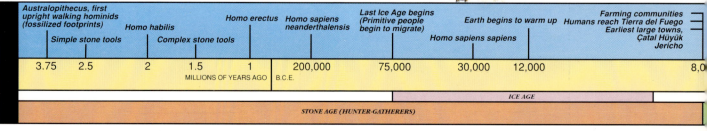

Australopithecus, first upright walking hominids (fossilized footprints)		Homo habilis			Homo erectus	Homo sapiens neanderthalensis		Last Ice Age begins (Primitive people begin to migrate)		Earth begins to warm up	Farming communities Humans reach Tierra del Fuego Earliest large towns, Çatal Hüyük Jericho
	Simple stone tools		Complex stone tools						Homo sapiens sapiens		
3.75	2.5		2	1.5	1	200,000	75,000		30,000	12,000	8,0
			MILLIONS OF YEARS AGO		B.C.E.						

ICE AGE

STONE AGE (HUNTER-GATHERERS)

Jericho grew into one of the world's first towns as people came to take advantage of its fertile location. But then, sometime around 700 B.C.E., the walls of Jericho "came tumbling down."

the fertile valleys of the Tigris and Euphrates rivers in Mesopotamia and the Nile in Egypt, where plentiful supplies of water and rich soil provided far greater potential for growth.

Thus, around 3600 B.C.E., in an area near where the Tigris and Euphrates empty into the Persian Gulf, there arose a great system of city-states known as Sumer.

Despite their careful research, there are some questions archaeologists are still striving to answer.

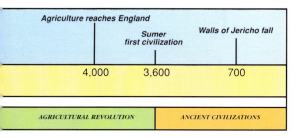

Agriculture reaches England

Sumer first civilization

Walls of Jericho fall

4,000   3,600   700

AGRICULTURAL REVOLUTION   ANCIENT CIVILIZATIONS

Quiz

1. The first hominid to appear on Earth was

Ⓐ Homo habilis.
Ⓑ Homo erectus.
Ⓒ Australopithecus.
Ⓓ Homo sapiens.

2. Hominids have been walking on Earth for approximately _____ of Earth's existence.

Ⓐ all
Ⓑ 1/100th
Ⓒ 1/1,000th
Ⓓ 1/10,000th

3. All human beings living today are members of *Homo sapiens sapiens*.

Ⓐ True
Ⓑ False

4. *Homo habilis* is Latin for "home-building man."

Ⓐ True
Ⓑ False

5. The volume of an average human cranial capacity is about _____ times that of a gorilla.

Ⓐ three
Ⓑ six
Ⓒ nine
Ⓓ twelve

6. The most recent ice age began about _____ years ago.

Ⓐ 75,000
Ⓑ 7,500
Ⓒ 750,000
Ⓓ 7,500,000

7. There are more than _____ human beings on Earth today.

Ⓐ five thousand
Ⓑ five million
Ⓒ five billion
Ⓓ fifty million

8. The Agricultural Revolution spread at a rate of about

Ⓐ one mile per year.
Ⓑ one mile per one hundred years.
Ⓒ one inch per mile.
Ⓓ one mile per decade.

9. Çatal Hüyük and Jericho were two of the earliest towns.

Ⓐ True
Ⓑ False

10. The walls of Jericho came tumbling down about

Ⓐ 1700 B.C.E.
Ⓑ 700 B.C.E.
Ⓒ 7000 B.C.E.
Ⓓ C.E. 700.

Chapter 3

The First Great Civilizations

Historians like to break history down into easy-to-handle chunks of time. The first piece of history we usually think of is called prehistoric, that is, the time before people began to keep written records. The Stone Age is what we call the several-hundred-thousand-year period of prehistory when humans roamed the earth as hunter-gatherers. Although we have no written records of the Stone Age, archaeologists tell us that many important advances were made by those early peoples. They learned to make and use tools and weapons of stone, they became the masters of fire, and they began to express themselves in language and in art.

About twelve thousand years ago, with the end of the last ice age and the advent of the Agricultural Revolution, farming communities began springing up all over the world, spelling the end of the Stone Age. Soon villages and towns appeared, some very sophisticated. But a scattering of villages is not quite a "civilization."

In order to qualify as a civilization, a social grouping must meet certain criteria over and above the establishment of relatively organized farming communities. In defining civilization, we look for a point at which all or most of the following have occurred: irrigation and fertilization are used in farming; the people have learned to make tools and jewelry from copper or bronze; advances in the arts and sciences have been made; a system of writing has been developed; mathematics and geometry have been put to practical use; and a common religion more complex than simple nature worship exists.

From the time that people first established farming communities, almost five thousand years passed before any of them began to display the earmarks of civilization. Archaeological evidence indicates that Sumer, which appeared in Mesopotamia around 3600 B.C.E., was the first true civilization in the world. Within the next five hundred years, the Egyptians more than matched the Sumerian achievements. The 2,500 years that followed saw a multitude of civilizations spring up all over the world.

How do we know exactly when a particular civilization began? In the case of the earlier civilizations, the dates can often be determined by carbon-dating of excavated remains. There might also be "king lists" written on clay tablets, or other written material that can be used

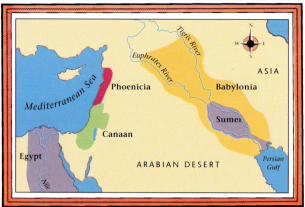

to confirm or supplement archaeological dating methods. As trade interaction between the various societies became more frequent, the people started keeping records of their business and finance. This information also helps us fill in the picture of these early civilizations.

During the three thousand years between 3600 B.C.E. and 600 B.C.E., the great ancient civilizations went through a period of almost constant change—rising and falling, expanding and shrinking, conquering and being conquered. Some appeared suddenly like a bright new star only to vanish just as suddenly from the face of the earth and from the pages of history. The many cultures of Mesopotamia, continually overrun by neighbors, fell only to rise time and time again with new characteristics, new ideas, and new developments. Babylonia was a dominant kingdom of Mesopotamia in 2000 B.C.E. It declined, rose, declined, and yet, by 600 B.C.E. it was again one of the mightiest empires in the region.

We have inherited much from those ancient peoples of thousands of years ago. They gave us the secrets of working with metals, laws to live by, governments to guide and protect us, art and religion to inspire us. And although they may seem as strange to us as creatures from another planet, it is clear from the remains of their writings, their art, and their daily lives that they were in most ways exactly like us. They worked hard to get ahead in business, government, or trade. They loved and fought as we do, enjoyed art and sport, and struggled to understand the world and their role in it. They wanted, more than anything else, the opportunity to provide for their families and to live good, simple lives, just the way we do today.

One thing history teaches us is that a major civilization seems to have a life cycle similar to that of an individual. Time after time a great society is born, matures, reaches a pinnacle of achievement, gradually loses its power, and finally fades away. Will this happen to our society, our culture? It's something to think about. But for now, our task is to see ourselves in the mirror of the past, not the crystal ball of the future. As you read on, ask yourself whether or not people have really changed that much since civilization first began.

The ziggurat of Ur towered over the city. As the people went about their everyday business they were constantly reminded of the gods.

Sumer—First in the Fertile Crescent

At first glance, the arid, windswept plain between the Tigris and Euphrates Rivers in modern-day Iraq might seem an unlikely place to have nurtured the tender shoots of the world's first civilized culture. Yet the soil was fertile, rich with the layers of silt deposited by the two mighty rivers over thousands of years. And an abundance of water was there, awaiting only the hand of humankind to put it to use transforming the bleak landscape into what some people think was the biblical Garden of Eden. The Greeks called the area Mesopotamia (the land between two rivers), and the civilization that grew there was called Sumer.

The native Semitic inhabitants of the region that we know as Sumer toyed with civilization for over a thousand years. They founded the villages that later became the majestic city-states of Sumer and achieved a relatively high degree of culture based on a settled agricultural economy. But it was the Sumerians themselves, an entirely different group of people whose original home was probably near the Caspian Sea to the east, who brought the culture of the region to full flower and created the civilization that bears their name.

As the Sumerians became the dominant people in the region, the existing communities gradually developed into cities, and then city-states. City-state is the name we give to a city with its own independent government and army, which grows so powerful that it can control the smaller communities around it. Among the most prominent city-states of Sumer were Lagash, Eridu, and Ur, close by the banks of the Euphrates. Biblical scholars had long believed that Ur was no more than a nomadic watering hole. But in 1854 the ruins of Ur were uncovered.

Much to the astonishment of the scholars and academics of the day, excavation revealed that Ur was a city of paved streets and large houses, many of them two stories high with as many as ten rooms. Ur thrived until the Euphrates shifted its natural course by about fifteen miles. The city and its people were left high and dry, and before long Ur was nothing more than a memory—abandoned to the ravages of the wind and the sand.

But that was much, much later. At first the Sumerians built their houses with the reeds that grew along the banks of the rivers (the Marsh Arabs who live in the area today *still* live in reed houses). Later they found they could construct sturdier houses with bricks molded from the alluvial mud of the rivers. The river mud was well suited to this purpose, since it dried hard in the sun.

Rising stark and vulnerable from the Mesopotamian tablelands, the cities of Sumer had no natural protection. So their inhabitants surrounded them with great walls to guard against invaders.

The Sumerians harnessed the water of the two rivers and sent it through canals to their crops and fields. This irrigation system was extremely complex but well worth the effort, since it immensely increased the size of their harvests. In time they designed dikes to hold back floodwaters during the rainy season and hydraulic systems to control the water supply.

The Sumerians were the first people we know of to domesticate sheep, cattle, and goats. We have learned from depictions in their art that they developed the wheel and used wagons pulled by wild donkeys. They even adapted their wagons for use as war chariots. And we know that their army was highly organized and regimented, fighting in close formation, armed with shields and long spears. You could say that they were just a little bit ahead of their time!

But they did not come by their success easily. Although Mesopotamia provided rich soil and plenty of water, it lacked many other resources necessary for the continued development of civilization. The land of the Sumerians was devoid of timber, metals, and even stone. How far could they have progressed without these vital materials? They could have thrown up their hands at the problem and satisfied themselves with their hardened mud bricks. Instead, they spread out in search of the

things they needed. They established trade relationships with neighboring peoples and built boats with which to ply the waters of the rivers and the sea. In this way an apparent obstacle to development became the impetus for a giant leap forward. Such is the nature of humankind.

Like that of all early societies, the religion of the Sumerians grew out of a need to explain and attempt to control the natural phenomena—both beneficial and destructive—that the people observed all around them. Sumerian religion involved the worship of a pantheon of greater and lesser gods and goddesses, each representative of some aspect of the natural world. The most important of the Sumerian deities were the protector gods and goddesses of the cities and villages. So important were these deities that a place was often referred to by the name of its god, such as the City of Enki, or the City of Inanna.

The priests of Sumer were almost as powerful as kings.

Central to each community was a shrine or temple where the native deity was

20

Sumer (Mesopotamia) first true civilization				
	Sumerians create writing system "cuneiform"		Sumer falls	
3600	3500		2000	
B.C.E.				
SUMER				
	EGYPT			

Sumerian war chariots were pulled by donkeys. Compared to the chariots of later cultures, they were clumsy and slow.

said to dwell, and to which offerings and gifts were brought. The temples were sacred places into which no ordinary mortal would dare venture. Only the priests, who acted as intermediaries between the mortals and the gods, were permitted access to the innermost holy of holies. As the only ones with access to the temples, they were also charged with taking care of the offerings that the people brought for the gods. More often than not, the priests ended up using the sacred offerings to line their own pockets and fatten their own bellies. Over time, the priestly class grew in power and wealth.

The temples, initially simple affairs built on raised platforms, evolved into enormous and elaborate monuments. The temples of the ancient Mesopotamian peoples were called ziggurats, and were probably the precursors of the pyramids of the ancient Egyptians. The increasing importance of the priests, and the growing complexity of religious worship and organization, led to advances in political and economic thought and practice. An extremely sophisticated governmental system became necessary for the maintenance of the physical structure of the temples and the administrative structure of the priestly class. The building of new temples

required large numbers of laborers and craftsmen. Large numbers of laborers and craftsmen needed supervision. Over time Sumerian society became stratified, with an upper class consisting of priests and political leaders, a middle class made up of merchants and artisans, and a lower class of common laborers. As the priests and rulers began to acquire excess wealth, they became patrons of the arts and sponsored the construction of ever more magnificent temples and buildings of all kinds.

The Sumerian city-states fought amongst themselves, and first one, then another might rise to a position of dominance for a time. But in those early days no single king was able to amass the power needed to establish an empire.

One of the first forms of writing! Symbols were pressed into soft clay with the end of a reed.

As Sumerian society became more and more complex, the need arose to find a way to keep records of the correct religious observances and the financial results of their trading endeavors. The ever-resourceful Sumerians responded to the challenge by inventing a system of writing. At first they contented themselves with drawing pictures on soft tablets of clay, which when dried in the sun became permanent records. In time they simplified the process so that the pictures became *symbols* which stood for things, rather than recognizable *images* of the things themselves. They imprinted the symbols into the clay with the wedge-shaped ends of reeds. The Latin word for "wedge" is *cuneus*, so the writing is called cuneiform.

More symbols were created as the need arose, and soon there were enough to allow the Sumerians to move beyond the simple recording of basic facts and figures to the construction of complete sentences. Thus was born the world's first literature. This, the invention of writing, is perhaps the most important of the famous firsts that can be attributed to the Sumerians. During the next two thousand years, other Mediterranean peoples picked up the Sumerian cuneiform system and adapted it to suit their own purposes. Many *thousands* of Sumerian clay tablets have been found by archaeologists in the last one hundred years. Their writing system, containing 350 symbols in all, has been deciphered, giving us detailed knowledge of the lives of these ancient people.

Observing the movements of the celestial bodies, searching for messages from the gods, the Sumerians became accomplished astronomers. Striving constantly to build ever more ambitious ziggurats and palaces, they developed sophisticated methods of surveying and construction. Finding themselves overwhelmed with the task of keeping track of financial matters, they invented the abacus, the earliest form of computer in the world! Concerned with maintaining peace and stability in their growing society, they established the world's first codified system of law and legal procedures.

They introduced silver as a medium of exchange and created a system of weights and measures to determine its value. (Coins with assigned monetary values would not come into existence for another several thousand years.) In addition to developing a decimal (base 10) counting system like ours, the Sumerians developed a base 60 counting system. This may seem like a peculiar way to approach mathematics, but in fact, our 60-second minute, 60-minute hour, and 360-degree circle are derived from the Sumerian counting system developed five thousand years ago!

Most of the Sumerian people were farmers. Attuned to the rhythms of nature and the seasons, they plowed their fields, maintained their irrigation canals, sowed their seeds, and reaped their harvests. By and large, women were charged with the task of maintaining hearth and home, but they had some basic legal rights (the right to hold property, to engage in business, to serve as a witness, to obtain a divorce), which gave them considerable status in the community. Slaves—either war captives or impoverished fellow citizens—did many of the hardest or most unsavory chores. Even slaves, though, were allowed some opportunity to better their lot: they could conduct business, borrow money, buy their freedom, and even marry a free person, thus guaranteeing the freedom of their offspring.

Artisans and craftsmen designed jewelry, worked with precious stones, and designed and built houses, temples, and boats. Boys who came from well-off families could even go to school. They learned to read, write, and do arithmetic. Successful students might become scribes and keep records for wealthy merchants, or they could work for the priests or the king's administrators.

Today the Tigris and Euphrates rivers empty into the Persian Gulf almost a hundred miles away from their exits of six thousand years ago. The "land between the rivers"—the modern-day nation of Iraq—is important not only for its vast oil resources, but for the incredible wealth of archaeological treasure that lies waiting to be discovered beneath the ever-shifting sands.

22

Sumerian students were harshly punished for poor performance.

Bowls held wet clay which was molded into tablets for writing.

The ancient Egyptians worshiped the light of Re, the almighty sun god.

Egypt—Gift of the Nile

Even before the beginning of recorded history, the Egyptians came up with a way, if not to tame, then at least to control the mighty Nile River. We call this technique basin irrigation. They divided the land up into low-lying basins, separated by earthen walls and connected by a series of canals and reservoirs. Floodwaters were held in the basins long enough to fertilize the land, and any excess was channeled off into the reservoirs. Over time, the need to develop and maintain this complex irrigation system led to the formation of larger settlements and a more centralized form of government. Ultimately the entire region coalesced into two kingdoms: Lower Egypt, centered around the low Delta lands, and Upper Egypt, the more mountainous region to the south.

Around 3100 B.C.E., King Menes of Upper Egypt conquered Lower Egypt and united the two kingdoms. Thus began the first recorded dynasty of the most cohesive unified nation-state the world had ever known. (A dynasty is a succession of rulers of the same family or ancestral line.) The Egyptian kings acquired the royal title Pharaoh, meaning "the Great House." The power of the pharaohs was such that they came to be thought of not only as absolute rulers, but as living gods.

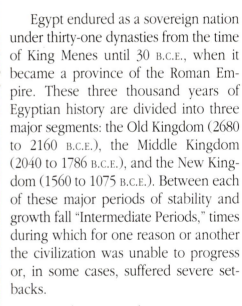

Egypt endured as a sovereign nation under thirty-one dynasties from the time of King Menes until 30 B.C.E., when it became a province of the Roman Empire. These three thousand years of Egyptian history are divided into three major segments: the Old Kingdom (2680 to 2160 B.C.E.), the Middle Kingdom (2040 to 1786 B.C.E.), and the New Kingdom (1560 to 1075 B.C.E.). Between each of these major periods of stability and growth fall "Intermediate Periods," times during which for one reason or another the civilization was unable to progress or, in some cases, suffered severe setbacks.

From the very earliest times, it was the practice of the Egyptians to bury kings and royalty in rectangular brick structures called mastabas. This remained the custom until around 2700 B.C.E., the beginning of the Old Kingdom. Pharaoh Djoser, the first pharaoh of the Third Dynasty, decided that his tomb would be the most glorious that anyone had ever seen. He enlisted the aid of his royal architect, Imhotep, and they set to work. The result was a six-tiered step pyramid—the first stone structure in the land—rising some two hundred feet above the desert floor. It still stands today. Imhotep, the brains behind Egypt's first pyramid, was so revered that he was elevated to the rank of a minor deity. The success of Pharaoh Djoser's pyramid set off a tremendous era of

23

pyramid building. The Pharaohs who came after Djoser went to enormous lengths trying to outdo their predecessors in the grandeur of their tombs. More than *seventy* pyramids were built over the ages.

The most famous of them all is the Great Pyramid of Giza, just outside the modern city of Cairo. It was built in about 2500 B.C.E. by the Pharaoh Khufu. This incredible monument, almost 500 feet high with each side over two football fields long, is by far the largest structure of any kind to be built before modern times. In ancient times the Great Pyramid and its two smaller companions were covered with polished white limestone. With the white-hot desert sun glinting off their polished sides, they must have looked like huge mirrors flashing out of nowhere, visible for miles around!

Next to one of the pyramids at Giza is a huge figure of a lion with a human head. This figure, called a sphinx, was a favorite monumental structure of the ancient Egyptians, and *thousands* of such statues rose up out of the desert sands. The giant sphinx at Giza was originally covered with plaster and painted with bright colors. Today the colors have long since worn away, and most of the nose is missing—used for target practice by Napoleon's army when it invaded Egypt in the 1800s.

The construction methods used to create the pyramids and other megalithic monuments of ancient Egypt continue to be foremost among the great mysteries of the ages. Archaeologists estimate that as many as 100,000 laborers, supervisors and planners would have been employed in building the Great Pyramid of Khufu over the course of twenty years. The Great Pyramid is made of more than one million blocks, each block weighing on the average two and a half tons. It would have taken ten men to drag such a block along level ground and twenty to pull it up the ramps they must have used. The blocks were somehow cut with such perfect accuracy that it is impossible to see daylight, or even slip a razor blade, through the cracks between them. How these ancient peoples achieved this degree of precision no one knows.

The Old Kingdom ended around the year 2160 B.C.E. with the reign of Pepi II, the last king of the Sixth Dynasty. Pepi II is said to have ruled for ninety-four years, and it is likely that the weakness of this aged pharaoh led to the breakdown of Egyptian society which characterized the First Intermediate Period. With the declining power of the centralized authority came a time of infighting among the local rulers, or nomarchs, as they struggled with one another to seize the pharaoh's throne.

The confusion in the land lasted for 120 years, until the mighty King Mentuhotep reunited Lower and Upper Egypt and began what is known as the Middle Kingdom. Mentuhotep set about the task of rebuilding and even expanding Egyptian society with vigor and enthusiasm. He made military expeditions into Syria, Lebanon, and the Sinai, and devoted special effort to subduing Nubia, a powerful neighbor to the south. He took full advantage of his role as all-powerful god-king to finance his dreams of foreign conquest and expansion.

Since the very beginning of the pharaonic system, the kings and nobility of Egyptian society had grown wealthy off the sweat and toil of the common people. They collected enormous tax revenue—crops from the farmers, and trade goods of all kinds from the merchants. Everything of value in the land was ultimately the property of the pharaoh. Pharaohs sat on thrones covered with gold and wore golden head-dresses, golden sandals, and even false golden beards. When King Tut's tomb was opened in 1922, archaeologists were shocked at the splendor they found inside. King Tut's coffin was made of solid gold and contained

Tutankhamen, the boy king

a golden death mask that revealed his beautiful facial features.

In addition to being by far the wealthiest citizen of the nation, the pharaoh was considered to be a god. This gave him incontestable authority in all things. The ancient Egyptians worshiped a large and bewildering collection of gods and goddesses, making first one, then another, preeminent at various times in their history. The gods were portrayed sometimes as humans, sometimes as animals, and often as a fascinating combination of both. One of the chief gods was Re, the sun god. His importance can be understood when you consider that the sun shines virtually every day in Egypt. Three other important Egyptian deities were Anubis, the judge and protector of the dead, who was often depicted as a jackal or a jackal-headed man; Thoth, the god of wisdom and truth, who had the head of a bird; and Osiris, the story of

25

100,000 workers labored for twenty years to build the Great Pyramid. No one knows for sure how they did it.

Isis

Horus

Hieroglyphics cover the walls of the tomb. They tell about Pharaoh's life.

Servants carry food, weapons, clothing and jewelry. Pharaoh will have what he needs for his journey to the land of the dead.

26

whose death and resurrection came to symbolize the yearly flooding and recession of the river. As time went on, the sacred animals that represented the gods became objects of veneration in their own right. Most important were crocodiles, bulls, birds such as falcons and eagles, and cats. Large cat cemeteries have been found throughout Egypt. One at Thebes contains the mummies of hundreds of thousands of cats!

The people of ancient Egypt did not view death as the end of existence, but as a transition from this world to another, in which the life of the deceased person would go on very much as it always had. Generally speaking, they enjoyed life and expected to go on enjoying life in the next world. They believed that after death a person's spirit continued to hover near the physical body. So it was of the utmost importance that the body remain in good shape lest the spirit become homeless (Wandering spirits could be dangerous!). In the early days the dead were buried in shallow pits, and the hot air and sand were sufficient to dry and preserve the bodies for hundreds and, in some cases, even thousands of years. But as the Egyptian people grew in sophistication, they developed a more effective way of preserving the bodies of the dead, a process we call mummification.

boat of the dead

Mummification was a major improvement over the naturally occurring preservation that took place in the arid desert environment. First, the internal organs were removed. The corpse was soaked in a preservative for about two months and then dried, stuffed with straw and rags, and wrapped in strips of linen that had been coated with a sticky substance.

The pharaohs and the nobility were mummified with great care and laid to rest in beautifully decorated vaults. Because of the Egyptian belief that the afterlife would be much like life on Earth, the deceased were entombed along with their most treasured possessions, which might include jewelry, furniture, weapons, their favorite pets, and sometimes even slaves. In some cases an entire *ship* might be carefully disassembled and placed in the tomb for use in the next world. Huge quantities of food and drink were left in the tomb to nourish the dead person during the voyage to the land of the dead.

By the time of the reign of Queen Sebeknefru, the last pharaoh of the Twelfth Dynasty, Egypt's reputation for wealth, prosperity, and power was so great that foreign adventurers began to contemplate the possibility of conquering the great kingdom and making it their own. Thus, ironically, it was the very success of Egyptian cul-

Following behind are Horus, the sky god, and Isis, the mother goddess.

A priest, wearing the jackal-headed mask of the god Anubis, makes final preparations to the mummy.

Osiris

Pharaoh

ture during the Middle Kingdom that brought about its downfall and led to the dark and violent times of the Second Intermediate Period.

Unlike the First Intermediate Period, a time during which local Egyptian rulers fought for control of the kingdom, the Second Intermediate Period is characterized by the appearance of foreign conquerors in the land. Foremost among these were the Hyksos (Shepherd Kings), Asiatic tribes who had over time established themselves in the Delta area. By the time of the Second Intermediate Period the Hyksos had become powerful enough to take control of the entire nation, founding a dynastic line that would rule for almost two hundred years. But Hyksos rule was resisted by a powerful group of native Egyptians based in the city of Thebes. There was constant conflict between these two groups until, around 1555 B.C.E., the Thebans drove the Hyksos interlopers out of the country (not before adopting many Hyksos' weapons and ways).

The New Kingdom commenced with the expulsion of the Hyksos and the reuniting of Egypt under King Ahmose, the first pharaoh of the Eighteenth Dynasty. Ahmose's imperial aspirations led him to make several

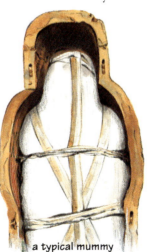

a typical mummy

military campaigns into Nubia and Cush in the south. Later pharaohs continued the militaristic tradition begun by Ahmose until, by the reign of Thutmose III in 1504 B.C.E., Egypt had established an empire that extended into Syria, Lebanon, Palestine, and the Mesopotamian plains.

Thutmose III was a great military leader. The story of his sixteen successful military campaigns is depicted on the walls of the temple at Karnak. Unfortunately for Thutmose III, during the early years of his reign he had to share the leadership of the country with his older stepsister, Hatshepsut. In fact, at one point the ambitious and scheming Hatshepsut took control of the throne completely and had herself crowned king. The story of her "divine birth" is depicted on the walls of her mortuary temple, where she is portrayed as a man. For twenty-two years she reigned with a firm hand, and Egypt prospered under her leadership. The temple she erected at Thebes is today considered one of the finest examples of Egyptian architecture.

It was only after Hatshepsut's death that Thutmose III was able to assume full control of the throne and forge his reputation as an empire-builder. Near the end of his reign, apparently out of anger at the way she had treated him in his youth, Thutmose III commanded that Hatshepsut's name be eradicated from all monuments and removed from all written records. Nonetheless her name and her story have survived.

During the Eighteenth Dynasty, under Pharaoh Amenhotep III, Egyptian civilization reached its peak. Its empire extended from Mesopotamia in the north to Nubia and Cush in the south. Its art and architecture were unsurpassed. Its culture was the envy of the ancient world. Nefertiti, the wife of Amenhotep's son Akhenaten, was acknowledged to be the perfect ideal of what a woman should be. Her beauty and regal dignity live for us in one of the most famous existing works of Egyptian sculpture. Notable among the kings of the Nineteenth Dynasty was Ramses II, who reigned for sixty-seven years and sired more than one hundred children. Today, four colossal statues of Ramses II stand as eternal and silent guardians of the temple he erected at Abu Simbel in honor of his most favored wife, Nefertiri (Nefertiti lived about one hundred years before Nefertiri).

Nefertiti

Ramses II and his wife Nefertiri.

We know much about the exploits of the pharaohs from their almost obsessive practice of recording the details of their lives in stone. But what about the daily comings and goings of the ordinary people? How did they dress? What did they eat? What were their dreams and their desires?

In the hot, dry climate of Egypt, it was not necessary to wear very much clothing. Most of the time, men and women wore short skirts made of linen, tied in front like a loincloth. On special occasions, women wore long pleated linen skirts with shoulder straps. Dressed in this fashion, a well-to-do Egyptian woman might go to dinner at a friend's house, where she would be considered impolite if she did not eat and drink until she felt sick. Just like today, the quality of the linen used in clothing depended on the wealth of the wearer. The finest and most costly linens were so light and comfortable that they were almost transparent. The poor laborer, on the other hand, would usually wear a simple loincloth made of animal hides or coarsely woven plant fibers. For lunch he might have three loaves of bread, two jugs of beer, and a couple of raw onions.

Egyptian men and women were extravagant in their use of jewelry, which they wore both to enhance their beauty and to invoke magical powers. The quality of the bracelets, necklaces, earrings, hair ornaments, and headdresses with which they bedecked themselves gave some indication of the class and wealth of the individual. Priests and other dignitaries often shaved their heads, and the rich never appeared in public without a cloth headcovering that hung to their shoulders, or some other type of wig or headdress.

The Egyptians were known to be among the world's cleanest people. They bathed several times a day and rubbed their bodies with many kinds of oils and perfumes. Egyptian women were the first to use lipstick, and they started the custom of painting their fingernails and toenails red. They also stained the palms of their hands and the soles of their feet. Men and women alike were accustomed to using heavy blue eye makeup. One trick of the beautiful people of ancient Egypt which thankfully has not survived through the ages, was that of wearing a cone of animal fat soaked with perfume on the tops of their heads. As the sun melted the fat, it dripped down into their hair, emanating a delightful fragrance.

How do we know so much about these ancient people? The answer to this complicated question can be found, like a secret code, hidden in three simple words: the Rosetta stone.

28

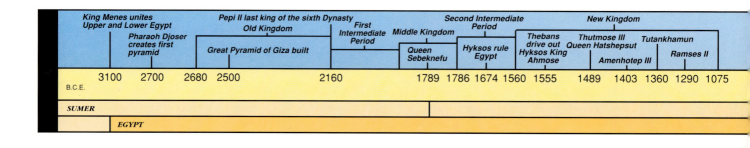

				Pepi II last king of the sixth Dynasty		First Intermediate Period		Middle Kingdom	Second Intermediate Period			New Kingdom			
	King Menes unites Upper and Lower Egypt			Old Kingdom							Thebans drive out Hyksos King Ahmose	Thutmose III Queen Hatshepsut		Tutankhamun	
		Pharaoh Djoser creates first pyramid		Great Pyramid of Giza built			Queen Sebeknefu		Hyksos rule Egypt				Amenhotep III		Ramses II
	3100	2700	2680 2500		2160		1789	1786	1674 1560	1555		1489	1403	1360	1290 1075
B.C.E.															
SUMER															
	EGYPT														

In 1799, a large flat stone with three sets of inscriptions was found at the Egyptian town of Rosetta. The Rosetta stone had one set of inscriptions in Greek, another in Egyptian hieroglyphics, and the third in an abbreviated hieroglyphic form called hieratic. By comparing the Greek writing, which was understood, to the two forms of the Egyptian system, scholars were able to break the code of the hieroglyphics and open the door to the detailed knowledge of ancient Egyptian culture that we possess today. The story of the twenty-year search to break the Rosetta stone "code" would make a book in itself. And in fact, many books have been written about this fascinating scientific quest.

With the end of the New Kingdom around the year 1075 B.C.E., Egypt's days as a sovereign empire were numbered. Egyptian society was weakened and drained of its resources by a succession of invasions. In the ninth century, Egypt fell briefly to its southern neighbors, the Ethiopians. In the sixth century, the Persians overtook the country. The Macedonian Greek conqueror Alexander the Great occupied the country in 332 B.C.E. His respect for Egypt's heritage was such that he permitted Egyptian pharaohs to continue to rule the nation, although they were now in a position of subservience to the ultimate authority of Greece. After Alexander's death his general, Ptolemy, founded the Ptolemaic Dynasty which ruled Egypt for nearly three hundred years. Finally in 30 B.C.E., in spite of the desperate maneuvering of Egypt's most notorious ruler, Queen Cleopatra, Egypt was subjugated by Julius Caesar. No longer a mighty empire, the land of the Nile, of the pyramids and the Sphinx became a province of the Roman Empire—its shining star faded from the world scene.

The Rosetta stone gave the French scholar Champollion the key to Egyptian hieroglyphics.

Ethiopians invade Egypt
Persians invade Egypt
Alexander the Great invades Egypt
Egypt becomes Roman province

| 900 | 600 | 332 | 30 |

Quiz

1. Which of the following is not necessary for civilization?

Ⓐ irrigation and fertilization Ⓒ a complex religion

Ⓑ use of copper or bronze Ⓓ a large standing army

2. Major civilizations seem to have a life cycle similar to that of

Ⓐ humans. Ⓒ plants.

Ⓑ solar systems. Ⓓ atoms.

3. The Sumerians were the first to develop farming communities.

Ⓐ True Ⓑ False

4. Which of the following was not a characteristic of Sumerian religion?

Ⓐ many gods and goddesses Ⓒ temples called ziggurats

Ⓑ belief in a single god Ⓓ Their priests were wealthy

5. Which of the following was not a prominent Sumerian city-state?

Ⓐ Lagash Ⓒ Ur

Ⓑ Eridu Ⓓ Thebes

6. Egyptian civilization grew in the valley of the _____ River.

Ⓐ Tigris Ⓒ Nile

Ⓑ Euphrates Ⓓ Yellow

7. The first king of the First Dynasty of Egypt was

Ⓐ King Sargon. Ⓒ King Menes.

Ⓑ King Minos. Ⓓ King Hammurabi.

8. The Great Pyramid at Giza was built by

Ⓐ Pharaoh Djoser. Ⓒ the architect Imhotep.

Ⓑ Pharaoh Khufu. Ⓓ Queen Cleopatra.

9. The Giant Sphinx at Giza was damaged by the armies of

Ⓐ Julius Caesar. Ⓒ Napoleon.

Ⓑ Alexander the Great. Ⓓ Sargon.

10. Three important Egyptian deities were

Ⓐ Anubis, Thoth, and Osiris. Ⓒ Zeus, Apollo, and Athena.

Ⓑ Enki, Astarte, and Baal. Ⓓ Brahma, Vishnu, and Shiva.

This boat has just returned from a trip to Egypt. The sailors are eager to get home to their families. But first they must unload the cargo.

Dolphins play in the harbor and follow the boats as they come and go! Many of the wall frescoes include dolphins in their designs.

Crete—Island of Light

The island of Crete floats like a solitary diamond sparkling on the deep blue waves of the Mediterranean Sea. In prehistoric times farmers sailed their tiny boats to this beautiful island. Isolated and alone for hundreds of years, their descendants were free to develop a way of life all their own. The culture of ancient Crete is called Minoan, after the mythical King Minos who is said to have ruled there. A famous legend tells of a terrible monster, half-bull and half-man called the Minotaur, which lived in a labyrinth, or maze, below King Minos' palace. Only the hero Theseus could find a way into the labyrinth, kill the Minotaur, and escape with his life. Although the truth of this legend is doubtful, many wondrous Minoan sites have been identified and excavated.

Beginning around 3000 B.C.E., Crete started to grow as a trading center. Its boats carried lumber, oil, and obsidian gathered from nearby lands to the mighty empires of Egypt and Mesopotamia, and returned home with the products of those distant and exotic places. The Minoans also made contact with the young cities of India and Asia. They gained knowledge from their neighbors and soon discovered bronze, a stronger metal than any known before. They made their pottery by hand, for the potter's wheel was still unknown. Gradually the people moved away from their tiny villages along the coast and built towns and cities in the center of the island.

The Minoan people learned quickly, and by 2500 B.C.E. Crete had practically monopolized the sources of tin (an important ingredient in the making of bronze) in the Mediterranean area. They became prosperous by

The volcano has been asleep since long before anyone can remember. They say it will never wake up again.

The Palace at Knossos is so beautiful! The frescoes are so bright they seem to be alive!

Almost every boy and girl on the island wants to be a fearless bull-leaper. They are the greatest athletes in the land!

Even the birds love the sound of the double flute when the king's musicians play!

These pots are full of wine and olive oil. You can see the olive trees and vineyards on the hills behind the palace.

trading this valuable metal along with their lumber and oil, their pearls and rare spices. They soon surpassed their neighbors in the art of working with metal, as well as in other arts and sciences. By 2000 B.C.E. a mature and impressive civilization had developed on the island, but our knowledge of it is limited by the fact that their system of writing remains a mystery to us.

During the period from 2000 to 1500 B.C.E. Minoan civilization continued to grow and develop, until it rose to heights of splendor and glory that rival any civilizations that have come and gone in the past four thousand years. The Minoans built palaces of two to five stories with sophisticated plumbing and drainage systems. Trade goods and the bountiful harvest of the many farms were kept in the palaces and then distributed to the people. In this way the rulers controlled the lives of their citizens and assured that nothing would go to waste.

Many heroic tales are told of the terrible man-bull monster that lived in the royal labyrinth below King Minos' palace.

The walls of the palaces were covered with bright frescoes bathed in sunlight shining in from central courtyards. The remains of the great palace of Knossos are awe-inspiring even to our modern eyes. Its corridors and staircases were supported by tapering wooden columns that seemed to reach into the sky, and its inhabitants could brag of their tiled baths, running water, and flush toilets. Built of expertly crafted stone, the palace's intricately decorated walls attested to Cretan ways of life and religious beliefs.

It is likely that the colorful and highly stylized Cretan paintings of the time were influenced by the art of the Egyptians. But otherwise the flow of Minoan culture continued to follow its own distinct path. Paintings and statues that have been unearthed depict Cretans engaged in a dangerous sport known as bull-leaping. Daring young men and women somersaulted between the horns of a charging bull! It's possible that this may have been the origin of the modern sport of bullfighting.

Bull-leaping may also have been a way in which Cretans paid homage to their gods. Although they believed in many gods, the Cretan people primarily worshiped a Mother Goddess, in whose honor they performed beautiful dances. One legend tells how the craftsman Daedalus made a special dance floor for the princess Ariadne.

The double-bladed axe was an important religious symbol, although we do not know its exact significance. It appears frequently as a decoration in frescoes and on various objects, and real axes have also been discovered.

Crete prospered and profited from its position as trading center of the Mediterranean world, and it seems that even the common people were able to live with some degree of comfort and luxury. Ordinary houses were decorated and enlivened with frescoes and other ornamentation. Besides wheat, barley, vegetables, and grapes, the farmers grew large quantities of olives. Oil from crushed olives became a staple of Cretan cooking. Since the Minoans lived close to the sea, fish was an important part of their diet. The fish were probably grilled on sticks over a fire.

Crete became a commercial giant during this time, establishing trading centers all along the coast of mainland Greece. The city of Troy, famous for the story of the Trojan Horse, may have been a Cretan trading post. The distinctive decoration of Minoan pottery is so easy to identify that we can trace the progress of Cretan traders by the presence of their pottery throughout the Mediterranean. Egyptian tomb paintings record the visits of Cretan traders. Often they are shown holding objects similar to those actually found at Minoan sites. No doubt the Cretans were daring sailors. In ancient times, the sailors of the mighty King Minos were said to be the rulers of the Mediterranean Sea.

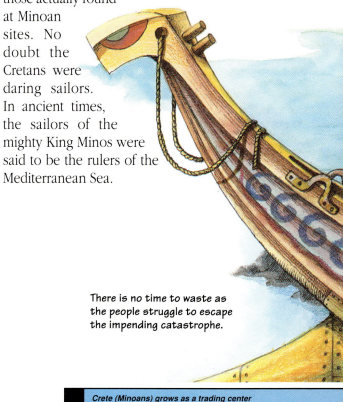

There is no time to waste as the people struggle to escape the impending catastrophe.

Crete (Minoans) grows as a trading center			
Crete monopolizes the source of tin			
Crete grows into a civilization			
3000	2500		2000
B.C.E.			
CRETE			
			HEBREWS

32

Some seventy miles north of Crete lay the small and sparsely populated island of Thera. Around 1500 B.C.E., a gigantic volcanic eruption blew much of Thera away. The houses were completely buried under a thick layer of lava and ash. Crete also sustained enormous damage from the great waves, earthquakes, and showers of debris that followed in the wake of the explosion of nearby Thera. As a result, Achaean invaders from the mainland of Greece soon were able to take over Crete. The great palace and other structures at Knossos, already damaged by the natural catastrophe, were probably completely demolished by these Achaeans in 1450 B.C.E. Three centuries later a new wave of Greek-speaking people called Dorians obliterated what little remained of Minoan culture, and Crete, the island of light, went dark, never to shine again. Today Crete is the largest of the many eastern Mediterranean islands that are part of Greece.

The wise ones were wrong! The volcano is awake! Already lava flows down the hillside like the boiling blood of an angry god!

volcanic eruption of Thera

Achaean invasion of Crete

1500   1450

PHOENICIA

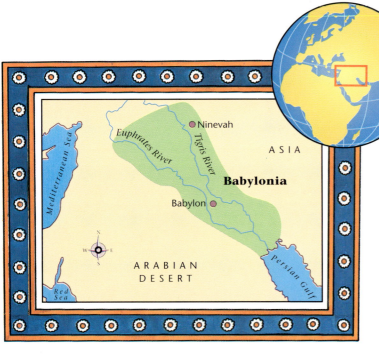

Hammurabi's army enforced the laws and conquered enemies!

Babylonia—Laying Down the Law

By 2350 B.C.E. the early city-states of Sumer were already well-developed, nourished and nurtured by the life-giving waters of the Tigris and Euphrates rivers. But in that year they were overwhelmed by Semitic conquerors from northern Mesopotamia, led by King Sargon of Akkad. Legend has it that, as an infant, Sargon was found in a basket floating on the Tigris River. (This story was created over a thousand years before the story of Moses being found in a basket!) He became a favorite of the king of Kish. Then when he grew up, he overthrew the king and took his place. We know that Sargon built a capital city called Akkad, but its site has not yet been discovered.

Sargon created an army the likes of which the world had never seen before. In the past, armies had been gathered together for short periods of time—a few weeks or months, or for the duration of a war. Rulers would force farmers to leave their fields and take up arms. When the fighting ended, the farmers who were still alive would return to their fields. Sargon changed that by establishing a standing army of professional soldiers. With that army, Sargon devastated the city-states of Sumer. Sargon's army was like a whirlwind appearing suddenly over the horizon. It completely destroyed many Sumerian cities. One Sumerian wrote that after Sargon's army attacked a city, "...even the birds could find no place to build their nests." In time Sargon's army conquered and united all of Mesopotamia. Thus Sargon is remembered as the founder of the world's first empire.

The Mesopotamian lands held attraction for all the surrounding peoples—where else could one find such a rich natural farming area? So it is not surprising that the Sumerians' unique position could not last. Around 2000 B.C.E., a people called the Amorites settled in Mesopotamia. They built their capital city on the banks of the Euphrates River. They called it Babylon, and they called themselves Babylonians.

Archaeologists have learned that Babylon was one of the greatest cities of the ancient world. It contained some of the most beautiful temples and palaces ever constructed. They were decorated with blue glazed bricks and pictures of mythical beasts. People would gaze about in wonder as they entered the city through huge bronze gates. Near the center of the city stood the Tower of Babel mentioned in the Bible. Not far from the tower were the famous Hanging Gardens of Babylon, built by a Babylonian king for his wife, who yearned for the beauty of her homeland in the mountains. These gardens were

With its blue tiles and gold trim, the Ishtar gate invited visitors into the city.

Under Hammurabi's code this doctor's hand is being cut off for the crime of causing a patient to die. He'll be more careful next time!

Hammurabi's code governed trade and made Babylon a good place to do business.

considered by ancient writers to be one of the Seven Wonders of the World.

Babylonia at the peak of its glory was an empire that included most of Mesopotamia. It was ruled by a king called Hammurabi. Hammurabi set up a strong government to run his vast empire. He sent officials far and wide to carry out his orders. They collected taxes, took charge of repairing dikes and dams, and supervised the digging of canals and the building of roads. Under the mighty King Hammurabi, a code of ethics and law was formulated and put into use. It is known as the Code of Hammurabi.

Here, in 1550 B.C.E., for the first time anywhere, there were laws to deal with almost every aspect of life. The Code of Hammurabi was the most complete law code known up to that time. It included nearly three hundred laws that dealt with marriage and divorce, property and business, taxes, wages, loans, military service, and many other areas of life. The Code also listed punishments for anyone who broke a law. Although they were created to protect the rights of private citizens, some of Hammurabi's laws may seem harsh to us. For example, if a surgeon performed an operation that caused the death of a patient, the surgeon's hand was cut off. Another law said that if an architect built a house that collapsed and killed its owner, the architect would be put to death. Harsh or not, Hammurabi's code was an important achievement. It gave all the people of the empire the same set of laws and the laws and punishments were written down for all to see. The laws of modern nations stem from this first set of legal guidelines, established over 3,500 years ago.

The people of Mesopotamia worshiped many gods and goddesses. Hammurabi made his god, Marduk, the most powerful god in all the land. Each year the victory of Marduk over the sea monster, Tiamat, was celebrated at the New Year Festival. Many Babylonian myths and legends survive today. Some became the source of stories from other religions with which we are more familiar.

One Babylonian story sounds very much like the Bible story of Noah and the ark. It says that once the gods were angry with humans and decided to destroy them in a great flood. They warned one good man, Ut-napishtim, to build a boat. The flood came and everything was destroyed except Ut-napishtim's boat, which came to rest on a mountain. He sent birds out, but they could find nowhere to settle. Finally, a raven was sent out and it did not return. This meant the earth was beginning to dry out. Ut-napishtim and his family gave thanks to the gods for having been saved.

The Epic of Gilgamesh is thought to be the first piece of literature ever written. In this story, Gilgamesh was the proud king of Uruk. His pride angered the gods and they sent a half-beast, half-man called Enkidu to destroy him. But after fighting, Gilgamesh and Enkidu became friends. They had many adventures, but then Enkidu was killed.

Ut-napishtim survived the flood that cleansed the world of sin.

Afraid of death for the first time, Gilgamesh went to visit Ut-napishtim, who had the secret of eternal life. The secret was a plant that grew at the bottom of the sea. Gilgamesh dived and plucked it, but on his way home it was eaten by a snake as he slept, so he did not achieve immortality!

In many ways the Babylonians were happy to learn from the people they conquered. They used Sumerian writing, adopted the Sumerian calendar, and built their cities like the Sumerians had. They also used the Sumerian number system. But in mathematics the Babylonians improved on the work of the Sumerians. The Babylonians developed the first multiplication and division tables and they used geometry to measure their fields and lay out boundary lines.

After Hammurabi died, the Babylonian empire collapsed. New invaders from the north and east moved in. With no natural barriers to keep invaders out, the flat plain of Mesopotamia lay open to such attacks. By 1530 B.C.E. a nomadic people known as the Kassites had overwhelmed Babylonia. Their leadership and influence were weak, and little or no cultural advancement took place during their reign.

The Hittites invaded Babylonia in about 1525 B.C.E. The Hittites came from Asia Minor and spoke an Indo-European language. They became the first people to learn how to process iron ore using a heating process called smelting. They brought the Iron Age to the Mediterranean world, starting a revolution in weapon making as earthshaking as that caused by the introduction of war chariots in previous centuries and of bronze in still earlier times. Yet by 1200 B.C.E. the Hittite empire, like so many before it, was crumbling, and Babylonia was conquered by another people, the Assyrians. Although the people and culture of Babylonia vanished from history, their far-reaching ideas about law and justice have survived and have given us guidance in creating the rules for our own society today.

36

The Assyrian conquerors of Babylonia inherited a legacy of greatness from their Sumerian predecessors.

Phoenician ships ventured where none had dared go before!

The Phoenicians and the Hebrews—The Wanderers

Constantly moving between the settled civilizations of the ancient world, like bees spreading pollen from one flower to another, were two important groups of Semitic nomads: the seafaring Phoenicians and the desert-wandering Hebrews.

THE PHOENICIANS

With the decline of Cretan civilization, the Phoenicians became the chief sea power of the Mediterranean. Originally nomadic tribes from the Sinai desert, by around 1100 B.C.E. the Phoenicians had built a number of city-states along the rocky eastern coast of the Mediterranean. Phoenicia was a narrow strip of land about one hundred miles long squeezed between the mountains of Lebanon and the shore. The region was inhospitable to agriculture, so the Phoenicians turned to the seas. They quickly grew to become wealthy seafaring traders.

The forests of the Lebanon Mountains, lush with cypress, fir, and cedar trees, provided Phoenicians with wood for ships. Timber was a vital building material, and it was scarce in most of the Middle East. So it became an important article of trade for the Phoenicians.

The Phoenicians were not warriors. They hired soldiers from other lands to do their fighting. Phoenician cities had splendid harbors and strong defenses. The greatest of them were Tyre, Sidon, and Byblos. Tyre was built on a rocky island just off the Phoenician coast, a location that made it virtually invulnerable to attack. According to the Bible, Tyre was a city of "perfect beauty."

The Phoenicians applied their energy to becoming the greatest seafaring traders in the ancient world. They learned to use the stars to navigate, and they mapped sea routes. This made it possible for them to be the first to sail beyond the sight of land. The Phoenicians sailed where no other people dared to go. Their ships, powered by oars and sails, journeyed to every corner of the Mediterranean and beyond. They reached the coast of Spain and then ventured beyond the Strait of Gibraltar into the Atlantic Ocean. They explored the west coast of Africa. Around 600 B.C.E. they may have sailed around the southernmost tip of Africa.

Phoenician ships carried the lumber from the forests of Lebanon to Egypt, Greece, and other lands. The ships returned to Phoenicia laden with silver from Spain, tin and copper from England, ivory from Africa, pottery from the island of Rhodes, and gold, iron, oil, figs, and wine from the lands of the Aegean. Wood was not the only valuable Phoenician trade good. The Phoenicians also became experts in manufacturing and working with glass. Craftspeople produced beautiful glass bottles, cups, and beads. Phoenicians also traded wool and linen cloth, iron goods, furniture, and jewelry.

But the most precious of all Phoenician resources was a rare dye used to color cloth. The dye was made from the shells of murex snails, which lived only along Phoenicia's rocky coast. Thousands of snails had to be boiled and processed to produce just a tiny bit of dye. Thus, the dye was very costly. Named for the city of Tyre, it was called Tyrian purple. It could be used to dye cloth an astonishing range of colors, from pastel pinks to deep purples. The Phoenicians grew wealthy trading the purple cloth. Royalty throughout the Mediterranean world draped themselves and their palaces with fabric of Tyrian purple. Eventually the color purple came to stand for power and wealth, and it has been the color of royalty ever since.

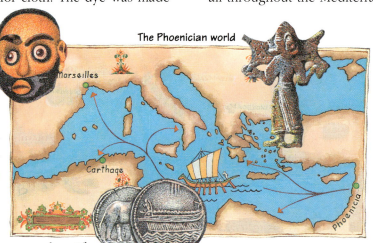

The Phoenician world

As the Phoenician merchants spread out across the Mediterranean, they set up trading posts in Spain, Africa, and other lands. The trading posts made long voyages easier. Ships could stop at the posts for fresh water and supplies before setting off for more distant lands. In time some trading posts grew into colonies. The largest colony was Carthage, near the modern city of Tunis in North Africa. Legend tells us that it was founded in 814 B.C.E. by the Phoenician princess Dido. When Dido landed on the coast of North Africa, she asked the local ruler for land on which to build a city. He graciously granted her only as much land as could be covered by one ox hide. Cleverly, Dido had the hide cut into very thin strips so she could mark off a large area of land. Eventually Carthage

grew to be a mighty kingdom of its own. Other important Phoenician colonies were Marseilles in France, and Cádiz in Spain. The colonies paid taxes to the Phoenician homeland. In this way the great Phoenician city-states of Tyre, Sidon, and Byblos grew rich and strong.

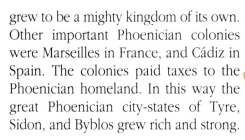

The Phoenicians are not known for developing an original culture of their own. They were experts at picking out and adopting the best of the art and religion of the peoples they visited in their travels. In this way they helped spread civilization all throughout the Mediterranean. The Phoenician traders carried the skills, knowledge, and culture of the Middle Eastern cultures to people living in other lands.

They did, however, come up with one original idea that has stood the test of time—the alphabet. At first the Phoenicians probably used both the Sumerian and Egyptian systems of writing. But those complicated systems with their hundreds of symbols were hard to learn. The Phoenicians created a simple alphabet of twenty-two letters. In fact, the word "alphabet" comes from their first two letters: aleph and beth. Many modern alphabets, including our own, are based on the Phoenician alphabet.

The Phoenicians maintained a close relationship with their neighbors to the south, the Hebrews. We know that Ahab, a Hebrew king, married Jezebel, a princess of Tyre, and that Phoenician craftsmen helped build a temple for another Hebrew king, Solomon. In the eighth century B.C.E. both the Phoenicians and the Hebrews were conquered by the Assyrians. Phoenicia became a part of the Babylonian, and then of the Persian empire. But even their conquerors respected the Phoenicians' knowledge of the seas—the Persians used Phoenician warships to fight great sea battles against the Greeks.

38

Did the Phoenicians discover America? This Phoenician-looking face appears on a drinking cup found in Guatemala!

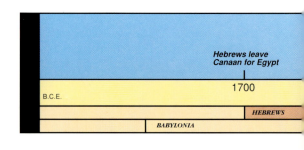

Hebrews leave Canaan for Egypt

1700

B.C.E.

HEBREWS

BABYLONIA

THE HEBREWS

"Hear, O Israel, the Lord our God, the Lord is One."
— Deuteronomy 6:4

Those words are from the Bible. They were spoken by Moses over three thousand years ago. Moses was speaking to the people of Israel. His words sum up the most important precept of Judaism: the belief that there is only one God. The belief in only one God is called monotheism. The Hebrews, or Jews, were the first society to practice this sophisticated religious idea.

The story of the Hebrews is written in the Old Testament of the Bible. It was written by a group of Jewish rabbis from tales that had been passed along orally for many centuries. The Bible says that a man named Abraham was the father of the Hebrew people. Abraham was a herder who may have lived near the Sumerian city of Ur. In the Mediterranean world most people believed in many gods. There were gods of death and gods of the sun and rain. But the Hebrews believed in only one God, and they longed for a homeland where they could worship in peace. The Old Testament says that God made an agreement with Abraham, telling him and his followers, "Leave your own country, your kinsmen and your father's house and go to a country that I will show you." There, God promised to make the Hebrews into "a great nation." So Abraham and his people packed up their belongings and struck off into the wilderness.

Even in our earliest records, there are references to tribes who wandered the edges of the Mesopotamian deserts with their flocks and herds. Such people are called nomads. The nomads carried all their belongings on the backs of donkeys. Sometimes nomads were able to settle among the farmers they encountered in their travels, but if too many arrived, the locals drove them away. Among the wandering tribes were the Hebrews.

Abraham and his followers moved into the land of Canaan, along the east coast of the Mediterranean Sea, just south of Phoenicia. The Hebrews farmed and herded in Canaan. But around the year 1700 B.C.E., drought struck Canaan. Crops and animals died. People were without food. So the Hebrews left Canaan and began their wanderings anew, in search of greener pastures—food for their livestock and for themselves. They headed for Egypt.

For a while they lived peacefully among the Egyptians along the Nile River, where food was plentiful. But eventually they were made slaves by the Egyptian rulers. Sometime between 1300 and 1200 B.C.E., a Hebrew leader named Moses (the Great Lawgiver) stood up to the Pharaoh Ramses II, and led his people out of Egypt. The Bible describes this movement out of Egypt in the Book of Exodus. According to the Hebrew scripture called the Torah, for forty years the Hebrews wandered the Sinai desert. Moses climbed up Mount Sinai to pray. The Bible says that he received two tablets of stone from God on which were written ten rules, or commandments—a code of civil and religious conduct. The Ten Commandments became the basis of the Hebrew religion, which today we call Judaism.

The first commandment says that people must believe in only one God: "Thou shall have no other gods before me." The Ten Commandments also tell how people should act toward each other. It is wrong to steal, the commandments say. It is wrong to kill. It is wrong to dishonor your father and mother. The Hebrews were the first society to look upon hurting others as a sin.

The Hebrews believed that God had made a covenant, or bargain, with them. They promised to honor the commandments and devote their worship only to God. In return, God would protect the Hebrews, and the land of Canaan would be theirs for all time.

39

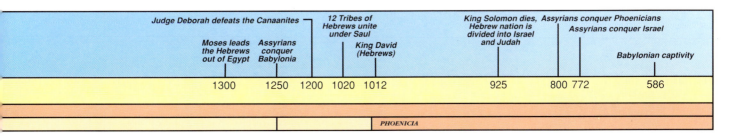

Moses finally led the Hebrews across the Red Sea and through the deserts of the Sinai Peninsula back to Canaan, which they called "The Promised Land." There they built towns, tended their flocks, and followed their religion.

But Canaan was already inhabited by a people called the Canaanites. For over one hundred years the Hebrews fought the Canaanites for control of Canaan. At that early time, the Hebrews were not a united people. They were divided into twelve tribes. Each tribe fought its own wars against the Canaanites. Each tribe had its own leader, called a judge. One great judge was a woman named Deborah. When a powerful Canaanite king attacked her people, Deborah raised an army that crushed the Canaanites. Her victory brought forty years of peace.

The peace ended when a warlike people called the Philistines attacked the Hebrews. The Philistines lived along the Mediterranean Sea in western Canaan. Divided into separate tribes, the Hebrews could not defeat the Philistine army. So the Hebrews decided to unite, and they chose a man named Saul to be their king. Saul united the twelve tribes into one kingdom called Israel. But still the Philistines could not be defeated.

40

According to the Bible, victory for the Hebrews came in the person of a young shepherd boy named David. He volunteered to do battle with the mightiest Philistine warrior, a giant named Goliath. David killed Goliath with a rock hurled from a slingshot, and the Philistines fled, vanquished once and for all.

David, the young hero, grew up to become king after the death of Saul in about 1012 B.C.E. The Hebrews achieved their greatest power during King David's reign. They conquered all their enemies and moved their capital from Hebron to Jerusalem, which became their Eternal City. Jerusalem was later to become a city sacred to Christians and Moslems, as well as to Jews.

When David died, his son Solomon became king. King Solomon was known to be good and very wise. He erected a fabulous temple in Jerusalem and built a fleet of fine sailing ships. Under his rule, Jerusalem became a mighty city and Israel prospered.

King Solomon increased the wealth of the kingdom by increasing trade with the Phoenicians, the Egyptians, and other peoples, but he also burdened his people with heavy taxes. When the king died in 925 B.C.E., civil war divided the Hebrews into two nations: Israel in the north and Judah in the south. Jerusalem was in Judah. The people of Judah were called Jews.

For the next two hundred years the two kingdoms fought with each other, and with the powerful kingdoms all around them. At last they could fight no more. In 722 B.C.E. the Assyrians conquered Israel and took many of the people as slaves. In 586 B.C.E. Judah fell to the Chaldeans, who were the rulers of Babylonia at that time. The Babylonian king destroyed Solomon's temple in Jerusalem, and the leaders of Judah were exiled to Babylon as prisoners of war.

Held captive in the huge city of Babylon, the Jews refused to adopt their conquerors' religion or way of life. They held true to the holy covenant and kept their faith alive. They met in places called synagogues to pray and study the Torah. Teachers called rabbis led the meetings. In 538 B.C.E. the more tolerant Persians conquered Babylon and allowed the Jews to return to Judah. Many did go back. But others stayed in Babylon or traveled to other lands. Wherever they went, wherever they have gone, the Jews have always kept their covenant with God.

It is more than 2,500 years since the Babylonians destroyed the temple of Jerusalem. The land of Canaan later became known as Palestine. Today a large part of Palestine has become the Jewish state of Israel. In many ways, little has changed in all that time. Different groups of people are still arguing over who should control the holiest of all cities. But none can deny Judaism its place as one of the preeminent religions of the world. Its teachings about the one and only God, about ethics and morality, and about the importance of the law influenced two other great faiths—Christianity and Islam. And the high standard of behavior and discipline set by the Hebrew people so long ago still stands as a guiding beacon for all of us today.

Quiz

1. The Minoan culture of ancient Crete is named after

Ⓐ a labyrinth.
Ⓑ King Minos.
Ⓒ Mesopotamia.
Ⓓ the Minotaur.

2. The hero who defeated the minotaur was named Theseus.

Ⓐ True
Ⓑ False

3. The downfall of Crete began with

Ⓐ a volcanic explosion.
Ⓑ the Trojan horse.
Ⓒ pirate attacks.
Ⓓ a plague of locusts.

4. King Sargon's greatest invention was

Ⓐ the professional army.
Ⓑ his code of ethics and law.
Ⓒ the Tower of Babel.
Ⓓ the Hanging Gardens.

5. King Hammurabi's greatest accomplishment was

Ⓐ the professional army.
Ⓑ his code of ethics and law.
Ⓒ the Tower of Babel.
Ⓓ the Hanging Gardens.

6. The Hittites, who invaded Babylonia in 1525 B.C.E., came from

Ⓐ the Indus Valley.
Ⓑ Rome.
Ⓒ Asia Minor.
Ⓓ Africa.

7. The largest Phoenician colony was

Ⓐ Carthage.
Ⓑ Tunis.
Ⓒ Marseilles.
Ⓓ Canaan.

8. The rare purple dye that made the Phoenicians wealthy was made from

Ⓐ hermit crabs.
Ⓑ murex snails.
Ⓒ giant squid.
Ⓓ starfish.

9. Which of the following was a characteristic of Hebrew religion?

Ⓐ many gods and goddesses
Ⓑ a belief in a single god
Ⓒ giant temples called ziggurats
Ⓓ wealthy priests

10. The "Promised Land" of the Hebrews was the land of

Ⓐ Egypt.
Ⓑ Babylon.
Ⓒ Canaan.
Ⓓ Mount Sinai.

Chapter 4

Early Civilizations of Asia and the Americas

India—The Twin Cities

Life is good in Mohenjo-Daro. You live with your family in a pleasant mud-brick house. Early each morning you go out to the well in the courtyard for a drink of fresh water. You play with your friends in the clean, straight streets, and later, when the sun is high and the day gets hot, you go to the public swimming pool or the bathhouse to cool off. Enormous fields of wheat and orchards of date palms rustle in the warm breeze on the farms outside the city. One day you're by yourself, thinking about how the swaying wheat fields look like waves on the water. You glance up and see them on the northern horizon—invaders! You rush home to warn the city, but it's too late. The barbarians show no mercy as

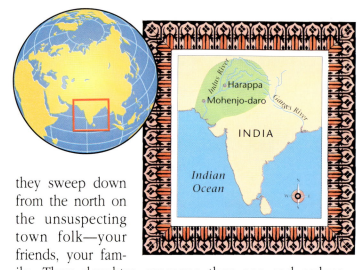

they sweep down from the north on the unsuspecting town folk—your friends, your family. They slaughter everyone they see and reduce Mohenjo-Daro to a smoking mound of rubble. There's nothing you can do but stay hidden until they're gone. Then you join the rest of the survivors as they pack up what little remains and head south.

Until 1921 no one even suspected that a great civilization once flourished in the Indus Valley. Although much has been learned about this ancient and fabulous Indian culture, many mysteries have yet to be unraveled. Between 3000 and 2800 B.C.E. small farming communities began to appear in the Indus River Valley and in the

The irrigated fields produced so much food that it had to be stored in the huge granary. From there it was distributed to all the people.

regions near its delta on the Arabian Sea. As had been the case with the earlier civilizations of Mesopotamia and Egypt, people were attracted to the Indus Valley because of the river. The yearly rising and subsiding of the river provided rich farmlands and a steady supply of fish. And transportation was easier by water than by land.

The nomads who wandered into the valley found it pleasing and settled into villages. Soon they were planting crops such as wheat and barley. The people learned to irrigate their fields in order to grow more crops. In

The first Indus people worshiped the Mother Goddess— the mystery of life!

time their tiny farm villages grew into towns and cities. With their hands they fashioned attractive pottery, which they used for cooking and storing food. Their houses were constructed of mud-brick and stone. Their religion seems to have been a combination of fertility rites and worship of a Mother Goddess.

By about 2500 B.C.E., the Indus people had developed an advanced civilization with two chief cities, Mohenjo-Daro and Harappa, located about 350 miles apart. Most of what we know about the Indus civilization has been learned from the remains of these two great cities, which we think were twin capitals. Smaller cities as far apart as a thousand miles have been found all along the Indus and its tributaries and scattered about the delta land near the Arabian Sea.

Cities such as Mohenjo-Daro and Harappa were carefully planned. Each city was laid out in geometrically exact patterns. The streets were wide, straight, and paved. Many houses had their own indoor wells and tile-lined baths. Some even had brick lavatories. The Indus people also built sewer systems for their cities very much like the ones we use today. Each house was connected by drainpipes to larger pipes running beneath the streets. The sewers carried wastewater away from the places where people lived. Mohenjo-Daro was defended by brick walls and towers. Piles of large clay missiles have been found behind the walls, still waiting to be used as ammunition for slings. Since farming was the primary source of wealth, the granary, where the grain was stored, was one of the most important buildings in the city. Besides wheat, barley, and vegetables, the Indus people were probably the first to domesticate cotton. Other large buildings, including a great bath, have also been found.

The total population of the Indus civilization at its height probably consisted of about 100,000 people who were most likely the ancestors of the dark-skinned Dravidian peoples who live in southern India today. Like the Egyptians, they were organized into a regimented society under strict government control, and were headed by priest-kings.

The Indus civilization drew its strength from the great Indus River, just as Sumer did from the Tigris and the Euphrates, and as Egypt did from the Nile. The products of its thriving agriculture were in great demand as far west as Egypt and Mesopotamia. We know the Indus people traded in Mesopotamia because their pottery has been found there.

43

The Indus River was the source of life. Along its banks the people bathed and prayed. Without it they could not live!

Warm winds filled the sails of the boats that traveled from the mountains to the sea.

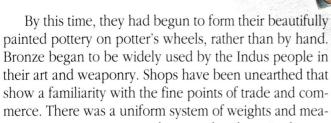

The Indus people were defenseless against the mounted Aryan invaders.

By this time, they had begun to form their beautifully painted pottery on potter's wheels, rather than by hand. Bronze began to be widely used by the Indus people in their art and weaponry. Shops have been unearthed that show a familiarity with the fine points of trade and commerce. There was a uniform system of weights and measures, unknown elsewhere in the ancient world. Indus Valley sailors took crows with them on their long voyages of trade and exploration. If the sailors became disoriented at sea, they set a crow free and followed it. They knew that a crow always flies toward land! Compare this to the Babylonian legend of Utnapishtim and the flood.

The people of the Indus Valley were skilled craft workers. They made jewelry, statues, and other objects of gold, bronze, and copper. Weavers wove cotton thread into fine fabric. Many clay seals have been unearthed,

proving that the Indus people could write, but so far no one has been able to read the script. Most likely the seals were used to impress the owner's name.

The Indus Valley civilization lasted over one thousand years. But then, around 1500 B.C.E., this grand and prosperous civilization was destroyed by Indo-European nomads known as Aryans, probably coming from Persia. The word *Aryan* means "nobleman" or "owner of land." And the Aryans believed that they were born to conquer

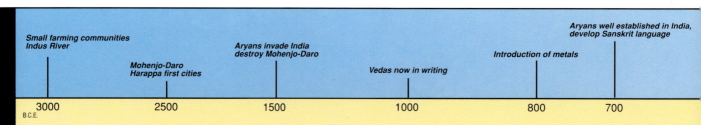

Small farming communities
Indus River

Mohenjo-Daro
Harappa first cities

Aryans invade India
destroy Mohenjo-Daro

Vedas now in writing

Introduction of metals

Aryans well established in India,
develop Sanskrit language

3000
B.C.E.

2500

1500

1000

800

700

and control. Having conquered the capital cities, they spread out to the east and to the south, overcoming one kingdom after another. The native people were forced to flee ever farther south. Soon the invaders controlled all of the Indus River valley. The Aryans were fierce warriors, but they also brought new ideas. They became known for making beautiful cloth embroidered with gold and silver. They also became known for their skill as doctors and mathematicians. By about 700 B.C.E. the Aryans were well established in the area.

The Aryan tribes settled in the lands that they conquered and formed several city-states. Each one was ruled by a raja, or prince. The rajas lived in fine palaces with highly trained armies to protect their domains. The Aryan people considered themselves entirely superior to the darker-skinned Dravidian people whom they had conquered, even though the Dravidians were in many ways far more advanced. The conquerors thought it sinful to have any physical contact with those they had vanquished.

The Aryans busied themselves with agriculture and cattle raising. Their kingdoms were often at war with one another, so the rajahs built walled cities into which all the people could withdraw during attacks. Their religious beliefs at this early time were a kind of nature worship which had been passed from one generation to the next in the form of poems, songs, and hymns. With no other way of preserving knowledge and culture, even minor changes in the oral tradition were strictly forbidden. Around 1000 B.C.E., these collected hymns and prayers, which were called the Vedas, were being written down in the Sanskrit language. They would come to form the basis of the religion that we know as Hinduism.

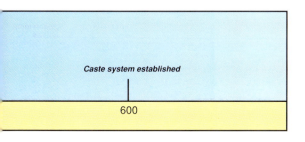

१ काकौ वृक्षे वसतः २ देवो वदति
३ किमर्थम्पितरम्पुत्रो न स्मरति

(1) Two crows dwell in a tree; (2) The God speaks;
(3) Why does the son not remember the father?

The translation is correct, but what does it mean?

Central to the Aryans' religious system, which included a belief in reincarnation, was a unique social system known as the caste system. Under this system people were divided into castes, or groups, according to their occupation and, to a certain extent, the color of their skin. There were four castes, ranging from highest to lowest: the Brahman (priests and scholars); the Kshatrya (rulers and warriors); the Vaisya (craftsmen, merchants and farmers); and the Sudra (unskilled workers).

The rajas lived lives of luxury in fine palaces surrounded by high walls. Their ancient songs, hymns, and poems were the basis of the Hindu religion.

45

Caste laws were strict and unbending. People remained in their caste for life, and children became members of their parents' caste. No one could move up to a higher caste no matter how they tried, since their soul had supposedly been born into the caste in which it belonged. The Aryans' name for people in the lowest levels of society was "outcastes," or "untouchables." Any Aryan who was foolish enough to befriend or marry an untouchable would be banished from the caste of his or her birth to join the ranks of the outcastes. Each caste had strict rules of conduct for its members. People in one caste could not eat, drink, or associate with people from other castes.

The caste system has remained the basic organizing principle of Indian life for thousands of years. Today it still affects the way many Indians live. In the twentieth century, there has been a concerted effort on the part of many Indian leaders to eliminate this unfair system, but tradition dies hard.

Caste system established

600

The Yellow River—"China's Sorrow"— often flooded, bringing death and destruction. But the river also made the soil rich and provided an abundance of grain.

China—The Hidden Valley

By about 3500 B.C.E. scattered groups of Stone Age peoples were settled along the valley of the Huang Ho, or Yellow River, in central China. They called themselves the Black-haired People, and used polished-stone tools and weapons. Northern China and the people of the Yellow River valley were cut off from other ancient peoples. Steep mountains, wide deserts, steppe regions, and deep seas encircled their homeland. Their society grew up apart from the rest of the world, and much about them remains a mystery. But archaeologists believe that by about 2500 B.C.E., in addition to hunting with bows and arrows, they had begun to farm. At first they built pit houses with roofs of woven grass. But the farmers of the Yellow River valley were often overwhelmed by floods which both enriched the soil and devastated their communities. (In fact, over time the Yellow River came to be known as "China's Sorrow.") So they turned to building their houses of mud and wattle (a framework of sticks plastered with mud), and surrounding them with thick walls as protection from the effects of the frequent floods.

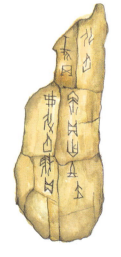

These early Chinese also developed a primitive writing system. The earliest form of Chinese writing was inscribed on animal bones. Like other peoples of all times and places, the Chinese have legends about their earliest forerunners. Some legends say that in the beginning the people were led by wise and powerful kings who lived in palaces of wood and mud. These legends refer to the time from 2852 B.C.E. to 2205 B.C.E. as the Age of the Legendary Five Rulers. According to the legends, it was these kings who taught the people to farm. They also taught the people the joy of music. One legendary king named Yu found a way to control the flooding rivers. "Without Yu," the Chinese say, "we would all have become fish." Another is said to have invented the calendar. This same king's wife taught the people how to weave beautiful silk cloth from the delicate filament of the silkworm.

The Hsia Dynasty is thought to have had its beginnings about 2200 B.C.E. in the valley of the Yellow River. After dominating the area for many years, so the story goes, the Hsia rulers fell to fighting among themselves, causing much misery for their subjects. About 1700 B.C.E., one thousand years after the beginning of civilization in India, the Prince of Shang conquered and unified China. The first Shang prince founded the Shang Dynasty, whose beginnings are dated from 1776 B.C.E. by some historians and from 1523 B.C.E. by others. When a Shang king died, his son became the new king. In that way they kept power in one family. The Shang dynasty ruled China for over five hundred years until 1028 B.C.E.

From 1500 B.C.E. on, Chinese history leaves the realm of legend and enters the world of scientific fact and definitive civilization. Archaeological findings and inscriptions upon shells, bones, and bronze have many tales to tell, and actual written historical records have been discovered dating back to 1300 B.C.E. The Shang built China's first cities. Their largest city was Anyang, in what is now Honan province. Anyang and other Shang

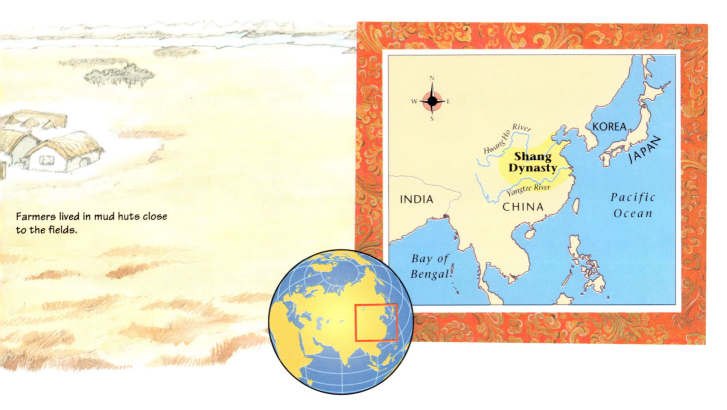

Farmers lived in mud huts close to the fields.

cities were protected by thick walls and divided into sections for different craftspeople. In one section lived the potters, who fashioned beautiful pottery from a fine white clay. To this day we call that type of pottery "china," regardless of where in the world it is made. Weavers lived in another section of the city. They wove silk thread into cloth. During the Shang dynasty cattle and pigs were domesticated, and millet, wheat, and rice were the basic cereal crops. Most of the Shang people were farmers who lived outside the city walls. They had no plows, but used wooden sticks to work the soft soil of the valley.

Warrior chiefs during the later Shang years carried bronze daggers and rode in chariots with bronze fittings. Shang civilization consisted of an area smaller than Honan province in what is today the vast nation of China. Shang warriors used their war chariots to conquer the entire Yellow River valley. Some archaeologists think that the Chinese learned of the chariot from the Indo-Europeans, who had already been using it for a thousand years. The reason so many centuries passed before the chariot appeared in China is that geographical barriers which kept invaders away also slowed down the importation of knowledge and new ideas. The abacus, first invented in Sumer, was either transported to China via trade or invented independently by the Chinese at a later date.

The Shang were the first people we know of to make systematic astronomical studies. They regularly observed and recorded eclipses, novas, comets, and other heavenly phenomena. They also made much progress in science and mathematics. And they developed a sophisticated writing system similar to that of the Egyptians, which used pictures to stand for words. Later they developed several *thousand* symbols to stand for both words and ideas. Chinese people today still use the system of writing developed by the Shang. It is the oldest and most complicated writing system still in use. Other peoples, such as the Koreans and the Japanese, have used and modified the Shang writing system.

Chinese students today still learn the thousands of symbols of the Shang writing system!

Like other ancient peoples, the Shang worshiped and sought the favor of many gods. They sometimes sacrificed animals and human beings as gifts to the gods. The Shang believed that when people died they became spirits, and that the spirits of dead people could help their living relatives. The Shang tried to please the spirits of their ancestors with prayers and gifts of meat and wine in bronze vessels. Jade ornaments were sewn to a dead person's clothes. Ornamental daggers and other objects were put in the graves of nobles and rich people. This practice became known as ancestor worship. Recently the tombs of the Shang kings near Anyang were opened. They contained the skeletons of charioteers complete with their horses and chariots.

The reverence that the ancient Chinese people felt for their ancestors led them to treat their homes, their families, and their land with honor and respect as well. They devised strict rules of courtesy, which made it possible for large families to live together peacefully. Because of the combined effects of geographical isolation and respect for tradition, Chinese culture changed very little over thousands of years. Many Chinese still venerate their ancestors today.

Around 1140 B.C.E., after an unbroken line of thirty generations of Shang rulers, the Shang dynasty began to weaken as the feudal state of Chou, a more warlike people, grew stronger. In despair the last Shang ruler burned himself to death, and in 1122 B.C.E. the Chou dynasty was established under the leadership of Wu Wang, who took the title of emperor over the collection of small kingdoms that then made up China. The Chou leaders developed systems of irrigation and flood control. And they extended their empire to reach from the Yellow River valley south to the Chang, or Yangtze, River. The powerful Chou dynasty ruled for more than 750 years. One reason for its longevity was the Chou emperors' practice of giving large areas of land to relatives and nobles in exchange for pledges of loyalty and military aid. This was a practice that would be used to great advantage one thousand years later by the medieval kings of Europe.

Toward the end of the Chou dynasty, Confucianism, the most ancient and revered philosophy of China, was devel-

48

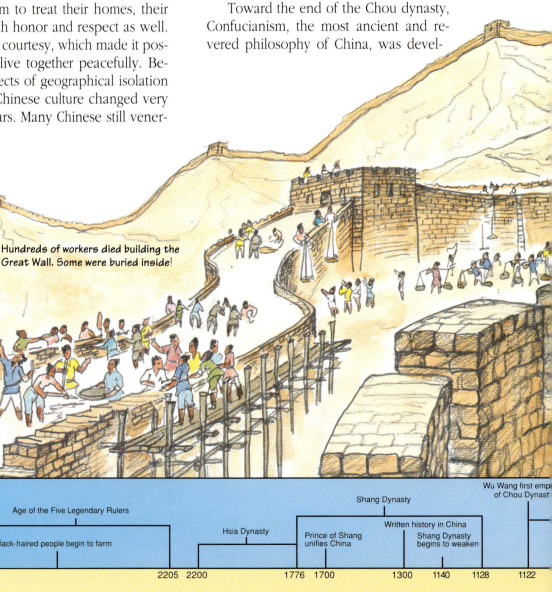

Hundreds of workers died building the Great Wall. Some were buried inside!

Neolithic peoples settle in Huang Ho (Yellow River) in central China, call themselves Black-haired people

Age of the Five Legendary Rulers

Black-haired people begin to farm

Hsia Dynasty

Prince of Shang unifies China

Shang Dynasty

Written history in China

Shang Dynasty begins to weaken

Wu Wang first emp of Chou Dynast

| 3500 | 2852 | | 2205 | 2200 | | 1776 | 1700 | | 1300 | 1140 | 1128 | 1122 |

B.C.E.

oped by a soldier's son named K'ung Fu-tzu. We know him by his Latinized name, Confucius. He lived from 551 to 479 B.C.E. Confucius wrote books of profound wisdom on philosophy, history, poetry, music, and just about every other aspect of life. His teachings about personal and political morality and conduct became the backbone of Chinese thought and culture, and remained so until the twentieth century. One of his sayings was the first known expression of the Golden Rule: "What you do not want done to yourself, do not do to others."

The name "China" may have come from Ch'in. This was the family name of a dynasty that ruled China briefly from 221 B.C.E. until 206 B.C.E. Shih Huang-ti was the first Ch'in emperor. Under his leadership, China was united under a strong central government for the first time. Shih Huang-ti is best remembered as the man respon-

sible for the building of the Great Wall of China. Although the land of China was hemmed in by natural barriers on three sides, the northern border provided easy access for enemies, who often came to raid Chinese farms. The Chinese of the Chou dynasty had tried to protect this border by building short walls. Shih Huang-ti decided to connect these walls. He envisioned one great stone wall stretching across the northern frontier of his vast empire.

The Great Wall of China is the only man-made structure on Earth that can be seen from outer space! It is fifteen hundred miles long, twenty feet high, and about fifteen feet wide at the top. It helped protect the northern borders from invaders, especially those on horseback. But it also further isolated China from the rest of the world.

Fifteen hundred miles long, from twenty to fifty feet high, and twelve to thirty-five feet wide—astronauts can see the wall from outer space!

The emperor Shi Huang-ti was determined to keep out the invaders from the north!

Chou Dynasty	Shih Huang-ti unites China, begins the Ch'in Dynasty	Ch'in Dynasty	
		Great Wall of China built	
	372	221	206

The central pyramid was as high as a twenty-story building. The Maya had no wheels, no beasts of burden. How did they build these incredible temples?

Pok-a-tok—the holy game. The winner was a hero, the loser lost his life!

The Americas—A World Away

THE OLMEC

One of the oldest and most baffling civilizations of the Americas was that of the Olmec. It rose up out of the dense rain forests of Central America around 1200 B.C.E. and endured for almost a thousand years. The Olmec were probably the builders of the first city in the Western Hemisphere, yet today these advanced people and their culture are shrouded in an almost impenetrable veil of mystery.

Early in their history the Olmec cleared the unimaginably thick jungle to make room for their crops of domesticated maize, an early ancestor of modern corn, which grew wild in Central America. They lived together in small villages and tended their fields. As the maize harvest grew increasingly bountiful, the people found themselves raising more food than they

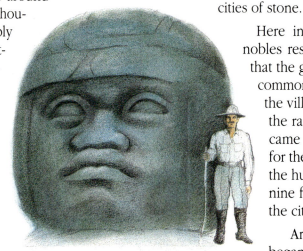

The colossal stone heads of the Olmec weigh ten tons or more! Olmec warriors wore helmets for protection against enemy war clubs.

could eat. Food surpluses meant that now some of the people could be relieved from the chores of survival and devote their attention and imagination to other things. Over time a form of government developed, and in a place called La Venta, for reasons that no one knows, a village became the first of many cities— cities of stone.

Here in the cities the priests and nobles resided. And it was here, too, that the gods were said to dwell. The common people continued to live in the villages, close to the maize and the rain forest. On holy days they came to the cities with offerings for the gods. They stared in awe at the huge stone heads—some over nine feet tall—that stood guard at the city gates.

Around 600 B.C.E., the Olmec began building shrines to their gods on top of enormous earthworks. It is difficult to believe that they could have constructed

Archaeologists slash their way through dense jungle to find the ruins of Maya temples. It's like a trip into a forgotten past!

these towering mounds using nothing but their strength and ingenuity and a few simple stone tools. They had not even invented the wheel. All the thousands of tons of dirt that went into the building of the earthworks, they carried themselves in woven baskets.

They became skilled artists, sculpting unique and vigorous works of stone, jade, and clay. Olmec art is easily recognized by the strangely haunting baby faces of the figures, the constant jaguar theme, and the African-looking features of their enormous stone heads. They also developed a calendar, a counting system, and a form of hieroglyphic writing, all of which would have a great influence on the later civilizations of Mesoamerica.

THE MAYA

With the end of the Olmec civilization came the rise of the Maya. Based in an area of Mesoamerica that is today southern Mexico, Belize, and Guatemala, the Maya drained the swamps and irrigated their fields of maize, beans, and other crops. As had been the case with the Olmec, surplus food supplies led to increased population and then the creation of large cities as centers of worship and trade.

The Maya devoted their cities to the worship of many gods—gods of rain, of the earth, of the plants and animals that were important to them. The largest Maya city was called Tikal. At its heart stood a flat-topped pyramid of stone crowned with a temple. Tikal's pyramid was as high as a modern twenty-story building, and a vast improvement over the earthen mounds of the Olmec. But like the Olmec, the Maya had no wheels, no horses or oxen. They were their own beasts of burden.

In each Maya city, adjacent to the central pyramid, stood a large stone court in which a religious game called *pok-a-tok* was played. Pok-a-tok players, heavily swathed in protective bandages, used their hips, elbows, and knees to hit a solid rubber ball back and forth. Priests helped the players dress and kept score. Archaeologists believe that the game was something like a cross between modern basketball and soccer. No one knows exactly how the game was scored or precisely what its religious significance was.

The Maya built on what they learned from the Olmec. They studied the Olmec calendar. Then they watched the sun, the moon, and the stars and recorded all that they saw. They were able to predict when such frightening things as an eclipse of the sun would happen. Their advanced astronomy helped them develop an extremely accurate calendar. Like ours today, their year consisted of 365 days. One important feature of the Maya calendar was that it spelled out the many feast days set aside to honor the gods.

The Maya also developed a sophisticated mathematical system based on the number twenty. It included the concept of zero, something the very advanced ancient Greeks and Romans never thought of. The Maya numbering system consisted of combinations of dots and bars: a dot equalled one, a bar equalled five, a shell-like symbol represented zero.

When it came to writing, the Maya again turned to the Olmec for inspiration. Maya writing, which has not yet been fully deciphered, was based on Olmec hieroglyphics. Writing on paper made from the bark of certain trees, the Maya wrote books on history, mathematics, science, and religion. They also wrote songs, poems, and plays.

The third important place in every Maya city was the marketplace. There the people congregated, loaded down with such trade goods as salt, honey, cotton, cacao beans, bird feathers, and various foodstuffs to be bought and sold. The Maya traded with other peoples as far away as northern Mexico to obtain highly valued items of gold, copper, and silver.

Maya society was divided into three classes. At the top were the rulers. Warriors and priests made up the second class—that of the nobility, the only group that learned how to write. The nobles collected taxes and made laws. They also organized armies in times of war. Priests helped the rulers run the government. They also guided the common people in appeasing their many gods. No farmer would plant and no army would march without the blessing of a priest. Most of the people were in the third and lowest class. Included in this class were craftsmen, businessmen, peasants, and slaves. Many slaves were convicted criminals who had been forced into slavery as punishment.

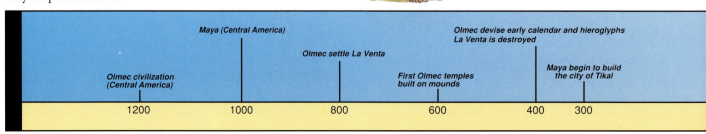

Olmec civilization (Central America)

Maya (Central America)

Olmec settle La Venta

First Olmec temples built on mounds

Olmec devise early calendar and hieroglyphs
La Venta is destroyed

Maya begin to build the city of Tikal

1200 1000 800 600 400 300

The Maya built mighty cities for millions of people, carved roads through the jungles, and raised glorious temples.

The caracol was an ancient observatory specially designed for star-gazing.

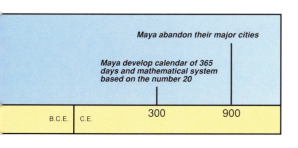

Maya abandon their major cities

Maya develop calendar of 365 days and mathematical system based on the number 20

B.C.E.	C.E.	300	900

Quiz

1. **The ancient Indus people worshiped**

   Ⓐ their ancestors.   Ⓒ a Mother Goddess.

   Ⓑ the god Marduk.   Ⓓ themselves.

2. **The Indus Valley civilization lasted for**

   Ⓐ ten years.   Ⓒ one thousand years.

   Ⓑ one hundred years.   Ⓓ ten thousand years.

3. **The Yellow River came to be known as**

   Ⓐ China's Glory.   Ⓒ China's Shame.

   Ⓑ China's Sorrow.   Ⓓ China's Fortune.

4. **Shih Huang-ti completed the Great Wall of China in about 210 B.C.E. to**

   Ⓐ keep invaders out.   Ⓒ keep diseases out.

   Ⓑ keep his subjects in.   Ⓓ keep the glaciers from coming.

5. **The Chinese writing system was invented during the**

   Ⓐ Hsia dynasty.   Ⓒ Chou dynasty.

   Ⓑ Shang dynasty.   Ⓓ Ch'in dynasty.

6. **Confucius was primarily concerned with**

   Ⓐ war preparations.   Ⓒ art.

   Ⓑ science.   Ⓓ morality and conduct.

7. **The Olmec civilization began around the year**

   Ⓐ 1200 B.C.E.   Ⓒ C.E. 1200.

   Ⓑ 200 B.C.E.   Ⓓ C.E. 1920.

8. **The largest Maya city was called**

   Ⓐ Chichén Itzá.   Ⓒ Tikal.

   Ⓑ Mohenjo-Daro.   Ⓓ Copan.

9. **The Maya played a religious game called**

   Ⓐ pok-a-tok.   Ⓒ tok-a-tok.

   Ⓑ tok-a-pok.   Ⓓ pop-a-top.

10. **The Maya number system was based on the number**

   Ⓐ ten.   Ⓒ zero.

   Ⓑ twenty.   Ⓓ sixty.

Chapter 5
Greece—The Quest for Perfection

The defenders of Troy lined the ramparts of the city and watched in disbelief. Their Mycenaean Greek enemies were dismantling their camp, loading their ships, and sailing away. The invading Greeks had laid siege to Troy for ten long years, and despite the help and counsel of the gods and goddesses, many heroes on both sides had fallen in mortal combat. Now they were simply giving up and going away? It hardly seemed possible. Even more mystifying, the Greeks had left at the gates of the city an enormous wooden horse. The Trojans held council to sort out the strange situation. The gods and goddesses who favored them were there. The Greeks, it seemed, had simply lost their spirit for the fight. And what else could the giant horse be but a gift of peace? After making certain the coast was clear, the Trojans opened the gates and wheeled the statue into the city. People gathered to marvel at the offering and then, still buzzing with the excitement of the day, went home to their first safe night's sleep in ten years. But in the middle of the still, dark night, the Greek soldiers hidden inside the hollow horse lowered themselves to the ground and opened the gates to their countrymen, who had secretly returned. Once inside the Greeks swarmed over the sleeping town, and such slaughter there was! Mighty Troy was laid waste, her people either dead or scattered to the ends of the earth.

54

Historians believe that there probably *was* a battle between Troy and the people of Mycenaean Greece that occurred sometime between 1150 B.C.E. and 1250 B.C.E. Over hundreds of years, stories about the war were passed along and embellished by countless storytellers. The *Iliad* and the *Odyssey*, the two epic poems that tell us about the Trojan War and the Greeks' adventures on their long trip home, were composed and written by the Greek poet Homer sometime around the year 725 B.C.E. For us, the fabulous story of the wooden horse is a lesson in trust—everyone knows that it's wise to "beware of Greeks bearing gifts." For the Greeks, though, these wondrous works of history and legend, fact and faith, laid the foundation for a thousand years of grandeur, courage, idealism, and honor.

Homer—the blind poet who saw into the distant Greek past.

The Trojans opened the city gates and brought about their own destruction.

Is this the burial mask of the famed king Agamemnon of Mycenae?

55

Around the year 2000 B.C.E., as the Minoan culture of Crete was reaching its apex, the Mycenaeans were settling in on the Greek mainland to the North. They established an impressive culture in Mycenae and several other cities. These people were, first and foremost, warriors. They built their heavily fortified and walled cities on imposing hills, and depended for their prosperity on both war booty and trade. When the pioneering archaeologist Heinrich Schleimann explored the ruins of Mycenae in 1876, he found an unbelievable cache of gold face masks, bracelets, and other precious objects attesting to their wealth. The Myceneans established settlements throughout the lands of the Aegean, and they vanquished Troy and probably Minoan Crete as well. Yet by 1100 B.C.E., their culture was destroyed—the cities desolated, the people dispersed, even their writing (today known only as "Linear B") erased from the annals of history. Among the many mysteries of their sudden demise, one certain reason was the incursion of the Dorians, a less civilized people from northern Greece, who overwhelmed them and rose to prominence in their place.

This was during a time known as the Bronze Age. Bronze was an alloy of tin and copper, two ores which are rarely found together. So the Bronze Age had been a time of trade and travel as people sought new sources of these important metals. But then the benefits of iron became known. The Iron Age began in Greece around the year 1000 B.C.E. The new metal was plentiful, easy to work, and stronger than bronze. As each community found a nearby source of iron ore it tended to become self-sufficient, growing independent from, and having little contact with, its neighbors.

As the villages grew, so did the population, and by the year 750 B.C.E. the Greeks were fighting among themselves for the land. They set out for other lands across the sea to conquer and colonize. Greek colonies were established to the west in southern Italy and Sicily and to the east along the coasts of the Aegean and Black Sea. The economic effect was astounding as trade exploded. By 700 B.C.E., thanks to its far-flung and flourishing colonies, Greece was one of the most important exporting countries in the world. The Greek villages prospered and grew into cities, and then city-states. Population pressure was eased as the gigantic land holdings of the ancient aristocracy were broken up and parceled out among the middle class of merchants and craftsmen.

The invention of coined money in the seventh century revolutionized the economic and political structure of the Greek world. Suddenly the measure of wealth was not land, but *money*, as it has been ever since. This changed everything. When money became the source of power, the aristocratic landowners lost their ability to dominate the city-states. Where before the aristocrats had been the only people who could raise and finance an army, now the increasingly wealthy craftsmen and merchants had the money and resources to mount their own military adventures.

The prosperous members of the rising middle class invested more and more of their money in slaves, which were cheap and abundant, until it became common for even small farmers and merchants to own as many as five slaves. As a result they found themselves with time to spare from the everyday business of life. In their art, in their writings, in their conversation, they started asking basic questions

Modern nations all over the world have been inspired by Greek ideas about democracy.

about their world. Why should it be only the landowners, or only the financial wizards of the city, who governed? What was true power, and who should have it? Was there a better way? By now the city-states of Greece formed a unified culture, sharing a common language, religion and the heritage of Homer. But in their quest for a better society, they experimented with a bewildering variety of forms of government.

Kings, monarchs, tyrants? The Greeks had done away with them long ago—monarchy, tyranny, these were things of the past. The land-owning aristocracy had had their turn, and now people were becoming unhappy with the "oligarchy" of a few rich farmers and businessmen that decided their fate. One thing that hadn't been tried was a "democracy," a system where the citizens themselves governed. Now that was *really* a radical innovation! No other civilization in history had even thought of it before, or if they had, they'd certainly never tried it.

As time went on, a basic pattern of government emerged from the democratic experiments of the various city-states. The government was divided into three sections: (1) a magistracy or civil authority, (2) a council or senate, and (3) an assembly. In the early years, both the magistracy and the council were dominated by the aristocracy. The assembly, for the first time ever, was made up of all the citizens, or men chosen to represent them. By the end of the Archaic Period (800-500 B.C.E.), the two largest city-states were Sparta and Athens. Although alike in their degree of power and influence, they could not have been more different in their execution of the concept of democracy.

Centered on the broad Lacedaemon Plain, landlocked and surrounded by mountains, Sparta was the principal city of a province of southern Greece called Laconia. As the city and its population grew, the Spartan kings conquered the neighbors in Laconia and then the province of Messenia to their east. The Messenians they forced to become serfs, or *helots*, to slave in the fields or die like flies on the battleground. In about 630 B.C.E. the Messenians rose up and with help from several other cities in the area, known as the Peloponnesian Peninsula, began an insurrection that lasted seventeen years. When the Spartans finally reimposed order, they had to ask themselves how, with 10,000 citizens at the most, they were going to maintain control of the 250,000 or so souls they had struggled to subdue. They could only do this, they decided, by devoting all their energy and resources to ensuring that every Spartan was a super-soldier . . . and super-soldiers they became.

Every free man, woman, and child in Sparta was trained for war. Military training began at birth. Each new-born infant was inspected by a special council for physical defects or sickliness. If found to be in any way unfit, the child was thrown onto a pile of jagged rocks to die. At the age of seven, Spartan boys were removed from their homes to begin their lives as soldiers. Early in their training they were taught to endure physical pain and deprivation, and to live off the land by any means, including theft. Beginning at the age of twenty, Spartan men lived their whole lives in army barracks. Encouraged to marry, they were prohibited from living with their wives. At the age of thirty, a Spartan man became a full citizen. Yet he continued to sleep and eat in the barracks with his fellow soldiers until at the age of sixty, his civic duty finally fulfilled, he was free to retire to his home and family. And as for the girls and women, aside from fulfilling the requirements of their own rigorous physical training programs, they were seldom seen in public. Their main role in Spartan society was to keep themselves in top physical condition in order to produce the strongest possible offspring. They were also expected to support their warrior husbands, sons, and fathers with total dedication. A Spartan mother's traditional farewell to her son about to enter battle was "return with your shield, or on it," in other words, "kill or be killed."

Credit for the unusual Spartan governmental system as it eventually evolved is generally given to a semimythical personage by the name of Lycurgus. Whatever its origins, it became one of the most peculiar and enduring governments of all time. The Spartan system was a unique combination of monarchy, aristocracy, and democracy. The most surprising aspect was the simultaneous rule of two kings. Never before in history had two kings successfully shared a throne for any extended period of time.

In Sparta the system worked for hundreds of years! Maybe it worked because, in most matters, the kings were subordinate to the senate and the will of the people.

With such total devotion to the cause of war, it's not surprising that Sparta became virtually invincible in battle. By the sixth century B.C.E. the Spartan system was well established and functioning smoothly, and Sparta was able to forge the Peloponnesian League, an alliance of all the Peloponnesian cities except Argos. Sparta remained the acknowledged super-power of Greece for several hundred years.

The city-state of Athens developed along very different lines. Ruled by several different aristocracies early on, by 621 B.C.E. the political situation in Athens was in such a shambles that the citizens asked a leader named Draco to assemble and codify a brand new set of laws for their society. Draco turned out to be a very hard egg. His laws were so repressive, his punishments so severe, that even today we refer to an unreasonable rule or law as "Draconian." Thanks to Draco's laws making slavery the punishment for nonpayment of debt, the economy was soon in ruins and the entire society near total collapse. In 594 B.C.E., Solon, a prominent businessman known for his practical good sense, was granted absolute authority to save the city of Athens. He rewrote the constitution, cancelled all debts, and revoked the laws which forced debtors into slavery. And most important, he established in Athens yet another new form of government—a "meritocracy," in which leaders were chosen solely on the basis of their intelligence and their ability to govern. Solon's system was often modified, but remained the backbone of the Athenian system for most of the next five centuries.

The Spartan phalanx— a human war machine!

As the Greeks worked their way through trial and error to develop their idea of the most perfect society, a monster empire was building nearby in the east. In 559 B.C.E. Cyrus became King of Persia, a small kingdom to the east of Mesopotamia. Cyrus joined forces with the king of Babylonia, and together they built by far the greatest empire the world had seen up to that time. The new empire was governed under a system that was unusually sophisticated for the time. Permitting the conquered peoples to maintain their own languages and customs, the Persian king divided the empire into twenty provinces and put a *satrap*, or governor, in charge of each one. It was the satrap's duty to collect enough taxes to make himself rich while also filling the treasure houses of the king. In many ways the Persian civilization was superior to that of the Greeks, yet the Greeks looked upon the Persians, as they did upon all other non-Greek peoples, as "barbarians."

By 546 B.C.E., the Persians had become an imminent threat to the Ionian Greek colonies of Asia Minor. The colonies called for help, and the mainland city-states, particularly Athens, responded with money and ships. In 499 B.C.E. the Ionians enlisted the help of Athens and Eretria to drive the Persians out, but after five years of struggle the Persians remained steadfastly in control. Only now they were angry. In 490 B.C.E. under King Darius I, they launched an attack on the Greek mainland that would culminate in one of the most famous military battles in history.

The Persian forces landed at the island of Naxos and quickly destroyed it in revenge for its resistance during the Ionian uprising nine years before. Then they burned Eretria to the ground and deported its inhabitants to Persia. The Athenians made a stand at the town of Marathon, only twenty-six miles from their beloved city. They begged Sparta for help, but the Spartans were celebrating a holiday and refused to come to their aid. Nevertheless, the Athe-

nians' superior military strategy led to a sound defeat for the Persians, who turned around and headed for home. A messenger ran to Athens to spread news of the victory. Today's marathon races duplicate that famous feat.

In 481 B.C.E., Xerxes, Darius' successor to the throne of Persia, gathered the largest army and navy the world had seen—over 150,000 men and 600 ships—for a fresh assault on the hated Greeks. But the Athenians, at the urging of their leader Themistocles, had prepared for the onslaught that was bound to come by building a fleet of two hundred ships.

The Persian plan was to destroy Athens and incorporate all Greek territory into the Persian Empire. Yet only thirty-one of the several hundred Greek city-states joined the fight. Sparta took the lead with principal help from Athens, Corinth and Aegina. The Greeks would try to defeat the Persians at sea, while holding the Persian army to a standstill at the pass of Thermopylae, a narrow passage between the mountains and the rocky coast. For two days the Greeks, led by the Spartan King Leonidas and his three hundred warriors, held the pass against the overwhelming Persian force. On the third day a traitor showed the Persians a mountain trail that brought them through the mountains and into the rear of the Greek defense. True to their tradition, Leonidas and his warriors fought to the last man, giving most of their Greek allies a chance to escape. The Persians marched into Athens and destroyed it, burning and smashing all the beautiful temples on the Acropolis.

Meanwhile, out on the water, storms came up that tossed the Persian ships like matchsticks, destroying a good portion of their fleet. When the big battle finally came off the coast of the island of Salamis, the Greeks annihilated much of the already-damaged Persian fleet. The tattered remains of the Persian navy fled, stopping to pick up part of the army in its retreat. The Greek fleet

58

Greeks and Persians waged war for a hundred years.
In the end, the Greeks were triumphant.

followed and at Mycale in southern Ionia, burned most of what remained of the mighty Persian fleet. A large part of the Persian army stayed behind, encamped near Thessaly after the destruction of Athens. The Greeks amassed their biggest army yet to drive the invaders from the land once and for all.

With the defeat of the Persian Empire in 479 B.C.E. begins the Classical Period in the history of Greece. In 449 B.C.E., the Persian King Artaxerxes agreed to give up Persia's drive to dominate the Greeks in Asia Minor. In the western Mediterranean, Greece made peace with the great empire of Carthage. For the first time the people of Greece lived secure in the knowledge that they were safe from attack. Their enemies were enemies no more. To ensure the peace more than 200 city-states throughout the Aegean banded together to form the Delian League. At the helm was Athens with her powerful fleet and her mighty victories.

This was the time of Athens' "Golden Age," when the city of Athena blazed with the glory of a hundred suns as the brightest, most innovative society the world had ever seen. It was a time when their forward-thinking leader, Pericles, could proudly boast, "as a city, we are the school of Greece." Pericles allotted some of the income from the Delian League to rebuild the Acropolis with new temples and gave more money to support the arts. Architecture, sculpture, poetry, drama—all the arts would be nourished by the government to yield the greatest achievements since civilized society came to be.

But even as Athens' sun blazed ever brighter, storm clouds were gathering in the skies above Sparta. Sparta and the Peloponnesian League came to feel threatened by the growing power of Athens and her allies. In 431 B.C.E., the Peloponnesian War broke out between the two great cities. The Athenians dug in to withstand the Spartan assault and the Spartans besieged the city, cutting down the surrounding olive trees, burning the farms, trying to starve the city into surrender. After the siege had gone on for a year, a terrible plague broke out that lasted four years and took the lives of one of every four Athenians, including the great leader Pericles. After horrific losses on land and at sea, Athens finally surrendered in 404 B.C.E.

In 342 B.C.E., King Philip II of Macedonia in northern Greece made his bid for conquest. In rapid succession he conquered the Greek provinces of Thrace, Thessaly and Chalkidike. The Greeks, led by Athens and Thebes, formed a new alliance, the Hellenic (Greek) League, to

stop the Macedonian invasion. But within four years Philip controlled all of Greece. The next year he announced that he was preparing to go to war against the perennial enemy, Persia. Philip died before he had a chance to carry out the Persia campaign, and the task of conquering Persia fell to his twenty-year-old son, Alexander.

Alexander solidified his mastery of Greece by taking control of the Hellenic League and ruling it with an easy hand that became an iron fist when someone stepped out of line. When Thebes tried to break away, that fine city was burned to the ground and the survivors sold into slavery. After that the Greeks decided that it made sense

Alexander the Great—
Greek empire builder.

60

to go along with Alexander! At the same time the Macedonian army was preparing for the coming war with Persia. Once they began their march they never stopped, and they never looked back. They were victorious in Asia Minor, in Egypt, all across the Persian Empire and beyond into India. Astride his famous black horse, Bucephalus, Alexander was a fearless and brilliant general, beloved by his troops and feared by his enemies. He never fought a battle that he didn't win. No wonder they started calling him Alexander the Great! Alexander wanted to press on through India to China, but his army begged him to stop and let them enjoy the wealth they had accumulated. He agreed. But what opposing armies could not do, natural causes could, and Alexander died of fever at the young age of thirty-three—for one brief moment ruler of the greatest empire the world had ever seen.

Greek culture continued to dominate the Mediterranean world for another three hundred years, until, in the year 146 B.C.E., both Greece and Macedonia became provinces of the mighty Roman Empire.

The achievements of the Greeks during the five centuries from 600 to 100 B.C.E., in almost all areas of human endeavor, survived to form the framework of what we know today as western civilization. Greece's time of glory, and that of the Romans who came after them and built upon their accomplishments, is referred to by western historians as the Classical Era of ancient history. Here we can only highlight some of the incredible innovations of the Greek mind.

According to Homer, the sporting events which became the Olympics were first organized to provide an outlet for grief at funerals. Beginning in 776 B.C.E. the Olympic games were held every four years almost without interruption until C.E. 394 when the Romans abolished them. The first games were held in the city of Olympia, only later moving from city to city as they do today. In the beginning, participation in the games was limited to free Greek citizens. But as their popularity grew, the Olympics became a great festival, and messengers were sent out all over most of Europe and part of Asia to announce the coming games and to invite competitors. During the Olympics a temporary truce was declared for any war that might be in progress, and the cities of Greece opened their gates to all visitors. The first Olympic contest involved a single running event, which was won by a very proud cook. But soon other events—the broad jump, the javelin and discus throw, boxing, wrestling, and chariot racing—were added to the bill.

No people in history has pursued truth and knowledge so earnestly, and perhaps so successfully, as the philosophers of ancient Greece. As early as the sixth century B.C.E., men like Anaxagoras and Thales of Miletus were casting the light of reason upon the myths and legends of the times, and rejecting traditional notions about the nature of existence. A class of professional teachers, the Sophists, arose. Using their ideas about virtue, wisdom, and the art of rhetoric (clear self-expression), they analyzed and dissected every belief, institution and religious concept they found in their world. There was nothing that the typical Athenian enjoyed more than a philosophical discussion.

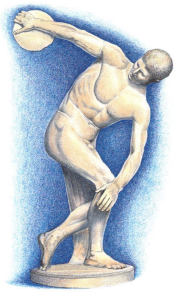

An Olympic discus thrower frozen in stone.

Perhaps the greatest thinker of the Golden Age of Greece was Socrates, who insisted on questioning absolutely everything. A popular teacher, he accepted no pay for his teachings. Socrates developed a new way of arriving at the truth by following a series of questions to its logical and unavoidable conclusion. He used logic to force his students to consider fundamental questions of human behavior, like "What is a good person?", "What is a good government?", or "Why do we act the way we do?" His devoted following of young students grew until he came to be seen as a threat to the stability of the society. In 399 B.C.E. an Athenian jury condemned him to death for "corrupting the youth." Socrates left behind no writings of his own, but lives for us in the books of his brilliant protégé, Plato. In his books, Plato recreated the dialogues between Socrates and his students, giving us a vivid picture of the "Socratic method" in action. Plato also founded the Athenian Academy, a school for statesmen, philosophers and scientists that existed for almost 1,000 years.

Plato's most famous pupil was Aristotle, who served as tutor to Alexander the Great, then returned to Athens to begin his own school, the Lyceum. His investigations into the realms of ethics, logic, the natural sciences and literary criticism remain unsurpassed to this day. Eratosthenes,

Socrates led the philosophers of Athens in pondering the meaning of life.

who headed the famous Alexandria Museum (which was also a center of Greek science) proved that the earth was round and calculated its circumference to an accuracy of 96 percent. Aristarchus of Samos deduced that the earth spins on its axis and revolves around the sun. Hipparchus of Nicaea divided the year correctly into 365¼ days.

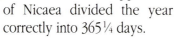
Decorated vases give us pictures of everyday life in ancient Greece.

In the arts, the Greek quest for perfection reached its zenith. Never before had the human form been depicted with such grace, depth, and realism as in the painting and sculpture of Classical Greece. Greek artists rendered facial expression, youth and age, and even physical deformity with exquisite attention to detail and an almost unbelievable sensitivity.

Their painting has survived for us in the hundreds of decorated vases which today are on display in museums all over the world. They provide us with vivid images of warfare, sports, social life, fashions, farming—every aspect of Greek life comes alive in the distinctive designs of their beautifully glazed pottery.

Sculpture played an important part in the public life of every Greek community, but it played its most important role in the temples, where statues of

Greek sculptors labored to capture the perfection of the human form.

the gods inspired awe and reverence. In the Parthenon, the central building atop the Acropolis in Athens, a statue of Athena (the goddess for whom the city was named) towered forty feet high, its perfect form of ivory clothed in sheets of gold. We are indebted to the Romans, who collected and copied many great examples of Greek sculpture, for the survival of this incredible body of work that would otherwise have largely been destroyed by earthquake, fire or the ravages of war.

The Greek passion for architecture burst into full flower in the sixth century. Their conviction that they could design the ideal building for every purpose drove them to create such masterpieces of light, space and proportion as the Parthenon, the arena at Olympia, and the Temple of Zeus, which was considered to be one of the seven wonders of the ancient world.

In Athens, one of the most important religious celebrations was the Dionysia, which featured drama competitions including both tragedy and comedy. The tragedies of Aeschylus, Sophocles and Euripides dealt with the universal themes of human frailties, passions and conflicts played out against the background of a universe seething with cosmic intensity. The comedies of dramatists like Aristophanes, for all their humor, took on equally ambitious themes, and included pointed satire of the people and events of the times as well. Modern theatre in the Western world is a direct extension of Classical Greek drama, and the works of the great Greek dramatists are still a standard part of theatrical repertory.

The enormous statue of Athena atop the Acropolis watched over the city.

62

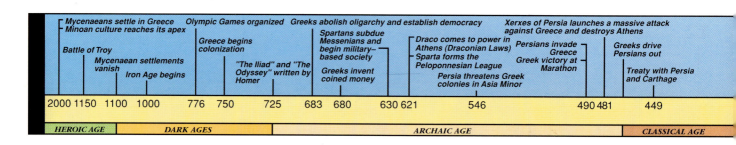

Mycenaeans settle in Greece — Olympic Games organized — Greeks abolish oligarchy and establish democracy — Xerxes of Persia launches a massive attack against Greece and destroys Athens

Minoan culture reaches its apex

Battle of Troy — Greece begins colonization — Spartans subdue Messenians and begin military-based society — Draco comes to power in Athens (Draconian Laws) — Persians invade Greece — Greeks drive Persians out

Mycenaean settlements vanish — Iron Age begins — "The Iliad" and "The Odyssey" written by Homer — Sparta forms the Peloponnesian League — Greek victory at Marathon — Treaty with Persia and Carthage

Greeks invent coined money — Persia threatens Greek colonies in Asia Minor

2000 1150 1100 1000 776 750 725 683 680 630 621 546 490 481 449

HEROIC AGE DARK AGES ARCHAIC AGE CLASSICAL AGE

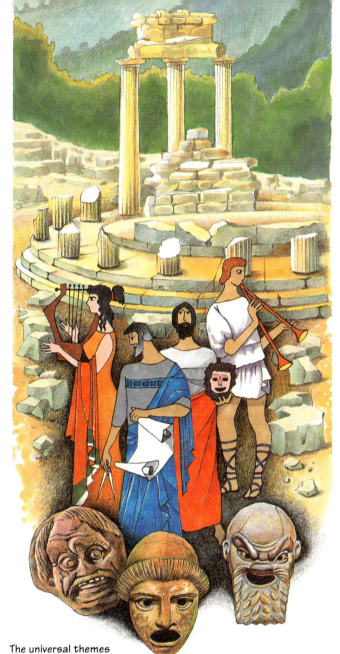

The universal themes
of Greek drama still move audiences today.

The Golden Age also nurtured the work of Herodotus, known today as the Father of History. He set out to chronicle the history of the Persian Wars, and in the process wrote the first factual history of the western world. Rejecting the histories of his predecessors, with their emphasis on legendary heroes and supernatural beings, Herodotus mostly recorded what he actually saw and heard, and only after subjecting it to rigorous and skeptical analysis. Thucydides' history of the Peloponnesian War is another masterpiece of objectivity which is still used as a textbook in many colleges and universities.

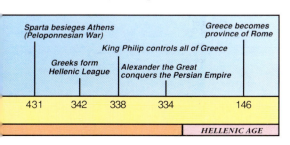

Quiz

1. The Trojan Horse was full of

- Ⓐ Greek soldiers.
- Ⓒ boiling oil.
- Ⓑ gifts.
- Ⓓ Trojan soldiers.

2. The poet who wrote the *Iliad* and the *Odyssey* was

- Ⓐ Heinrich Schleimann.
- Ⓒ Plato.
- Ⓑ Homer.
- Ⓓ Pericles.

3. Which form of government did the Greeks invent?

- Ⓐ aristocracy
- Ⓒ monarchy
- Ⓑ oligarchy
- Ⓓ democracy

4. The people of Sparta devoted all their resources to

- Ⓐ art.
- Ⓒ war.
- Ⓑ the Olympics.
- Ⓓ thinking.

5. King Leonidas and his army held off the Persians at

- Ⓐ Thermopylae.
- Ⓒ Naxos.
- Ⓑ Salamis.
- Ⓓ Mycale.

6. What Athenian leader boasted, "as a city, we are the school of Greece"?

- Ⓐ Alexander
- Ⓒ Pericles
- Ⓑ Themistocles
- Ⓓ Darius

7. Alexander the Great was from the Greek province of

- Ⓐ Thrace.
- Ⓒ Chalkidike.
- Ⓑ Thessaly.
- Ⓓ Macedonia.

8. Socrates was condemned to death for the crime of

- Ⓐ murder.
- Ⓒ robbery.
- Ⓑ corrupting the youth.
- Ⓓ not paying his debts.

9. Herodotus is known as the Father of History.

- Ⓐ True
- Ⓑ False

10. The first Olympic games were held in the year

- Ⓐ 776 B.C.E.
- Ⓒ 100 B.C.E.
- Ⓑ 600 B.C.E.
- Ⓓ 146 B.C.E.

Chapter 6

Rome—The Drive for Conquest

To find the legendary origins of Rome, we return to that horrible night in the city of Troy, when a gift of peace became a scourge of death and absolute defeat. As the Greek invaders ran wild in the streets and the city went up in flames, Aeneas, carrying his ailing father on his back, grabbed his son's hand and fought his way through the panic-stricken crowd to safety outside the city walls. Together with the few other survivors, they escaped in a boat and, after a long and difficult voyage, settled in an area of Italy known as Latium. Many years later Aeneas' twin grandsons, Romulus and Remus, were born. Their uncle, King Amulius, fearing that one day they would overthrow him, ordered that the babies be thrown into the Tiber River. But the gods saw them safely to shore where a she-wolf raised them as her own until they grew up. Romulus and Remus argued over who would be the leader of the city they planned to build. To stake his claim Romulus began building a wall on the crest of the Palatine Hill, one of seven hills in the area. Remus mocked Romulus by jumping over the wall and Romulus, in his anger, killed his brother. Romulus went on to build the city called Rome, which was destined to rule the mightiest empire in the history of the world.

This, anyway, is the story created by the Romans themselves to explain who they were and where they came from. It was set down as an epic poem called the *Aeneid* by the Roman poet Virgil, who used the *Iliad* and *Odyssey* of Homer as his source and inspiration. The archeological evidence presents us with a somewhat less dramatic scenario.

Sometime around 2000 B.C.E. a tribe of people moved from Central Europe across the Alps and into what we know as Italy. These farmers and herders, called Latins, settled on a broad plain beside the Tiber River. Their land became known as Latium. By about 750 B.C.E. one settlement on the Tiber had grown into a village called Rome.

Then sometime around the year 600 B.C.E. a people known as the Etruscans moved south from northern Italy to take over Rome and the other villages in Latium. No one knows where the Etruscans came from originally, although the oriental features of their culture give evidence of an eastern origin. The Etruscans ruled Rome for a hundred years. During that time the quiet village grew into a bustling city. The Etruscans were a much more advanced society than the Romans of those times. They erected a wall around the city, drained the nearby swamps, and built plumbing and sewer systems. They taught the Romans how to build roads and how to use arches in building bridges and aqueducts. The Romans used the Etruscan alphabet to write their own language, called Latin.

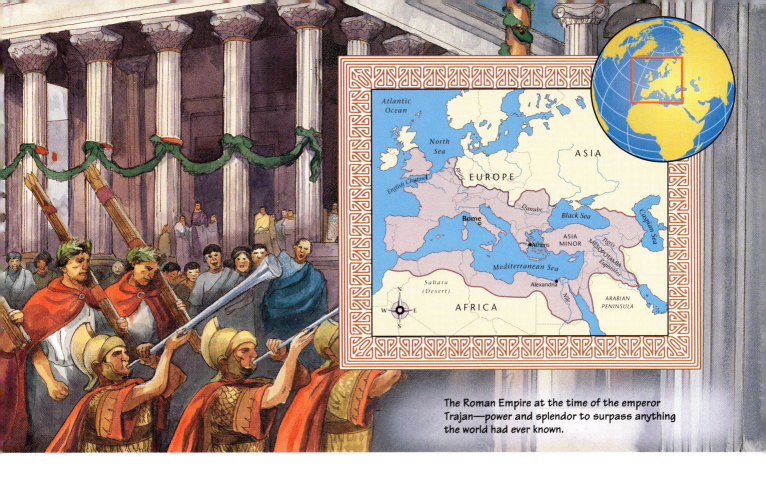

The Roman Empire at the time of the emperor Trajan—power and splendor to surpass anything the world had ever known.

In 509 B.C.E. the Romans rebelled against the harsh Etruscan king, Tarquinius Superbus, and drove the Etruscans from Rome. Tired of being ruled by kings, they set up a Republican form of government. In the Roman Republic three hundred elected representatives met in a senate, or council. These "senators" were usually wealthy landowners. They held office for life. The Senate proposed laws and elected and advised the "consuls," who were the highest officials in the government. The consuls commanded the army, saw to the collection of taxes, and enforced the laws. Consuls could hold office for only one year. This way no single person could acquire too much political power.

Just as had happened in Greece, two classes soon developed in the early Roman Republic. The Patricians, or wealthy landowners, were the only ones eligible to be elected consul or become members of the senate. They controlled the government. The Plebian class, made up of farmers, merchants and workers, at first had virtually no rights at all. But over time they demanded and received a greater role in governing the city. Eventually they were given the right to create their own assembly, the Assembly of Tribes, which met alongside the Senate and gave final approval for all new laws.

Rome grew in wealth and power as it moved out to establish trading posts and colonies throughout the Mediterranean. But in do-ing so it threatened the already established masters of the Mediterranean trade routes, the North African city-state of Carthage. Carthage had been founded by Phoenician colonists from Tyre around 800 B.C.E., and by the time of the Roman expansion, had taken control of the greater part of the North African coast, southern Spain, and certain regions of what is today the country of France.

The leaders of Carthage proposed to the Romans that the two cities set up "spheres of influence" to prevent interfering with each other. The contesting powers maintained an uneasy peace until 264 B.C.E., when the people of the Sicilian city of Messana (today called Messina) asked both the Carthaginians and the Romans for help in their fight against invaders from the Greek colony of Syracuse. The inevitable confusion that followed led to the first Punic (Latin for Phoenician) War,

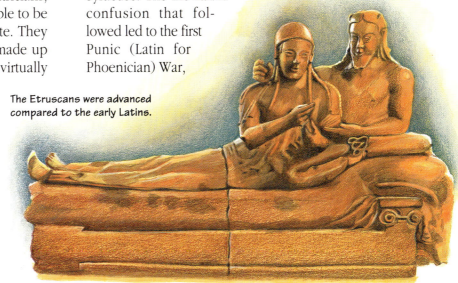

The Etruscans were advanced compared to the early Latins.

Hannibal's elephants braved the
Alpine winter to enter Roman territory.

66

which the Romans finally won in 241 B.C.E., acquiring the Greek island of Sicily as spoils of war.

Carthage neither forgot nor forgave the defeat it had received at the hands of the Romans. In 218 B.C.E., under the leadership of the remarkable military leader Hannibal, the Carthaginians made a bid for revenge with an incredible attack on Rome. The Second Punic War began when Hannibal landed in Spain with an army of 50,000 soldiers, 9,000 horsemen, and thirty-seven fighting elephants. From there he moved north and then south again through the narrow mountain passes of the snow-covered Alps into Italy. Hannibal routed several Roman armies, but could not capture the prize—the city of Rome itself. Rome responded by sending its own army to the North African coast, threatening the very gates of Carthage. Hannibal was forced to hurry home to defend the city, and in the year 202 B.C.E. the Roman army again defeated the Carthaginian forces. Hannibal fled to Tyre to escape death at the hands of the conquering Romans. In 149 B.C.E., Rome decided to rid itself of its old enemy once and for all. In the Third Punic War, after three years of fighting, it reduced the city of Carthage to ruins, in the process adding the lands of North Africa to its ever-expanding empire.

Within a relatively brief period of time, Rome found itself the possessor of a vast and far-flung empire. Spain, the southern coast of France, Greece, North Africa, Egypt, and most of Asia Minor had fallen under the domination of the seemingly invincible Romans. As immense riches poured into the city from the conquered lands, a few notables became fabulously wealthy. Yet conquest had its price. The farmers, the merchants, and especially the common workers were replaced by the sudden influx of slaves from the conquered lands and found themselves in ever more dire straits. The increasingly sharp division between the wealthy few and the struggling multitudes led to a period of constant riots, rebellions, and civil war that lasted for a hundred years.

In 49 B.C.E. the Senate, desperate to restore order to the crumbling republic, declared Julius Caesar (a popular and successful general), temporary dictator of Rome. Julius Caesar (102-44 B.C.E.) is without doubt one of the towering figures of antiquity. Besides being a brilliant military leader, he possessed a keen intellect and an original and inventive mind. He wrote two books of history that are still considered classics: *Commentaries on the Gallic War* and *Commentaries on the Civil War*.

He also wrote poetry and was much admired as an orator. He began his official career in 68 B.C.E. as a minor financial official. Seven years later he was appointed Governor of Further Spain. Soon thereafter Caesar accepted a five-year post as commander of the Roman army in Gaul. His exploits and his success in subjugating all of Gaul and making the first Roman invasion of Britain won him the loyalty of his legions and the admiration and respect of the entire citizenry.

From 49 to 45 B.C.E., Caesar was embroiled in a civil war with a rival general, Pompey, and his forces. When Caesar departed Rome for the war with Pompey, he left Mark Antony, his close friend and comrade from the Gallic Wars, in charge at home. With the defeat of Pompey, Caesar returned triumphantly to Rome and began the process of reorganizing and reforming the government. He helped the poor, created jobs, and gave farms to farmers who had lost their lands. He became immensely popular with the people and in 44 B.C.E. declared himself sole ruler and dictator for life. A group of senators that included men he had trusted, angered by his tyrannical behavior, assassinated Caesar on the steps of the Senate building. It was Mark Antony who delivered one of the most famous funeral orations of all time, arousing the populace against the conspirators.

After Caesar's death, civil war erupted again. The struggle for power was between Mark Antony and Caesar's adopted son, Octavian. Antony was bitterly disappointed when the Senate declared Octavian the new consul and took an assignment in Egypt where he, like Caesar, fell under the spell of the bewitching Cleopatra. Antony and Cleopatra married and began making plans to depose Octavian. When Octavian learned of their plot, he declared war on Egypt, and Roman ships decisively defeated the Egyptian fleet at the battle of Actium in 31 B.C.E. Within a year both Mark Antony and Cleopatra had committed suicide. In 27 B.C.E. the Roman Senate proclaimed Octavian Consul, Tribune, and Military Leader for Life with the title "Augustus," meaning "revered." Although he was not immediately given the title, it was not long before Augustus was in fact the Emperor of Rome. Under Augustus, the Roman Republic came to an end—the Senate had given away its power to govern.

At that time nearly one hundred million people were under Roman rule. In the north, the empire extended from Britain to the Rhine and Danube rivers. In the south, Rome controlled the Mediterranean Sea, much of North Africa, and Egypt. To the west Rome's control extended to the Atlantic Ocean, and to the east to the Euphrates River.

Augustus reorganized the government as a monarchy. He personally supervised every aspect of life in the empire. He tried to restore family values in the turbulent society by nurturing religion—old temples were repaired, new ones were built, and emperor worship was established—and marriage, and by discouraging divorce. He devoted special attention to balancing the budget, restructuring the distribution of grain, and improving highways and flood control. Ultimately Augustus the dictator accomplished what the Senate could not: He brought peace, law, and order to a weary Roman world. The system he set up remained effective for two hundred years, and his reign ushered in the Pax Romana ("Roman Peace"), which lasted until around C.E. 180.

This was the time of greatest expansion for the empire. By 51 B.C.E., Julius Caesar had conquered Gaul as far north as the Rhine River, Pompey had subdued Syria, and the frontier had been pushed back in Asia Minor. Egypt was annexed after the defeat of Antony and Cleopatra in 31 B.C.E. During the reign of Augustus, the boundary of the empire in Central Europe was extended to the Danube River. Rhaetta, Noricum, Pannonia and Moesia (comprising parts of modern Switzerland, Germany, Austria, and Hungary) were also annexed. One of Augustus' successors,

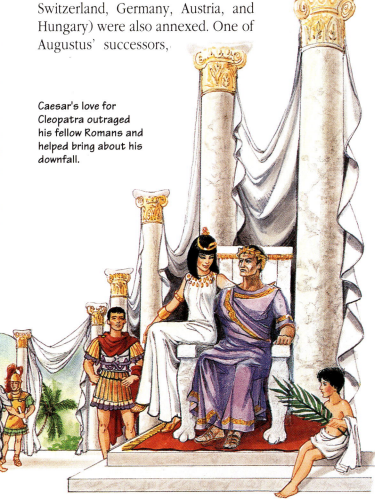

Caesar's love for Cleopatra outraged his fellow Romans and helped bring about his downfall.

Claudius added Thrace (Rumania and Bulgaria), Numidia, (an area south of Carthage), and Britain, which Caesar had invaded earlier but had not conquered.

As Rome conquered and occupied more and more distant lands, its original religion, an adaptation of ancient Etruscan beliefs, came to encompass many of the beliefs of the conquered peoples. From the most ancient times, the veneration of the Magna Mater, the "Mother Goddess," continued to be a major source of spiritual strength. From Greece the gods and goddesses of Mount Olympus were introduced into the Roman world with little change. From Egypt, Isis and many other deities became popular with the people of Rome. With the end of the republic and the birth of the empire under Augustus, the emperor himself became the god of gods, and emperor worship became the official state religion.

Side by side with the state-sanctioned religion, the old beliefs persisted as mystery cults. Highly secretive and open only to chosen initiates, their existence fostered a society in which unusual and exclusive religious practices were generally tolerated, if not fully accepted. The only group in the entire empire that did not have to—at least superficially—pay obeisance to the emperor were the Jews. The Jews had a long history of belief in one god, and in the interest of maintaining peace and stability in the land, the government of Rome respected this belief. It was into the religious melting pot of imperial Rome that Jesus was born.

For most of Jesus' life he was viewed by the Roman authorities as just another in a long line of Jewish prophets—slightly mad, occasionally annoying, essentially harmless. But as his teachings became more radical, he came to be viewed as a dangerous influence. Finally he was tried and executed as an enemy of the state. It was only after his death that a small following grew into a large and vociferous cult which, for a time, was again misunderstood by the Romans as simply another mystery cult— peculiar, but of no consequence

Gladiators fought to the death as the people of Rome enjoyed the show.

to the smooth running of the empire. It was only when the Christians' strict code of conduct led them to openly deny the divinity of the emperor that the persecution began. And it continued for three hundred years. Yet despite the constant harassment, economic hardship, torture, and wholesale slaughter, Christianity not only survived but flourished. All over the empire the poor and downtrodden heard the "Good News" of the apostle Paul and flocked to the new religion with its promise of a glorious eternal life in heaven.

During the reign of the emperor Trajan (98 - 117) the empire reached the outer limits of growth. The government, in addition to supporting a huge standing army and maintaining an enormous and intricate web of public works, provided free public entertainment, free grain to the poor, and low-cost loans to farmers—all subsidized by a constantly increasing tax burden. As many as 300,000 applicants received a monthly ration of grain at less than half the normal market price. When there was cause for celebration, this monthly ration was free. And as for the public entertainment, money was virtually no object in keeping the masses distracted. From the times of the republic to the second century, the number of national festivals rose from sixty to one hundred and thirty! And of what exactly did this free entertainment consist? Here is just a sample of what the ancient Romans found amusing: gladiator death-fights lasting one hundred days and involving as many as 19,000 combatants; fashionably dressed women in hand-to-hand combat with dwarves and invalids; unarmed men battling lions or bears; victims being tossed from tall towers into cages full of hungry animals; and so much more!

The empire began to spin in a vicious circle as the heavy taxes swelled the ranks of welfare recipients, in turn creating the need for ever more tax revenue. By the time of Marcus Aurelius (emperor from 161–180) Rome had expanded beyond the resources it had available to maintain it and beyond the ability of its government to govern. The far-flung borders could no longer be defended and the first of the outlying territories were relinquished. As the economic situation worsened, the government took increasingly severe measures in a desperate struggle to set things right. In the third century, the vast estates of wealthy landholders were confiscated and declared property of the state. Eventually the heavy taxes and the apparent breakdown in the administration of the empire turned the people against their rulers.

When Emperor Marcus Aurelius died without naming a successor in C.E. 180, the long standing system for ensuring a smooth transition from one ruler to the next fell apart. The empire entered a period of civil strife as rival generals with their private armies fought for the right to the emperor's throne. Reigns became shorter and often ended in assassination, further destabilizing the society.

Diocletian, who ruled from 284 to 305, took the most drastic measures to stop the disintegration of the empire. In 301, he issued a price-control edict that made it a crime to raise prices on anything. Finally recognizing that the empire's size made it impossible to govern effectively, he split it into two parts, with himself ruling in the west and a subordinate ruler in the east. It was the beginning of the end.

Diocletian's successor, Constantine, threatened by the European barbarians to the west and by the resurgent Persian Empire in the east, made two moves that were to have a direct effect on the future course of the empire. Aware that Christianity had grown to become a powerful economic and political force, in 313 he personally converted to the new religion and ended the persecutions. In 330, having declared Christianity the new state religion, he moved the capital of the empire from Rome to the ancient Greek city of Byzantium in the east (which he renamed Constantinople), the more effectively to deal with the growing Persian threat.

For more than a hundred years, there had been almost constant warfare along Rome's eastern frontier. Neither side had ever been able to seriously damage the other, but the vicious battles strained the resources and tested the might of Rome. Over the years three Roman emperors had been lost to the fierce Persians.

At the same time, the northern and western borders were being repeatedly tested by the unconquered European tribes. As the empire's internal problems increased, less and less attention was devoted to maintaining the borders, and a trickle of barbarian tribes began settling in the Roman hinterlands. The Romans made the foolish mistake of establishing a policy of hiring mercenary barbarian warriors to fight other invading barbarians. In 378, a barbarian tribe known as the Goths defeated the Roman army and killed the

The banner of Christianity flew over Constantine's victorious troops.

emperor Valens, and from that day forth the western empire became prey to a succession of powerful barbarian invaders. In 410 Alaric I, a Visigoth who had served in the Roman army, led his troops into the city of Rome itself and pillaged it for three days before being repulsed. In 476, the last emperor of Roman birth, Romulus Augustus, surrendered the throne to the barbarian king Odoacer. That date is considered the official end of the Roman Empire. The great civilization had endured for more than one thousand years. Although the eastern Byzantine Empire carried on, the glory that was Rome was no more. By the sixth century the city of Rome, which had once been home to a million people, was a small town of 50,000 souls, strewn with the broken statues and dilapidated monuments that were the only reminders of its time in the sun.

Perhaps the most enduring of Rome's many lasting contributions to Western civilization was the Roman concept of law that, simply put, was common sense generalized. For Romans the law was more than a system for punishing wrongdoers: It served to protect lives and property. Any Roman citizen could ask for and obtain a ruling direct from the emperor himself. This notion brought a new level of sophistication to the idea of law and order. In 527, the Byzantine Emperor Justinian, fearing that the Roman system of law would eventually disappear, ordered that all Roman laws be organized and codified. Justinian's law code became the basis for the legal systems of many modern countries, including the United States.

Slavery was a fact of life in ancient Rome. Slaves served as teachers, doctors, architects, gladiators, or as workers in mines and quarries. In the times of the Republic the treatment of slaves was despicable—probably the worst in the history of the world. As a result, rebellions and uprisings killed as many as one million people. The last major slave rebellion, led by the gladiator Spartacus, lasted for two years as 90,000 slaves terrorized

Crucified slaves lined the Appian way for miles when the rebellion led by the gladiator Spartacus was finally crushed.

Latins move from Central Europe into Italy

Settlement on the Tiber grows into Rome

Etruscans from Northern Italy take over Rome

Romans rebel against Etruscans and form Republic

Punic (Phoenician) War
Rome defeats Carthage

Second Punic War
Rome defeats Carthage

Caesar declares himself ruler for life
Caesar assassinated, Octavian becomes consul
Julius Caesar Emperor of Rome

Third Punic War
Rome leaves Carthage in ruins

Octavian declares war, defeats Egypt

Octavian (now Augustus) proclaimed ruler for life, Republic ends

Emperor Marcus Aurelius, Decline of Rome

Emperor Trajan, Rome reaches its limits of growth

Marcus Aurelius dies without naming a successor, civil strife begins

| 2000 | 750 | 509 | 264 | 218 | 149 | 49 | 45 | 31 | | 27 | 98 | 161 | 180 |
| | | | 241 | 202 | 146 | | | | BC | AD | | | |

the Italian countryside. During the middle years of the republic, a vast number of slaves were prisoners of war. Rome acquired 70,000 slaves from the First Punic War and as many as 500,000 from Caesar's Gallic Wars. The slave markets were also well supplied by the pirate kidnappers who infested the Mediterranean. Wealthy Romans often owned as many as five hundred slaves. In Augustus' time, one fourth to one third of the population were slaves. Compare this with the southern states of the U.S. prior to the Civil War, when one third of the population were slaves. In the second century a proposal to make slaves wear distinguishing clothing was defeated in the Senate for fear that, once the slaves realized how numerous they were, they would be uncontrollable.

The Romans' skill as innovative engineers can be seen today in their incredibly well-built bridges, aqueducts, and roads, many of which are still in use. Their use of poured concrete and high-vaulted ceilings in architecture enabled them to build larger buildings than any of their predecessors. One example, still standing, is the Pantheon in Rome. The Romans also implemented the first health care system, under which doctors paid by the government helped care for the poor. Yet they never developed a public education program. In the early years of the empire, male children were taught at home by their parents

Roman engineering skills were unsurpassed for centuries.

using the Twelve Tables, an ancient law code analogous to the Ten Commandments, as the standard text. Later, Greek slaves served as teachers in schools where rhetoric, oratory, agriculture, law, medicine, and military studies were taught. As opposed to the early Greeks, the Romans never developed science to any great degree, since scientific inquiry was considered sacrilegious.

Latin, the language of the Romans, became the common tongue of all the people in the empire, and from it many modern languages—Italian, French, Spanish, Portuguese, and Rumanian—evolved. Many English words were derived from Latin roots, and to this day Latin is the universal language of the legal and medical professions.

71

| 301 | 313 | 330 | 378 | 410 | 476 | 527 |

- **Diocletian splits Roman Empire into two** (301)
- **Emperor Constantine converts to Christianity** (313)
- **Capital of Rome moved to Greece (Byzantium renamed Constantinople)** (330)
- **Goths defeat Romans kill Emperor Valens** (378)
- **Alaric I's troops pillage Rome** (410)
- **Romulus Augustulus surrenders to barbarian king Odoacer** (476)
- **Byzantine Emperor Justinian codifies Roman Law** (527)

Four Emperors of the Pax Romana Who Ruled the World

To read a short summary of the first four emperors after Augustus is like reading a soap opera written by an imaginative madman:

•TIBERIUS (14-37) Augustus adopted Tiberius and made him heir to the empire. It is widely assumed that Augustus' wife, Livia, poisoned or otherwise dispensed with a number of relatives who might have had preference over her son Tiberius as Augustus' successor. An experienced military commander, Tiberius was readily accepted as the second emperor. For the most part he followed Augustus' policies, strengthened the frontiers and governed the provinces well. In C.E. 26 he decided to govern from his home on the island of Capri. Historians report that he indulged in murderous family quarrels motivated by his suspicious nature. Upon hearing of a plot against him instigated by Sejanus, leader of the Imperial Guard, Tiberius instituted a frightening period of terror in which many of Sejanus' friends, and Sejanus himself, were killed. Rome hoped the terror would end when Tiberius died.

Tiberius

72

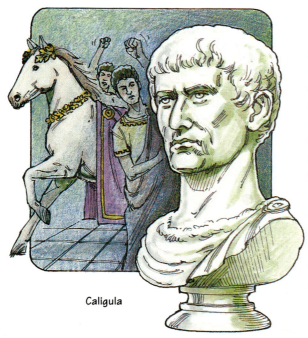

Caligula

•CALIGULA (37-41) Caligula was much, much worse. Tiberius' grandson had been declared joint heir along with Caligula. However, the Senate declared the will to be invalid, and Caligula became emperor. His short reign was marked by autocratic rule and savagery toward his enemies. He had Tiberius' grandson executed. Some senatorial records claim that after an illness during his first year he became mentally unbalanced. Where Tiberius had been frugal, Caligula quickly squandered the treasury. Convinced he was a god, he demanded that he be worshiped. When his favorite sister died, he insisted that she be deified as well, the first woman to be given that honor. The Romans were horrified, but had to obey. He gave his horse a marble stable, an ivory stall, and a jewelled collar—to flaunt his power over the Senate he declared this trusted companion to be Consul! In the year 41, members of the Praetorian Guard assassinated him and declared his uncle, Claudius, to be emperor.

•CLAUDIUS (41-54) Claudius had no aspirations to become emperor. In fact he was lucky to have survived the many family intrigues under Tiberius and Caligula. Physically limited by a partial paralysis that affected both his face and his legs, he was considered unfit for a public career and was usually not allowed to be seen in public. When Caligula was assassinated by the Praetorian Guard, the leaders of the plot declared Claudius emperor, perhaps as a joke. This action thwarted the Senate, which wanted to restore the republic.

Claudius entrusted a great deal of power to his manipulative wives and to his trusted inner cabinet members—in several key instances former slaves. But he was an able leader, founding a number of new Roman cities in the far-flung provinces. He added Britain, Mauritania (northern Africa), and Thrace (north of Greece) to the empire. Claudius was probably the most literate of the Roman emperors, having studied

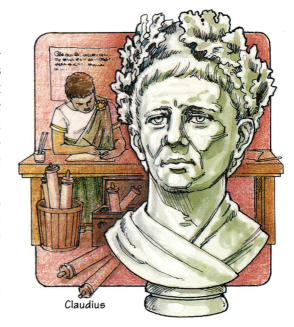

Claudius

history, linguistics, and antiquities. He wrote histories of the Augustan era, and of the Etruscans and the Carthaginians, which unfortunately have not survived.

Claudius' third wife, Messalina, was executed when she married her lover in the hopes of making him emperor in place of Claudius. Claudius then married his niece, Aggripina. She convinced him to adopt her son, Nero, thus excluding his own son from succession. Claudius is believed to have been poisoned by Aggripina when he had second thoughts about who his successor should be.

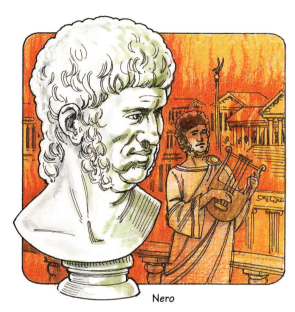

Nero

• NERO (54-68) Nero continued the reign of murder established by his predecessors. First he did away with Brittanicus, Claudius' surviving son. Then he had his meddlesome mother, Aggripina, murdered. He divorced and then murdered his first wife. In 64 a great fire consumed ten of fourteen districts in Rome. It was believed that Nero himself had arranged the fire in order to clear land for an enormous new palace. Nero blamed the fire on the Christians, at that time a very small sect. The result was the first major persecution of the Christians.

Nero was excessively proud of his meager abilities as an actor, athlete, artist, singer, poet, and musician. In 67 he toured Greece and participated in numerous chariot races and musical competitions. Since Greece was under Roman domination it should come as no surprise that he *always* won first prize. In 68, the governors of three provinces revolted against Nero's profligate rule. Returning from Greece only to find that the Praetorian Guard had deserted him, he committed suicide.

Quiz

1. The Etruscans took over Rome in the year

  Ⓐ 2000 B.C.E.   Ⓒ 509 B.C.E.

  Ⓑ 750 B.C.E.   Ⓓ 600 B.C.E.

2. The Punic Wars were fought between Rome and

  Ⓐ Greece.   Ⓒ Tyre.

  Ⓑ Carthage.   Ⓓ Troy.

3. The Assembly of Tribes included members of which class.

  Ⓐ Plebian   Ⓒ Republican

  Ⓑ Patrician   Ⓓ Slaves

4. The great fire of 64 occurred during the reign of

  Ⓐ Tiberius.   Ⓒ Nero.

  Ⓑ Caligula.   Ⓓ Claudius.

5. When he became emperor, Octavian was given the name

  Ⓐ Augustus.   Ⓒ Mark Antony.

  Ⓑ Julius Caesar.   Ⓓ Hannibal.

6. The Roman Empire reached its greatest size during the reign of

  Ⓐ Augustus.   Ⓒ Trajan.

  Ⓑ Marcus Aurelius.   Ⓓ Cleopatra.

7. The first Roman emperor to declare Christianity the state religion was

  Ⓐ Diocletian.   Ⓒ Valens.

  Ⓑ Jovian.   Ⓓ Constantine.

8. The Byzantine Empire continued to carry on after the barbarian conquest of Rome.

  Ⓐ True   Ⓑ False

9. The Roman legal system was codified during the reign of

  Ⓐ Justinian.   Ⓒ Shapur II.

  Ⓑ Trajan.   Ⓓ Romulus Augustus.

10. The last Roman emperor of Rome was

  Ⓐ Alaric I.   Ⓒ Romulus Augustus.

  Ⓑ Odoacer.   Ⓓ Justinian.

Chapter 7

The Expansion of Religion

What is the meaning of life? How did the universe begin? How will it end? Can we control the forces of nature around us? What happens when you die? All the scientific evidence points to the conclusion that, since the very earliest times, human beings have pondered

time or another. The next step in the development of religious thought seems to be to an attempt to control the forces of nature by communicating with the gods and goddesses that represent them. This communication takes the form of prayers, offerings and sacrifices which will convince the gods to make the rain come, or to stop floods, or to keep the sun shining, or to give warriors success in battle. Hinduism, the first religion to be discussed in this chapter, is an extremely sophisticated form of what began as a simple form of nature worship. From

Relative concentrations of World Religions

- ✝ Christianity
- ☪ Islam
- Hinduism
- Buddhism

questions like these—questions to which there are no certain answers. It is easy to understand why people have always searched for better ways to provide themselves with shelter from bad weather, water to quench their thirst, food to satisfy their hunger. The *hunger for meaning* is a more complicated phenomenon. It is this spiritual hunger from which the need for religion springs. And it is this hunger that defines us as human beings, a kind of animal so different from all the others.

Scientific research tells us that the earliest form of religion is the worship of life itself in the form of a Mother, or Earth, Goddess. Primitive people witnessing the miracle of birth envision the power of creation as a mother constantly giving birth to all the things they need to survive. The Mother Goddess, in her many guises, has reigned over almost every culture in the world at one

Hinduism sprang Buddhism, a religion based on the teachings of a single remarkable person.

With the development of human culture comes increasing sophistication in religious belief. Monotheism, the belief in one supreme god, is an idea which was brought to full development by the Jewish people thousands of years ago. From Judaism came Christianity, and then Islam.

Several hundred million people today describe themselves as non-religionists, and several hundred million describe themselves as atheists. (They do not believe there is a supernatural guiding spirit.) However, the majority of people in the world do profess belief in one of the four religions discussed in this chapter. We summarize these four because they have come to predominate in influence, impact, and membership.

From left to right, the three main gods of Hinduism: Brahma the Creator, seated on a lotus blossom; Vishnu the preserver astride Garuda, his winged servant; and Shiva the destroyer crushing the demon of ignorance underfoot.

Hinduism

Of all the world's religions, none is older, more shrouded in mystery, more difficult for the westerner to comprehend, than Hinduism, the ancient religion of India. Hinduism has evolved over the course of three thousand years. Its special beauty is the way in which, with no single charismatic founder, no organized church, no specific leadership, it continues to grow. It has absorbed the gods and goddesses, the traditions and beliefs of the thousands of minor cults that have come and gone in the land over the centuries. Nearly all of the more than 700 million Hindus in the world live in India. Today Hinduism is the third largest religion in the world.

Like all early peoples, the first people of India deified the forces of nature, which had such a direct influence on their lives: the sun, the moon, the wind, the rain, the yearly cycle of the seasons. The plants and the animals came to be symbolized and worshiped as gods and goddesses. Myths were born to explain how and why things had come to be the way they were. Many tribes inhabited the vast Indian subcontinent, each with their own gods and goddesses, each with their own set of myths.

That's the way it was about 1500 B.C.E. when the Aryans swept down from the north and, with sword and fire, imposed their will upon the land. Over the course of the next several hundred years, the religion that the Aryans brought with them gradually gathered unto itself the smaller local cults of the conquered peoples. Trees, stones, animals such as monkeys, peacocks and cobras, rivers, mountains, the stars, all these and untold other divinities came to be included in a pantheon of, according to some interpretations, literally millions of different sacred objects, gods and goddesses.

Early Hindus combined all of their elemental deities into one all-pervasive, all-powerful spirit—Brahman, the spirit of the universe itself, which resides in all living things. Hinduism portrays the spirit of Brahman as manifesting itself in three different guises: Brahma, the Creator of the universe; Vishnu, the Preserver; and Shiva, the Destroyer.

In the Hindu tradition, the major gods often come to Earth in numerous forms called manifestations. One of the most beloved of the Hindu gods is Krishna who, according to Hindu legend, is a manifestation of the god Vishnu. Krishna loves humanity, which in turn loves him for his follies, his passions, and most of all, his human ways. Many legends describe him as a mischievous young boy who is as apt to sneak a lick of butter from his mother's kitchen as to mind his parents. He has great strength which he uses to fight monsters, demons, and jealous rulers. His heroics take on superhuman dimensions—he can inhale deadly fires and conquer giants. He is handsome, too. When he plays his flute in the dark of night he can woo women from all parts of India to his side.

The complexities of Hindu belief are explained in a collection of writings known as the Vedas, or Books of Knowledge. These, among the oldest living religious texts in the world, are believed to have been written beginning around 1500-1200 B.C.E. The four Vedas—the *Rig Veda*, the *Sama Veda*, the *Yajur Veda*, and the *Athara Veda*—contain immense riches of prayers, hymns, theology, mythology, and philosophy which, together, make up this intricate system.

One of the unique concepts of Hinduism is that of reincarnation. Reincarnation is the belief that the soul does not die with the body, but that after one physical life comes to an end, the soul is eventually reborn in another body. Belief in reincarnation is closely linked to the caste system. Hindu doctrine says that people with good "karma,"—people who have led good lives—may be reborn into a higher caste. But people with bad karma are reborn into a lower caste. A person might even be reborn as an animal or an insect. Hindus believe that after many rebirths, some souls can achieve a level of spiritual development that surpasses even the

Krishna and his consort, Parvati.

highest caste. These pure and clean souls are liberated from the cycle of birth and death and become one with the spirit of Brahman forever.

Another important Hindu concept is that of "dharma," which may be interpreted as "the Law," "the Right Path," or "Proper Behavior." This simply means that there are rules to follow which will create good karma. Not drinking alcohol is one. Not eating meat is another.

Hindus have a reverence for all animals, but particularly cows. For Hindus it is a major offense to kill or harm a cow. They treat cattle with the utmost respect, hanging garlands of flowers around the animals' necks and sometimes allowing them to roam freely into and out of their homes. This custom may date all the way back to the original Aryan conquerors of India who depended heavily on cattle for their well-being.

Another expression of Hindu philosophy that is more readily understood by non-Hindus is yoga. Many westerners today practice yoga as a form of exercise. But in its true and essential form it is much more than that. Given to humanity by Ishvara, the Hindu god of supreme knowledge and goodness, yoga is a technique of meditation that through various "asanas," or postures, allows one to gain control of the mind and the senses. The positions are difficult and require long practice and training, but while in control, the mind and the senses can no longer interfere with the progress of the soul along the road to ultimate liberation.

We can barely glimpse the beauty of the ancient and intricate Hindu religion in the pages of this book. Yet perhaps a glimpse is sufficient to set the stage for the entrance of a young Indian prince who could not abide the suffering that he saw in the world.

76

In Hinduism, cows are considered sacred, and treated with veneration and respect.

The goal of Yoga is to free the soul by controlling the body.

Buddhism

In the sixth century B.C.E., the region of Magadha lay nestled in the long shadows of the mighty Himalaya Mountains in Northeast India. Today it is the small country of Nepal. It was here that Siddhartha Gautama, the Great Liberator, was born into the established social and political milieu of Hinduism. Siddhartha Gautama is better known to us as the Buddha—the Enlightened One, the serene figurehead of a religion that today bears his name, and the spiritual hopes and dreams of more than 300 million devotees.

The historical facts of Siddhartha's life are hopelessly enmeshed in a web of legend and myth. Yet the story of his birth to an illustrious noble family and his transformation into the greatest holy man in an eternally holy land, serves as a model by which those who wish to follow him might judge their own spiritual progress.

The Buddha found enlightenment while meditating in the shade of a Bo tree.

Even before Siddhartha was born, a prophet told his father (a wealthy member of the Kshatrya, or warrior, caste) that his son would one day renounce his family and his royal legacy to live the life of a holy man. His father wished to prevent this, so from the very start Siddhartha was sheltered behind the walls of his father's palace, distracted by pleasure and luxury, and given the finest education and training that money could buy. He was forbidden nothing, except that he was not permitted to leave the palace grounds. Before he was twenty he married a beautiful woman who bore him a son of his own.

As the sheltered young prince grew, so did his curiosity about the outside world. Finally he convinced his servant to take him out to see what was there to be seen. As they traveled about he saw four sights that he had never seen before and that he did not understand. He saw an old man, twisted and bent with age, a sick man suffering in pain, and a dead man being mourned by his grieving family. He asked his servant to explain the meaning of these things, but the servant could tell him only that old age, sickness, and death were misfortunes that no one could avoid. Finally Siddhartha saw a holy man—a monk. The simple garments of the holy man, the way his hands were raised to heaven as he held his alms bowl, and the calm smile on his face convinced Siddhartha that this was the way he too must follow. So in the dark of night, when everyone else in the household was asleep, Siddhartha and his faithful servant rode away from the palace, forever renouncing his life of luxury, and even his wife and son.

This, the Great Departure of Gautama, as it is known in Buddhism, took place when Siddhartha was twenty-nine years old. He put aside his rich garments and dressed himself in the rags of a beggar. He cut off his hair, dismissed his servant, and, with nothing but his alms bowl and the robe on his back, set off along the banks of the holy river Ganges. Traveling the length and breadth of India in search of enlightenment, he would not rest until he had discovered the reason for all the suffering in the world and the way to eliminate it.

He devoted himself to the study of Hinduism and other religions that he encountered, but none held the answers he sought. He joined a group of five other monks and for six years lived a life of asceticism, or extreme physical denial, in the hope that it might lead to ultimate knowledge. But one day he realized that this path, too, was a road to nowhere. He ate some simple food to regain his strength and resumed his wanderings. Soon he had a dream which told him that enlightenment was near. Seating himself at the foot of a Bo tree, or Tree of Knowledge, he meditated for forty-nine days.

When at last he emerged from his deep meditation, he had broken through to a Great Awakening. He understood the why of suffering, and the how of freeing oneself from it. From that day forth he has been known as the Buddha—the Enlightened One. The answer to the why of suffering he called the Four Truths: 1. all existence is suffering; 2. all suffering is caused by desire; 3. suffering can be overcome by eliminating desire; 4. the way to eliminate desire is to follow the Eightfold Path.

The Eightfold Path was the Buddha's answer to freeing oneself from suffering. By striving always to maintain the right views, the right purpose, the right speech, the right conduct, the right livelihood, the right effort, the right awareness, and the right meditation, people could rid themselves of the desire for false or unimportant things. By eliminating desire, one also eliminates the anguish that unfulfilled desire begets. And when desire and anguish are gone, one is left in a condition of total and perfect inner happiness, and released forever from the cycle of reincarnation, a philosophy that Buddhism shares with Hinduism.

The Buddha disclosed to his five disciples the Four Truths and the Eightfold Path. They

became the Buddha's first monks, moving out to spread his message among the people. The great Siddartha Gautama Buddha himself preached for forty-five years, bringing to everyone in India, regardless of caste or inheritance, a message of peace and compassion.

Many Hindus, especially of the lower castes, quickly became converted to the new religion. This gentle faith offered them a way out of their unhappiness, both in this life and in lives to come. Buddhism rejects the caste system. It teaches instead that reincarnated souls move through a *cycle* of higher and lower births in order to learn that pain and suffering are part of every life, whether rich or poor, male or female, human or animal.

After the Buddha's death, his saffron-robed monks continued to share his message, and the number of his followers quickly grew. Eventually, though, the deeply-embedded Hindu faith reasserted itself as the premier religion of India. But in China to the north and east, Buddhism grew to be a major faith of the land, and from there it spread to Japan, Korea, Ceylon, Thailand, and all the countries of Indochina. Today, it is the fourth largest religion in the world. Tibet, a tiny country tucked between China to the north and India to the south, came to be the spiritual center of the Buddhist world.

78

Buddhist monks live in poverty and devote their lives to spiritual growth.

Christianity

Five hundred years after the passing of the Buddha, in the province of Judaea in the heart of the Roman Empire, another liberator of the spirit was born. The Roman Empire embraced the entire Western world at that time, and Augustus, the Roman emperor, ruled supreme. The Romans imposed peace and discipline on the peoples they conquered, promoting law and order, good roads, and rich commerce. The empire, from the Middle East to the British Isles, flourished under the "Pax Romana," the Roman Peace.

One way the Romans maintained peace in their vast empire was to allow the conquered peoples to retain their culture, customs, and religious beliefs. Provincial Roman governors saw to it that the business of the empire prospered and that taxes were paid on time. As long as things went smoothly, the people were free to live as they wished and worship whatever gods they chose. Unlike most other conquering nations, the Romans had no interest in forcing their religion on those they defeated. They saw that this often caused dissent and rebellion, which could easily be avoided by adopting a policy of tolerance. However, for those who rebelled or opposed the Romans, death was quickly meted out, often by crucifiction.

Judaea was populated by the Jewish people, with a cultural and religious heritage that was some two thousand years old. With their unshakable faith in the one God, Jehovah, and the Torah (the first five books of the Old Testament) to guide them, the Jews remained steadfast in their beliefs and in their unity as a people even under the full weight of Roman domination.

This was the world into which Jesus of Nazareth was born, the son of a Jewish carpenter named Joseph and his wife, Mary. The story of the life of Jesus is told in the first four books of the New Testament of the Bible, the Gospels according to Matthew, Mark, Luke, and John. The Gospels say that Jesus was born miraculously when the spirit of God entered into Mary to create a child. He grew up as a normal Jewish boy of the times, studying the Torah, attending synagogue, and helping his father with his work. At an early age, he displayed exceptional understanding of the wisdom of the Torah.

When he was about thirty years old Jesus was baptized—immersed in the waters of the River Jordan—by his cousin John the Baptist, a Jewish prophet. An important part of Jewish belief was the idea that a Messiah, or Saviour (The Greek word for Messiah is "Christ.") would one day come to rescue them from their long captivity. John the Baptist proclaimed to the crowd gathered on the banks of the river that the Messiah had come, and that Jesus was the Christ.

When the baptism was over, Jesus began his life mission, traveling all over the land of Judaea teaching about love and the eternal life of the spirit. As he traveled he chose twelve men—rich men and poor men, fishermen and tax collectors—to follow him and be his disciples. Moving from village to village, Jesus began to gather a following. People crowded around to listen to him speak. What they heard sounded strange and new. Jesus emphasized to the Judaeans that their God was one of love and mercy. Like the first followers of the Buddha, most of the people that flocked to hear Jesus speak were the poor, the sick, the dispossessed, those living harsh and desperate lives. They were inspired by his declaration that "the meek shall inherit the earth," and given hope by his promise of a "kingdom that is not of this world."

Jesus asked the people to follow him, and some did. Enough, anyway, to alarm the Jewish elders and even to draw the attention of

Beautiful churches inspire Christians in their faith.

On Easter, Christians celebrate the death and resurrection of Jesus.

and anyone else who believed in him—would gain eternal life.

Jesus' disciples continued spreading word of the new way, moving throughout the Roman world gathering believers among any people who would listen. At first the Romans ignored the Christians, with their strange ideas and their meddlesome ways. But as their numbers grew and they carried on their ceaseless preaching and proselytizing, they came to be seen as a threat to Roman security. For almost three hundred years they were subjected to intermittent persecution, torture, and death by the Roman authorities in a futile attempt to stamp out this new religion. But still it slowly grew.

the local Roman magistrate. When Jesus began referring to himself as the Son of God the priests became alarmed, fearing that Jesus would become a dangerous challenge to their authority. They also feared that unruly demonstrations might threaten their delicate peace with Rome. As the Jewish high holy day of Passover approached, Jesus made his way toward Jerusalem, the Holy City. He was accused of trying to start a rebellion against Roman rule and Pontius Pilate, the Roman magistrate, ordered Jesus arrested. He was tried as an enemy of the state, found guilty, and crucified with two other criminals.

According to the New Testament, the great miracle of the story of Jesus takes place three days after his followers take his dead body down from the cross and lay him in his tomb. It goes on to tell us that on this day, later to be known as Easter, Jesus returned to life, walked out of his tomb and visited his closest disciples, showing them that he lived on after death and promising that they—

One of the worst persecutors of the early Christians was Saul of Tarsus. But then he himself converted to the new religion, changed his name to Paul, and became the greatest of the early Christian missionaries. He traveled all over the Middle East winning converts for the new religion. In fact some historians believe that Christianity would have died out had it not been for Paul's missionary zeal.

In the year 313, the Roman Emperor Constantine had a vision the night before a major battle. In a dream he saw the name of Christ and the words, "By this sign you will conquer." His victory the next day convinced him that the Christian God was, if not the one and only, certainly the most powerful. In the following year he decreed Christianity the official religion of the empire. The persecutions ceased and Christianity leapt forward. Over time the Roman Empire crumbled and disappeared, but Christianity flourished. Today it is estimated that 30 to 35 percent of the world's people find peace in the words of Jesus, making Christianity the largest religion in the world.

Islam

Several centuries after the Roman Empire disintegrated, a slumbering giant in the vast Arabian deserts to the east began to stir. Compared to life in the Empire, life in the scorching desert was harsh and spartan. The fiercely independent nomadic tribes were constantly on the move, grazing their flocks of sheep wherever they could, drinking, gambling, and fighting amongst themselves, with no uniting authority or central government. Most devoted little thought to the subtleties of religious philosophy or the well-being of their souls.

Many tribes engaged in trade by organizing caravans of camels. At home on the desert sands, the Arabs and their caravans formed an important link in the chain of commerce between Europe and Asia. The most important city in Arabian lands was Mecca, near the Red Sea. It was the wealthy center of the caravan trade and the location of the Kaaba, the holiest Arab shrine—a place where many gods were worshiped. The more than 360 idols that the Kaaba contained testify to the variety of religious belief among the "sons of the desert."

Mohamed, the Prophet of Islam, the Messenger of Allah, was born to a humble family in Mecca about 570 C.E. His parents died while he was still very young, and he was raised by an uncle. As a young man Mohamed was a camel driver in the employ of a wealthy widow fifteen years his senior. She so respected his work and his character that she took him as her husband, thus transforming him into a prosperous and prominent member of the community.

Mohamed often went to a cave in the desert to be alone and to contemplate the wickedness and iniquity that he saw all around him in the bustling city. He saw that the people had grown selfish and greedy, and he was deeply troubled. During a period of deep meditation in his cave, Mohamed had a vision in which the angel Gabriel appeared before him. In the vision, Mohamed said, the angel told him that he had

been selected to be the prophet of God. "Tell your people there is but one God and His name is Allah," the angel commanded.

At first Mohamed wondered if he'd gone mad, or if he'd been possessed by an evil spirit. But the vision was persistent. The angel kept appearing to him, always with the same message. Finally Mohamed became convinced that he had actually been chosen as God's messenger. For ten years Mohamed preached in Mecca, passing on the messages of Allah as they were given to him by the angel Gabriel. Few people chose to listen to him in those early years, but he was treated with respect because of the prestige of his wife's family.

When his beloved wife died, Mohamed found himself vulnerable to the wrath of the many he had offended with his strict teachings. So in the year 622, he fled from Mecca to the city of Yathrib, some three hundred miles to the north. His followers call Mohamed's flight from Mecca the Hegira, or withdrawal. The year 622 C.E. is the year 1 A.H. (Anno Hegira) of the Islamic calendar. In Yathrib, Mohamed's message gained a great following. The city changed its name to Medina, or "City of the Prophet." The religion of Islam was born. The word "Islam" means "submission to God." Those who follow the faith are called Muslims or Moslems. They do not worship Mohamed, they worship only Allah.

81

As Mohamed's following grew, he forged an army. He had been driven from Mecca by force and he would use force to return. In

Several times a day, Moslems the world over turn to face Mecca with their humble prayers.

The Koran—the holy book of Islam

630, Mohamed made his triumphant return to the city of Mecca. His first act was to go to the Kaaba and smash the hundreds of idols there. Only the Black Stone* remained, the destination of pilgrims for centuries, as it is to this day.

With the victory at Mecca, Mohamed became the most powerful man in Arabia, and Islam became its sole religion. Within two years Mohamed had died, and leadership of Islam was assumed by Abu Bakr, one of Mohamed's first disciples.

The holy book of Islam is the Koran and no book has

*Many western observers believe that the black stone is a meteorite fragment which was recovered from the desert many hundreds of years before Mohamed's time.

been treated with greater awe. To Moslems the only correct Koran is in Arabic because that is how Gabriel passed Allah's words to Mohamed. To translate it to other languages might result in errors in the true words. The Koran enumerates the Five Pillars of Faith upon which Islam stands: 1. The announcement of faith ("There is no God but Allah, and Mohamed is his prophet."); 2. Prayer (Five times each day every Muslim must face Mecca, prostrate himself, and pray.); 3. Charity (A portion of every believer's income must be given to the poor.); 4. Fasting (During the thirty-day holy month of Ramadan, no Muslim may eat between sunrise and sunset.); 5. Pilgrimage (All Muslims who are physically able must visit Mecca and the Kaaba at least once in their lives. Those who do so are given the title, "Hajji," which means "Assured of Heaven.").

Similar in many ways to Judaism and Christianity, Islam includes a strict moral code and a detailed system of ethics. Like the Bible the Koran prohibits lying, stealing, adultery, and murder, then goes a step further by completely prohibiting the consumption of alcoholic drink or of any food from the pig. Central to Islamic faith is the belief that this life is a period of testing and preparation for the true and eternal life to come, which waits on the other side of death's door. The believer need only submit completely to Allah's will to be assured a place in

Within one hundred years, believers had spread the new faith of Islam from Spain to India.

82

Aryans invade India		Siddhartha Gautama is born in Nepal					Jesus of Nazareth born		Roman Emperor Constantine converts to Christianity
	Hindu Books of Knowledge, the "Vedas"		Buddha's Great Departure		Augustus the Roman Emperor "Pax Romana" begins		Jesus baptized—proclaimed the "Messiah"		
				Buddha's Great Awakening				Pontius Pilate orders Jesus crucified	
1500 1200		563	534	528		27 B.C.E.	C.E. 30 40		313

| HINDUISM |
| BUDDHISM |
| JUDAISM → |
| CHRISTIANITY |

paradise. Especially esteemed by Allah are the holy warriors who die fighting in His name.

Mohamed considered himself the last and greatest in a long line of prophets stemming from the Judeo-Christian tradition, including Adam, Abraham, Noah, Moses, and Jesus. He differed from Christian beliefs in insisting that the great prophets, including Jesus and himself, were not divine, but ordinary mortals inspired by the divine word of God. In particular, he regarded the story of the resurrection and ascension of Jesus as pure fiction.

In the historical eye-blink of one hundred years, Islam spread like brushfire. From the Arabian Desert, Arabs professing the new faith traveled east all the way to the banks of the Indus River in India. To the west, they moved along the shores of North Africa and through Spain into France. The expansion of Islam into western Europe was stopped by Charles Martel and an army of Frankish knights in 732 at the Battle of Tours.

For the next six hundred years the Islamic world remained a bright flame of enlightenment as Europe groped its way through the darkness of the Middle Ages. Islam continued to attract new followers in Africa and the far reaches of Asia. Today Islam, the youngest of the world's major religions and the fastest growing, is second only to Christianity in the number of its followers.

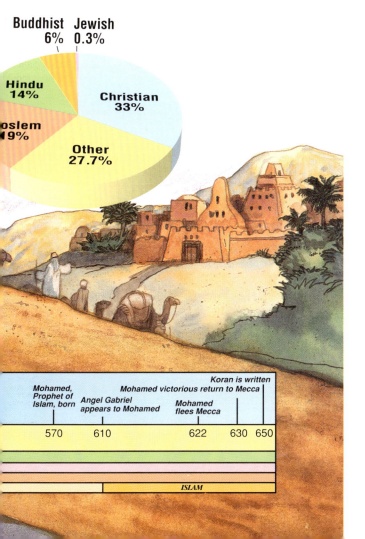

Quiz

1. In the Hindu religion the Creator is

- Ⓐ Buddha.
- Ⓒ Brahma.
- Ⓑ Vishnu.
- Ⓓ Shiva.

2. Hinduism is the world's oldest living religion.

- Ⓐ True
- Ⓑ False

3. The Vedas are the Hindu books of

- Ⓐ knowledge.
- Ⓒ prophecy.
- Ⓑ awareness.
- Ⓓ mystery.

4. Buddhism originated in

- Ⓐ Japan.
- Ⓒ Tibet.
- Ⓑ China.
- Ⓓ India.

5. That all existence is suffering is the first of the _____ Truths.

- Ⓐ Three
- Ⓒ Five
- Ⓑ Four
- Ⓓ Seven

6. Right conduct is one of the steps on the _____ Path.

- Ⓐ Fourfold
- Ⓒ Sevenfold
- Ⓑ Fivefold
- Ⓓ Eightfold

7. Jesus was born in the Roman province of

- Ⓐ Judea.
- Ⓒ Bethlehem.
- Ⓑ Nazareth.
- Ⓓ Galilee.

8. The Roman emperor who made Christianity the official religion of the empire was

- Ⓐ Pontius Pilate.
- Ⓒ Constantine.
- Ⓑ Augustus Caesar.
- Ⓓ Herod.

9. Islam is a _____ religion.

- Ⓐ monotheistic
- Ⓒ desert
- Ⓑ purely Arabic
- Ⓓ Hindu

10. The holy book of Islam is the

- Ⓐ Bible.
- Ⓒ Vedas.
- Ⓑ Koran.
- Ⓓ Torah.

Chapter 8

Asia and the Americas: 500 B.C.E. to C.E. 1300

Persia

Spread out on the vast Iranian Plateau, standing at the cross-roads between East and West, the Persian Empire steadily rose to take its place as one of the great ancient civilizations. In the fourth century B.C.E., its rulers succumbed to the Macedonian Greek conqueror Alexander the Great. But with Alexander's death at the age of thirty-three, Greece quickly lost its grasp on the vast Persian lands to the Parthians, a native Persian group that ejected the Greeks and established its own dynasty in 247 B.C.E.

Clinging to the memory of the glorious sixth and fifth centuries as their inspiration, the Parthians ruled until C.E. 224, when they were overthrown by Ardashir, who took the ancient title "King of Kings." Ardashir established the Sassanian dynasty and set about the task of returning Persia to its former might and splendor. He succeeded in restoring Persia's wealth and power by consolidating its position as the most vital link in the trade route that stretched between Europe and the Orient. At its height the Sassanian Empire extended from the Euphrates River to the valley of the Indus, and Persian traders routinely traveled to India and China, returning with the fine fabrics, the rare spices, and the advanced tech-

The Persian world blossomed as the Roman Empire collapsed.

84

Map labels: Black Sea, MACEDONIA, ANATOLIA, Caspian Sea, Royal Road, Sardis, Euphrates, Tigris, Persian Empire, Mediterranean Sea, Ecbatana, Sidon, Babylon, Susa, Egypt, Persepolis, Persian Gulf, Red Sea

Extent of Persian Empire under Darius I

Darius I rules Persia		Ardashir I overthrows the Parthians and establishes the Sassanian Empire in Persia		Persian war with Byzantium		Islamic Empire overthrows the last of the Persian rulers
	Alexander the Great dies		Ardashir I dies			
		Emperor Trajan of Rome invades Persia	Persians capture Roman Emperor Valerian			
	Parthians eject Greeks, establish Parthian Empire					
		Persian peace with Rome		Rome falls to barbarian king Odoacer		
521	323	247	114 120	224 244 256	476	540	641
		B.C.E.	C.E.				

nology so highly coveted by Europeans. The Sassanians revived ancient Persian customs and made the native religion, Zoroastrianism (named for the Persian prophet Zoroaster, who was a possible early influence on Christianity) the official religion of the empire.

It was the Sassanian Persians who thwarted the ambitions of the Roman Empire, always eager to extend its eastern frontier. These two giant empires, neighbors and mortal enemies, fought many times over the course of centuries. At one point the Persians even captured the Roman emperor Valerian along with tens of thousands of other prisoners, and put them to work building roads, bridges, and irrigation systems for their empire. With the collapse of the Roman empire in the west the tables turned, and now it was the Persians who eagerly sought westward expansion. The burden of resisting Persian expansion fell upon the shoulders of the Byzantine inheritors of Rome's legacy. Frequent warfare with Byzantium and internal quarrels during the sixth and seventh centuries weakened Persia and made it an easy target for the Islamic Empire pushing in from the west, which conquered Persia in 641.

India

Around 320 C.E., the northern part of the Indian subcontinent was conquered and united by Chandragupta Maurya, the founder of the Mauryan Empire and the first ruler of the Gupta Dynasty. His son, Samudragupta, expanded the empire eastward into areas known as Bengal, Assam, and Nepal, and south across the Deccan—the harsh grasslands that cover India's central plateau. The Hindu Guptas ruled most of India for about a hundred years, during which time they brought about peace and prosperity—rarely seen in its turbulent history. It was under their rule that the young and fast-growing Buddhist religion was overwhelmed by a resurgence of Hinduism in the empire.

Hindu themes dominated—indeed consumed—the art of the Gupta period. Carvings of animals, flowers, and figures of the gods covered Hindu shrines and temples. Elephants, monkeys, bulls, dancing women, jovial men, warriors, lovers, and countless other figures, all intricately intertwined, occupied every inch of stone. Stupas, the burial chambers of Buddhist monks, were surrounded by gates and railings that were ornately decorated with drawings, paintings, and sculpture. Gupta lit-

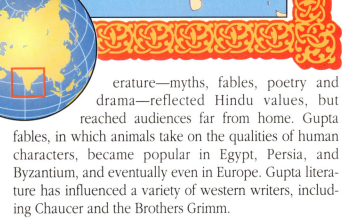

erature—myths, fables, poetry and drama—reflected Hindu values, but reached audiences far from home. Gupta fables, in which animals take on the qualities of human characters, became popular in Egypt, Persia, and Byzantium, and eventually even in Europe. Gupta literature has influenced a variety of western writers, including Chaucer and the Brothers Grimm.

Young Gupta Brahmins studied at special schools and universities that were established throughout the

Hindu art and architecture flourished under the Gupta dynasty.

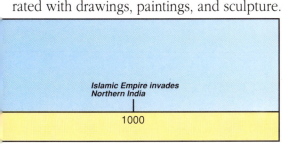

Islamic Empire invades Northern India

1000

empire. Because of this commitment to scholarship, the Gupta dynasty excelled in science and mathematics. Gupta astronomers correctly measured the size of the moon; they understood the principle of gravity; they knew that the earth was round and that it rotated on its axis. Europeans would not come to grips with these concepts for almost another thousand years! Gupta mathematicians developed a ten-digit system of numbers. Later this system was adopted by the Arabs, who in turn introduced it to Europe. The Europeans, who used Roman numerals up to that time, called the new kind of numbers Arabic numerals, but the real credit goes to India's Gupta Dynasty. The Guptas made strides in medicine too. They were the first to use inoculation as a way to prevent disease. (Inoculation would not be independently discovered in Europe for another thousand years.) Their very advanced doctors derived medicines from plants, set bones, and performed surgery.

By the year 500, the glory days of the Gupta dynasty were past. Weakened by constant assaults from the northern Huns, it could not withstand the southern kingdoms' attempts to retake the Deccan. Finally, in the 600s the empire fell apart, to be replaced by many small Hindu kingdoms, each ruled by a local prince. For the next seven hundred years the people of India endured internal warfare and almost continuous attacks from peoples outside its borders. One kingdom, the Pala dynasty, ruled northeastern India from the eighth to the twelfth century. The Buddhist Palas were an exception in Hindu-dominated northern India, and maintained strong ties with Tibet, the homeland of Buddhism. Meanwhile the vigorous Is-

The three lions—symbol of the Maurya Empire.

lamic Empire posed the most serious external threat to the Hindu kingdoms of India. In 711, after nearly a century of constant friction, the Arab followers of Islam overtook part of the Indus River valley in northwestern India, only to be stopped finally by the Rajputs, a clan of fierce Hindu warriors.

When the Hindus and Moslems weren't fighting, they were trading. India traded its silk, ivory and pearls for Arabian horses, known throughout the world for their speed and beauty. Indian merchants crossed the Indian Ocean to ports in Asia and the Middle East. Eventually they formed colonies in the Malay Peninsula and Indonesia, introducing Hinduism and Buddhism into those areas. They focused their economy increasingly on shipbuilding and overseas commerce.

The Hindus and Buddhists of India and the Arabs of the Islamic empire lived in uneasy yet profitable coexistence until around the year 1000, when Moslem warriors from Persia and Afghanistan began making incursions into northern India. The Persians and Afghans were bent on converting the vanquished Hindus to Islam. They destroyed Hindu idols, replacing them with Moslem mosques and universities, and installed a Moslem teacher in every town and village. Now there was little positive interaction between Moslem and Hindu. Monotheistic Moslems came to detest the caste system and the Hindu pantheon of gods. Hindus found Islamic exclusivity and militarism practically incomprehensible. By the 1200s the Ottoman Turks had ousted other Moslem invaders and set up sultanates throughout most of India.

86

Chandragupta Maurya unites northern India, establishes Gupta Dynasty

Dravidian kingdoms retake the Deccan in India

India ruled by small Hindu kingdoms

Gopala establishes the Pala dynasty in India

320

B.C.E.   C.E.

500   600   700

Southeast Asia

India's influence on the peoples of Southeast Asia went well beyond trade. Travelers and traders, monks and merchants who passed through the colonies in Indonesia, Burma, and Malaya brought the seeds of India's culture—her religions, her art, her science—with them.

One place where these seeds bore fruit was at Angkor, the splendid capital of the Khmer people of Cambodia. The entire city was built to replicate the Hindu view of the universe. Khmer kings came to be thought of as living incarnations of Shiva, the minor Hindu god that became the greatest god of Khmer civilization. The Khmer constructed huge temples to Shiva in which their god-kings rested after death. Among the grandest of these temples was Angkor Wat, built in the first half of the twelfth century. The Khmer prospered until the 1400s when they were overcome by their Thai neighbors and were forced to abandon their beautiful city. But although they might fight among themselves, the nations of Southeast Asia—Cambodia, Thailand, Laos, Vietnam—share one thing forever in common: the cultural legacy of their giant neighbor to the north, China.

China

By the third century C.E., the many feudal kingdoms of China had been consolidated into three: the Wei kingdom in the North; the Wu, in the mid- and lower-Yangtze River valley; and the Shu, in Szechwan, the midwestern region of China. Each king claimed to be emperor of the whole of China. This, the "Time of the Three Kingdoms," was a period of great instability and war. During this time Confucianism, by now a philosophy used by the ruling class to justify itself, lost its appeal and its authority. Some Chinese turned to a more mystic philosophy called Taoism. Others became followers of the new, gentle religion imported from India, called Buddhism.

China was finally united when the Sui dynasty came to power in 589. Sui Wen-ti, the dynasty's first emperor, established a new capital city and began renovating and rebuilding the empire that had suffered for so long under the siege of war. He assembled over a million workers to build the largest canal system in China, linking the Yangtze and the Yellow rivers. The Sui continued the Confucian tradition of using civil servants who had passed a series of difficult exams to run the government bureaucracy. Landowning nobles held much of the power in the country, as they would continue to do for centuries. Unsuccessful military adventures eventually brought about the downfall of the Sui dynasty in 618.

T'ai Tsun, the emperor whose reign began the T'ang Dynasty, ushered in what has been called China's "Golden Age." T'ai Tsun reorganized the government to give himself direct control over every aspect of administering the vast country. Each and every one of China's civil servants was directly responsible to the emperor. As China's armies pushed the borders out into Korea, Manchuria, and India, the need for competent civil ser-

87

Angkor Wat—the crowning achievement of Buddhism in Southeast Asia.

Islamic Empire overtakes the
Indus River valley in India

Ottoman Turks drive out
Islamic invaders and
establish Sultanates in India

Rajputs drive out Moslems in India

Chola Empire of Southern India

711 724 750   1200

vants grew. T'ai Tsun built more schools to prepare students for the grueling series of civil service exams that tested everything from creative writing skills to mathematics. From 618 to 900, the T'ang ruled a China that was the richest and most powerful country in the world. T'ang society was wide open to foreign people and ideas. From Persia, Korea, and Japan, they came to live and learn in Ch'ang-an, the T'ang capital city.

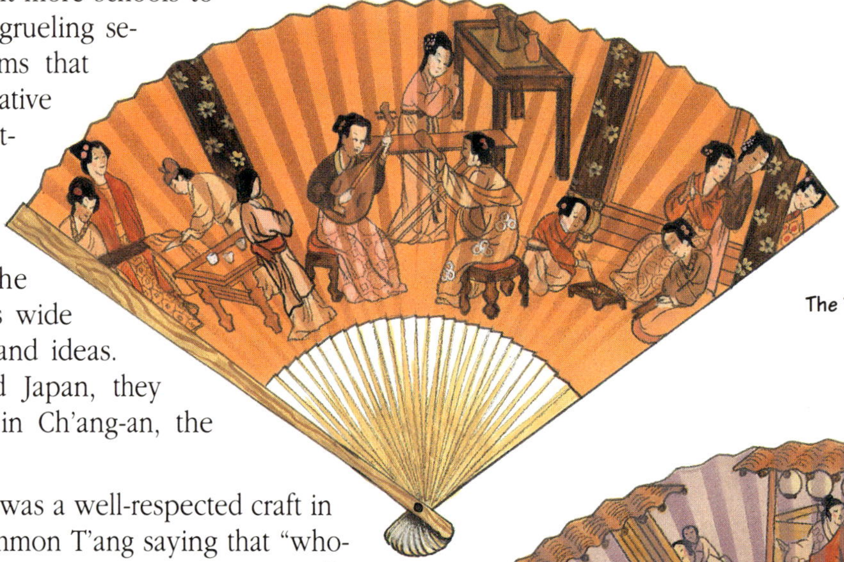

The T'ang dynasty ushered in China's "Golden Age."

The writing of poetry was a well-respected craft in T'ang China. It was a common T'ang saying that "whoever was a gentleman was a poet." Poems were usually short and poetic themes usually reflected nature or the lives of ordinary people. Painting also achieved a marked degree of sophistication. Artists practiced their craft on paper or silk scrolls, depicting natural landscapes in which human figures appeared appropriately small and insignificant when set against breathtaking vistas of mountains, trees, rivers, and valleys.

One of the most significant achievements of the T'ang dynasty was the invention of block printing. In block printing, each individual page of text was carved into a block of wood before ink and paper were applied to the block to print a finished page. Using this technique, the Chinese lay claim to the oldest printed book in existence, which dates from 868. And of course, Chinese pottery was always in demand. Orders for T'ang porcelain poured in from Africa, India, and Europe.

As the northern provinces were attacked by surrounding steppe invaders, the leaders developed their own strong armies. Inevitably these warlords refused to accept directions from a central government. The T'ang dynasty finally fell in 900, to be replaced by that of the Sung. Unlike the T'ang, the Sung were not interested in aggressive military exploits. They moved the capital to Hangchow in the Yangtze River Valley and concentrated on improving their society. Hangchow was a very modern city with wide streets and streetlights. The streets were cleaned daily, and the city had its own fire department. Medieval European cities with their narrow, garbage-strewn streets, could not compare!

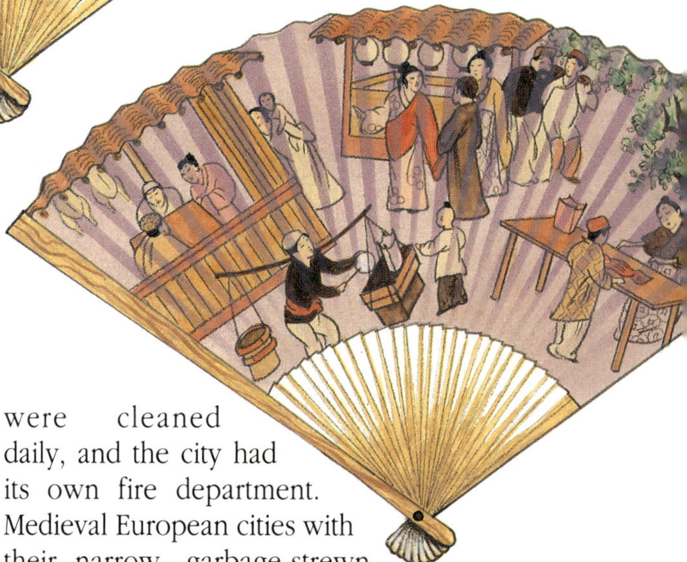

Around 1050 a printer named Pi Sheng discovered a new way of printing that made the printing process easier and faster. Instead of carving a page of text into a wooden block, which was time consuming and had to be done for each page in a manuscript, Pi Sheng carved individual Chinese characters into clay blocks. These blocks were set on a tray and could be moved around to form a new page of print. This was the world's first printing press (hundreds of years before the Gutenberg press in Europe), and once in standard use, it

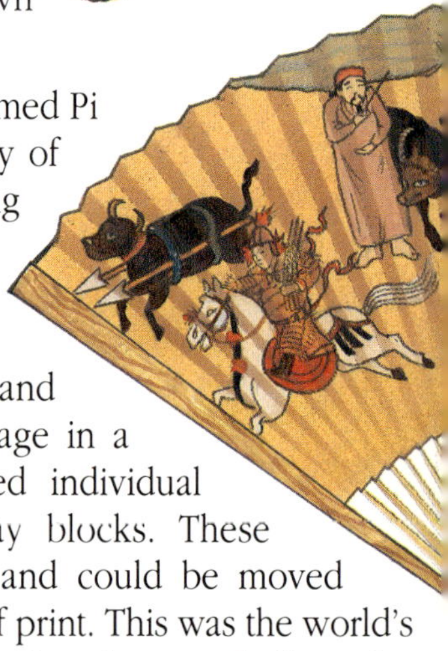

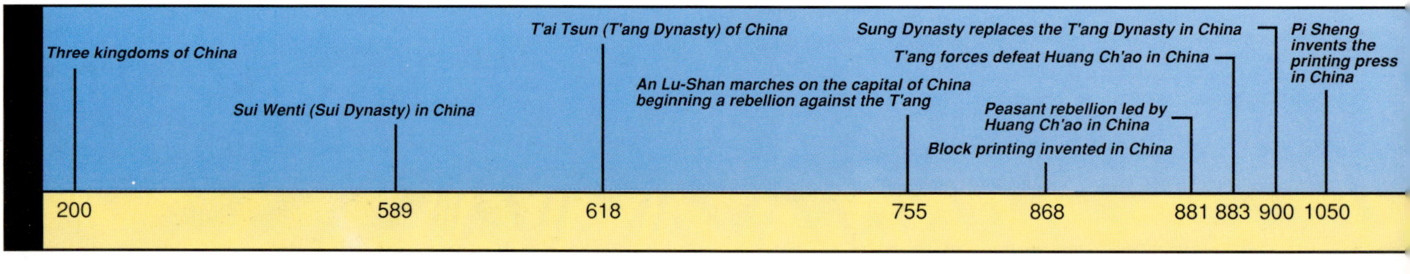
Three kingdoms of China
200
Sui Wenti (Sui Dynasty) in China
589
T'ai Tsun (T'ang Dynasty) of China
618
An Lu-Shan marches on the capital of China beginning a rebellion against the T'ang
755
Block printing invented in China
868
Peasant rebellion led by Huang Ch'ao in China
881
T'ang forces defeat Huang Ch'ao in China
883
Sung Dynasty replaces the T'ang Dynasty in China
900
Pi Sheng invents the printing press in China
1050

helped circulate knowledge more quickly throughout the empire. The Sung also invented the magnetic compass, a new kind of clock, and even a machine that measured earthquakes.

Sung court life with its intrigue, glamor and complex social code rivaled or surpassed anything Europe had to offer. Much of that social code pertained to proper modes of behavior for women. Women who lived as the wives, daughters, or concubines of the royal court were carefully instructed in the social graces and manners of correct living. They were expected to be demure, reserved and submissive, and spent most of their time making themselves conform to the ideal of Chinese beauty. They powdered their faces to make themselves pale, wore rouge and lipstick, painted their eyebrows, and fixed their hair in the fashionable styles of the day. Small feet were considered highly desirable, so an infant girl's feet would be kept tightly wrapped in cloth. As the girl grew, the bandages forced her feet to curl in upon themselves. By maturity the feet would be curled so that the toes could almost touch the heels. The results were crippling and painful. Bound feet came to symbolize the wealth of a young girl's family—only a rich girl with many servants could afford the luxury of being crippled for life! Usually, marriages were arranged between a woman's family and that of her future husband. In many a peasant family, a girl child was often looked upon as a useless burden and left out to die. Although the daughters of some wealthy families did learn to read and write, most young girls were taught practical skills like spinning yarn and embroidery. There is no doubt about the inferior status of women in Chinese society. Introductions of female characters in Chinese literature often included the phrase, "unfortunately she was born a woman . . ."

The Sung dynasty was a time of introspection and re-evaluation in Chinese history. The study of Confucian philosophy once again became popular, and the

emphasis was on looking inward, not on military expansion. Unfortunately, the Manchurians on China's northern border had other ideas. Even though the Chinese used gunpowder in warfare for the first time, the Manchurians overran northern China and the Sung court fled south. The southern Sung dynasty survived and even prospered in the south. But soon the two mighty kingdoms of China would face an even more deadly threat—the Mongols.

The Mongols were herders who lived on the Asian Steppe—the broad, dry grasslands of northern Asia. They were organized into family groups called clans. In the thirteenth century a clan chief named Temijii united the Mongols under his control. Temijii became known as Genghis Khan, the feared Mongol leader who went on to subdue people from Eastern Europe, the Middle East, and the Asian continent. Genghis Khan may have had little formal education, but he was a talented and ruthless military leader. The rumble of horses' hooves was usually heard too late to save the unlucky villagers who were the targets of a Mongol attack.

The Mongols traveled light and fast, and fought on horseback using bows and arrows and clubs to subdue their enemies. They also used gunpowder and cannons (technology borrowed from China) to shoot large rocks into the walls of besieged cities. Those foolish enough to resist the Khan and his warriors were utterly destroyed— every man, woman and child killed. Genghis Khan lusted for power and conquest: "The highest joy is in victory," he said. "To conquer one's enemies, to take their goods, to ride their horses, and to make their loved ones weep." He invaded China in 1211. By the time he had captured the north from its Manchurian rulers, ninety cities had

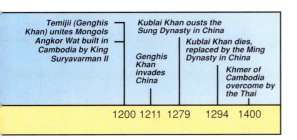

Temijii (Genghis Khan) unites Mongols Angkor Wat built in Cambodia by King Suryavarman II	Kublai Khan ousts the Sung Dynasty in China		
		Kublai Khan dies, replaced by the Ming Dynasty in China	
	Genghis Khan invades China		Khmer of Cambodia overcome by the Thai
	1200 1211	1279	1294 1400

been *completely* destroyed.

Genghis Khan died in 1227, but his grandson, Kublai Khan, completed the conquest of China by overthrowing the southern Sung. He founded the Yuan dynasty in 1279. By 1300, Kublai Khan had created the largest empire the world had ever seen. At its height, it stretched from the Danube River to the Pacific Ocean and played host to that most flabbergasted of travelers, Marco Polo. But with the death of Kublai Khan, his empire, the "Golden Horde," was quickly toppled and replaced by the native Chinese Ming dynasty. The invasion of the Mongol outsiders left a deep and lasting impression in the Chinese psyche. Under Ming rule the importation of any foreign-made products or currency other than gold and silver was prohibited, and China closed its doors to the outside world.

90

Japan

East of the Asian mainland, five hundred miles from China and a mere hundred miles from the coast of Korea, lies the island nation of Japan, a land of mountains, hills, and valleys. Although Japan is made up of more than three hundred islands strung out for 1,500 miles over the Pacific Ocean, most of it's people live on the four major islands—Honshu, Hokkaido, Kyushu, and Shikoku. Since it is very mountainous only about one-fifth of Japan's land can be used for farming, so early in their history the Japanese turned to the sea for their food and livelihood. Although warm ocean currents keep the climate moderate, natural cataclysms like earthquakes, floods and volcanic eruptions have troubled the Japanese since the earliest days. Little is known about ancient Japanese history, although most scientists believe that the first inhabitants came to Japan from the Asian mainland during the Stone Age. Prior to the introduction of the Chinese writing system in C.E. 500, the Japanese had no written language but developed their history and culture through myth and the oral tradition. In just this way has Shinto, the ancient religion of Japan, been preserved. Shinto

means "The Way of the Gods" and developed out of the earliest tradition of gods inhabiting streams, rocks, and other natural phenomena.

In ancient times Japanese society was organized into basic family groups called clans. In the year 400 the Yamato clan gained control of Japan and their chief became Japan's first emperor. Incredibly, this family has maintained its pre-eminent status to the present day: the current Japanese emperor is a descendant of the Yamato clan. According to one Japanese myth, the first Yamato emperor was related to the most powerful of the Shinto deities, Amaterasu, the sun goddess. Up until the twentieth century the emperor was considered to be a god. Japan's emperors have always been honored as the leaders of their society, though many times in Japan's history, as in that of other nations, the ruling power has been in the hands of powerful aristocrats.

In the sixth century, frequent contact with China began to have a significant influence on the Japanese way of life. China's T'ang dynasty maintained strong ties with Japan, and the Japanese admired the music, art, poetry, cooking styles, and architecture of the T'ang. Japanese scholars traveled to China to study medicine, mathematics, and science, and returned with a wealth of new knowledge and two of the most precious gems of Chinese philosophy—Confucianism and Buddhism. Eventually the efforts of Chinese and Korean missionaries placed Buddhism alongside Shinto as one of Japan's two major religions. Japan's love affair with Chinese culture continued over the next few centuries.

The Japanese adapted part of China's legal structure for their own law code, and even tried instituting the Chinese civil service system. But the bureaucratic method did not fit the Japanese temperament, and Japan quickly returned to the established system of government by powerful nobles. Under this system the emperor owned all the land, and the nobility paid for their use of it with

Japan

Hokkaido

Honshu

Kyoto

Edo
(Tokyo)

Nagasaki

taxes and service. But nobles living in the farflung provinces of the empire came to resent paying tribute to the emperor, and the emperor lacked the power to enforce their obedience. Eventually the system broke down as one noble clan after another openly refused to acknowledge the emperor and declared ownership of their ancestral lands. There followed a period of civil war which ended when the powerful Fujiwara clan reunited the nation. Fujiwara Motosume, the chief of the Fujiwara clan, was a powerful military leader. Until 1156 he and his descendants controlled Japan's army as well as the daily administration of the government. This phase of Japanese history is known as the Heian Period.

When the Fujiwara dynasty collapsed in the 1100s, the country deteriorated once again into civil war as the noble families vied for power. General Yoritomo, leader of the Nimamoto clan, assumed control of the nation in 1185, naming himself Shogun, or "Barbarian-subduing Great General." Yoritomo assured that his family line would continue to rule Japan by making the position of Shogun inheritable by the most worthy son or other heir. He did not want family rivalry to break up the government. Yoritomo worked carefully behind the scenes, making sure that in all outward appearance the emperor was governing, while in truth it was the shogun who was calling the shots. He sent his loyal followers out to oversee the government in Japan's wealthiest provinces so that the nobles would not try to usurp the shogun's power as they had that of the emperor. This system of shadow government that Yoritomo put in place lasted until 1867.

The next most powerful group under the shoguns were the noble landowners, called daimyos, who dominated the Japanese countryside. They controlled their

Peace and tranquility were the ideal in Heian Period Japan.

land and the people who lived on it in ways similar to the feudal society of Europe during the Middle Ages. Their rule, and not the rule of the emperor, was law to the common people who lived and worked on their lands. Powerful daimyos gave part of their land to loyal supporters and to warriors called samurai. Samurai protected the lives and interests of the daimyos, who were often at war with rival clans.

The samurai were a highly respected class in Japanese society. They followed a code of honor called Bushido, which stressed courage, discipline, loyalty, and obedience to their daimyo masters. Unlike European knights, whose duty to their lord was basically a legal obligation, the samurai believed the daimyo had an almost divine right to rule—their obligation was a deeply moral one. The samurai's job was to protect the peasants that lived on the daimyo's land as well as to fight for the daimyo's interests. It was not only an honor for a samurai warrior to die in the name of his daimyo, it was expected. In return for such devotion, the samurai warrior and his family were usually given land and material wealth. Honor was a very important concept in Japanese society. As ferocious as samurai warriors could be in battle, they were also skilled in the arts. Unlike Medieval European knights who found learning "unmanly," the samurai respected learning. These warriors were known for their skill in painting and poetry.

The nobles of the emperor's court rarely left the capital city. Life was often quiet, even boring, at the imperial court, so Japanese royalty filled their time partaking in court ceremonies, playing games, and exploring the arts and literature. The writing of poetry—tanka and haiku were two common poetic forms—was a popular pastime. Japanese poets, always observing the changing of the seasons, the opening of the cherry blossoms, the rustling of the leaves of the maple tree, expressed their love of nature in their work. The court poets of imperial Japan also sought to capture fine subtleties of mood and emotion in their poetry, which was often written for celebrations at court. Many of the most accomplished writers of poetry and fiction were women. The popular *Tale of Genji*, considered by many to be the first novel ever written, was the work of Murasaki Shikibu, a lady of the Japanese court.

Russia and Eastern Europe

As early as the fifth century numerous tribes of people collectively known as Slavs had migrated from central Asia to settle in Eastern Europe. The largest Slavic community developed along the banks of the Dnieper River and its tributaries. The Dnieper was an important north-south trading route that connected the Vikings of the Scandinavian Peninsula to Constantinople, and the Slavic cities that grew alongside the river became prosperous as a result. The city of Novgorod rose to prominence as the largest of the early Slavic settlements. Legend tells us that the citizens of Novgorod, after being occupied by and then ridding themselves of Viking raiders, found that they could not govern themselves, and invited the Scandinavians back to restore peace and order. Invited or not, a Viking prince named Rurick assumed leadership of Novgorod in 862. The Slavs called the Vikings the "Rus," so the land of the Rus and Slavs became known as Russia.

Historians date the beginning of Russian history to Rurick's rise to power. Upon his death, Prince Oleg succeeded to power in Novgorod and extended his rule to encompass all the land between Novgorod and the city of Kiev, which he captured and made the new capital of his

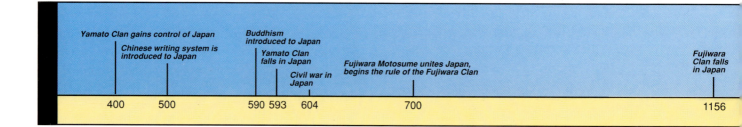

Samurai warriors were known for their skill in painting, poetry and calligraphy.

Yamato Clan gains control of Japan	Buddhism introduced to Japan		Fujiwara Motosume unites Japan, begins the rule of the Fujiwara Clan		Fujiwara Clan falls in Japan
Chinese writing system is introduced to Japan	Yamato Clan falls in Japan				
	Civil war in Japan				
400 500	590 593 604	700			1156

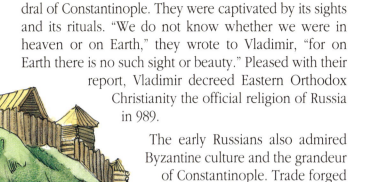

Vikings, Slavs and Mongols contributed to early Russian culture.

dral of Constantinople. They were captivated by its sights and its rituals. "We do not know whether we were in heaven or on Earth," they wrote to Vladimir, "for on Earth there is no such sight or beauty." Pleased with their report, Vladimir decreed Eastern Orthodox Christianity the official religion of Russia in 989.

The early Russians also admired Byzantine culture and the grandeur of Constantinople. Trade forged increasingly strong ties be-

93

fledgling kingdom, known as Kievian Russia. The next ruler of Russia, Rurick's great grandson Vladimir I, decided to unite all the different peoples under his rule by establishing a state religion. The only question was: What religion should it be?

According to legend, Vladimir sent some of his officials on a journey to study the religions of Europe and the Middle East. They investigated Judaism, Roman Catholicism, and Islam, but found none of them particularly appealing. But then they went to an Eastern Orthodox Church service at the Hagia Sophia, the beautiful cathe-

tween the two. Besides traders and travelers, Russia was often visited by Byzantine missionaries eager to convert the Slavs to Orthodox Christianity before the Roman Church could reach them. Around the year 900, two Greek monks named Cyril and Methodius succeeded in converting many Slavs by creating a writing system that would allow them to study the words of the Bible and the directives of the Church in their own language. This system is still used in Russia today.

Russia's ties to the Eastern Church and the Byzantine Empire isolated it from the Roman Catholic Church, and ultimately cut it off from the mainstream of western European culture. Yet for the first two hundred years after Vladimir, the country prospered under a series of strong,

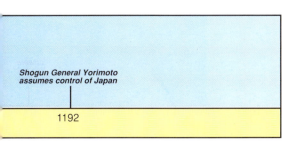

Shogun General Yorimoto assumes control of Japan

1192

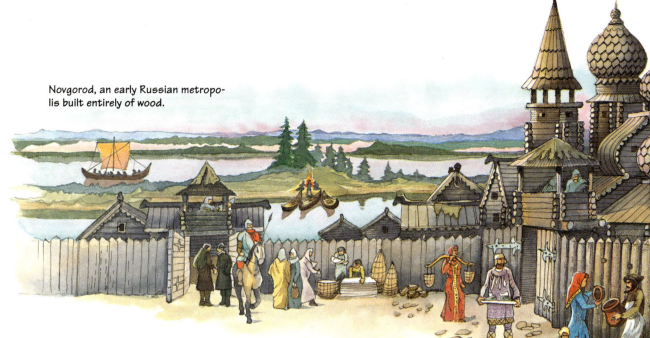

Novgorod, an early Russian metropolis built entirely of wood.

effective leaders. By 1000 Kiev was the largest city in Europe and by 1050 Russian life was, in many ways, more advanced than life in the rest of medieval Europe.

But in the thirteenth century Russia's luck took a turn for the worse. In 1237 Mongolian horsemen invaded Russia, turning life upside down. Many cities, including Kiev, were completely destroyed. Refugees from Russian cities fled north, finding shelter in a small town named Moscow. The Mongols captured all of Russia and demanded slaves, soldiers, and tribute—money paid in return for peace and "protection" against attack (mainly against another attack from the Mongols themselves).

Those who refused to yield to the

Mongols' demands were killed. The Moscovite rulers won favor with the Mongols by collecting the tribute from other Russian cities for their Mongolian masters. In return, the Mongols helped Moscow's leaders expand their rule within Eastern Europe, and by the 1400s Moscow had replaced Kiev as the most powerful city in Russia. But in 1462, the reigning prince of Moscow defied the Mongols by refusing to pay tribute. The Mongols sent an army to attack Moscow, but when they saw the huge army that the rebellious prince had sent to meet them, they decided it would be better to retreat than fight. This prince who broke the Mongol stranglehold on Russia was a descendant of the esteemed Rurik who earned his own place of esteem in the hearts of Russia's people. His name was Ivan the Great.

94

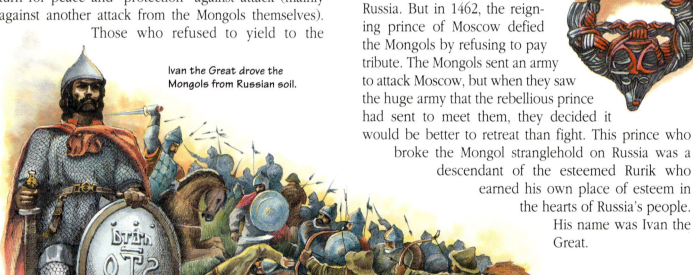

Ivan the Great drove the Mongols from Russian soil.

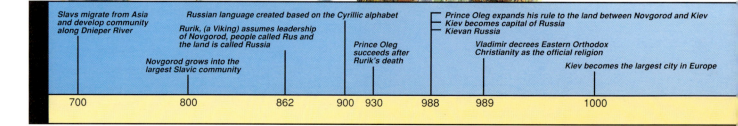

Slavs migrate from Asia and develop community along Dnieper River

Russian language created based on the Cyrillic alphabet

Rurik, (a Viking) assumes leadership of Novgorod, people called Rus and the land is called Russia

Novgorod grows into the largest Slavic community

Prince Oleg succeeds after Rurik's death

Prince Oleg expands his rule to the land between Novgorod and Kiev
Kiev becomes capital of Russia
Kievan Russia

Vladimir decrees Eastern Orthodox Christianity as the official religion

Kiev becomes the largest city in Europe

700   800   862   900 930   988   989   1000

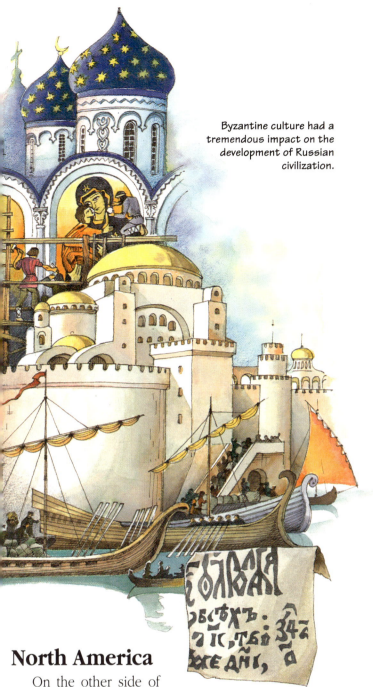

Byzantine culture had a tremendous impact on the development of Russian civilization.

their own toil they created earthen monuments to rival the pyramids of Egypt or the grandest stoneworks of the Maya. Today we call them the Mound Builders.

It began with a humble tradition of personal respect. When a family member died, the body was left exposed on a platform until the bone was cleansed of flesh by scavenging birds. Then the bones were buried—along with personal effects like jewelry, masks, pipes, and weapons—in a clay-lined pit or a hollowed-out log under the floor of the family dwelling. When a generation or two had passed, and the ground beneath the house could accept no more remains, the house was burned and the entire area covered over with soil to form a small mound. As the Adena grew in numbers and became settled in their way of life, the burial mounds grew larger and higher, sometimes twenty to eighty feet tall. There are between three and five hundred known mounds still in existence, dotting an area stretching from Kentucky to New York. Archeologists believe that more than ten thousand mounds may have been built by the mound-building tribes, but we will never know. Most of them have either been leveled to clear the way for modern roads and buildings or worn away by time and the elements.

After enduring for almost 1,500 years the Adena culture faded, and another, the Hopewell, rose to prominence in its place. The Hopewell people created bigger and more elaborate mounds, and filled them with elegant burial offerings. These huge earthworks—some more than a quarter of a mile across—come in a variety of shapes: circles, squares, or octagons. The best-preserved Hopewell mound, which covers almost two square miles, is in Newark, Ohio. Among the artifacts found there are fine carvings, tools, pottery, and ornaments made of copper or mica. It also seems that servants were sometimes buried with their deceased masters. The elaborate burial costumes are incredibly rich and varied. Hopewell dead have been found adorned with grizzly bear teeth, freshwater pearls, obsidian from the Rocky Mountains, mica from North Carolina, conch shells, sharks' teeth and sea turtle shell, all providing ample evidence of a vast trade network stretching from the Atlantic Ocean to the Rocky Mountains, from the copper mines of Lake Superior to the Mississippi River delta.

By the beginning of the first century the introduction of agriculture had led to a settled society and changing ways of life for the people. They cultivated corn, made better tools and weapons, and built fortifications to protect their land. This phase is known as the Mississippian. During Mississippian times, burial mounds became flat on top (resembling early Mayan pyramids), society became stratified into several ranks, and arts and crafts achieved new levels of sophistication. Villages became

95

North America

On the other side of the world, the rolling hills and fertile soil of the Ohio Valley nurtured a North American society which archeologists call the Adena. The Adena were Indians of various tribes who intermingled and traded ideas and goods. It is their dedication to memorializing the dead that makes them unique among the early civilizations of the Americas. With nothing more than woven baskets and

Ivan the Great (reigning Prince of Moscow) defies and defeats the Mongols

Moscow becomes the most powerful city in Russia by collecting tribute money for the Mongols

Mongols overtake Russia

Mongols invade Russia

| 1227 | 1260 | 1400 | 1462 |

towns buzzing with activity and the comings and goings of traders from distant tribes—cities of earth and wood.

The greatest of the mound cities was at Cahokia, near St. Louis, Missouri. The site lies in the middle of the continent, where the Ohio and Missouri Rivers merge with the Mississippi on its way to the Gulf of Mexico. At Cahokia, the common people buried their dead in cemeteries. Only the elite families built mounds and took their most precious possessions with them to the grave. Cahokia's central mound, called Monks Mound, must have taken about three hundred years to complete. It covers fifteen acres and rises in four steps to a height of one hundred feet. Monk's Mound was the site of a temple, a council house, the ruler's residence, and several other buildings. More mounds and dwellings surrounded this city center. Other areas were used for games, processions, and commerce. The Mississippian societies flourished until they were destroyed by the strange diseases and barbarity of European adventurers and the colonists who followed in their wake.

Mesoamerica

In the lush, tropical rain forests of Central America—in what is now southern Mexico, Guatemala, and parts of San Salvador and Honduras—the ruins of magnificent temples and pyramids give us a glimpse of the grandeur that the mighty Maya civilization achieved in the centuries prior to its dissolution. Maya tradition dates back 5,000 years and is one of the most remarkable in the world. The early Maya were stable farmers who devoutly worshiped their gods of fertility, rain, and sunshine. Around C.E. 300 they built the first of their great temples and ceremonial cities. Imposing buildings fifteen stories tall with massive staircases appeared deep in the near-impenetrable jungle, protected from attack by the tangles of vines and creepers that surrounded them. Because of the remoteness of these Maya cities, archaeologists once believed the Maya were an isolated people. It is now known that they had frequent contact with other Mesoamerican cultures.

Later temples were built on the limestone plains of Yucatan. Subterranean streams run close to the surface there, and from time to time the ground caves in to form a deep well. These wells, called cenotes, were sacred to the Maya, who built cities around them and not only

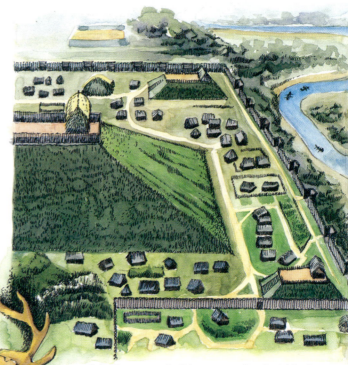

Cahokia—moundbuilder metropolis of middle America

We will never know how many mounds have been plowed under or paved over, or what secrets they might have held.

drew water from them but used them as places of sacrifice as well! Human sacrifice was rare: more likely to be offered to the dark waters were food and flowers. In the extreme case that a human was sacrificed, it was usually at dawn. If the person was still alive at noon, he was considered blessed, rescued from the water and allowed to live with honor. At one famous city the cenote is 170 feet wide and 700 feet deep. From its depths archaeologists have recovered priceless gold artifacts intended as offerings to the gods.

By C.E. 550 Maya civilization had entered its Classical Period. The Maya had far outstripped their neighbors in their writing and architecture, painting and

96

sculpture. Jewelry and headdresses made of shells, feathers, and jade showed elaborate craftsmanship. Like the Olmec, the Maya strapped boards to the heads of infant children to give them elongated heads. Maya mothers also dangled beads in front of their babies' faces to give them crossed eyes, which were considered attractive. Tattoos were also fashionable. Maya men wore loincloths or long cotton skirts and capes. The women wore long skirts or simple dresses.

Of all Maya achievements, their advances in astronomy and mathematics were the most impressive. Maya priests tracked the movement of the stars and planets. Their records were so complete that they could actually forecast solar and lunar eclipses. Using this knowledge they could tell when a sacrifice was needed, when farmers should plant, and could even determine the most auspicious day for a young couple's wedding. The calendar was arranged so that every twenty days there was a religious festival and market day. Carved stone pillars, called stelae, have been found at every Maya city. Each stelae is engraved with the date and relevant astronomical data. They also tell us a great deal about the many Maya gods.

The Maya Classical Period achieved a grandeur to rival that of any early civilization.

Archeologists still don't know why, around c.e. 900, the Maya cities were suddenly abandoned, the people vanishing like shadows back into the jungles and the mountains. Did the people flee in terror from a natural disaster or an enemy army? Did they grow tired of paying taxes and rebel against their leaders? The answer may never be known. Whatever happened, the cities vanished. The vines and creepers reclaimed the stone walls and temples, and a blanket of silent mystery concealed the light of Classical Maya splendor. But the Maya people survived. Their descendants lived on, dispersing throughout the region and reverting to the simple lifestyle of earlier times. Today they are working to rebuild their identity and their culture.

In northwest Mexico, around the year 900, a group of warlike nomad tribes settled and established a city they called Tula. The people of Tula, the Toltec, showed great prowess at warfare and overpowered most of their neighbors. Their preoccupation with conquest is evidenced by the symbols most prominent in their art—jaguars, skulls, eagles devouring hearts. Perhaps we could consider them the Hell's Angels of the ancient Americas. Their two most honored gods were Tezcatlipoca, god of war, and Quetzalcoatl, the feathered serpent personified in the morning star. Early in the twelfth century the bloodthirsty Toltec fell victim to a new wave of invasion by the unstoppable armies of the most powerful society in the history of pre-Columbian America—the Aztec.

It was the Aztec who united most of Mexico into a vital and successful empire. They had it all: a powerful monarchy, an efficient war machine, and a merchant class that gave the kingdom a solid economic base. They eventually ruled an empire of twelve million people and nearly four hundred states.

The Aztec quickly made enemies out of the neighboring peoples with their constant military forays, so they built a virtually impregnable city on the islands of Lake Texcoco and named it Tenochtitlan. Tenochtitlan was a marvel of architecture with huge temples and buildings glittering with magnificent metalwork in gold, silver, copper, and bronze. A giant hydraulic system brought fresh water to the city and a dike kept the salt water in the lake from polluting the fresh water reservoirs. Irrigated and fertilized crops grew in terraced fields. At first the inhabitants of the city could only reach the mainland by canoe, but later they built three causeways of stone and soil. They cleverly left gaps in the causeways and spanned them with unique bridges. Canoes could pass under and in times of danger the bridges could be removed. Living in a city in the middle of a lake, the Aztec soon ran out of useable farmland. They solved this prob-

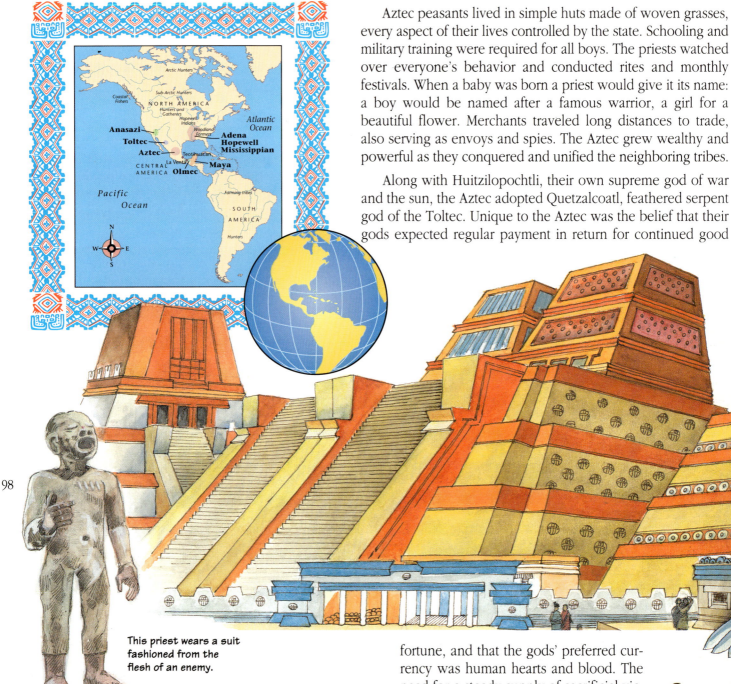

Aztec peasants lived in simple huts made of woven grasses, every aspect of their lives controlled by the state. Schooling and military training were required for all boys. The priests watched over everyone's behavior and conducted rites and monthly festivals. When a baby was born a priest would give it its name: a boy would be named after a famous warrior, a girl for a beautiful flower. Merchants traveled long distances to trade, also serving as envoys and spies. The Aztec grew wealthy and powerful as they conquered and unified the neighboring tribes.

Along with Huitzilopochtli, their own supreme god of war and the sun, the Aztec adopted Quetzalcoatl, feathered serpent god of the Toltec. Unique to the Aztec was the belief that their gods expected regular payment in return for continued good

This priest wears a suit fashioned from the flesh of an enemy.

fortune, and that the gods' preferred currency was human hearts and blood. The need for a steady supply of sacrificial victims led the Aztec to escalate their military exploits. They often went to war for the sole purpose of obtaining captives to sacrifice. Aztec society became a military

lem by making rafts of wood and leafy reeds and piling thick mud on top. These floating gardens were called *chinamps* and they worked so well that the farmers could have two or more crops a year without even having to worry about the irrigation.

The Aztec became increasingly warlike as their need for sacrificial victims grew.

98

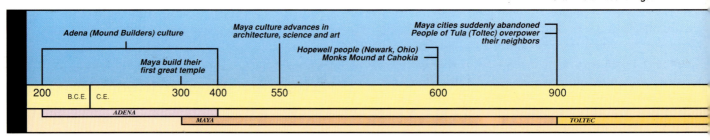

Adena (Mound Builders) culture

Maya build their first great temple

Maya culture advances in architecture, science and art

Hopewell people (Newark, Ohio) Monks Mound at Cahokia

Maya cities suddenly abandoned People of Tula (Toltec) overpower their neighbors

| 200 | B.C.E. | C.E. | 300 | 400 | 550 | 600 | 900 |

ADENA

MAYA

TOLTEC

state, taxed to the limit to finance the wars, and dripping with blood. Eventually a terrible rumor began to be whispered among the people: Quetzalcoatl had become disgusted by the atrocities of the Aztec and had abandoned them, returning to his home across the great water to the east. That awful myth reflected the self-doubt of a society blinded by its own power. It turned out to be one of the main reasons that in the early sixteenth century, the Spanish explorer Cortés and his small band were able to bring the mighty Aztec empire to its knees.

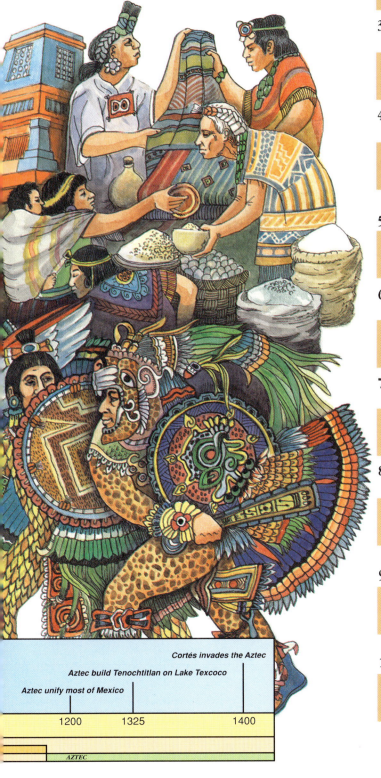

Aztec unify most of Mexico
Aztec build Tenochtitlan on Lake Texcoco
Cortés invades the Aztec

1200   1325   1400

AZTEC

Quiz

1. The Islamic Empire conquered Persia in the year

- Ⓐ 224
- Ⓑ 641
- Ⓒ 320
- Ⓓ 247

2. What religion underwent a resurgence during the Gupta dynasty?

- Ⓐ Islam
- Ⓑ Buddhism
- Ⓒ Hinduism
- Ⓓ Christianity

3. The Moslems lived in peaceful coexistence with the _____ and _____ until around the year 1,000.

- Ⓐ Christians and Jews
- Ⓑ Christians and Buddhists
- Ⓒ Christians and Hindus
- Ⓓ Buddhists and Hindus

4. The two main influences on Cambodian culture were India and China.

- Ⓐ True
- Ⓑ False

5. In T'ang China, "whoever was a gentleman was a ____."

- Ⓐ warrior
- Ⓑ poet
- Ⓒ philosopher
- Ⓓ civil servant

6. Genghis Khan united the Mongol tribes during the _____ century.

- Ⓐ tenth
- Ⓑ twelfth
- Ⓒ thirteenth
- Ⓓ fourteenth

7. The most important influence on early Russian culture was

- Ⓐ the Persian empire.
- Ⓑ the Roman empire.
- Ⓒ the Mongol empire.
- Ⓓ the Byzantine empire.

8. Beginning in the 1100s, the most powerful person in Japanese society was the

- Ⓐ daimyo.
- Ⓑ monk.
- Ⓒ samurai.
- Ⓓ shogun.

9. Two common Japanese poetic forms are

- Ⓐ tanka and haiku.
- Ⓑ sonnet and haiku.
- Ⓒ lyric and sonnet.
- Ⓓ tanka and sonnet.

10. The island city of the Aztec was named

- Ⓐ Texcoco.
- Ⓑ Tezcatlipoca.
- Ⓒ Tenochtitlan.
- Ⓓ Quetzalcoatl.

Odoacer and his barbarian warriors were merciless in their attack on Rome.

Chapter 9

The European Middle Ages

The occupation of the city of Rome by the barbarian king Odoacer in 476 signaled the disintegration of the western Roman Empire. The center of power shifted to Byzantium in the East, where the imperial legacy would survive for another thousand years, but western Europe was abandoned to the many barbarian tribes that had already infiltrated the area. The Visigoths took over the Iberian Peninsula, and the Ostrogoths—Odoacer's tribe—conquered and settled the Italian Peninsula. The Great European Plain with its dense forests and its many rivers was occupied by one of the largest of the Germanic tribes, the Franks. This tribe lived along the shores of the Rhine River before moving west to what today is called France. By the 600s, the Angles, Saxons and Jutes had crossed the North Sea and taken control of the British Isles. Collectively these tribes became known as the Anglo-Saxons.

For three centuries after the fall of Rome, constant warfare among the barbarian tribes plunged Europe into what is called the Dark Ages. The social systems created by the Romans and the order that Roman will had imposed gave way to chaos and anarchy. Laws were unenforceable, public records were destroyed, and artistic treasures were desecrated. The monumental Roman roads fell into disrepair. Learning became a thing of the past as books containing the wisdom of the ages were used to fuel cooking fires.

Death, destruction, and instability came to shape the way the people of medieval times viewed their world. Their lives filled with pain, loss and confusion, they turned to Christianity for solace, with its promise of a glorious golden afterlife. They truly believed in heaven and strove to live the lives of faith, sacrifice, and good deeds that would get them there. As for life in the here and now, there was little to be done. Everything that happened on Earth was in accordance with God's plan: The rich were rich, the poor were poor, and nothing could be changed. The constant reality of death and the very real terror of judgment also made many superstitious. Ghosts, demons, and spirits of every description dwelt in the minds and the folklore of the people—how else could the unpredictable and unfathomable happenings in their lives be explained?

Europe was divided into many kingdoms, each led by a ruler who was usually a great warrior. Only the strongest and craftiest survived. The common people came to see that their only hope for survival lay in placing themselves in the hands of a powerful protector. In time a new social and political order developed in the vacuum created by the absence of imperial government. There was an implicit agreement—an unspoken understanding—between ruler and subject: The ruler would govern and protect his subjects, and in return the peasants would pledge the fruits of their labor, their loyalty, their very lives if need be, to the ruler. Medieval society assumed the form of a pyramid, with the most powerful rulers, the kings, at the top, and the defenseless peasants at the bottom. In between were various classes of more or less powerful nobles, each class pledging allegiance to the class above. Ultimately everyone was loyal to and dependent on the king. This system is known as feudalism.

Kings gave favored nobles large grants of land in exchange for loyalty and support in times of war. The land a noble received in this way was called a fief, or manor, and along with it came everything it held, including the people. The noble who received land in this way was subservient to the king—he was the king's "vassal." At the same time, he was the lord and absolute master of his fiefdom. The common people were at the mercy of their lord, who might be benevolent and paternal, but was more often cruel and predatory. News traveled slowly in the Middle Ages,

and the largely self-sufficient fiefdoms tended to be isolated from one another, so the lords took more and more power to themselves, often even disregarding the king's wishes with impunity. It was a common saying in medieval society that the only law between a peasant and his lord was God—and the only justice was in heaven. During this time 90 percent of the people of Europe were peasants, tied in service to their lords and forbidden to leave their villages. Most peasants worked in the fields growing food for the lord's table. When their work in the fields was done, the women sheared the sheep, spun the thread, fashioned the clothing, and tended to all the needs of the house and family.

Central to every fiefdom was the manor house or castle of the lord. Basically a castle was an armed fortress, built to defend the people—and especially the nobles—against enemy attack. In times of danger the peasants could leave their village to find safety behind the castle's stone walls. A drawbridge, which could be hauled up in case of emergency, led across the murky water of the moat that encircled the battlements to the castle gate. Castles were cold, damp, and dreary places, especially in the winter. Small windows in thick stone walls allowed bitter winds but little light. Shadowy passageways were dimly lit by the flickering light of smoky torches. The huts of the peasants were even less pleasant. Sparsely furnished, perhaps with a few stools and a table, their thatched roofs often leaked in stormy weather. They were always filled with fumes and smoke from the crude fireplaces that were used for warmth and cooking.

101

The manors and castles provided villagers refuge from the dangers of medieval life.

Huddling at the feet of the grim and imposing castle, the village was where the peasants gathered and where the craftsmen and artisans plied their trades. The miller ground grain into flour. The cobbler made shoes, the cooper made barrels, and the tinker mended pots and pans. Certainly the blacksmith was always busy with his work. Beside making horseshoes, nails, tools, and dozens of other important everyday items, he constructed the armor that protected the lord and his knights in battle.

The knight was a highly honored member of the medieval society. Warrior, police officer, judge, and soldier, he belonged to an exclusive society and swore an oath of loyalty to his lord, his king, and the Church. Knights had a special set of rules called the "code of chivalry." Every knight was expected to comfort the suffering, help the needy, rescue those in distress, behave with humility, and follow a whole host of guidelines concerning conduct and dress. It was a tall order to follow, and the privilege of knighthood was granted to none but

a chosen few. Only a boy of noble birth could become a knight. Around the age of seven a young lad aspiring to become a knight went to work as a page in the house of a noble lord. Once in his teens, a page became a squire. Having learned to ride and to fight with sword and lance, he became a knight's servant, caring for the armor and weapons and even following his master into battle. If a squire served his knight well, at the age of twenty-one he himself was knighted in a ceremony sanctioned by the lord and the Church. Kneeling before his lord, he was sworn to knighthood and received the touch of the noble's sword on his shoulders and his bowed head. If a knight was lucky, he would obtain land from his father or from some other noble which he could rule as a fiefdom of his own.

The Christian church had been the only established institution to stay intact when the Roman empire collapsed. The Church had continued to grow in power since the time of Emperor Constantine, and Christian missionaries had been persistent in traveling the hinterlands of the Empire and beyond, to convert the barbarians. With the social upheaval that followed the fall of Rome, the Church's stability and its message of salvation brought hope to many

A knight dedicated his life to defending his lord and the king.

whose lives had been uprooted, who had lost what few possessions they had ever possessed, who daily faced death from disease or the attack of a warring tribe. By 1000 most of Europe had been converted to the way of the cross.

In the early days of Christianity, Jesus' disciple Peter had traveled to Rome to lead the missionary effort in the empire. He became the first pope—the leader of the Roman Catholic church. Over time the popes became very powerful and wealthy. During the Middle Ages the pope and other Church leaders were able to secure their lands in Rome as an independent state. The Papal State, as it was called, lasted for many centuries. The popes held near-total authority, both spiritual and earthly, over all Christians from the lowliest peasant to the most powerful king, and the Church was deeply involved in the politics of the time.

Indeed, the Church played a strong role in all segments of the society. Each village usually had a parish priest who led his community through various rites of passage such as birth, marriage, and death. He helped settle disputes and comforted those in need. Women who wanted to devote their life to spiritual pursuits became nuns. They lived apart from the rest of the world in communal dwellings called convents, and took strict vows that set them apart from the rest of society. They vowed not to marry, to give up material possessions, and to obey their leaders without question. They gave shelter to travelers, helped the poor, cared for the sick, and divided their days between work, study, and prayer. Men who took similar vows were called monks, and their dwellings were called monasteries. Some convents and monasteries became wealthy because they received land and other gifts from noble benefactors.

The village fair was a welcome relief from the cares and drudgery of peasant life.

Priests acted as advisors and assistants to the nobles, who like most medieval people were illiterate. Book-learning was considered trivial—even unmanly—by the nobility, and for the peasants, whose every ounce of effort was dedicated to survival, it was an impossibility. Common folk learned the teachings of the Bible through plays and pageants. History and folklore were passed on by storytellers and traveling musicians—troubadours. And the clergy ("clerics," or clerks) gained power as they tended to the nobles' written accounts and provided counsel in matters of state. Attitudes about education didn't begin to change until the twelfth century. The first schools were opened in monasteries to prepare boys to enter the clergy. Later, schools were started in the main churches of the towns and cities. A typical medieval student might take courses in Latin, rhetoric, logic, math, astronomy and music.

Living off the labor of the peasants, the nobility had plenty of time between battles for recreation and entertainment. On fine summer days they could revel in the spirit of the hunt, enjoying the prime hunting grounds that were off limits to the peasants. Or there might be a tournament and jousting match, followed by a banquet where wine flowed in abundance and music and laughter filled the great hall. In quieter moments, chess and backgammon were popular games. The life of a peasant was drab and dull by comparison, but once a year, singers, jugglers, acrobats and musicians made the village fair a joyous occasion. The village fair brought much needed relief for the peasants and gave them rare contact with the outside world. During the fair, the villagers had a chance to buy some trinkets from, or sell their wares to, the traveling merchants and perhaps, get a pot mended by a tinker passing through.

103

City life all but disappeared with the end of Roman rule, and the village became the focal point of the peasant's tiny world. It was only in the eleventh century that the development of the iron plowshare and other innovations in farming made planting easier, and crops healthier. For the first time Europe was producing food in some abundance. Farmers had extra crops to sell and money to buy things from merchants and craftsmen. More people had the opportunity to choose the life of an artisan or a trader, and consume the surplus food that others had produced. The population grew. Over time some villages became towns, some towns became cities, until the cities were once again a significant part of the European landscape. No matter their size, medieval cities were still considered to be part of a fief, and thus under the control of the lord of the manor, to whom they paid high taxes. In return, the townsfolk expected the lord to provide security and protection from the bandits and rogues who prowled the narrow streets and roamed the lawless countryside. As the towns and cities grew in wealth and power, they were able to influence the actions of the nobles, and sometimes even of the king.

But for the average town dweller, medieval cities were small, cramped, and dirty places. The streets were narrow dirt or cobblestone paths. There were no organized waste disposal or sewage systems; people just threw their garbage and waste out of their windows. Diseases spread quickly through the filthy, crowded streets. Most of the houses were made of wood, making the cities susceptible to disastrous fires. In the French city of Rouen, fire destroyed the city twelve times within a period of twenty-five years! Yet with all the problems of urban living, many peasants still found it better than life in the rural village. The lord had less control over his subjects in the city than back in the village. If a runaway serf could evade the lord's grasp for a few years by losing himself in the crowds of the city, he became a free man.

As the cities grew and the buying power of the people increased, artisans and craftsmen prospered. They began to band together in guilds, the better to protect the interests of each craft or trade. The guilds established guidelines to insure the quality of their members' work, set prices and established business hours. Girls and boys

who wanted to practice a particular craft became apprentices to trained craftsmen, or masters. Apprentices lived and worked with the masters while they perfected their skills. After seven years they became journeymen, and for the first time could earn wages. To gain official entry into a guild, every journeyman had to produce a piece of work that he considered to be his "masterpiece." If the masterpiece passed the guild's test a journeyman became a full-fledged member of the guild. Guild leaders grew to become powerful citizens of medieval cities.

One of the strongest and largest of the Germanic tribes to emerge in Western Europe with the break-up of the Empire was that of the Franks. In 485 the Frankish king Clovis united all the Franks under his rule. He was the first of the Germanic kings to adopt Christianity. When Clovis died his kingdom was divided among his three sons. It would be another two hundred years before the

Then as now, bustling cities provided opportunities for a better life.

Franks were again united under a strong leader. His name was Charles Martel, and he was an influential high court official to a weak and ineffective Frankish king. Martel's son, Pepin the Short, was Mayor of the Court to the Frankish king Childeric, a religious man whose fondest dream was to join a monastery. After taking pains to confer with the pope and win the support of key members of the nobility, Pepin gave Childeric his wish. In 751, with the blessing of the Church, Pepin the Short, the former court official, became king of the Franks.

"A giant of a man! About seven feet tall!" This was the way a medieval writer described Pepin the Short's son, Charles the Great, or Charlemagne. Under Charlemagne's rule, the Franks ruled the largest European empire since the fall of Rome. Frankish dominion extended from the North Sea to the Pyrenees Mountains and on into northern Italy. Charlemagne did more than perhaps any other single individual to pull western Europe out of its Dark Ages and start it on the road to the bright light of the Renaissance. Un-

like most other Germanic rulers, he encouraged art and education. At his command, schools were started in monasteries, convents and churches throughout the kingdom, the first of which was held at the royal castle and led by the brilliant court scholar, Alcuin. At Charlemagne's behest, Alcuin also set out to collect and preserve the writings of ancient Greek and Roman thinkers. Charlemagne's love of knowledge helped save ancient history, literature, and philosophy for future generations—all this from a man who could barely read or sign his own name!

Charlemagne—a giant towering over the medieval world.

In 799 Pope Leo III was attacked in Italy, and rescued by a group of Charlemagne's knights, who saw the pope safely back to his palace and quieted the angry crowds. The pope never forgot the Franks' kindness. On Christmas Day, 800, Pope Leo III bestowed the greatest honor imaginable upon Charlemagne, crowning him "Emperor of the Holy Roman Empire." During his thirty-year reign, Charlemagne's strength, diplomacy and skill with the sword kept the land free of invaders and held internal rivalries in check. But great men eventually die. The empire was broken up as Charlemagne's grandchildren fought for power, leaving the lands that he had worked so hard to unite vulnerable to a new and fierce barbarian tribe—the Vikings.

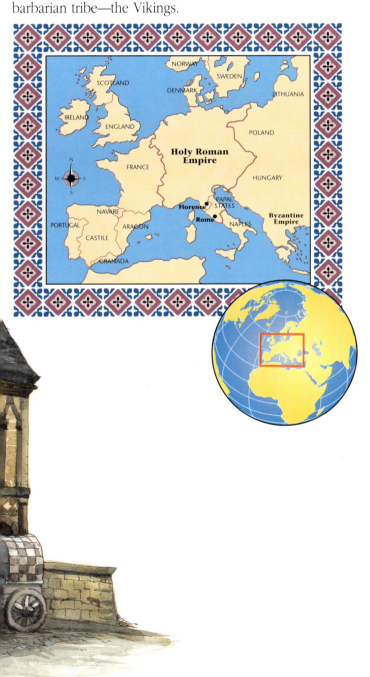

Quiz

1. Which of the following barbarian tribes did not settle in England?

- Ⓐ the Angles
- Ⓑ the Saxons
- Ⓒ the Jutes
- Ⓓ the Franks

2. A noble who pledged allegiance to the king was called a

- Ⓐ vassal.
- Ⓑ fief.
- Ⓒ peasant.
- Ⓓ knight.

3. A fiefdom included the land and everything on it, except the people.

- Ⓐ True
- Ⓑ False

4. In a medieval village, the cobbler made shoes, the tinker mended pots and pans, and the cooper made

- Ⓐ weapons.
- Ⓑ hats.
- Ⓒ barrels.
- Ⓓ jewelry.

5. By the year _____, most of Europe had been converted to Christianity.

- Ⓐ 500
- Ⓑ 1000
- Ⓒ 1500
- Ⓓ 1066

6. The only class of people in medieval society who could read and write were the

- Ⓐ nobles.
- Ⓑ peasants.
- Ⓒ knights.
- Ⓓ clergy.

7. Guilds were organizations of

- Ⓐ craftsmen and artisans.
- Ⓑ nuns and monks.
- Ⓒ knights and nobles.
- Ⓓ criminals and outlaws.

8. Charlemagne was the grandson of

- Ⓐ Charles Martel.
- Ⓑ Pepin the Short.
- Ⓒ Clovis.
- Ⓓ Childeric.

9. In the year 800, Charlemagne was given the title "Emperor of the Holy Roman Empire."

- Ⓐ True
- Ⓑ False

10. Although Charlemagne could barely read or write, he encouraged

- Ⓐ art and music.
- Ⓑ art and education.
- Ⓒ war and conquest.
- Ⓓ science and religion.

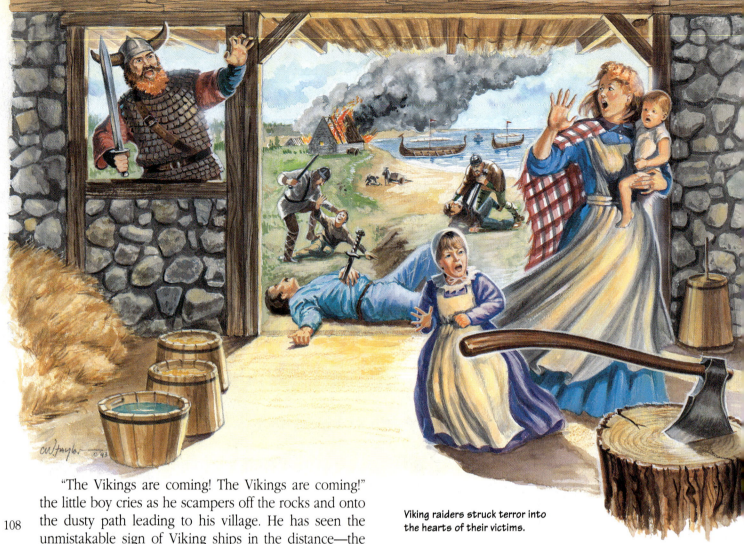

Viking raiders struck terror into the hearts of their victims.

"The Vikings are coming! The Vikings are coming!" the little boy cries as he scampers off the rocks and onto the dusty path leading to his village. He has seen the unmistakable sign of Viking ships in the distance—the billowing blaze of purple and red sails and rows of long oars moving as one. The Vikings travel with incredible speed. Hearing the cries of alarm, young and old gather in the village church, praying, crying, hoping that their village might be spared. Viking raiders have attacked villages all along the coast. Usually by the time help arrives the Vikings are gone, along with all that is of value. The men are dead, and the women taken captive. Burned-out huts stand like vacant shells in villages once alive with the squeals of children and the hearty laughter from the ale house. The ships are closer now, the dragons and sea serpents carved on their prows rearing up like demons. Viking yells reach the village. Now there is no hope. Now there will be no mercy.

By the year 800 the barbarian inheritors of the legacy of Rome had developed a culture and a civilization of their own. The descendants of the warlike Franks and Angles and Saxons and Goths, who had carved out the kingdoms, were peace-loving farmers and prosperous merchants. Now they in their turn felt the sting of invasion as the Vikings, or Norsemen, swept down from the Scandinavian Peninsula in their long boats and hit the shores of Europe like a tidal wave. In 793 Vikings sailing south from the North Sea began raiding England, Ireland, and Scotland. In swift, violent, and ruthless attacks, the Viking raiders

targeted various destinations along the European coastline. Appearing suddenly, they burned down villages and took everything of value they could find, then vanished as quickly as they'd come. Those who were not killed by the Viking attack were taken to be sold as slaves.

The Vikings, who at home were farmers, herders, fishermen, and expert shipbuilders, inspired fear throughout western Europe and beyond. By the middle of the ninth century they had looted and plundered the coastlines of France, Spain, and Italy. Moving by sea and by land they seemed to be everywhere. Their ships rounded the Strait of Gibraltar and sailed the Mediterranean to terrorize North African shores. From Sweden they followed the rivers to the Black Sea and even attacked Constantinople, the capitol of the Byzantine Empire.

The Vikings were explorers and adventurers as well as ocean-going warriors. They sailed west past the British Isles into the cold unknown and established colonies in Iceland and Greenland. Around the year 1000 a Greenlander named Leif Ericson stepped ashore on the east coast of North America, in what is now known as Newfoundland. He called the region Vinland because of

Back at home, the Norsemen celebrated successful raids with feasts and stories in song.

the grapes that grew there in abundance and from which his crew made wine. As far as anyone can say with certainty, he was the first European ever to reach the Americas.

At the beginning of the tenth century Charlemagne's empire was splintered into three kingdoms, the areas which make up modern day France, Germany, and part of Italy. The Frankish rulers were divided and weak—helpless against Viking attack—and they knew it. With a fleet of ships bearing the warriors of the Viking Rollo waiting just off-shore, the king of France offered a compromise: he would give Rollo the French province of Normandy if Rollo would promise to leave the rest of France in peace. Rollo agreed. It was probably the easiest battle that he ever fought. Rollo's descendants were known as Normans, and like their ancestors they gazed out across the sea in search of new lands to conquer. And the land that they saw was England.

In 1066 Edward the Confessor, King of England, died, and Harold, Earl of Wessex ascended the throne. William, the Duke of Normandy, protested that Edward had promised the throne to him and immediately set out across the English Channel with five thousand men. At the Battle of Hastings, William defeated Harold and his Anglo-Saxon army, and became the new king of England.

William the Conqueror brought the Norman way of life to England and completely changed the course of English culture and language. Under William the Normans established a strong centralized government, and the Great Council, which would come to be known as Parliament, was formed.

As all this was going on in western Europe, the Byzantine Empire was developing a personality of its own—a blend of Roman, Greek, and oriental influences. And further east, Islam was transforming the Arab world. Soon after the death of Mohamed, the leaders of Islam had declared "jihad," or holy war, to conquer the world for the glory of their faith. Thus did the Islamic nations set their sights on empire. Soon the armies of Islam had snatched Palestine and Syria out of the grasp of the Byzantine Empire. Asia Minor, Egypt and North Africa converted to Islam, and Jerusalem, a holy city for Christians and Moslems alike, fell to the conquerors. In 711 Islam made its first thrust into western Europe when the Moors, North African Moslems, took over much of the Iberian Peninsula (today's Spain and Portugal). By 750 the Islamic empire was larger than the Roman empire had ever been!

Unlike the West, the Arab world had not suffered through a dark age. While Rome crumbled and western Europe descended into chaos, the nomads of the Sinai had simply kept herding their sheep, goats and camels across the endless desert. Always on the move, they had adapted less to Roman ways, so they did not lose their footing when left on their own—they did not have to create a new culture, they already had one. Unified under the banner of Islam were incredibly wealthy traders, scholars light-years ahead of their western contemporaries, and scientists making huge advances in astronomy, medicine, and mathematics. Certainly Arab nobility lived more comfortably than medieval kings and lords. Their palaces were made of white plaster, which reflected the sun's strong rays and kept the lavishly furnished interiors cool. The splendid work of Arab artisans was displayed everywhere, on carpets and tiles and columns. The palace grounds were beautifully designed with lush gardens and gushing fountains.

Mounted on swift steeds and armed with the finest steel, Moslem warriors spread the new religion.

For four hundred years of relatively tolerant Islamic rule, Moslems and Christians shared the holy city in peaceful coexistence, and Islamic leaders respected the rights of Christian pilgrims to visit sacred sites. But in 1071 another Moslem group, the Seljuk Turks, overran the Arab Islamic empire and took control of Palestine. They were less hospitable to the Christian pilgrims in Jerusalem, and soon stories of attacks on Christian pilgrims and the destruction of Christian churches reached western Europe. Although the rumors were probably untrue, they made European blood boil. The Seljuk Turks also directly threatened the entire eastern Byzantine Empire.

In 1095 the Byzantine Emperor appealed to Pope Urban II for help in stemming the tide of Turkish conquest, and the pope responded by issuing a call to arms to Europe's faithful—they would wage holy war to drive the Moslems out of Christian lands and recapture Jerusalem for the glory of God. So began the Crusades, a period of war between Christians and Moslems that lasted for two hundred years.

The pope's clarion call stirred feelings of anger and vengeance toward the Moslems and indirectly, toward all non-Christians—the *infidel*. The rich and the poor, the nobles and the serfs, clamored to meet the Pope's challenge. Religious zeal was not the only reason Europeans flocked to join in the Crusades. Although many fought with the sincere belief that they were defending their faith, others went in search of adventure, glory, and wealth. Nobles saw the Crusades as a way to gain power and ease debts. For the serfs, tied to the land on which they were born, the Crusades were a way to escape the hardship of village life. And for those fleeing the long arm of the law, the costume of a Holy Crusader was the perfect disguise.

Whatever their motives, all the crusaders quickly discovered one great truth: that they had embarked on a difficult, dangerous, and often deadly mission. Fully 90 percent of the crusaders never made it to the Holy Land that they had sworn to protect and liberate. Disease and

Pilgrims, adventurers, beggars, kings—the crusaders flocked in pursuit of the glory and riches of the holy land.

starvation were common threats. The many who set out with little or no money were forced to work their way across the continent, or to steal in order to survive. Because of this, many people who lived along their routes grew wary of, and even hostile toward, the crusaders.

The first group to leave for the Holy Land was led by a man named Peter the Hermit. The expedition consisted of zealous peasants, ignorant and untrained in warfare. They traveled overland, killing any Jews they could find along the way and creating much ill will for crusaders to follow. The last of the rag-tag group died in Hungary. The first official Crusade was led by French nobility. Knights from all over western Europe joined in the effort. By 1099 the crusaders had taken the city of Jerusalem, and established four Christian states in the Middle East. Flushed with victory after the conquest of Jerusalem, they slaughtered all the non-Christians they could find and then looted the city.

Saladin, the ruler of Egypt and leader of the Islamic armies, was determined to recapture Jerusalem. He united the Moslems for a massive attack on the Christian defenders of the city, and in 1187 succeeded in taking it back. Unlike the crusaders, he did not massacre Christian civilians. Instead he allowed them to leave the city. When news of Saladin's victory reached the West, there was a renewed surge of enthusiasm to continue the fight. This time the crusaders would be led by the rulers of three of Europe's nations—Richard the Lionheart of England, Frederick I of the Holy Roman Empire, and Philip II of

France. Like all crusaders, they struggled to endure the hardships of the journey to the Holy Land. Frederick I drowned when his ship went down in a storm, and soon after that, Phillip II became ill and returned to France, leaving the burden of the entire mission on the shoulders of England's Richard Lionheart.

Saladin and Richard eventually met on the battlefield. Both men were great warriors, and each had the utmost respect for the martial skills of the other. After a period of heavy fighting, Saladin's troops gained the upper hand, but the armies of Christ were not willing to admit defeat. Suddenly a messenger came with the news that Richard was

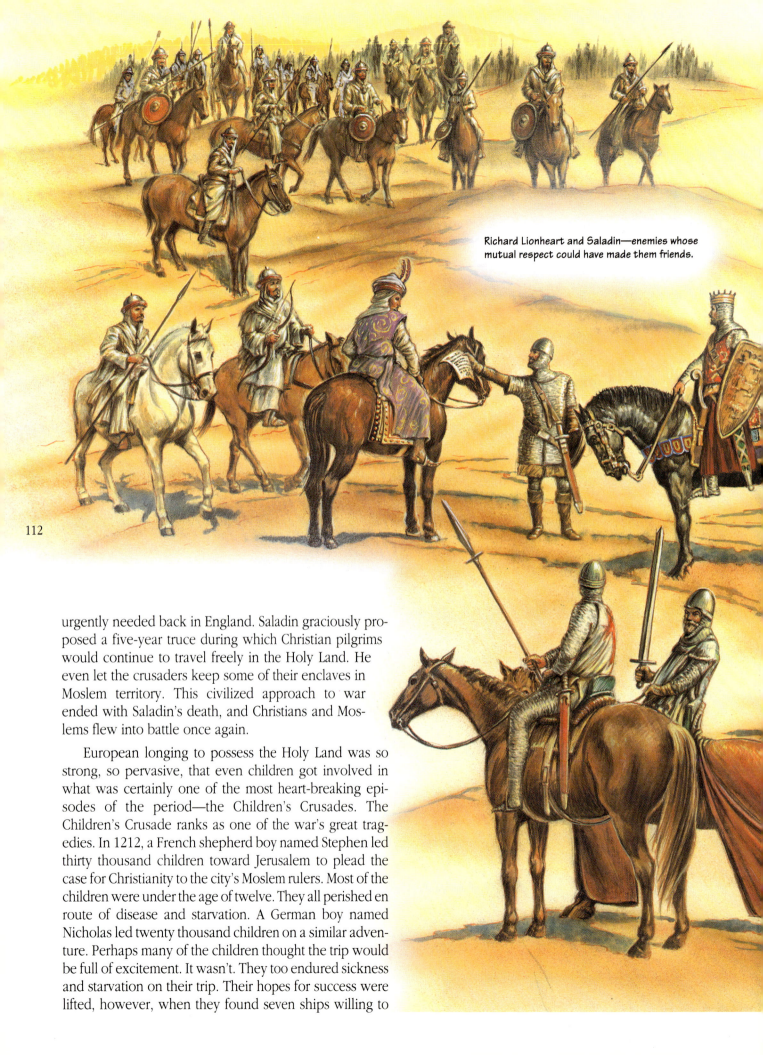

Richard Lionheart and Saladin—enemies whose mutual respect could have made them friends.

urgently needed back in England. Saladin graciously proposed a five-year truce during which Christian pilgrims would continue to travel freely in the Holy Land. He even let the crusaders keep some of their enclaves in Moslem territory. This civilized approach to war ended with Saladin's death, and Christians and Moslems flew into battle once again.

European longing to possess the Holy Land was so strong, so pervasive, that even children got involved in what was certainly one of the most heart-breaking episodes of the period—the Children's Crusades. The Children's Crusade ranks as one of the war's great tragedies. In 1212, a French shepherd boy named Stephen led thirty thousand children toward Jerusalem to plead the case for Christianity to the city's Moslem rulers. Most of the children were under the age of twelve. They all perished en route of disease and starvation. A German boy named Nicholas led twenty thousand children on a similar adventure. Perhaps many of the children thought the trip would be full of excitement. It wasn't. They too endured sickness and starvation on their trip. Their hopes for success were lifted, however, when they found seven ships willing to take them to Jerusalem. The ships started on their course. During the sea voyage high winds and heavy rain sank two of the seven ships, taking the lives of all the children on board. The surviving children, though shaken, still had great hopes of reaching Jerusalem. But their hopes were soon dashed when, instead of achieving their noble goal they were taken to Egypt and sold into slavery.

By 1291 Jerusalem was under Moslem control for good. The Crusades had cost many hundreds of thousands of lives—mostly of innocent bystanders—but they changed European society in positive ways, too. The crusaders' eyes had been opened to a new and different world. They had gained a new sense of independence, and a renewed interest in exploration.

Quiz

1. The Vikings came from

Ⓐ Greenland.
Ⓒ England.
Ⓑ the Scandinavian Peninsula.
Ⓓ the Iberian Peninsula.

2. The Norman conquest of England occurred in the year

Ⓐ 1066.
Ⓒ 1660.
Ⓑ 1606.
Ⓓ 1099.

3. The French province of Normandy was given to a Viking named Rollo.

Ⓐ True
Ⓑ False

4. In 750 the Islamic Empire was larger than the Roman Empire at its height.

Ⓐ True
Ⓑ False

5. One of the holiest cities for both Christians and Moslems is

Ⓐ Rome.
Ⓒ Jerusalem.
Ⓑ Constantinople.
Ⓓ Athens.

6. The Crusades primarily spanned which centuries?

Ⓐ twelfth and thirteenth
Ⓒ fourteenth and fifteenth
Ⓑ ninth and tenth
Ⓓ thirteenth and fourteenth

7. A famous leader of the Moslems in their fight against the crusaders was Saladin.

Ⓐ True
Ⓑ False

8. Which of the following European rulers never participated in the Crusades?

Ⓐ Richard Lionheart of England
Ⓒ Frederick I of Germany
Ⓑ Philip II of France
Ⓓ King John of England

9. The Moslem group that posed the greatest threat to the Byzantine Empire in the eleventh century was

Ⓐ the Seljuk Turks.
Ⓒ the Moors.
Ⓑ the Arab Islamic Empire.
Ⓓ the Ottoman Empire.

10. Which was not a reason why people joined the Crusades?

Ⓐ to escape village life
Ⓒ to escape the law
Ⓑ to ease debts
Ⓓ to see Athens

"Ring around the rosie,
a pocket full of posies,
ashes, ashes,
all fall down."

The sickness is everywhere. In every city and every town, the stench of death and decay fills the air. "Bring out your dead.... Bring out your dead...." You can see the horses pulling carts piled high with corpses slowly clip-clopping toward the bonfires where the bodies are being burned. There are not enough people left alive to bury those that have died. There are no doctors to care for the sick, no priests to minister to the dying and the dead. The mournful tolling of the bells in the church tower never stops.

The sickness is everywhere, and no one can escape. The lords and la-

dies hide behind the high walls of their castles and manor houses, but somehow death finds them too. You watch helplessly as the people you love fall one by one. And now you look at yourself and the signs are there. The little ringed spots—as red as rosebuds—are all over your skin. Soon they will swell, blister, and turn black. Soon after that you too will die.

Durham 1349
London 1349
Paris 1348
Marseille 1347
Venice 1348
Rome 1348
Seville 1348
Sicily 1347
Constantinople 1347
Southern Russia 1345
From Asia
Mediterranean Sea

The grim spectre of death was everywhere as the Black Plague spread across Europe.

The Magna Carta limited the power of the king.

The crusaders brought many things back with them when they returned from the Holy Land: new ideas, new inventions, new foods, new treasures, but also a new disease—the devastating Black Death. The plague came first to the port cities of Italy, borne by flea-ridden rats aboard the ships returning from the East. From there it spread quickly to France, Germany, England, and the other countries of Europe. The people did not know what caused the terrible illness, but they could see the horrible results. Between the years 1347 and 1350, one out of every four Europeans fell victim to the dread disease! England alone lost nearly a third of its people.

The Black Death caused major upheavals in the economic life of Europe during the fourteenth century. People fled the infected towns and cities for the clean air of the countryside. Governments had less money since dead citizens, after all, don't pay taxes. There were fewer workers so employers were forced to pay higher wages, and many businesses failed. Less food was needed for the population so food prices dropped and farmers suffered.

The fabric of Europe's rigid feudal society was destroyed. Peasants, for generations chained to the land they worked, began to wander about seeking escape from the sickness, or some way—any way—to improve their desperate lives. Nobles lost their wealth and, along with it, the fearful respect of the common folk. The clergy, powerless in the face of the scourge that left no one untouched, came to be looked upon with disdain.

Desperate lives led to desperate acts, and the people began to express their outrage and their discontent. English peasants rebelled against their king, Richard II. The uprising was quickly suppressed, but the Peasants' Rebellion was a clear warning of the storms of change that were about to sweep across the continent. The people had lost faith in their leaders, in their religion, in a way of life that was all they had ever known. With the loss of faith came questions—and defiance.

It had started almost a century before with Richard Lionheart's brother, King John of England, neither a very wise nor a very agreeable man. By raising taxes sky high and relying too much on the executioner's skills, he managed to make himself unpopular with nobles and commoners alike. With no talent for war, he lost England's holdings in France, including the highly prized province of Normandy (This was an especially bitter loss since Normandy was the very same land that his warrior ancestor, Rollo the Viking, had won from the king of France long ago.). With no aptitude for diplomacy, he fought constantly with Pope Innocent II. At one point he was excommunicated and endured the humiliation of publicly begging to be readmitted to the fold.

In 1213 a group of dissatisfied English nobles asked King John to listen to their grievances. He refused, so the nobles raised a large army which they brought to the

115

King's doorstep. Then they asked him to reconsider his decision. This time John was more cooperative and a meeting was arranged on June 15, 1215, at a place called Runnymede on the bank of the Thames River. King John, the nobles, and representatives of the Church met face to face. The nobles put before the king a document with a list of sixty-three demands. This document became known as the Magna Carta, or Great Charter. The Magna Carta limited the power of the king and defined his responsibility to his subjects. More importantly, it set a precedent by which no one—not even the king—was above the law. King John signed the document, but not surprisingly went back on his word at the first opportunity. When he died the nobles made his son King Henry III sign it as well.

116

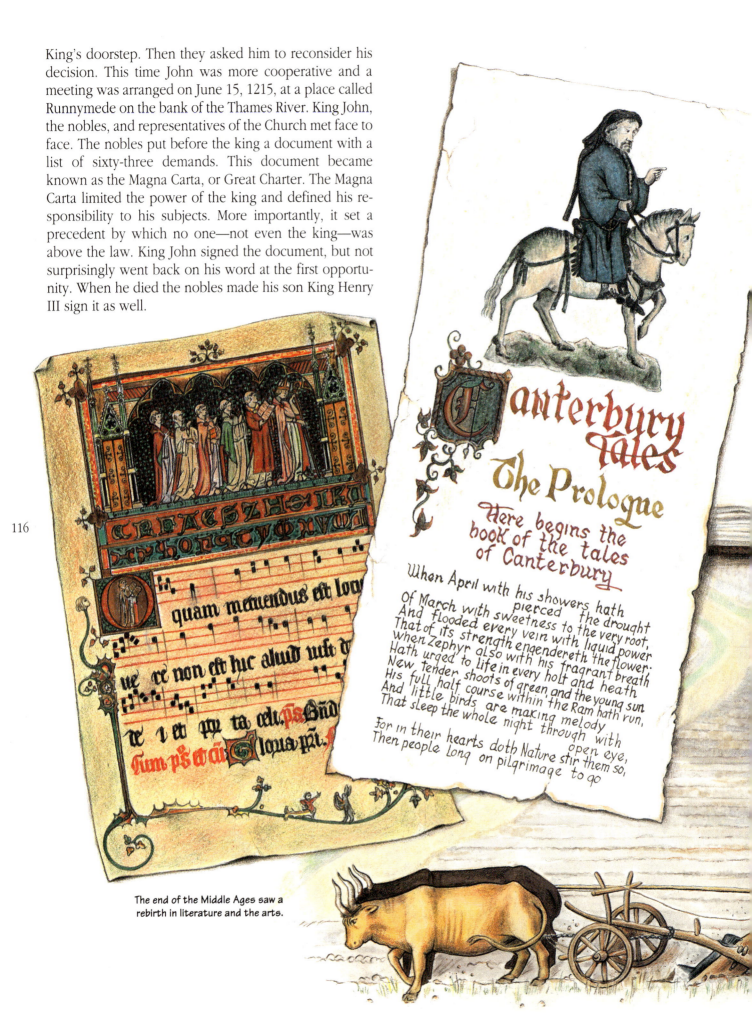

The end of the Middle Ages saw a rebirth in literature and the arts.

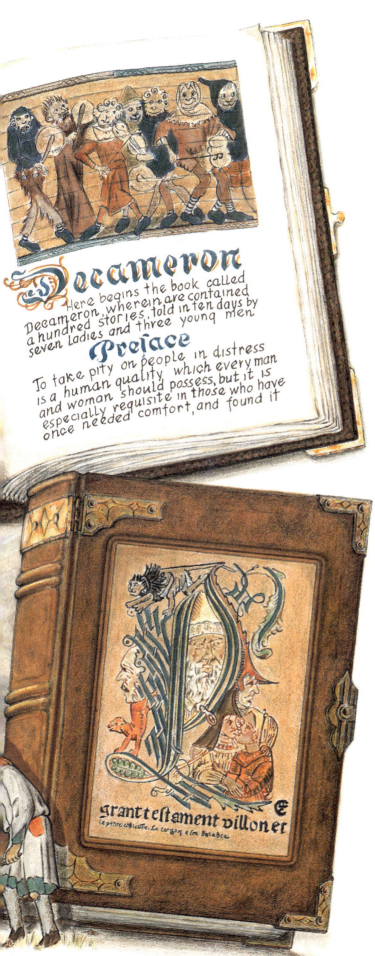

Decameron
Here begins the book called Decameron, wherein are contained a hundred stories, told in ten days by seven ladies and three young men

Preface
To take pity on people in distress is a human quality which every man and woman should possess, but it is especially requisite in those who have once needed comfort, and found it

grant testament villonet

Next to be challenged was the political power of the Church. In 1303, the powerful King Phillip IV of France actually dared to arrest Pope Boniface VIII because of a dispute over the Church's refusal to pay taxes. Six years later King Phillip installed a Frenchman, Clement V, as pope and moved the pope's residence from Rome to Avignon in France. For the next sixty-five years the leaders of the Catholic church lived in the city of Avignon, under the complete domination of the French throne. It was not until 1377 that a pope returned to Rome.

But still the conflict continued. From 1378 to 1417, a period known as the Great Western Schism, there were two popes—one in Avignon, the other in Rome. At one time there were as many as three popes, each with his own College of Cardinals and his own center of administration! This struggle for power and for domination divided and weakened the Church.

While the secular rulers of Europe tested the Church's political power, challenges to its religious authority came from within. In England, John Wycliffe criticized bishops and priests for neglecting their religious duties and charged that Church leaders were greedy, corrupt, and hungry for temporal power. He declared the Bible, not the Church, to be the only true authority for Christians. He made the first English translation of the Latin Bible so the common people could read it for themselves. His followers were known as the "Poor Preachers," a name that indicated their disdain for material wealth.

In Italy a lyric poet and scholar, Francesco Petrarch, chose to focus not on the traditional religious doctrine of the Church, with its emphasis on sin, salvation and the afterlife, but rather on *humanity.* It was Petrarch who first put forth the notion, strange and revolutionary as it seemed at the time, that every human being, rich or poor, great or humble, was important and deserved to be treated with dignity and respect. These ideas earned Petrarch the title "Father of Humanism" and forever changed the face of religion, the arts and the sciences in the western world. Other writers like Giovanni Boccaccio in Italy, Geoffrey Chaucer in England, and Francois Rabelais in France followed Petrarch's lead. Their earthy and robust books, *The Decameron, The Canterbury Tales,* and *Gargantua and Pantagruel,* realistically depict the times in which the authors lived, and portray people with all their foibles and weaknesses as inherently important and good at heart.

But in spite of the revolutionary changes taking place in their world—perhaps even entirely unaware of them—most people carried on with the day-to-day business of war and the never-ending war of business.

In 1328 King Edward III of England made a claim for the vacant throne of France. (His mother was the daugh-

ter of the previous French king.) The French people refused to accept an Englishman as their king, so in 1337 the two countries went to war. The aptly named Hundred Years' War lasted, in fact, more than a century. Through thick and thin, good times and bad, the French and the English fought. During these many years of battle, new weapons and modes of warfare evolved. At the Battle of Crécy in 1346, British archers, with their new and powerful longbows, were able to pierce the heavy armor of the French soldiers, and in no time at all heavy armor became a thing of the past. The English won victory after victory until by 1400 much of France was in English hands. Obviously, though, this state of affairs was not to last.

To the south the Moors were driven out of much of Spain, maintaining a foothold only in Granada at the southern tip of the Iberian Peninsula. The kingdoms of Aragon and Castille rose to become the most powerful of the many Christian kingdoms that shared the Spanish lands.

And in Byzantium the Ottoman Turks led by their chief, Osman, surprised everybody by defeating the mighty army of the Byzantine Empire. The Ottomans began to build a new Islamic empire, which continued to grow after Osman died. By 1340 the Ottomans controlled all of Asia Minor, and the days of the Byzantine empire, the last fragile remnant of the glory that was Rome, were numbered.

118

The battle of Crécy proved armored knights obsolete, bringing an end to the age of chivalry.

Occupation of Rome and disintegration of Roman Western Empire

Vikings raid England, Scotland, and Ireland

Clovis unites all Franks

Pepin the Short becomes King of the Franks

Rollo acquires Normandy (Normans)

Most of Europe converted to Christianity

Leif Erickson reaches North America

William the Duke of Normandy defeats Harold Earl of Wessex and becomes the King of England

Crusades

Crusaders take over Jerusalem

Magna Carta is signed by King John of England

Angles, Saxons, and Jutes control British Isles (Anglo-Saxons)

Islamic Nation larger than Rome

Charlemagne crowned Emperor of the Holy Roman Empire

Saladin of Egypt unites the Moslems and takes back Jerusalem

Jerusalem under Moslem Control

Islam in Europe

476 485 500   711   750   751 793   800   1000   1066 1095 1099   1187   1213   1295 12

Quiz

1. The plague, also known as the Black Death, was carried to Europe by

Ⓐ monks.
Ⓒ traders.
Ⓑ rats.
Ⓓ Crusaders.

2. Between 1347 and 1350, _____ of the people of Europe died of the plague.

Ⓐ one half
Ⓒ one fourth
Ⓑ one third
Ⓓ one million

3. Governments during the plague years had less money because there were fewer people to pay taxes.

Ⓐ True
Ⓑ False

4. For 65 years, the popes of the Catholic Church lived in the French city of

Ⓐ Paris.
Ⓒ Toulon.
Ⓑ Marseilles.
Ⓓ Avignon.

5. John Wycliffe made the first _____ translation of the Bible.

Ⓐ English
Ⓒ French
Ⓑ Latin
Ⓓ Greek

6. Boccaccio, Petrarch, Chaucer, Rabelais—how many were great humanist writers?

Ⓐ one
Ⓒ three
Ⓑ two
Ⓓ four

7. English nobility forced _____ to sign the Magna Carta.

Ⓐ King John
Ⓒ Rollo the Viking
Ⓑ Richard Lionheart
Ⓓ Pope Innocent II

8. The most important concept in the Magna Carta is that no one is above the law.

Ⓐ True
Ⓑ False

9. The Italian scholar, _____, is known as the Father of Humanism.

Ⓐ Boccaccio
Ⓒ Chaucer
Ⓑ Petrarch
Ⓓ Rabelais

10. The Hundred Years' War was fought between

Ⓐ England and Italy.
Ⓒ England and France.
Ⓑ Italy and France.
Ⓓ Byzantium and France.

Ottoman Turks control all of Asia Minor

Great Western Schism

King Edward III of England claims the throne of France

100 Years' War

Most of France in English hands

Black Plague

1328   1330 1337   1350   1378   1447

Chapter 10

The Renaissance—Out of the Dark

With the dawn of the fourteenth century came the awakening of the people of Europe from the deep and troubled sleep of the Middle Ages. The crusades, ruinous and wasteful in many ways, did have the positive effect of opening the eyes of Europeans to the many wonders of the world beyond their own front door. Contact with the Islamic world and the rich and vibrant cultures of the East stimulated the Europeans to develop a taste for the finer things in life—and a hunger for knowledge—that could be satisfied only by further exploration. By the end of this century, the people of Europe would be astonished to find themselves inhabitants of a world much larger and more diverse than previously imagined. Nowhere was the impact of Europe's interaction with the East more evident than in the economic and cultural flowering of the city-states of Italy.

As the exotic products of China and India became ever more popular among the people of Europe and trade with those lands continued to grow, the cities of Venice, Genoa, Pisa, and Florence, already prominent financial centers because of their location at the crossroads of the Mediterranean trade routes, prospered as never before. These Italian cities became leaders in the great reawakening interest in life called the *Renaissance*, which means "revival" or "rebirth." The people of Europe, isolated and withdrawn

Lorenzo the Magnificent—the most famous member of the powerful Medici family.

since the collapse of the Roman Empire in the West, began to ask questions—about life, the cosmos, themselves, their history—and the arts and sciences came alive, straining for answers. They found inspiration in what they began to view with nostalgia—the Golden Age of ancient Greece and Rome.

The city most important in initiating this upsurge of cultural activity was Florence. In addition to its fame as a

FLORENCE

the financial and cultural heart of
fourteenth century Europe

This is Leonardo da Vinci's sketch for a flying machine similar to modern helicopters. Leonardo always wrote his notes in mirror images. No one knows why.

During the Renaissance, Europe was bursting with new developments in science, the arts, and philosophy.

producer of fine fabrics, Florence reigned supreme among the financial giants of Italy. Although nominally a republic, Florence was dominated by the immensely wealthy Medici family who were the leaders of the banking guild. Led by its most brilliant and insightful member, Lorenzo the Magnificent, the Medici family supported the work of many great artists and thinkers and devoted much of their wealth to the construction of magnificent buildings and public monuments. They helped foster the most brilliant intellectual and artistic outpouring since the days of classical Greece and nurtured the careers of people like Leonardo da Vinci (scientist, engineer, inventor, and painter of the *Mona Lisa*), Michelangelo Buonarroti (painter, architect, poet, and sculptor of the *David* and the *Pietà*), Niccoló Machiavelli (political theorist, statesman, and author of *The Prince*) and many others.

The advances made by painters and artists during this time were especially impressive. Renaissance artists began to study nature and

The construction techniques used by the artist Brunelleschi in building his famous dome remained a mystery for hundreds of years.

the human body to help them draw things more accurately. They also made the revolutionary discovery of perspective, a technique for showing distance in their paintings by creating the illusion of a three-dimensional space on a two-dimensional surface. Sculptors were inspired by the statues of ancient Greece and Rome. Architects built wonderful new palaces and churches based on the style of Greek and Roman temples.

Scholars began to study Greek, Latin, and Hebrew texts that had been retrieved from the Islamic world by the crusaders. They were thrilled to discover the exciting ideas and concepts of the ancient philosophers, which had been lost to them for many generations. Many new universities and schools were founded. The Dutch scholar Erasmus devoted his time to studying the writings of early Christian leaders and came to the conclusion that

Printing was developed in China as early as the eighth century. But Gutenberg's movable-type printing press was a major advance that boosted the spread of knowledge throughout Europe.

the Catholic Church and clergy of his time had strayed far from the original teachings of Christianity.

It became the standard for a properly educated person to be accomplished in many areas. It was not unusual for a young Renaissance man to understand and collect art, write poetry, play a musical instrument, read and write Latin and Greek, speak several languages, fight if neces-

Patrons like the Medicis stood by to give guidance and support.

Artists like Michelangelo filled Florence with grandeur and beauty. His "David" is probably the most famous and admired statue in the world.

sary, be familiar with political issues, excel at sports, and display gallant manners. So today when we call a person a "Renaissance man" (or woman) we laud him or her for being well-rounded, with many interests and capabilities.

Although the Renaissance began in Italy, its influence spread quickly to the other nations of Europe. One invention of the time did more than anything else to hasten the dissemination of knowledge. In 1454 Johann Gutenberg, a German, developed the printing press, which allowed books to be made and copied quickly and cheaply. Reading, which had hitherto been a specialty of monks and scholars, became a pastime enjoyed by many, and the rare and costly hand-copied manuscript was replaced by the less expensive and more easily obtained printed book.

Renaissance painters developed new techniques for showing depth and perspective, adding greater realism to their work.

During the fourteenth century, central Europe had degenerated into a loose collection of hundreds of small kingdoms, constantly at war with one another. One family, the Hapsburgs, became so powerful that it was able to overcome and unite all the other rulers in the region. True to the spirit of the Renaissance, the Hapsburgs looked back in time for their inspiration, and found it in the model of the mighty Romans. Thinking back to the example set by Charlemagne, they gave themselves the title of emperor and called their kingdom the Holy Roman Empire. However as the French wag Voltaire once remarked, it was in fact neither holy, Roman, nor an empire. In 1516 the Hapsburg archduke, Charles V, inherited Spain and the newly won Spanish territo-

123

Men and women of the Renaissance took pride in their ability to excel in many areas of endeavor.

In imitation of the masterworks of ancient Greece and Rome, the subject matter of Renaissance art shows a fascination with the human form.

Joan of Arc believed that God called her to lead France to victory in the Hundred Years' War.

124

ries in America. When Charles died, his empire was divided between his son Philip II of Spain, and his brother Archduke Ferdinand of Austria. From then on Spain and Austria were ruled by separate branches of the Hapsburg family.

Farther west, the Hundred Years' War between France and England ended in 1453, with England finally driven from France. France and England had battled continuously for more than a century over England's claims to certain French territories. The French troops had been inspired by Joan of Arc, a teenage girl who claimed divine guidance. With no military experience she led the French to victory in several important battles. She later became a prisoner of the English and in 1431 was condemned as a witch and burned at the stake. But her martyrdom only served to unify and strengthen French

resolve against the presence of the English on their soil. Wars between France and England continued sporadically for the next four centuries. It would not be until the twentieth century that they would come to be close allies.

England, temporarily freed of its long conflict with France, quickly became embroiled in the War of the Roses, which lasted from 1455 to 1485. The colorfully named War of the Roses was a civil war in which two powerful families—the Lancasters, whose symbol was the red rose, and the York family, represented by the white rose—fought for the throne of England. Henry Tudor of the house of Lancaster finally defeated Richard III and began the reunification of the English nation under the leadership of the Tudor family.

In Eastern Europe changes were taking place that would have lasting impact on the relationship between Europe and the countries of Asia. In Russia the rulers of the city of Moscow gained power by cooperating with the fierce Mongols, who had invaded Russia two centuries before. The princes of Moscow helped the Mongols collect tribute from other conquered cities. In return, the Mongols helped the Russian princes increase their territory. By the 1400s the princes of Moscow were the most powerful rulers in Russia.

In 1462 Ivan III, a descendant of the esteemed Viking, Rurik, became prince of Moscow and determined to rid his homeland of the foreign invaders. After driving the Mongols and their satellite Russian princes from Moscow in 1471, he declared himself czar of all Russia and made Moscow its capital. Like the other European leaders he sought to emulate the Romans and chose the title *czar* because it was the Russian word for "Caesar." In 1480 the Mongols set out to destroy Ivan. But when they saw Ivan's huge army, they fled without a fight. That ended Mongol rule in Russia. When Ivan III died in 1505, he left Russia a free and united nation. For that reason he is remembered as Ivan the Great.

The city of Constantinople, capital of the Byzantine Empire, had been the last bastion of the Roman Empire and the center of the Orthodox Christian Church since the fall of Rome in the West almost one thousand years before. But in 1453 the Ottoman Turks, who were Moslems, conquered Constantinople. The last Byzantine emperor died in the struggle. The Ottomans renamed the city Istanbul and made it the capital of their empire.

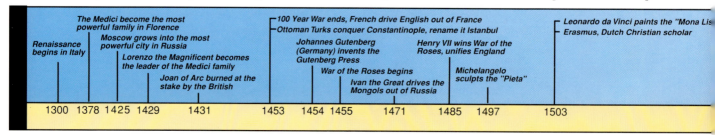

		The Medici become the most powerful family in Florence		100 Year War ends, French drive English out of France		Leonardo da Vinci paints the "Mona Lis
		Moscow grows into the most powerful city in Russia		Ottoman Turks conquer Constantinople, rename it Istanbul		Erasmus, Dutch Christian scholar
	Renaissance begins in Italy			Johannes Gutenberg (Germany) invents the Gutenberg Press	Henry VII wins War of the Roses, unifies England	
		Lorenzo the Magnificent becomes the leader of the Medici family		War of the Roses begins	Michelangelo sculpts the "Pieta"	
			Joan of Arc burned at the stake by the British	Ivan the Great drives the Mongols out of Russia		
1300	1378	1425	1429	1431	1453	1454 1455	1471	1485	1497	1503

As the torchbearer of the civilization of Rome, Constantinople had been the keeper of the documents sacred to Christianity and much of the culture of the Western world. It had also served as an effective barrier against Asian Huns, Magyars, Mongols, and Turks. In the same way, trade with India and China had remained open to Europeans as long as Constantinople guarded the gateway to the East, the Strait of Bosphorus. Increasing contact between Europeans and other cultures would soon lead to conflict, growth, and tragedy.

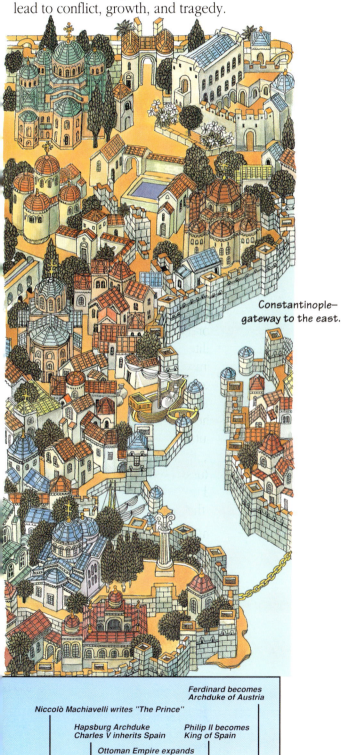

Constantinople—
gateway to the east.

Niccolò Machiavelli writes "The Prince"

Ferdinard becomes
Archduke of Austria

Hapsburg Archduke
Charles V inherits Spain

Philip II becomes
King of Spain

Ottoman Empire expands

1513	1516	1520	1556	1619

Quiz

1. During the Renaissance, the most influential of the Italian city-states was

- Ⓐ Rome.
- Ⓒ Florence.
- Ⓑ Venice.
- Ⓓ Genoa.

2. The wealthy Medici family is best known for being

- Ⓐ doctors.
- Ⓒ lawyers.
- Ⓑ supporters of the arts.
- Ⓓ very large.

3. The printing press was invented in 1454 by

- Ⓐ Johann Gutenberg.
- Ⓒ Erasmus.
- Ⓑ Charles Hapsburg.
- Ⓓ Lorenzo Medici.

4. Who did Ivan III drive out of Russia?

- Ⓐ Turks
- Ⓒ Chinese
- Ⓑ Armenians
- Ⓓ Mongols

5. Renaissance sculptors were inspired by the statues of ancient

- Ⓐ Greece and Rome.
- Ⓒ India and China.
- Ⓑ Sumer and Babylon.
- Ⓓ Crete and Phoenicia.

6. The Dutch scholar, _____, studied early Christian writings.

- Ⓐ Leonardo da Vinci
- Ⓒ Niccolò Machiavelli
- Ⓑ Erasmus
- Ⓓ Michelangelo

7. Joan of Arc helped the French in their Hundred Years' War against

- Ⓐ Germany.
- Ⓒ Byzantium.
- Ⓑ Russia.
- Ⓓ England.

8. The Ottoman Turks conquered the city of _____ in 1453.

- Ⓐ Paris
- Ⓒ Constantinople
- Ⓑ Venice
- Ⓓ Moscow

9. The War of the Roses was fought between the Lancaster family and the York family.

- Ⓐ True
- Ⓑ False

10. The Holy Roman Empire was begun by the Hapsburg family.

- Ⓐ True
- Ⓑ False

Chapter 11

The Reformation—Back to Basics

October 31 was warmer than usual in Wittenburg, Germany in 1517. The cobblestone streets of the city were thronged with people going about their daily chores. Martin Luther, a monk and teacher from the nearby university, approached the local church. His determined stride told the townsfolk he passed that he was on a serious errand. He reached the entrance to the church, but instead of going inside he carefully nailed a piece of paper to the outside of the heavy door and walked away. With this one simple yet defiant act, he began the period of upheaval in Christianity that we call the Reformation.

As a young man, Martin Luther was almost killed when a savage storm overtook a boat he was traveling on. With the fury of the wind and the water raging all around him, he vowed to become a monk if only he survived. The storm passed and Martin made it safely home. In 1507 he bade farewell to worldly things to enter the Augustinian order of monks, thus fulfilling his near-death vow. A few years later he became a professor of religious studies at the University of Wittenburg.

By the dawn of the sixteenth century the Roman Catholic church had achieved a position of immense wealth and political power. The pope could make or break kings. Priests and church officials had grown rich from the taxes they collected on their vast land holdings. And still there was not enough money flowing into the coffers of the Holy City to pay for the construction of St. Peter's Cathedral, the great monument to faith that Pope Leo X believed must be built.

In 1515 the Pope declared that the Church would begin selling "indulgences" in order to raise money. An indulgence was a church document that could be bought by anyone, which was considered an official pardon for any sins a person might have committed—sort of a free pass

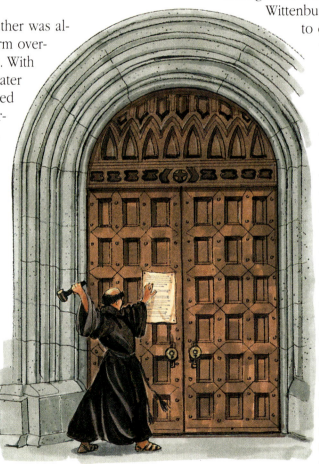

Martin Luther shook the Christian world when he hammered his *95 Theses* to the door of the Catholic church.

for guilt and punishment. According to the pope people who bought indulgences were doing good deeds for the Church, so they deserved to have their sins excused.

Martin Luther devoted his studies to the question of salvation—that is, how a Christian should act to be forgiven of his or her sins and saved from hell to enter heaven. The Church taught that salvation could be gained by following Catholic rituals and by doing good deeds. But the more Luther studied the Bible the more he became convinced that only *faith*—a sincere belief and trust in God—could lead to salvation. He was also convinced that the indulgences being sold by the Church not only were of no good whatsoever to a person's soul, but were directly opposed to the pure Christianity of the Bible.

In 1517 a monk named John Tetzel began selling indulgences at his church near the University of Wittenburg. Martin Luther did not hesitate to express his opinion on the matter, and animosity developed between the two men. The whole thing came to a head when Martin Luther nailed his *Ninety-five Theses* to the church door on that warm October day.

Luther's *Ninety-five Theses* was a list of serious criticisms of things that the Catholic church was doing, including selling indulgences. No one had ever dared to criticize the Church like this before. Although Luther wrote the document in Latin, the official—and confidential—language of the Church, it was quickly translated into German and news of it spread, creating a stir all over Germany. The decrease in the sale of indulgences that came in the wake of Luther's deed was enough to alarm Church officials in Rome, and they were none too pleased with his thoughts on other things, either. They decided to keep an eye on this Martin Luther fellow.

Luther continued to speak out and write against Church practices. When in 1520 he received an order from the pope to cease questioning the authority of the Church, he publicly burned the document. The pope then promptly excommunicated him. The following year the Holy Roman Emperor convened a meeting of Church officials and royalty from all parts of Europe in the city of Worms,

Germany. Luther was found guilty of heresy (denying the teachings of the Church) and declared a criminal—an outlaw.

Fortunately Luther had a rich and influential friend, Frederick the Wise, a German prince. Frederick kept Luther safely hidden from the authorities in his castle for almost a year. During this time Luther devoted himself to translating the Bible from Latin, which only priests and scholars could read, into German so that common people could read the words for themselves.

Among the German people Luther's popularity grew to the point that he eventually formed his own church. Lutheranism was a new form of Christianity that did away with elaborate ritual and formal language and went directly to the hearts of ordinary people. The beliefs of the Lutherans were simple and clear: salvation is based on faith alone; the Bible is the source of religious truth; no priest, not even the pope, is necessary for a true understanding of the Bible. Services in Luther's church were conducted in German, the language of the people. Leaders of congregations were called ministers instead of priests, and they were allowed to marry. In 1529 the Catholic church declared a ban on Lutheranism. But by then the new sect had gained the support of several German princes with enough power to protest the Church's edict. These protesters became known as Protestants.

The wave of protest swept out in all directions from that small church in Wittenburg. In Switzerland it was John Calvin who harnessed its power and sent it down a channel of his own design. He established a set of rules that he felt would help his followers attain salvation. The rules were strict and rigidly upheld: no gambling, no card playing, no swearing, no drinking. Church leaders made regular visits, almost tours of inspection, to the homes of Calvinists, and when one broke a rule, it was not uncommon for the infraction to be noised about by an informer who had once been thought a friend.

In some ways Calvin was even more influential than Luther. His ideas influenced Protestants all over Europe, including France, where his followers called themselves Huguenots. The Huguenots were persecuted and reviled by the majority Catholic population of France. The bitterness between the two factions grew so heated that violence frequently broke out. The conflict reached its zenith on the eve of St. Bartholomew's Day, August 23, 1572. Most of the Huguenot leaders were assembled in Paris for the marriage of King Charles IX's sister Margaret of Valois to the Protestant Henry of Navarre, who would one day become King Henry IV. There was hope that this alliance would bring peace to the land. Instead a group of militant Catholics pressured the king into ordering a massacre of the Huguenot leaders. The St. Bartholomew's Day Massacre set off a month-long spree of blind religious zeal in which Protestants were wantonly murdered all across the country. About seven thousand Huguenots lost their lives. Calvinism survived, but France remained a bastion of the Catholic Church.

In England the forces of the Reformation took an altogether different twist because of the stubborn and irrepressible King Henry VIII. In the beginning Henry was a loyal Catholic. For his writings denouncing the heresies of Martin Luther, the pope had awarded him the title Defender of the Faith in 1521. But affairs of the

127

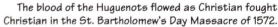

The blood of the Huguenots flowed as Christian fought Christian in the St. Bartholomew's Day Massacre of 1572.

heart—and of the throne of England—would prove to be the undoing of the bond between the pope and his royal majesty the King of England.

When Henry's queen Catherine of Aragon seemed unable to bear the king a son to inherit the throne, he became determined to divorce her and marry a woman named Anne Boleyn. But the Catholic Church did not allow divorce, and Catherine did not wish to be divorced. Henry appealed directly to Pope Clement VII for an annulment of the marriage. But Catherine was a

powerful person in her own right—the aunt of Charles V the Holy Roman Emperor, who just happened to have an army stationed rather too close to Rome for comfort. The pope realized that no matter what he did he would anger either Henry or Charles, so he did nothing.

With a stony silence the only reply from the pope, Henry proceeded to marry Anne Boleyn secretly in 1533.

Then he handpicked a new Archbishop of Canterbury, the highest religious authority in all of Catholic England. The new archbishop annulled the king's marriage to Catherine, and Anne Boleyn was crowned queen. Like Martin Luther, whose ideas he despised, Henry VIII was excommunicated from the Church.

With his power and his pride, Henry scornfully brushed off the excommunication and set about establishing a church of his own. In 1534 Parliament passed a law naming him head of the Anglican Church, or the Church of England. He confiscated all lands held by the Catholic Church and directed the composition of a new definition of faith and a Book of Common Prayer. But he made only a few modifications to the doctrine and rituals of the Church itself. Many of the more committed Protestants in England were unhappy with the king's compromise. These "puritans" were fervent in their desire to purify the Christian faith, and they would later play a prominent role in American history.

The conflict between Catholic and Protestant in England ended only after Henry's death when Elizabeth, his Protestant daughter by Anne Boleyn, became queen. England has remained a Protestant nation since that time.

The combined efforts of the established Catholic Church to stem the tide of Protestant reform are called the Counter-Reformation. More often than not it took the form of forceful,

Catherine of Aragon

Daughter Mary died childless...

...and Elizabeth became the Queen.

When the Catholic church prevented his divorce, Henry VIII became a Protestant and formed the Church of England.

Anne Boleyn

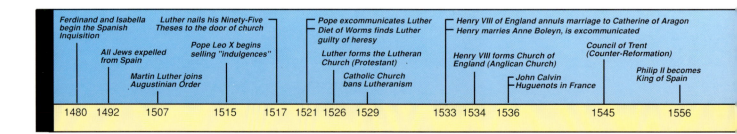

Ferdinand and Isabella begin the Spanish Inquisition

Luther nails his Ninety-Five Theses to the door of church

Pope excommunicates Luther
Diet of Worms finds Luther guilty of heresy

Henry VIII of England annuls marriage to Catherine of Aragon
Henry marries Anne Boleyn, is excommunicated

All Jews expelled from Spain

Pope Leo X begins selling "indulgences"

Luther forms the Lutheran Church (Protestant)

Henry VIII forms Church of England (Anglican Church)

Council of Trent (Counter-Reformation)

Martin Luther joins Augustinian Order

Catholic Church bans Lutheranism

John Calvin
Huguenots in France

Philip II becomes King of Spain

1480 1492   1507   1515   1517 1521 1526 1529   1533 1534 1536   1545   1556

The Spanish Inquisition—torture and mass execution in the name of a compassionate God.

even brutal repression and elimination of unorthodox sects. Historians place the beginning in Spain around the year 1480, when, during the reign of the Catholic monarchs Ferdinand and Isabella, the Spanish Inquisition began. Its purpose was clear enough: to eliminate or convert to Catholicism all Jews and Moorish Muslims in the land. Because of the Inquisition and the massive terror imposed by the Catholic majority in Spain, several hundred thousand Jews were killed, about one and half million were forced to renounce their faith, and about a half a million were driven from Spain. A similar fate befell the Moors. The elimination of the Jews and Moors was a dress rehearsal for what the Spanish crown would soon accomplish in the Americas—the complete destruction of alien cultures and traditions.

The Inquisition became a form of institutionalized savagery through which anyone who earned the disfavor of the Church or the Crown or society in general might be imprisoned, tortured, and killed in the name of God. While it scoured the countryside for signs of sin and heresy, the Inquisition cleaned its own house as well, and by 1517 the Church in Spain was effectively purged of the ills that had ignited the movement for reform in Germany.

Perhaps the most important event of the Counter-Reformation was the Council of Trent, which took place from 1545 to 1563. After subjecting Catholic dogma and practice to the most searching scrutiny in Church history, the council reaffirmed almost every doctrine challenged by the Protestants. With the lines drawn and the division clear, the dream of a reconciliation between the traditionalists and the reformers faded forever.

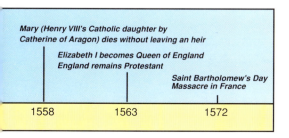

Mary (Henry VIII's Catholic daughter by Catherine of Aragon) dies without leaving an heir

Elizabeth I becomes Queen of England
England remains Protestant

Saint Bartholomew's Day Massacre in France

| 1558 | 1563 | 1572 |

Quiz

1. The person who wrote the *Ninety-five Theses* was

Ⓐ John Tetzel. Ⓒ Martin Luther.
Ⓑ Pope Leo X. Ⓓ John Calvin.

2. Martin Luther was

Ⓐ a monk. Ⓒ a doctor.
Ⓑ a lawyer. Ⓓ a king.

3. The official language of the Catholic church was

Ⓐ Italian. Ⓒ Latin.
Ⓑ German. Ⓓ English.

4. Which of the following was not a rule in the Calvinist Church?

Ⓐ no gambling Ⓒ no swearing
Ⓑ no dancing Ⓓ no card playing

5. Calvinists in France were called

Ⓐ Astronauts. Ⓒ Lancelots.
Ⓑ Argonauts. Ⓓ Huguenots.

6. The St. Bartholomew's Day Massacre was a fight between Catholics and Protestants.

Ⓐ True Ⓑ False

7. Henry VIII of England wanted to divorce Catherine of Aragon because

Ⓐ she was from Spain. Ⓒ she spoke poor English.
Ⓑ she was Catholic. Ⓓ she had not borne him a son.

8. The highest Catholic authority in England was

Ⓐ the Archbishop of Canterbury. Ⓒ the pope.
Ⓑ the king. Ⓓ Parliament.

9. Henry VIII's daughter Anne became Queen of England.

Ⓐ True Ⓑ False

10. The Catholic church's reaction to the Reform movement was called

Ⓐ the Spanish Inquisition. Ⓒ the Counter-Reformation.
Ⓑ the Index of Forbidden Books. Ⓓ the Council of Trent.

European explorers scoured the world for new sources of wealth.

Chapter 12

The Age of Exploration— Worlds in Collision

With Byzantium fallen and the Ottoman Turks breathing down their necks, the merchants of Europe began to look for new routes to the exotic trade goods of Asia—spices, jewels, jade, tea, porcelain, silk—routes which would be less hazardous than the remaining land routes. Portugal and Spain, with direct access to the Atlantic Ocean, were the first nations to make a concerted effort to reach Asia by sea. Their efforts would have been doomed to failure without the improvements in ship construction and navigation fostered by the Portuguese prince, Henry the Navigator.

First and with relative ease, Portuguese sailors crossed the Mediterranean and established trading posts in North Africa. In 1498 another Portuguese explorer, Vasco da Gama, sailed south from Europe, around Africa's Cape of Good Hope and then, proceeding north and east, made his way to the fabled land of India. Da Gama had discovered a new route to the treasures of the East, long sought by European traders.

Some Spaniards believed a more accessible route to India might lead across the Atlantic Ocean. It was this belief that led Christopher Columbus, an Italian seaman, to plant the flag of Spain on the shore of an island in the Caribbean and discover what would eventually be known as the Americas.

Africa

Imagine if you can the splendor and grandeur of the caravan of the great African king Mansa Musa. Watch as he rides majestically by, leading 60,000 warriors and 12,000 slaves, all dressed in flowing robes of silk. Five hundred of those slaves are carrying six-pound staffs of solid gold. Eighty camels carry three-hundred-pound bags of gold dust on their backs.

The year is 1307, and Mansa Musa is on a pilgrimage from his West African Kingdom of Mali to the holy city of Mecca, the center of the Muslim world. Perhaps he notices you by the roadside in your peasant clothes, your eyes wide with wonder, your mouth agape. He smiles and tosses a bit of gold your way. It lands in the dust at your feet. Only after the incredible procession has passed are you able to gather your wits, stoop and pick up the small nugget that represents more wealth than you have ever seen before in all your life.

Mansa Musa ruled Mali from 1312 to 1337 during the period of its greatest power and glory. After the fall of the Empire of Ghana, Mali, with the richest gold mines in the world, became the mightiest kingdom in Africa. Mansa Musa became a Muslim, and like all followers of the religion of Islam, he wanted to make a pilgrimage to Mecca to show his devotion to his faith. But the pilgrimage of Mansa Musa was no humble affair. His flamboyance and generosity during the trip and upon his arrival in Mecca made him legendary throughout Africa, Europe, and Asia.

Under the reign of Mansa Musa, Mali became a center of Islamic learning and trade. Sometimes it didn't come easily. One visitor was especially impressed by the fact that children of Mali who did not learn the Koran—the holy book of Islam—were put in chains until they had memorized it!

At a time before Western Europe even had universities, Mansa Musa set up a great center of Islamic learning in Timbuktu. He invited the greatest scholars of Arab lands to come and teach, and seekers of knowledge from all over the world went to study there.

Mansa Musa was a great and special man, but he could not live forever. After his death there was civil war in Mali. Within 150 years the great kingdom was lost.

When Prince Henry the Navigator of Portugal arranged the first voyage to explore the west coast of Africa in 1420, he opened the door to a whole new area of trade for the nations of Europe. When news of the expedition spread, other adventurers quickly followed the trail he had blazed, eager to buy the ivory, gold and slaves that were to be had from the two great West African kingdoms of the time—Benin and Songhai.

Today Benin is a small town in Nigeria, but between 1450 and 1850 it was the capital city of a great kingdom, a notable center in the manufacture of cotton goods and the working of bronze, and an important crossroads in the intricate maze of trading routes that crisscrossed Africa. European explorers brought back reports that Benin's warriors were highly disciplined and very brave, and were constantly fighting to win more land and slaves. Although many African peoples traditionally enslaved captive members of other tribes, the arrival of European traders eager to pay high prices for slaves elevated the slave trade to new heights of cruelty and barbarism. The demand for slaves became so great that it decimated the population of the entire region of West Africa and resulted in the virtual extinction of entire tribes. With the termination of the European and American slave trade in the mid-1800s the Kingdom of Benin, which had become dependent upon the selling of captives into slavery, rapidly lost its power.

By way of contrast the Moslem Kingdom of Songhai had little contact with European adventurers, was not deeply involved in the slave trade, and rose to become the third most powerful empire in the history of West Africa,

Mansa Musa's pilgrimage to Mecca lives in history for its lavish display of wealth.

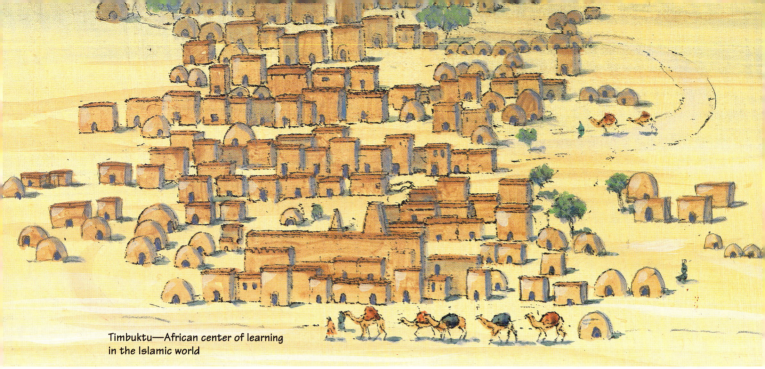

Timbuktu—African center of learning in the Islamic world

overshadowed only by its two mighty predecessors Ghana and Mali. At one time Songhai was a district of the Mali kingdom, but under the leadership of a strong leader named Sonni Ali, Songhai broke away from Mali and eventually conquered its former rulers.

Sonni Ali was Songhai's greatest king—an effective but harsh ruler. From 1464 to 1492 he never lost a battle. He divided the empire into provinces and appointed officials to carry out his laws. He also implemented a standardized system of weights and measures, which greatly simplified trade and exchange. King Sonni Ali transformed Songhai into the largest of the West African empires. At its height it stretched from the Atlantic Ocean eastward nearly 1,800 miles. The city of Gao was the capital of Songhai, and salt was its most important product on the trans-Saharan caravan routes. Ali's armies captured the important cities of Timbuktu and Djénné. Under his rule Timbuktu continued as a center of trade and learning. Students from all over the Muslim world went to study in its colleges. The Songhai city of Djénné was famous for its medical school.

The Songhai Empire flourished until 1589, when an army from Morocco in North Africa crossed the Sahara intent on conquest. Because the Songhai had little contact with the European visitors to West Africa, they had not learned of the power of the gun. Armed only with swords and spears they were no match for the firepower of the Moroccan forces and were quickly and decisively defeated. After that a Songhai scholar wrote "Peace gave way to sorrow, disaster and violence."

Asia

"I've gone places where no one else has been. I've seen things that no one else has seen."

The strange old man in the dark corner of your cell begins to speak. You are both innocent travelers, taken captive in a local war. Now you are locked in a prison in Genoa, Italy. Who knows how long it will be before you are set free? Time passes slowly. You may as well listen to the old man talk.

"Tell me your story, friend," you say. "I am a writer. I will set it down for all to read."

He replies, "My name is Marco Polo. I have not seen my home in Venice since I was fifteen years old. That was the year I set out with my father and my uncle seeking new places to trade our wares."

He proceeds to tell you tales so fabulous and incredible that you can scarcely bring yourself to write them down. But you do, and soon the book becomes a sensation not just in Italy, but throughout all Europe.

Marco Polo was not the first European to see the Orient. Many others had traveled to those fabled lands over the preceding 1,600 years, ever since the Old Silk Road was established in the third century B.C.E. But he may have been the first European to live there for most of his life. He became a trusted official of the great Mongol ruler Kublai Khan, who had completed the conquest of China in 1279. The Mongols were a nomadic tribe who had already conquered much of Persia and Russia. They usually took what they wanted and left the natives to fend for them-

132

Prince Henry the Navigator—patron of exploration

selves. But Kublai Khan was different. Kublai Khan spent almost all his life in China. He adopted many Chinese ways and lived more like the Chinese emperors before him than the nomadic peoples from which he was descended. He took the Chinese name Yuan for his dynasty.

When Marco Polo, his father and his uncle arrived in Kublai Khan's capital city of Ta-tu (present-day Beijing), they could not believe what they saw. They were ushered into the emperor's presence in a palace that Marco Polo described as "the largest that ever was." Unlike many Eastern leaders Kublai Khan was in the habit of welcoming foreign visitors. He knew that there was much he could learn from them. He took a liking to young Marco Polo and invited him to stay. Soon he was sending Marco Polo on official missions all over his empire.

Everywhere Polo went he saw a smoothly run, well-organized kingdom. Kublai Khan had built great highways that made it easier for merchants and travelers to get about. There were stones to mark the way, and the

distance from one place to the next. Trees were planted by the roadside to give shade to travelers. The roads were good, and traveling on them was a pleasant experience—unlike the misery of riding the muddy, rutted, and dangerous roads to which the young European visitor was accustomed.

Kublai Khan developed a postal service, too. He knew it was important for people throughout his empire to be able to communicate. Horsemen carried messages along China's Great Wall. Every twenty-five miles along the wall stood a post-house where messengers could

Marco Polo became a friend and adviser to the mighty Kublai Khan.

The Forbidden City—dream world of the Ming Emperors

change horses and rest. He was responsible for building an 850-mile-long Grand Canal. Chinese boats called junks constantly traveled up and down the waterway, carrying people and merchandise. Travel and trade increased.

134

For over one hundred years—from 1260 to 1368—the Mongols ruled China. When word spread of Marco Polo's life in China and of the wonders he encountered there, more traders from Europe and the Middle East came to China. Some Chinese and Mongols traveled and settled in the Middle East and Europe. This increased contact with foreigners changed the course of world history. From the Chinese, the Arabs and Europeans learned about paper, porcelain, gunpowder, and many other inventions. From the outsiders China received glass, cotton, silver, and honey.

Traditionally Mongol rulers did not trust the people they conquered. In this Kublai Khan was no different. He did not allow Chinese to hold government positions.

While Ming royalty enjoyed all the luxuries life could offer, the people suffered.

Rather he gave these posts to other Mongols or to foreigners like Marco Polo. He was a Buddhist who believed in religious freedom, so his government was filled with Muslims, Hindus, Christians, and Jews. This policy allowed great freedom for new ideas and ways of thinking.

It also meant that Chinese scholars and officials found themselves with time on their hands. So they turned to the arts. They elevated the writing of plays and operas to a level of great sophistication. Their shows combined singing, acting, and dancing. The music was played by an on-stage orchestra. There was little scenery, but the actors wore very colorful, elaborate costumes. As in the Elizabethan theater in England three hundred years later, all the parts, even those of women, were played by men.

After Kublai Khan's death in 1294 the Yuan Dynasty weakened, and in 1368 the Mongols were driven out of China. This was to be the end of foreign rule in the land of China for many centuries. Beginning with the Ming Dynasty, which followed the Mongols, China was again governed by its own people. The Ming emperors built themselves a new palace, known as the Forbidden City, in Beijing, and ruled there for nearly three hundred years. The Forbidden City can still be seen today.

In 1324, many years after his stay in the Genoan jail, Marco Polo lay dying in Venice, the city of his birth. He was asked if, just perhaps, he might not have exaggerated his reports about China. He smiled weakly and said, "You only know the half of it. If I'd told everything, no one ever would have believed me."

During the 1400s Europeans were eager to buy Chinese trade goods, but the price was steep because the Chinese were not especially interested in anything Europe had to offer in return. Most of the emperors of the Ming Dynasty looked down on all foreigners as uncivilized barbarians and tried to isolate their empire from what they considered the damaging influences of the outside world. In order to do business with the Ming Dynasty it was necessary to pay a hefty tribute in gold or silver over and above the cost of the goods themselves. The Ming emperors lived in the Forbidden City surrounded by richly decorated buildings and lovely gardens. They cut themselves off from even their own people and were content to remain hidden in a dream world of their own creation while their subordinates governed the empire.

Yung Lo, third in the line of Ming rulers, broke the pattern of isolation. He sent out armies to reconquer the territories of China's empire that had been lost to the Mongols, hoping to restore the empire to its full size and splendor. He also sent expeditions to India, Southeast Asia, and the islands of Indonesia, demanding that tribute be paid to the Emperor of China. Perhaps the most remarkable of the Ming Dynasty expeditions was Admiral Cheng-Ho's exploration of the coastline of Africa. Some scholars believe that China could have become a major player in the race for colonial supremacy had it not been for the Ming Dynasty's strange decision to isolate itself from the rest of the world.

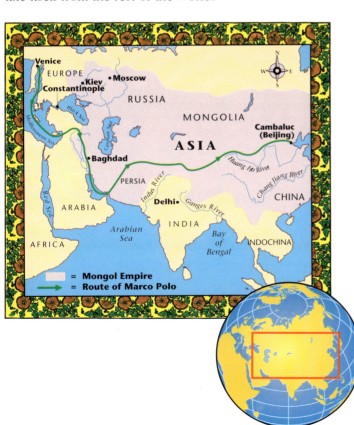

= Mongol Empire
= Route of Marco Polo

Quiz

1. Which great kingdom was led by Mansa Musa?

Ⓐ Mali Ⓒ Egypt
Ⓑ Ghana Ⓓ Nigeria

2. Marco Polo was born in

Ⓐ Genoa. Ⓒ China.
Ⓑ Venice. Ⓓ Persia.

3. Kublai Khan was a

Ⓐ Korean. Ⓒ Chinese.
Ⓑ Mongol. Ⓓ Japanese.

4. Which of the following people encouraged improvements in navigation and shipbuilding?

Ⓐ Christopher Columbus Ⓒ Vasco Da Gama
Ⓑ Prince Henry the Navigator Ⓓ King Ferdinand of Castile

5. The first European explorer to sail around the Cape of Good Hope was

Ⓐ Prince Henry the Navigator. Ⓒ Vasco da Gama.
Ⓑ Christopher Columbus. Ⓓ King Ferdinand of Castile.

6. The two great kingdoms of Africa during the fifteenth century were

Ⓐ Benin and Songhai. Ⓒ Benin and Mali.
Ⓑ Ghana and Mali. Ⓓ Mali and Songhai.

7. One important reason for the Songhai kingdom's success was

Ⓐ its silver mines. Ⓒ its gold mines.
Ⓑ its copper mines. Ⓓ its salt mines.

8. What did the arrival of Europeans do to the already existing African slave trade?

Ⓐ made it less cruel Ⓒ increased it
Ⓑ ended it Ⓓ decreased it

9. Which item listed below was not one of the valuable trade goods of Asia?

Ⓐ jade Ⓒ silk
Ⓑ tea Ⓓ bronze

10. The Forbidden City was inhabited by

Ⓐ Ming emperors. Ⓒ Japanese pirates.
Ⓑ Mongol invaders. Ⓓ samurai warriors.

India

In 1320 the Turkish Moslem leader, Ghiyas-ud-Din, established the Tughluk Dynasty in northern India. He reigned for five years before being murdered by his son, Muhammad Tughluk. Muhammad was one of the most fascinating characters among all the Moslem rulers of India. He was a scholar, an excellent writer, an eloquent speaker, and a military genius. He was also extremely cruel and established a code of law that was simple yet effective: the penalty for any crime, no matter how minor, was death, sometimes inflicted in especially painful ways. He considered himself a great visionary and began several monumental projects, all of which, unhappily, turned out to be dismal failures and caused great misery among his subjects. His solution to the problems created by his kingly arrogance was to increase the already harsh burden of taxation placed upon his subjects.

The only positive effect of his reign was that his oppressive rule eventually caused several large-scale revolts, one of which succeeded in creating the independent Vijayanagar kingdom in Southern India in 1336.

The state of Vijayanagar quickly grew to become a handsome and prosperous military state, which caused no end of grief to Muhammad Tughluk's successors.

The immediate successor of Muhammad Tughluk, Firuz Tughluk, reigned from 1351 to 1388. He was a refreshing change from Muhammad Tughluk, and he distinguished himself by making some actual improvements in the state of the kingdom. Under his rule several new cities were founded, a system of irrigation canals was built, and many parks, hospitals, bridges, and other public works came into being. The good name of the sultanate was restored and peace came to the land. But with his death there followed several weak and ineffective rulers who allowed things once again to fall to pieces. In 1398 Timur the Lame, or Tamerlane, the fierce and ruthless Mongol warrior who had already conquered Persia and portions of Asia Minor, descended upon this disorganized and vulnerable north Indian kingdom and reduced it to a wasteland.

Tamerlane and his warriors slaughtered thousands of Hindus and Muslims and left piles of human skulls where villages had been. But by about 1460, Mongol military control of northern India began to wane and was replaced by a host of small Muslim kingdoms. The southern areas of the subcontinent were still inhabited by the Hindu descendents of the Dravidian peoples who had settled there thousands of years before. Between the Hindus who dominated the south and the Moslems who ruled the north there was mistrust, hostility, and very often bloody war. Yet Islam, the Moslem religion, held great attraction for Hindus of the untouchable caste because it welcomed all colors and classes. At the same time, it repelled devout Hindus with its stubborn insistence that it was the only true religion. Conflicts between these two groups continue to plague India to this day.

Mongols on the move. Huge teams of oxen towed mongol yurts like modern day mobile homes.

Japanese sea raiders caused havoc with their Chinese merchant victims.

Japan

In fourteenth century Japan, the rule of the Ashikaga shoguns was a study in contrasts. Side by side with continual warfare and political disruption, there came significant economic development and expansion. In spite of heavy taxes and war, new industries came into being and trade guilds flourished. Kyoto was once again the capital city of the land.

Japanese pirates caused much consternation by raiding cities along the Chinese coast and preying upon Chinese vessels in the Sea of Japan. It was a time of great lawlessness and disorder in Japan, which was torn by a civil war that lasted one hundred years. The local barons, called *daimyos*, were constantly at one another's throats in a vicious struggle for power. They built huge castles—half-fortress, half-palace—where they lived with their warriors, the samurai. Eventually, around 1600 a powerful daimyo named Ieyasu Tokugawa succeeded in uniting Japan. He became shogun and ruled from his capital in Edo, which today is the city of Tokyo.

The arrival of Columbus foreshadowed the destruction of the culture of the Americas.

Columbus is often mistakenly credited with being the first European in the Americas.

The Americas

When Christopher Columbus found himself on a small island off the coast of Florida in 1492, it was for the people of Europe the discovery of a new world. Of course, it wasn't really new at all. By the time of his arrival, both the Toltec empire and the great civilization of the Maya had grown, flowered, and withered.

In Mexico the Aztec Empire was at its peak of power and size, consisting of an estimated five million people. 300,000 of them lived in Tenochtitlán, the island capital of the Aztecs, making this city about five times larger than London at the time. According to legend, the Aztec people wandered for many years without a home until they were visited by the sun god, who told them to build a city where "an eagle sits on a cactus holding a snake in its beak." The Aztecs continued to roam until they saw the sign of which the sun god had spoken. Then they settled and made that place their home. They built their city on an island in the middle of a lake and connected it

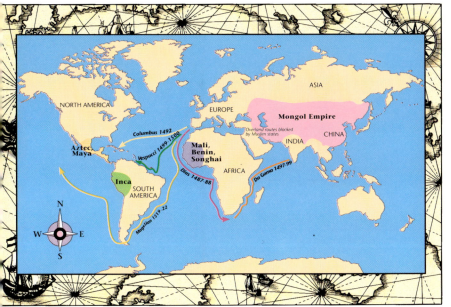

sun. Aztec priests believed the sun god demanded human sacrifice. They believed that if they did not make these sacrifices, the sun would not rise again. This was such a disturbing prospect that they never considered skipping a sacrifice to see what would happen. For the nearly two hundred years of their existence as a great empire, the Aztec warred with neighboring peoples, in large part to acquire victims for sacrifice to their hungry god.

In the Andes Mountains, far to the south, another American civilization developed. The Inca had settled in a valley of the Andes around 1100. They built their capital, Cuzco, high in the mountains of what today is the country of Peru. In 1438 a man called Pachacutec, whose name means "He Who Changes the World," became their king, and they spread out from the city of Cuzco to create a huge empire. The Inca conquered a vast area, which they ruled under the best organized political and social structure of pre-Columbian America. The Inca state at its greatest extent covered what is now Ecuador, Peru, and Bolivia, as well as parts of Chile and Argentina.

Throughout this immense region, a network of highways permitted the Incas to exercise tight control over their empire. One Inca road ran about 2,500 miles from present-day Ecuador to Chile. There were hanging bridges made of twisted straw and vines stretched across the deep mountain chasms. These roads and bridges

to land by paved roads called causeways. Visitors could enter the city only by walking along the causeways or by canoe. Today this site is Mexico City, the largest city in the world, and the Mexican flag depicts the eagle, the snake, and the cactus.

The Aztecs were great builders. In Tenochtitlán they erected temples and pyramids similar to those of ancient Egypt. Palaces, gardens, and markets were located near the temples. The emperor's palace was the largest structure. It housed the emperor's family and thousands of servants and officials. The palace also had a large library and even a zoo!

Like the Maya before them, the Aztec worshiped many gods. They had gods of corn, rain, war, and the

139

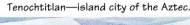

Tenochtitlan—island city of the Aztec.

One of the bloodiest civilizations ever, the Aztec sacrificed many to appease their hungry gods. To be a sacrificial offering to the gods was considered a great honor.

With the death of the last "rememberer," the quipus of the Inca became insoluble puzzles.

were built and repaired by peasants sent from their villages to serve the emperor. Since there were no wheeled vehicles, goods were carried by llamas, and fast runners carried messages all across the Inca Empire.

The ruler of the Inca Empire was called the Sapa Inca. It was believed that he was descended from the sun, and when he died his body was preserved and treated with great honor. The Inca emperor was very rich. He wore clothes made of gold thread. His royal guard had armor made of gold. Even the poles of the litter on which he was carried were covered with gold. All of the land in the Empire belonged to the emperor even though it was distributed to the people to farm.

With as many as twelve million inhabitants, it was necessary to divide the Empire into provinces. Governors were appointed for each province. Their primary function was to collect taxes. All the governors answered to the Inca, who had total power. The people grew crops on their portion of the emperor's land to pay their taxes. Most of the men had to serve some time in the army. They also had to give some of their time to work on government projects. A young man was required to marry. If he didn't (or wouldn't!) choose a wife, the government chose one for him. In many other ways it was quite an advanced society. For example, the sick, the poor, and the aged were cared for by the government.

Although the Inca Empire never reached the heights of astronomical knowledge and mathematical skill achieved by the Maya or the Aztec, it equaled them in engineering and architecture. In addition, Inca woven textiles were unsurpassed. Their medical knowledge was also highly developed. Inca doctors could set broken

bones, and even knew how to perform brain surgery! Like the other American empires, the Incas built incredible structures of stone. They fitted stone blocks weighing as much as two hundred tons tightly together without cement. To make up for the lack of flat land for farming, Inca farmers built wide step-like areas called terraces in the mountains.

Until recently it was believed that the Incas had no system of writing, but new discoveries indicate that some form of written communication may have been concealed in their intricate fabric patterns. We do know that they used *quipus*, or knotted strings, to help them record things. Colored strings stood for objects. Knots tied in the strings stood for numbers. Much information could be conveyed in this way. The quipus could only be deciphered by specially trained "rememberers." Valuable historical knowledge was lost forever with the death of the last rememberer.

The Inca Empire was a great and powerful civilization that flourished for one hundred years. However, like the Songhai in West Africa, it had no guns. When a small group of Spaniards led by Francisco Pizarro arrived in 1535, they used their superior weaponry to quickly and efficiently annihilate the Inca people. Then they plun-

Inca stonework rivaled that of the pyramids of Egypt.

141

dered the Inca cities and returned to Spain in ships laden with treasure of every description.

The native peoples of North America, as yet undisturbed by strangers from across the sea, continued in the ways of life cherished by their ancestors from time immemorial. They spoke more than three hundred distinctly different languages. They lived in housing as varied as portable tents (tepee), blocks of ice (igloo), community wooden homes (Iroquois long house), and houses made of earth and rocks (Navajo hogan). They made their tools of wood, bone, and shell.

The Eskimos of the far north were hunters. The peoples living in the American Southwest, in the Mississippi River valleys, and in the Southeast developed agricultural and pastoral communities. In between were a wide variety of hunting, fishing, and food-gathering peoples, ranging from the salmon fishers of northern California, Oregon, and Washington to the buffalo hunters of the Great Plains to the hunter-fishers who inhabited woodlands everywhere.

In the far north, the Inuit built dwellings of ice and snow.

142

The nomadic Indians of the Great Plains developed portable tepees and lightweight birchbark canoes.

Mongol Kublai Khan conquers China

The Polos arrive in China

Marco Polo becomes ambassador of Kublai Khan's court

Fall of Ghana (Africa)

Mansa Musa of Mali (Africa)

Ghiyas-ud-Din establishes the Tughluk Dynasty (Northern India)

Mali (Africa) becomes center of Islamic learning

Aztecs build Tenochtitlan

Vijayanagar Kingdom (Southern India)

Ashikaga rule (Japan)

Mansa Musa (Africa) dies

Mongols driven out of China

Yung Lo reconquers Chinese territories (Ming Dynasty China)

Tughluk Dynasty falls (India)

Tamerlane (Mongols) invades Northern India

Ming Dynasty (China)

Prince Henry of Portugal sends ships to W. Africa

Portugal and Spain search for new trade routes

Pachacutec becomes the king of the Incas

| 1279 | 1275 | 1279 | 1300 | 1312 | 1320 | 1324 | 1325 | 1336 | 1338 | 1346 | 1368 | 1388 | 1398 | 1400 | 1403 | 1419 | 1420 | 1438 |

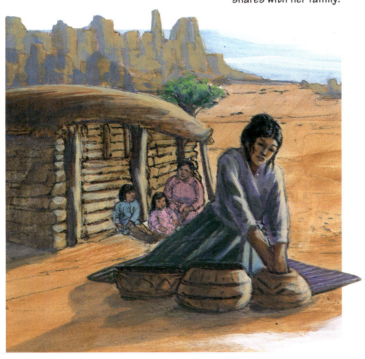

Above, an Iroquois longhouse under construction. Below, a Navajo woman tends to her chores outside the hogan she shares with her family.

Mongolian rulers replaced by small Moslem kingdoms (India)

Vasco da Gama sails around the Cape of Good Hope

Christopher Columbus discovers America

Benin becomes the center of trade (Nigeria)

Songhai last great empire of Africa ruled by Sonni Ali

Portuguese establish posts in N. Africa

Japanese civil war

| 1440 | 1450 | 1460 | 1464 | 1467 | 1492 | 1498 |

Quiz

1. In 1492, Tenochtitlan was about five times larger than the city of

- Ⓐ Timbuktu.
- Ⓒ Paris.
- Ⓑ Florence.
- Ⓓ London.

2. An eagle sitting on a cactus with a snake in its beak is depicted on the flag of what modern nation?

- Ⓐ Ecuador
- Ⓒ Mexico
- Ⓑ Peru
- Ⓓ Chile

3. The Mongol warrior chief Tamerlane was a follower of what religion?

- Ⓐ Hinduism
- Ⓒ Christianity
- Ⓑ Islam
- Ⓓ Buddhism

4. The powerful daimyo who united Japan was

- Ⓐ Tokugawa.
- Ⓒ Tughluk.
- Ⓑ Hideyoshi.
- Ⓓ Tamerlane.

5. Many Hindus were attracted to Islam because of its strict caste system.

- Ⓐ True
- Ⓑ False

6. The quipus, or knotted strings of the Incas, were used

- Ⓐ to make bridges.
- Ⓒ to keep records.
- Ⓑ to weave fabric.
- Ⓓ as hair ornaments.

7. The two great civilizations of the Americas during the fifteenth century were

- Ⓐ Maya and Toltec.
- Ⓒ Aztec and Toltec.
- Ⓑ Maya and Aztec.
- Ⓓ Aztec and Inca.

8. The Indians of North America during the fifteenth century spoke more than _____ different languages.

- Ⓐ three hundred
- Ⓒ one hundred
- Ⓑ two hundred
- Ⓓ four hundred

9. Which of the following was not a type of dwelling built by North American Indians?

- Ⓐ tepee
- Ⓒ yurt
- Ⓑ hogan
- Ⓓ longhouse

10. Inca medical knowledge was so advanced that they could even

- Ⓐ replace bad teeth.
- Ⓒ perform heart transplants.
- Ⓑ cure cancer.
- Ⓓ perform brain surgery.

English sea dogs nipped at the heels of Spanish ships laden with gold and riches from the Americas.

Chapter 13

Trade, Conquest, and Colonialism

When Christopher Columbus returned from his first voyage with vivid reports of the wonders he'd seen in the Americas, he inspired dreams of wealth, adventure, and empire in the minds of European leaders. Columbus himself led three more trips across the Atlantic over the course of the next nine years. He explored Hispaniola (today the countries of Haiti and the Dominican Republic), Cuba, Jamaica, and Puerto Rico, but remained stubbornly convinced until the end of his life that he had discovered a new route to India and the Orient. But as the dominant European powers—Spain, Portugal, England, Holland, France—raced to send expeditions in his wake, it soon became clear that it was the path to a brand new world.

At first Spain and Portugal were the most aggressive in laying claim to the new lands. It became apparent that conflict between the two was inevitable. So the pope intervened by drawing a "Line of Demarcation" down the middle of a map of the immense new territory, giving all lands west of the line to Spain and all lands to the east to Portugal.

It was not until Queen Elizabeth I ascended the throne in 1558 that England became a serious contender in the game of world discovery and conquest. There had been tension between Spain and England for many years, culminating in 1588 with England's total annihilation of the supposedly invincible Spanish Armada. Now, with England becoming a Protestant nation, Spain, still whole-heartedly Catholic, came to be looked upon as the "evil empire" bent upon global domination. Advisers to the Queen warned that Spain was turning all the Indians into Catholic converts and that they, the English, had a duty to show the Indians the "right" way.

England had entered a period of tremendous prosperity, due in large part to a growing manufacturing and exporting economy. England's small navy had become its pride and joy—boasting the fastest ships, the best guns, and the most efficient crews in the world. England was bursting with wealth and power and ached to put Spain in its place once and for all. England ached too for the ". . . plentie of excellent trees for mastes, of goodly timber

to build shippes and to make great navies, of pitche, tarr, hempe, and all things incident for a navie royall," which the New World was said to possess.

But rather than declare open war, Queen Elizabeth sent private adventurers out in their sleek, fast ships to harass and torment Spanish ships and colonies. These buccaneers, or privateers, with names like Sir Francis Drake, John Hawkins and Richard Grenville, took to the high seas and for nearly twenty years waged a relentless campaign of terror against the Spanish in the New World. Pirates, we call them. They called themselves sea dogs because they were ". . . as fast and fleet as a dog stealing a bone." On one voyage alone Drake pillaged towns and ships throughout the Caribbean and sailed around South America, looting settlements as far north as northern California. Then he circumnavigated the globe and returned to England with a rich cargo that rewarded both the Queen and the businessmen who had financed his voyage. Queen Elizabeth professed her inability to control the English raiders and kept the Spanish king Philip II,

from retaliating by promising to consider marrying him.

Elizabeth's advisers suggested that if England established colonies in the north they could then move southward to take the West Indies from Spain. So Sir Walter Raleigh was dispatched to establish the first English colony in the New World. He named it Virginia after the virgin Queen. This first attempt at colonization was a

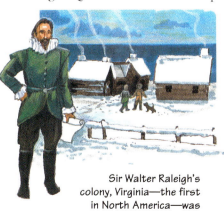

Sir Walter Raleigh's colony, Virginia—the first in North America—was a total failure.

dismal failure, and the surviving colonists beat a hasty retreat to England at the earliest opportunity. The next group was better prepared. The colonists included women and children, and settled nearby at a place called Roanoke Island. It was here that the first American child,

When the Pilgrims stepped ashore at Plymouth Rock, they had no idea of the suffering and hardship they would endure in their new world.

146

Virginia Dare, was born. The governor of the Roanoke colony had to return to England for supplies, and when he returned three years later, the colonists had vanished. What became of them remains a mystery to this day.

It continued to prove more difficult than had been expected for the English to establish a foothold in North America. The Jamestown settlement, named for King James I, was the first to succeed, but only after surviving near-total disaster. Three small ships left England in December 1606 and arrived in Virginia in April of the following year. By the following September, only 46 of the 104 people who had started out were still alive. By the end of the year, eight more had died. The original leaders had

Pocahontas kept peace between her people and the colonists by saving the life of Captain John Smith.

chosen to settle in a low, swampy spot that was thick with trees, infested with malaria-carrying mosquitoes, and surrounded by hostile Indians. It was only the sheer force of John Smith's stern personality that saved the few colonists that were left.

Smith became leader of the party after most of the other eligible candidates had died. He demanded that the colonists stop dreaming about gold and begin taking measures to ensure their survival. He insisted that the men build a blockhouse, dig a well, construct permanent houses, plant crops and tend to their chickens and livestock. He managed, after being saved from death by Pocahontas, the daughter of an Indian chief, to establish peaceful relations with the Indians.

Smith returned to England, and in the absence of his strong leadership the Jamestown settlement soon found itself in dire straits once more. These years, from 1609 to 1611, were called the starving time. Things were so bad that the settlers ate horses, dogs, mice, snakes, and at least one human body. The population dropped from five hundred to sixty. Much of the suffering stemmed from the fact that most of the men argued constantly over who should be doing the work. A new governor was appointed to the colony and set about the task of setting things right. He assigned each settler a small parcel of land and instituted a simple but effective rule: no work,

no food. He also met another challenge by choosing tobacco as the colony's money crop.

The Spanish had long been importing tobacco from the New World, and it was already popular in Europe. The Virginia colonists began planting tobacco in 1612. One of the colonists, John Rolfe, developed an improved method of curing it, and the financial success of the colony was thereby assured.

Few women of the time were daring enough to strike out for the colonies, but in 1619 ninety young women were sent to Jamestown to be bought as brides. The price per bride was 120 pounds of tobacco, which covered the cost of their transportation. In the same year, a Dutch vessel arrived with twenty Africans aboard. Since they had been baptized, they could not legally be made slaves, but rather became servants to the colonists. It would be almost another hundred years before slavery would become an established fact of life in North America.

Back in England, some Puritans acted upon their dissatisfaction with the Church of England by emigrating to Holland. But they were unwilling to adapt themselves to the ways of their adopted homeland, and soon began to yearn for a place of their own. A small group decided to go to America and establish a colony where they would be free to live and worship as they chose. They pooled their resources and bought a ship, the *Mayflower*. On the appointed day, the thirty-five Pilgrims, as they called themselves, and sixty-six others set sail from London. They stepped ashore at Cape Cod in November of the year 1620 and named their settlement Plymouth.

From the start they realized the importance of having an organized system of governing themselves, so they agreed to the Mayflower Compact, a document setting forth the rules and regulations of their colony. But in spite of their forethought and careful planning, they were totally unprepared for the difficult winter they faced, and by spring half were dead of starvation and disease. When the first governor died, William Bradford was elected to take his place. He governed wisely and well, and the neighboring Native Americans became friends and teachers to the colonists.

Squanto, an American native who had been to England, showed the colonists how to plant their corn in the Native American style. Another American, Samoset, introduced them to Massasoit, the leader of many tribes. Because of the help of Massasoit, Squanto, and their peoples, by the next fall the Pilgrims were well-organized and enjoying a bountiful harvest. They declared a three-day holiday and invited Massasoit and ninety other friends to a feast of "thanksgiving," a tradition that, for most Americans, endures to this day. Tragically, the tradition of goodwill between the Native Americans and the Europeans was not to endure.

Without Squanto's help the Pilgrims would have perished.

George Calvert founded the first Catholic settlement in North America.

One by one, more colonies started to appear. In 1632, George Calvert founded Maryland as a haven for the Catholic faithful. At first there was friction between the newcomers and the established Protestant colony of Jamestown nearby. But Calvert, who by then had become Lord Baltimore, defused the situation by requiring his colonists to avoid Jamestown in particular, and religious disputes in general. Maryland was the first colony to be successful right from the start. The Quakers, led by William Penn, received a charter from King Charles II in 1681. Penn widely publicized his colony, Pennsylvania, and welcomed colonists from Wales, Germany, and Ireland. Georgia was chartered to James Oglethorpe, a member of the British Parlia-

The first Thanksgiving—for one brief moment in time, Indians and Europeans shared food and understanding.

ment, who wanted his colony to be a place where people who had been imprisoned for debt in England could get a fresh start.

A second group of Puritans pestered the English King Charles I until he finally granted them permission to form a colony of their own. They established the Massachusetts Bay Company and called their new town Boston. Boston soon became a center of intellectual activity in the colonies. Harvard College was founded there in 1636, and the first printing press in America arrived in Boston Harbor in 1639. But despite the intellectual atmosphere, the Boston Puritans proved unwilling to grant the same religious tolerance to others that they had demanded for themselves.

A radical thinker named Roger Williams was banished by the town fathers for expressing the outlandish idea that freedom of religion was for everyone. He also held that the King of England could not parcel out land that already belonged to the original Americans! Williams bought land from the Indians of the region and founded Rhode Island. Here religious tolerance really was universal, and Native Americans were treated with dignity and respect. Another European who bought land from the Indians was Peter Minuit, a Dutchman. He must have been a ruthless trader because he paid only about twenty-four dollars in beads and trinkets for the Island of Manhattan. He named it New Amsterdam, but today we know it as New York.

Just as the southern colonies had found their money crop in tobacco, for those in the north it was wood. For every town and every farm that sprang up, many trees were felled, and the lumber could be sold as fuel, for shipbuilding, and for many other uses.

As the colonists continued their relentless expansion to the west, they became increasingly apprehensive about the Indians, with whom relations were becoming ever more strained. The Europeans told themselves that the land was theirs by right of their laws and their firepower. At the same time, the Indians continued to be good trading partners, and in some cases they were brave allies in battles with the French.

When Chief Massasoit died, his sons began to see that the endless influx of Europeans was endangering their way of life. In 1675 several tribes formed an alliance and attempted to stop the westward expansion of the northern colonies. Most of the outlying western rural settlements were destroyed, and many people on both sides

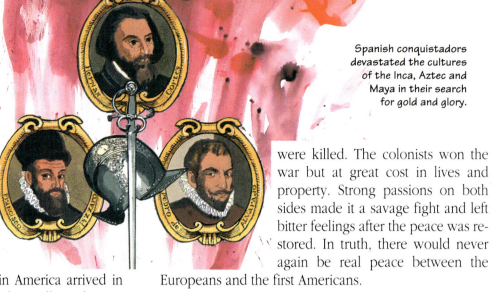

Spanish conquistadors devastated the cultures of the Inca, Aztec and Maya in their search for gold and glory.

were killed. The colonists won the war but at great cost in lives and property. Strong passions on both sides made it a savage fight and left bitter feelings after the peace was restored. In truth, there would never again be real peace between the Europeans and the first Americans.

The English colonizers of America dreamed of freedom of religion, a parcel of land to call their own, a new society. The Spanish conquistadors dreamed of gold and glory. When the Spanish began their invasion of South and Central America—and it can only be called an invasion—three advanced and magnificent civilizations dominated the land. The Aztecs were the dominant kingdom in Central America. They were strong and disciplined. Theirs was a smoothly run society with well-planned cities and elaborate religious rituals.

The second civilization, the Inca, controlled an empire that extended over parts of Peru, Ecuador, Bolivia, Chile, and Argentina. Cuzco, the capital city of the empire, sprawled out over thirty square miles and held some 200,000 people. Just prior to the arrival of the Spanish, the Inca empire had been torn apart by civil war. The "War Between Brothers" left Atahualpa as the new ruler, but 150,000 Inca were killed in the fight. Their spirits broken by the devastation and the personal grief, many of the Inca prayed for salvation from the strangers who were coming from over the sea. Unfortunately for them, the strangers were the Spanish conquistadors.

The third civilization, the Maya, had flowered much earlier and was located in the deepest jungles of Central America. The Maya was the oldest, most complex, and most successful society in the Americas. There was virtually no crime in Maya society. As an example of Maya justice, if someone was hungry, he could take two ears of corn from anyone's field. If, however, he took more, he was not fit to live, and anyone who wanted could kill him. By the time of the arrival of the conquistadors Maya civilization had declined, but the people remained, having returned to a peaceful agricultural way of life.

It was the adventurer Hernán Cortés who first encountered the Aztec Empire. His devastating conquest of this mighty civilization with no more than a handful of

148

troops has entered the realm of legend. The accounts of his adventures tell that when he landed in what is now Mexico, the native people were astonished by the sight of men riding horses. They believed, the legend goes, that horse and man were combined into one strange creature. Legend goes on to say that Montezuma, the supreme ruler of the Aztec Empire, thought that Cortés was the reincarnation of an important figure in Aztec religion—a white-skinned visitor who had become a god. So at first he welcomed the invaders with open arms. He sent them twenty women, including Marina, who became Cortés' wife and official translator. He sent jewels and a chest of gold, but still Cortés asked for more. "We Spaniards," he said, "suffer from a disease of the heart for which gold is the only cure."

Cortés and his men seized Montezuma as a hostage. Then they looted the city and massacred hundreds of the Aztec nobility. The Aztec tried to fight, but they had no chance against the Spanish guns. Cortés became the governor of New Spain and forced the vanquished survivors to build Mexico City atop the ruins of Tenochtitlán. Strangely, though he had been ruthless in his conquest of the Aztec, he was unusually moderate in his administration of them as conquered peoples.

Francisco Pizarro, the man responsible for the obliteration of the Inca civilization, grew up as the illiterate child of a destitute woman in Spain. Then as now, service in the army was one of the few ways that a young man of such circumstances could claw his way up and out of a life of poverty. Fearless, greedy, and incredibly cruel, he had the makings of a fine conquistador. In Spain he was nothing. In the New World he could become a rich and powerful man.

Pizarro had lived as a soldier in Central America for many years when he heard of a land to the south "flowing in gold." He obtained a license from King Charles I of Spain, gathered a small army, and boldly entered Peru. With him were his four half brothers. While in Spain making preparations for the expedition he consulted with Hernán Cortés, a distant cousin and the conqueror of the Aztec, who gave him some tips on this business of conquest and plunder.

When the Spaniards first approached the Inca city of Cajamarca, they were terrified. Their party of 170 soldiers and forty horses was surrounded by a huge encampment of between thirty thousand and eighty thousand Inca, spreading out as far as the eye could see in all directions.

Many historians doubt the story that Montezuma believed Cortés was a god.

Hernando de Soto, one of Pizarro's party who would go on to fame and fortune of his own, charged his horse straight at Atalhualpa and skidded to a halt in from of him. The Sapa Inca did not flinch, but some of his soldiers did. Along with their wives and children, these soldiers were executed for their lack of courage.

That evening the Spaniards cordially invited Atahualpa and his nobles to their camp. The Inca came unarmed. At once the Spaniards seized Atahualpa and killed his bodyguards. He offered to ransom himself by having his subjects fill a room seventeen feet wide, twenty-two feet long, and as high as he could reach, once with gold and twice with silver. Pizarro happily agreed to this arrangement and then, with the gold and silver secure, proceeded to murder the Inca leader!

The fortune was incredible, but the greed of the explorers was even more so. They fought amongst themselves over the loot they'd stolen from the Inca. Pizarro and three

The Sapa Inca, Atahualpa, was waiting with gifts to greet the strangers. The Inca were curious about these visitors, with their white skin and bushy beards, their shining armor and prancing horses. In a demonstration of horsemanship,

Pizarro's treachery led to the downfall of Inca civilization.

of his brothers were killed by their own soldiers. The fourth brother died in Spain while in prison for his crimes against the Inca.

The scourge of the Maya was Pedro de Alvarado, who forced a confrontation with these peace-loving people by stealing their women, killing their children, and burning their crops. The Maya quickly realized that they had no chance in a battle against the mounted, heavily armed and armored invaders, so the Maya prince Tecum Uman challenged Alvarado to man-to-man combat. Alvarado accepted the challenge. Tecum Uman, wearing only a loincloth and armed with a stone-tipped lance, faced the charging horse of the Spaniard encased in full armor and wielding an iron pike. The prince was dead in seconds. Alvarado went on to brutally subdue the peoples of Guatemala, Honduras, and Nicaragua. He was killed many years later when his horse fell on him during a trip to California.

The Spanish went on to establish colonies in the conquered lands and continued to strip the New World of its wealth. The surviving natives became slaves working in the gold and silver mines and on the large plantations. The Spanish landowners were supposed to take adequate care of their slaves and to see that they became converted to the Catholic religion. But they didn't. Harsh treatment, back-breaking labor, and European diseases resulted in the decimation of the native population. When the Spanish first set foot in the Americas, more than twenty million people lived there. Within a hundred years the indigenous population had been reduced to four million!

People have been enslaving one another since the days of the first civilizations. But no other society has ever developed the institution of slavery to such a grand scale, to such a level of savagery and inhumanity, as the Europeans in their enslavement of the peoples of the Americas and Africa between the years 1500 and 1860. The Europeans saw the limitless riches of the New World just sitting there waiting to be taken. But they needed help. The colonizers were not simply unwilling to do the dirty work required to make their dreams come true. It was their inability to do the work that led them to enslave others.

The first African slaves taken by Europeans were kidnapped by a Portuguese sea captain exploring the African coast in about 1444. He and his men saw a group of na-

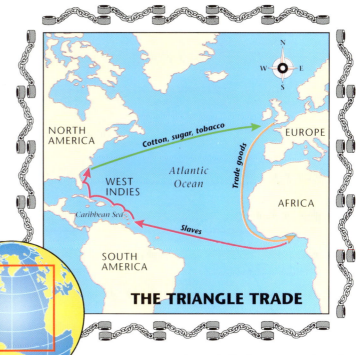

THE TRIANGLE TRADE

tives, crept up on them, killed some, and took 165 of them. Slavery on a small scale was already a fact of life in many parts of Africa, but by the middle of the sixteenth century, Portugal had a great many African slaves—so many, in fact, that slaves outnumbered masters in some parts of Portugal. But slaves were at least allowed to retain some dignity. They were treated no worse than indentured servants and were given opportunities to buy their freedom. It is likely that Pedro Alonso Niño, a pilot of one of Columbus' ships, was black.

But with the conquest of the New World, a new and profitable market for African slaves opened up. By 1540 about ten thousand black slaves a year were arriving in the West Indies, brought by British, Dutch, and French traders. In Brazil by the year 1600 about 44,000 slaves were being imported each year, and the numbers continued to grow. It has been estimated that at least five million and perhaps as many as twenty million Africans were brought as slaves to the New World. And since only 50 percent of those taken survived the ordeal, it is possible that as many as forty million in all were abducted. Of those who did not survive, some were killed resisting capture, some committed suicide, and many died in the dreadful transatlantic crossing.

The slave trade soon evolved into a major industry. Ships left Europe loaded with guns, ammunition, rum, cloth, tools, and trinkets, which they traded for slaves in Africa. The slaves were then taken to the West Indies to be sold at auction, and the ship's holds were in turn filled with the sugar (in the form of molasses), tobacco, and cotton which were the main products of the Islands. The ships made their way north to New England, where the raw materials were processed and then shipped back to

151

Europe to be sold. This incredibly profitable system became known as the Triangle Trade, and it contributed to the immense wealth of several European nations, particularly England.

In the Spanish and Portuguese colonies slaves were usually allowed to retain their religious beliefs and customs. Generally the owners kept families together, and a government agency was set up to protect the slaves from excessive abuse. The slaves could earn money on the side and in time buy their freedom.

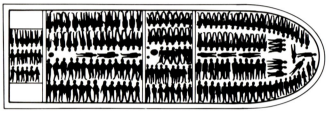

African captives were packed in slave ships literally like sardines in a can. Many died during the agonizing trip across the Atlantic.

But in the English colonies to the north, it was a different, and far more heartbreaking story. There most slaves were treated as "things," not as human beings. Some owners dehumanized the slaves by breeding them like cattle, whipping them like dogs and controlling them like horses. Most slaves were kept illiterate, forbidden to leave their owner's plantation, and prevented from attending religious or social gatherings of any kind. They were denied their own culture and prevented from adopting that of their masters. Their spirits were broken when their families were separated. They found themselves in a living hell with no past, no present, and no future—no opportunity to express themselves spiritually, politically, or artistically. They had absolutely no rights.

Even under such conditions the slaves fought back when and how they could. Work slowdowns, passive resistance, flight, spontaneous insurrection, and organized rebellion were some of the ways they found to resist their oppressors. But resistance led to even more brutal oppression. Any violent act by a slave might be returned tenfold by the master.

Slavery in the Americas lasted for almost four hundred years. The slaves of Haiti were liberated by the great leader Toussaint L'Ouverture in the 1790s. Slavery continued in the United States until 1863, when Abraham Lincoln signed the Emancipation Proclamation. The slaveholders of Brazil held out until 1870.

The world is still paying for the damage that resulted from the American slave system. The nations of Africa suffered the loss of millions of their youngest, strongest, and brightest men and women, devastating their social

152

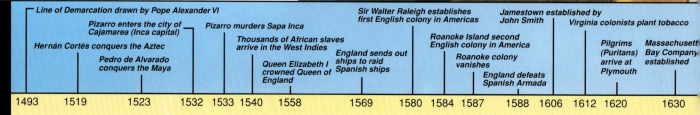

systems and rendering them vulnerable to the imperialist onslaughts of the Europeans in the decades to come. The nations of Latin America are still struggling to find alternatives to slavery that will allow them to prosper economically. And the United States is still, more than a hundred years after the Civil War, beset with immense difficulties in integrating African Americans fully and equitably into American society.

To the Europeans, buying a slave was no different than buying a goat or a horse.

Warfare breaks out between Indians and colonists

George Calvert establishes a colony in Maryland

William Penn establishes Pennsylvania

Rhode Island established by Roger Williams

First printing press arrives in Boston

| 1632 | 1636 | 1639 | 1675 | 1681 |

Quiz

1. The European nations first in the Americas were

Ⓐ England and Spain.   Ⓒ Portugal and France.

Ⓑ Spain and Portugal.   Ⓓ Spain and Holland.

2. England established its first colonies during the reign of

Ⓐ Queen Elizabeth I.   Ⓒ King James II.

Ⓑ King James I.   Ⓓ King Phillip I.

3. The first successful English colony was called

Ⓐ Roanoke.   Ⓒ Jamestown.

Ⓑ Plymouth.   Ⓓ Jamaica.

4. The leader of the Indians who helped the pilgrims was

Ⓐ Squanto.   Ⓒ Hiawatha.

Ⓑ Pocahontas.   Ⓓ Massasoit.

5. The Quakers founded the city of Boston.

Ⓐ True   Ⓑ False

6. The three major civilizations in the Americas when the Spanish arrived were

Ⓐ Olmec, Maya, and Inca.   Ⓒ Maya, Olmec, and Aztec.

Ⓑ Maya, Inca, and Aztec.   Ⓓ Aztec, Inca, and Olmec.

7. Francisco Pizarro conquered the Inca.

Ⓐ True   Ⓑ False

8. The leader of the Aztec was

Ⓐ Atahualpa.   Ⓒ Montezuma.

Ⓑ Massasoit.   Ⓓ Tecum Uman.

9. The first African slaves were kidnapped and taken from Africa about

Ⓐ 1650.   Ⓒ 1760.

Ⓑ 1544.   Ⓓ 1444.

10. The system of trade between Europe, Africa, the West Indies, and New England was called the Triangle Trade.

Ⓐ True   Ⓑ False

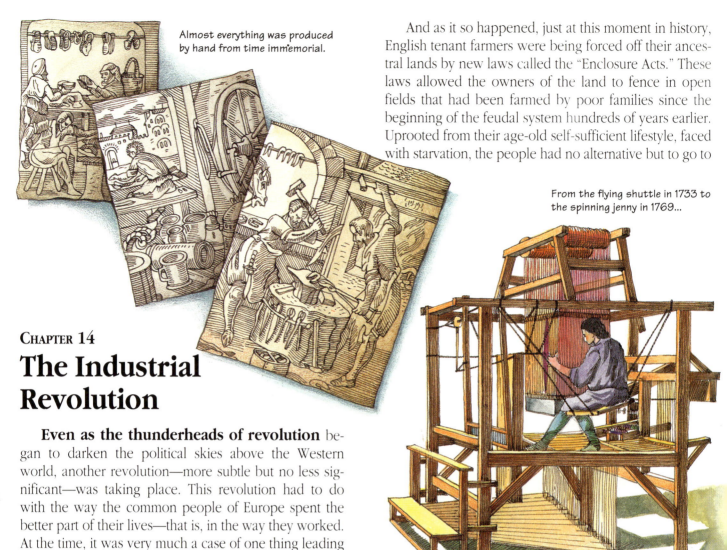

Almost everything was produced by hand from time immemorial.

From the flying shuttle in 1733 to the spinning jenny in 1769...

CHAPTER 14
The Industrial Revolution

Even as the thunderheads of revolution began to darken the political skies above the Western world, another revolution—more subtle but no less significant—was taking place. This revolution had to do with the way the common people of Europe spent the better part of their lives—that is, in the way they worked. At the time, it was very much a case of one thing leading to another. Today we call it the Industrial Revolution.

Prior to the beginning of the eighteenth century, almost everything was produced by hand. Craftsmen made products of all kinds, from swords to plowshares, one at a time in their homes or in small workshops. This was the way it had always been. But then in England around 1750, ideas and circumstances came together in such a way as to transform almost beyond recognition the very concept of work. People began to build *machines* to do certain kinds of work. The machines needed power, and so new sources of power were found. The new power sources were adapted to transportation and communication, which paved the way for bigger and better machines, which generated the search for more and more power, which. . .well, you get the picture.

Why in England? Because England, more than any other nation at that time, possessed the resources to nurture the seeds of industry. There was an abundance of rivers and streams to drive waterwheels, coal to fuel steam engines, and iron ore from which to fashion the big machines. But without people to set the waterwheels in motion, to shovel the coal, and to build the machines, there could be no industry.

And as it so happened, just at this moment in history, English tenant farmers were being forced off their ancestral lands by new laws called the "Enclosure Acts." These laws allowed the owners of the land to fence in open fields that had been farmed by poor families since the beginning of the feudal system hundreds of years earlier. Uprooted from their age-old self-sufficient lifestyle, faced with starvation, the people had no alternative but to go to the cities and become wage-earners. Men, women and children alike thought themselves lucky to find any job, for any wage, under any conditions.

At the same time that thousands of English farmers were struggling to survive, the upper classes were prospering as never before, thanks to England's success as a colonial power. There was plenty of money just waiting to be invested in the equipment and factories that the Industrial Revolution was about to spawn.

So all the elements were in place when in 1733 John Kay, a weaver, invented the "flying shuttle," a kind of loom that cut in half the amount of time it took to weave cloth. The British textile industry was suddenly able to produce twice as much cloth as before. As soon as the new machine was put into use, the textile business took off. But it soon became evident that there was a problem. The old-fashioned spinning wheels that spun the thread could not keep up with the new machines that wove the cloth. Business owners offered prizes to the inventor of a machine that could spin yarn faster. In 1769 John

Hargreaves invented the spinning jenny, which allowed one worker to spin as many as eighty strands of thread at one time. So far, the spinning and weaving were still done in the homes and cottages of the workers, although at a much accelerated pace. But the days of the "cottage system," as it is called, were numbered.

Because at just about the same time that Hargreaves introduced his spinning jenny, Richard Arkwright, a barber, came up with a device he called the waterframe, which produced a much stronger thread than had been possible before. This machine was bigger and heavier than Hargreave's machine. It was so big that it could not be kept in a home or operated by hand. Its power source was a waterwheel and it needed a

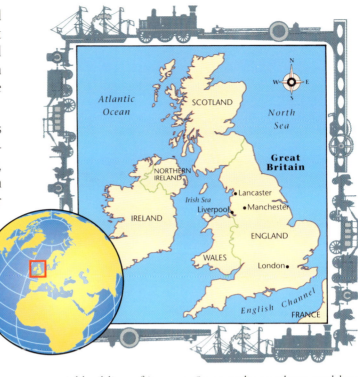

special building of its own. So now the workers could not stay at home. They rose each day and went off to work in the textile mills that appeared everywhere near streams and rivers. This was the very beginning of both the modern factory system and what we know today as the working class.

In 1779, Samuel Crampton combined the spinning jenny and the waterframe into one machine he called the "mule." This machine could spin a thread 150 miles long from a single pound of cotton. Now the weavers had to catch up with the spinners. And in a few short years Edmund Cartwright invented the steam-powered loom.

155

...to the steam engine in 1804, one development led to another in the explosion of ideas that we call the Industrial Revolution.

As the textile industry developed, it became clear that the available waterpower was limited—good locations on fast-flowing streams were getting hard to find. So factory owners looked for a new source of power, and they found it in the steam engine. Steam engines had been used for years to pump water from mines, but this was the first time anyone had used one to power a heavy machine. The Scottish engineer James Watt developed a steam engine specially designed to run machinery. The textile industry's quest for a better steam engine soon led to a major innovation in the way the English got from one place to another.

In 1804 Richard Trevithick mounted a steam engine on a set of wheels and called it a "locomotive." Like the steam engine itself, the locomotive served an apprenticeship hauling coal in the mines. The first successful commercial railroad came twenty years later, running cargo back and forth along twenty-five miles of track. By 1830 it was carrying passengers, and by 1850 some 6,600 miles of track crisscrossed the English countryside.

John McAdam came up with a way to pave roads that made them usable even in bad weather, and between the good roads and the fast trains, the canals which had long been the best alternative when it came to mass transportation, quickly fell into disuse.

As long as the American states had remained British colonies, they had been prohibited from competing with industries in England. In fact, the main purpose of the colonies, from the mother country's point of view was first, to be a convenient source of raw materials, and then to be a ready market for the finished goods. This was how England and the other European colonial powers were able to grow so wealthy. But with the coming of independence, and the help of a few expatriate Englishmen, the Americans quickly caught up in the race to industrialize.

The British government tried to keep the secrets of the new industrial technology to itself. The exportation of textile-making machinery was forbidden.

Workers who were familiar with the machines were not allowed to leave the country. But some made it to America anyway, and their knowledge came with them. Samuel Slater, who had once worked for Richard Arkwright, memorized the designs of the new textile machines before he made the trip. Soon after he arrived in New York in 1789, he hooked up with a businessman named Moses Brown, and before long they had America's first textile mill up and running in Pawtucket, Rhode Island. The factory system had arrived.

There was no influx of displaced farmers into American cities as there had been in England, so American factory owners, especially in the textile industry, began hiring children. In those days there was no law that said children had to go to school, and many did not. If their families were poor, they worked in the home or on the farm. When they were able to put more bread on the table by working in the mills than by working in the fields, they took work at the mills, despite the long hours, harsh conditions, and the risk of being injured by the machines.

A Boston merchant named Francis Cabot Lowell tried using young, unmarried women from nearby farms as his workforce. They lived in dormitories provided by Lowell and were taught reading, writing, and other subjects during their off hours. Obviously all of this was expensive, and although women were hired in large numbers at other mills, they were not usually treated so well.

156

Increased production led to improvements in transportation.

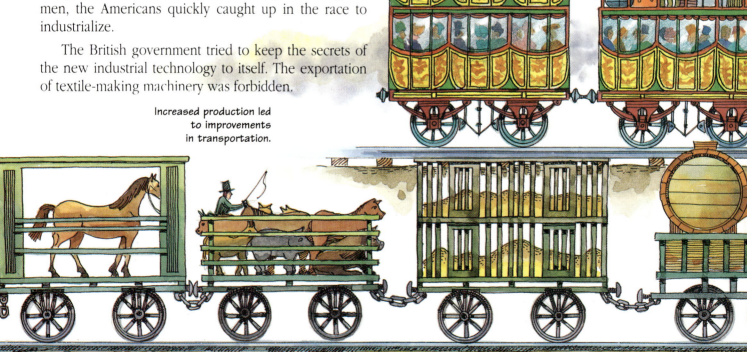

In 1793, Eli Whitney, an American, invented the cotton gin, which cleaned raw cotton fibers fifty times faster than could be done by hand. Finally the entire process of making cloth, from the cotton plant to the finished product, was mechanized, industrialized, and speeding along at an unheard rate of production. Then Whitney developed another process that would lead directly into the modern age. He began making guns with identical, interchangeable parts. Now if your gun broke, you could replace the broken part with the same part from another gun just like it. And the guns could be made faster and cheaper, too. In no time at all other industries were using Whitney's idea of mass production.

The airplane, a car with wings, sprang from the invention of the automobile, a train without tracks.

The 1800s saw an explosion of new technology that led to incredible advances in energy production, communication, and transportation. In 1807 Robert Fulton built the first successful steamboat. In 1831 Englishman Michael Faraday invented a machine called the dynamo, which generated electricity by using the powerful fields of force from magnets. In 1837 Samuel F.B. Morse built on Faraday's work to create the telegraph, which used electricity to send messages over wires with lightning speed. Then came Alexander Graham Bell and his telephone—not just messages, but actual voices moving through the wires. In 1895 Italian Guglielmo Marconi invented radio, doing away with the wires and sending sound waves through the air itself.

In 1856 Englishman Henry Bessemer discovered that blowing compressed air into molten iron burned out the impurities to produce a new product called steel. Steel was stronger and more flexible than iron. Steel could, and would, bear the weight of the world.

In the 1850s America discovered the miracle of petroleum, or unrefined oil. It was the perfect lubricant for fast-moving machine parts. It could be made into kerosene for light and heat. In 1886 a German scientist, Gottlieb Daimler, took what the Americans had learned about oil and invented the internal-combustion engine, which ran not on steam, but on gasoline, yet another form of petroleum. With wheels, the internal combustion engine became the automobile. With the wings that the Wright brothers gave it in 1903, it could fly.

Children and women were often exploited in early factories.

The transformation to the factory system turned independent workers and craftspeople into "wage slaves" with little control over their work environments.

What difference did all this change make in the daily lives of the people? How did they fare when the "Revolution" had been won? Under the cottage system, they had worked at home and owned their tools. They'd had some measure of control over their work and the part it played in their lives. When they began to work in the factories, the new tools and machines belonged to the factory owner, since they were too expensive for most people to buy. The owner not only decided who would work but how long they would work and how much they would be paid.

In England it took new laws called the Factory Acts to remove young children from the factories and to limit the hours that women and children could work. Factory owners gave little thought to the safety of their workers. Insurance for the workers was virtually nonexistent. Eventually workers banded together to protest poor working conditions. Out of protest came the labor unions, that demanded, and got, better wages and fairer treatment for their members.

The rapid flow of people into the cities and mill towns created overcrowding, which led to the formation of slums with inadequate sanitation, bad drinking water, and hogs and goats rooting through the piles of garbage in the streets. Epidemics were frequent, and many people died. Cities went gray from the soot and ashes that spewed from the smokestacks of the new coal-burning factories. In many ways we're still coping with problems that were born out of the Industrial Revolution. But the cities have survived to become the focal points of culture in the industrialized nations. Average life expectancy has gone from 39 years to 78 years. Many major diseases have been wiped out because of advances in science and technology.

The Industrial Revolution was a revolution in every sense of the word. Yet no shots were fired, no declarations were made, not one general ever issued a single command. It happened by itself almost as if it had to. One idea led to another, one machine made other machines, and suddenly, over the course of a hundred or so short years, one world was gone forever, and another world was here to stay.

158

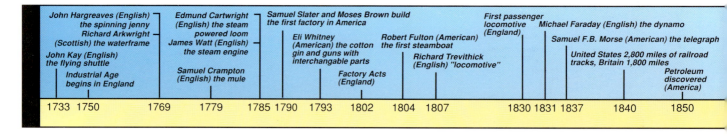

John Hargreaves (English) the spinning jenny	Edmund Cartwright (English) the steam powered loom	Samuel Slater and Moses Brown build the first factory in America		First passenger locomotive (England)	Michael Faraday (English) the dynamo
Richard Arkwright (Scottish) the waterframe	James Watt (English) the steam engine	Eli Whitney (American) the cotton gin and guns with interchangable parts	Robert Fulton (American) the first steamboat		Samuel F.B. Morse (American) the telegraph
John Kay (English) the flying shuttle				Richard Trevithick (English) "locomotive"	United States 2,800 miles of railroad tracks, Britain 1,800 miles
Industrial Age begins in England	Samuel Crampton (English) the mule	Factory Acts (England)			Petroleum discovered (America)
1733 1750	1769 1779 1785	1790 1793 1802	1804 1807	1830 1831 1837	1840 1850

The rapid flow of people into the cities led to overcrowding, slums, and frequent outbreaks of disease.

At first, no one knew how dangerous pollution was.

Alexander Graham Bell (American) the telephone

Gottlieb Daimler (German) the "internal combustion engine"

Henry Bessemer (English) produces steel

Wright brothers (American) the airplane

Guglielmo Marconi (Italian) the radio

1856 1876 1886 1895 1903

Quiz

1. The three things needed for modern industry are resources, workers, and investors.

   Ⓐ True   Ⓑ False

2. John Kay invented the

   Ⓐ flying shuttle.   Ⓒ waterframe.
   Ⓑ spinning jenny.   Ⓓ mule.

3. The waterwheel was replaced as a source of power by

   Ⓐ the internal-combustion engine.   Ⓒ the dynamo.
   Ⓑ the steam engine.   Ⓓ the telegraph.

4. Eli Whitney built the first successful steamboat.

   Ⓐ True   Ⓑ False

5. The Revolutionary War was important for industrialization in the U.S.

   Ⓐ True   Ⓑ False

6. He developed the idea of mass production.

   Ⓐ Robert Fulton   Ⓒ John McAdam
   Ⓑ Cabot Lowell   Ⓓ Eli Whitney

7. Iron is stronger and more flexible than steel.

   Ⓐ True   Ⓑ False

8. The Wright brothers invented the

   Ⓐ gasoline-powered airplane.   Ⓒ radio.
   Ⓑ automobile.   Ⓓ telephone.

9. In the cottage system, people had some control over their work.

   Ⓐ True   Ⓑ False

10. Labor unions were formed to demand

    Ⓐ vacations and short hours.   Ⓒ easier work.
    Ⓑ better pay and conditions.   Ⓓ different bosses.

Chapter 15

The Age of Revolution

THE AMERICAN REVOLUTION

"We hold these truths to be self-evident, that all men are created equal, that they are endowed by their Creator with certain inalienable Rights, that among these are Life, Liberty and the pursuit of Happiness.—That to secure these rights, Governments are instituted among Men, deriving their just powers from the consent of the governed.—That whenever any Form of Government becomes destructive of these ends, it is the Right of the People to alter or to abolish it, and to institute new Government...."

With these words, the Congress of the United Colonies of America voted to declare themselves free and independent states. The ideas embodied in the Declaration of Independence are the principles upon which democratic government is based.

The American Revolution was the result of the clash between the pompous insensitivity of the British government and the brash, even foolhardy defiance of the American patriots. To the British the colonies were nothing more than a source of extra income. To the colonists, who had worked hard and suffered much to build these new societies, the New World was home, and they deserved to reap the fruits of their labors.

For the first 150 years of the English presence in North America, England allowed her thirteen colonies the freedom to develop politically and economically. But after the long and costly French and Indian War during which England and France battled for supremacy in North America, King Charles III and the British Parliament decided that the colonists should bear a large part of the burden of the cost of that war.

In 1763 the British Prime Minister hit on a new way to increase income from the colonies. The Sugar Act put an import tax, or duty, on sugar, wine, textiles, and coffee. The colonies had no representation in the English government, and the colonists were enraged by these new taxes that had been forced upon them. To avoid the unfair taxes the colonists turned to smuggling on a grand scale, reducing even further the flow of money back to the mother country.

The English responded by imposing yet another odi-

160

It is hard to imagine a less likely band of revolutionaries than the wealthy planters and businessmen who succeeded in liberating the American colonies from England.

ous tax. The Stamp Act of 1765 required a special stamp to be put on all wills, newspapers, diplomas, marriage licenses, and playing cards. The colonists, of course, would foot the bill. The stamp tax created additional hardship for the settlers, and their discontent grew. Many Americans refused to buy anything made in England and some even raided tax-collecting offices. In the big cities the people rioted and hung government officials in effigy. The protesters became so violent that no one dared to sell the stamps. Since no ship could leave an American port without properly stamped papers, trade came to a standstill.

As the colonists began to discuss more organized forms of resistance, the English reaction was to impose the Quartering Act, which forced Americans to provide free lodging in their own homes to English troops. The colonists resented this invasion of their privacy. They knew it was the King's way of punishing those who spoke out in protest.

In 1767 the English government created a new set of tax laws for the colonies. Import taxes were placed on necessities like paper, paint, glass, lead, and tea. The colonies were prohibited from manufacturing any product that might compete with the same thing made in England. The colonists stood fast in their resistance to the ever more oppressive taxes and prohibitions. They smuggled Dutch tea or switched to coffee, and they continued their boycott of English-made goods.

Fiery Samuel Adams and a group of Boston men called the Sons of Liberty began to stir up dissension among the public at mass meetings. Adams and his friend James Otis wrote open letters to all the colonies calling for united action in defense of their liberties. The British considered their actions traitorous.

Violence erupted all through the colonies as the disagreements intensified. In Boston in 1770 a group of boys threw snowballs at a British soldier standing sentry. A detachment of twenty soldiers came to his aid, and a crowd of men gathered. The Bostonians grew bolder. Some of them threw rocks. The soldiers opened fire. A black man named Crispus Attucks was

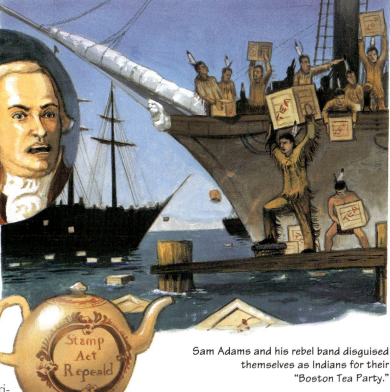

Sam Adams and his rebel band disguised themselves as Indians for their "Boston Tea Party."

killed and earned his place in history as the first casualty of the American Revolution.

Sam Adams hastened to spread the news of the clash, brimming with descriptions of the soldiers firing ". . .without provocation into a group of respectable citizens." He labeled it the "Boston Massacre." Tempers ran so hot that the governor ordered the British regiments out of the city until calm was restored.

For two years after that, things were quiet. But it was the quiet before the storm. Then Lord North, the British Prime Minister, granted the English-owned East India Company exclusive rights to sell their tea directly to agents in the colonies. Although this actually lowered the price of tea for the colonial consumer, it also effectively gave one company a monopoly on all the tea trade in North America. Again the colonists' anger exploded. In Philadelphia and New York City they mobbed the wharves and prevented the ships from being unloaded. In Boston one night, one hundred and fifty men disguised themselves as Indians and boarded three English tea ships in Boston Harbor. They dumped 342 chests of tea overboard while delighted crowds of people watched this "Boston Tea Party."

The English Parliament struck back swiftly at this latest American outrage with the Coercive Acts of 1774. These laws were so oppressive, so clearly aimed at punishing the people of Boston and the entire state of Massachusetts, that the Americans called them the "Intolerable Acts." Until now only a minority of Americans had thought it wise to rebel against the king. But the sparks

British troops found their way across the Concord Bridge blocked by a small but resolute band of minutemen.

that flew when the Coercive Acts were announced lit the flame of rebellion in many a timid and wavering heart.

English troops moved in to occupy Boston, and it became a city under siege. Sam Adams inspired groups called the Committees of Correspondence to keep up the call for united action and demonstrations of support. Donations of food and money poured in from the other colonies, helping the Bostonians remain firm in their defiance.

Virginia was the first colony to call for a meeting, or Congress, to discuss the crisis. So it came to pass that the First Continental Congress, with delegates from all the colonies except Georgia, met in Philadelphia. They agreed that the English Parliament had no authority to pass laws governing the colonies without the colonies' consent. They declared the Coercive Acts illegal. Massachusetts radicals advised the people of Massachusetts to form their own government, collect their own taxes, form a militia, and continue to boycott all trade with Britain.

As tensions grew, the colonists began to collect guns and ammunition and plan for armed rebellion. Sam Adams and James Otis continued to write passionate articles demanding independence from England. Otis wrote that, "Taxation without representation is tyranny." Local groups of ordinary farmers and townsmen created militia companies and began to drill. They were called minutemen because they were ready for action on a moment's notice.

The English Parliament declared Massachusetts to be in a state of rebellion and tried to isolate Boston, the hotbed of discontent, from the rest of America by closing the port and forbidding all trade. The patriots knew that

the rebellion was near. In Virginia, Patrick Henry demanded that his colony form a militia too, so they would be ready when the time was at hand: "Our brethren are already in the field! Why stand we here idle? Is life so dear or peace so sweet as to be purchased at the price of chains and slavery? I know not what course others may take, but as for me, give me liberty or give me death!"

In 1775 English troops were dispatched from Boston to nearby Lexington to seize the supplies of guns stored there and to place Sam Adams and John Hancock under arrest. But the Americans learned of the plan, and Paul Revere and William Dawes rode on horseback through the night to warn the farmers and the militia that the soldiers were coming. As the British approached the bridge at Concord they saw forty minutemen resolutely blocking the way. Shots were fired, blood was spilled. The Revolutionary War had begun.

Some of the minutemen were armed with only hoes and pitchforks, but others carried the new Kentucky rifles which had been introduced during the French and Indian War. They were deadly accurate compared to the European guns, and they gave the Americans a distinct advantage over the highly regimented English forces.

English General Thomas Gage placed Boston under martial law and declared any armed American a traitor. He promised pardon to anyone who was willing to lay down his arms except for Sam Adams and John Hancock. The rebels ignored the general and occupied Breed's Hill in Boston so that they could train cannon on the British warships in the harbor. The British tried to take the hill by marching 2,400 soldiers straight up the slope in three broad lines, hoping to intimidate the inexperienced Americans.

162

The British soldiers—the Redcoats—looked dashing and dangerous in their bright red jackets. But they were also easy targets. Colonel William Prescott told his ragtag band of rebels not to fire until they ". . .could see the whites of [the enemies'] eyes." Twice the British tried to take the hill. Twice they were driven back. They charged again. This time the Americans were out of ammunition and the Redcoats took the summit.

The Second Continental Congress met in June of 1776, with representatives from all thirteen colonies in attendance. Now they were all ready to join in the fight. John Adams of Massachusetts, the radical leader of the Congress, suggested a southern delegate from Virginia as Commander-in-Chief of the newly formed Continental Army. Tall, athletic, and serious, George Washington was an outstanding military man and a good leader. He had proven himself as a soldier in the French and Indian Wars. The vote for Washington was unanimous in a Congress that included most of the leaders of the rebel cause. From Massachusetts there were Sam Adams, John Adams, and John Hancock; from Pennsylvania, Benjamin Franklin. Representing Virginia were Patrick Henry, Thomas Jefferson, and Washington himself.

Thomas Jefferson was the chief author of the Declaration of Independence.

Another major contributor to the spirit of rebellion was Thomas Paine. His pamphlet, "Common Sense," which had just been published the previous January, inspired the delegates with its insistence on the natural right of the people to rule themselves. Paine's ideas had a major influence not only on the American patriots but also on the leaders of the French Revolution, which was soon to follow.

The Second Continental Congress also chose Benjamin Franklin, John Adams, and Thomas Jefferson to prepare the written declaration of the independence of the rebellious colonies. Jefferson did most of the writing. The Declaration of Independence was adopted by the Congress on July 4, 1776. As the delegates, patriots one and all, signed the monumental document, each was well aware that he was signing his own death warrant should the colonies lose the war. With a dramatic and defiant flourish John Hancock signed his name in big, bold letters, so that ". . .King George [could] read it without his spectacles."

Now the war began in earnest. The British sent an army of 32,000

troops, including hired Hessian mercenaries (German soldiers fighting for England), supported by a navy of more than four hundred warships. At the same time Washington was struggling just to keep his fledgling army alive. There was never enough money, and the part-time soldiers of the Continental Army were apt to leave their posts at any time to help on their farms

163

George Washington—surveyor, farmer, soldier, father of the American Revolution.

164

back home. But
Washington's mighty will
to fight became the will of the
army itself, and it held together. Early
on the British won many battles, but
they could not break the spirit of rebellion
in the hearts of the Americans.

Things continued to fare poorly for the rebels in the
early part of the war, and Washington knew he needed a
dramatic victory to keep hope alive. On Christmas night
of 1776 in the midst of a snowstorm, he secretly ferried
his army of 2,400 men across the Delaware River in small
boats. At dawn they surprised a force of Hessians camped
on the outskirts of Trenton, New Jersey. None of the
Americans were killed, and nine hundred Hessians were
taken prisoner.

General John "Gentleman Johnny" Burgoyne was still
in England when he devised a plan that he was sure
would scuttle the American upstarts once and for all. He
would make his way with his troops down the Hudson
River from Canada and join forces with General Howe in
lower New York. In this way they could isolate and
subdue the northern colonies. Burgoyne and his troops
managed to capture Fort Ticonderoga, near Lake
Champlain. For the next seventy miles they moved
through almost impenetrable forests, harassed by rebels

who remained invisible in the trees but
who slowed their progress to one mile a day by
demolishing bridges and blocking the path with fallen
trees. The Americans defeated Burgoyne's army in several pitched battles as he struggled to make his rendez-
vous with Howe. Finally, after the battle of Saratoga, he
surrendered, giving the Continental Army a great victory.

Things were going better for the British in the South,
despite the fact that they were being continually outwit-
ted by guerilla fighters like Francis "The Swamp Fox"
Marion and Thomas Sumter. General Charles Cornwallis
had met with success in Georgia and South Carolina by
using the colonists' own tactics against them. Now he
was moving into position to take all of North Carolina.
But backwoodsmen from what is now Tennessee crossed
to the east side of the Blue Ridge Mountains and attacked
Cornwallis' forces. Even though the British were in an
almost ideal position at the top of a mountain, the Americans drove them back. Sharpshooters all, they moved
from rock to rock, from tree to tree, picking off the
redcoats one by one.

Washington's most difficult time was at Valley Forge
in the winter of 1777, when the supplies of food and

Washington crossed the Delaware River to victory at Trenton on Christmas Night, 1776 and kept the Revolution alive.

Ben Franklin served as ambassador to France during the war. Greatly loved by the French people, he obtained crucial support for the cause of the Revolution.

clothing were so poor that thousands of his men were starving and barefoot. Thomas Paine wrote: "These are the times that try men's souls. The summer soldier and the sunshine patriot will, in this crisis, shrink from the service of his country, but he that stands it now, deserves the love and thanks of man and woman. Tyranny, like hell, is not easily conquered; yet we have the consolation with us, that the harder the conflict, the more glorious the triumph."

Money, or the lack of it, continued to be an enormous problem for the colonists, until Robert Morris, the Superintendent of Finances, finally managed to get substantial help from France, Spain, and Holland, who bitterly opposed England in Europe. Morris also used his own money to buy supplies to keep the army in the field. Another patriot who used his own money to aid the difficult cause was a man named Haym Solomon. He advanced over $700,000 to the cause of the Revolution—

huge amount in those days. He was never repaid and died almost penniless.

Benjamin Franklin had been named American ambassador to France during the war, and he used his position to plead the American cause at the court of the French king. A remarkable character with a brilliant mind and a penetrating wit, Franklin was already much loved by the French and was well known as a scientist, inventor, writer, and philosopher. France, traditionally at odds with England since the time of the Norman Conquest, agreed to Franklin's suggestion of a treaty of alliance and joined the war on the side of the United States in 1778. Spain and Holland also joined in the war against England.

Even prior to France's official entry into the war, many French adventurers had come to America to be a part of the birth of a new nation. Among them was the 19-year-old Marquis de Lafayette. Charged with youthful enthusiasm and dedication to the idea of democracy, he was also extremely wealthy. So eager was he to be a part

Winter at Valley Forge—the dark night of the Revolution's soul.

Charles Cornwallis—one of the more successful British generals—for a time.

of the fight for freedom that he bought his own ship in which to cross the Atlantic. Lafayette with his sword, like Thomas Paine with his pen, was a true freedom fighter in both the American and the French revolutions.

Cornwallis kept moving through the mountain wilderness and the swampy lowlands of the South, winning more often than not in skirmishes with the rebels, but steadily losing men and equipment. Tormented by the constant hit-and-run attacks of the backwoodsmen, Cornwallis abandoned all nonessential supplies in order to move his troops faster. But when he stripped his army down, he sealed his fate. Mired in the swamps, short of food and sick from drinking brackish water, the English made less progress than before. Cornwallis decided to make a stand and chose Yorktown, a small port on the

166

The world turned upside down when Cornwallis surrendered to Washington at Yorktown in 1781.

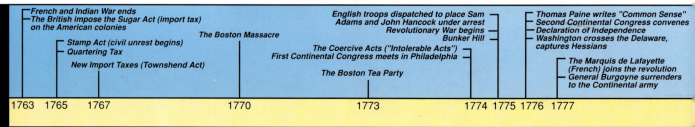

French and Indian War ends
The British impose the Sugar Act (import tax) on the American colonies

Stamp Act (civil unrest begins)
Quartering Tax

New Import Taxes (Townshend Act)

The Boston Massacre

English troops dispatched to place Sam Adams and John Hancock under arrest
Revolutionary War begins
Bunker Hill

The Coercive Acts ("Intolerable Acts")
First Continental Congress meets in Philadelphia

The Boston Tea Party

Thomas Paine writes "Common Sense"
Second Continental Congress convenes
Declaration of Independence
Washington crosses the Delaware, captures Hessians

The Marquis de Lafayette (French) joins the revolution
General Burgoyne surrenders to the Continental army

1763   1765   1767   1770   1773   1774 1775 1776 1777

coast of Virginia, as his base. It was here that his exhausted and disheartened army was overwhelmed and defeated by the combined forces of the French army under Lafayette and the Americans commanded by General Washington himself.

Cornwallis surrendered to Washington at Yorktown in the year 1781. The British band played a song called "The World Turned Upside Down." The Marquis de Lafayette had the American band strike up "Yankee Doodle." With the Treaty of Paris in 1783 the war was officially over, and a new nation was born.

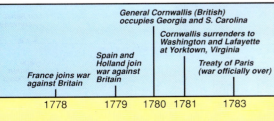

	General Cornwallis (British) occupies Georgia and S. Carolina		
		Cornwallis surrenders to Washington and Lafayette at Yorktown, Virginia	
	Spain and Holland join war against Britain		Treaty of Paris (war officially over)
France joins war against Britain			
1778	1779	1780 1781	1783

Quiz

1. The "Quartering Act" forced all colonists to pay taxes on sugar, textiles and coffee.

Ⓐ True   Ⓑ False

2. The Sons of Liberty was a group of patriots in

Ⓐ New York.   Ⓒ Philadelphia.
Ⓑ Boston.   Ⓓ Lexington.

3. Who was the first person killed in the Boston Massacre?

Ⓐ Sam Adams   Ⓒ John Hancock
Ⓑ James Otis   Ⓓ Crispus Attucks

4. Where did the first battle of the Revolutionary War take place?

Ⓐ Boston   Ⓒ Lexington
Ⓑ Philadelphia   Ⓓ Concord

5. The bright red jackets of the British soldiers made them easy targets.

Ⓐ True   Ⓑ False

6. Who wrote "Common Sense"?

Ⓐ Thomas Paine   Ⓒ John Adams
Ⓑ Thomas Jefferson   Ⓓ Benjamin Franklin

7. Who did most of the writing of the Declaration of Independence?

Ⓐ Thomas Paine   Ⓒ John Adams
Ⓑ Thomas Jefferson   Ⓓ Benjamin Franklin

8. Benjamin Franklin was the ambassador to what country during the war?

Ⓐ England   Ⓒ Spain
Ⓑ France   Ⓓ Holland

9. What two revolutions did the Marquis de Lafayette fight in?

Ⓐ American and French   Ⓒ French and Russian
Ⓑ American and Mexican Ⓓ French and Mexican

10. The English general who surrendered to Washington at Yorktown was

Ⓐ Howe.   Ⓒ Cornwallis.
Ⓑ Burgoyne.   Ⓓ Gage.

THE FRENCH REVOLUTION

The success of the American Revolution served as an inspiration for the people of France, still suffering under the yoke of tyranny placed on their shoulders by Louis XIV, the "Sun King," who had ruled as absolute monarch for 72 years. The current king, Louis XVI, was less the evil tyrant than the careless and lazy monarch. Full of good intentions, he was a weak and ineffective ruler. His wife, Queen Marie Antoinette, was the daughter of the Empress Maria Theresa of Austria. She occupied herself with frivolities like dancing, gambling, giving lavish parties, and spending money in any way she could. The French people did not like Austria, and they did not like her. The outrageous spending of "Madame Deficit," as they called her, made their own poverty an even more bitter pill.

And the poverty of the French people could not be denied. Half of a typical peasant's daily wage paid for a single loaf of bread. The other half went for taxes. While the peasants were taxed into starvation the nobles and clergy paid no taxes at all! The king and queen were draining the royal coffers as quickly as they could be filled, so Louis decided to require the clergy and nobles to pay taxes. They refused. After all, they had never paid taxes before. Louis then called for a meeting of the Estates-General—the first such meeting in over 150 years—in the hope that

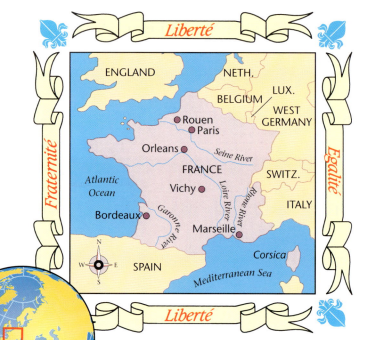

they could settle on a plan to squeeze more taxes out of the kingdom.

The French Parliament was divided into three groups called *estates*. The First Estate consisted of the clergy, the nobles made up the Second Estate, and into the Third Estate fell the rest—merchants, craftsmen, and peasants among them. Usually the three estates met separately, with each Estate casting one vote on a given issue. In the normal course of events, the Third Estate was always outvoted by the other two. Now they declared themselves the "National Assembly" and insisted upon including six hundred delegates in their group, each with a vote of his own. Many of the lower clergy and even some members of the nobility supported them. Encountering potentially dangerous opposition from the King, they met secretly at an indoor tennis court. There they took an oath not to disband until a constitution had been created.

All through the countryside of France the unrest grew. The high prices and food shortages caused riots and rumblings of protest. The King grew concerned and called up the army—both for his own protection and to prevent insurrection. But the presence of troops in the streets of Paris only served to incite the crowd. Word spread that there were weapons to be had at the Bastille—an age-old prison and symbol of the tyrant's fist. On July 14, 1789, a mob stormed the Bastille. This marked the beginning of the French Revolution, celebrated today as Bastille Day.

The National Assembly seized the moment and wrote their *Declaration of the Rights of Man* and a new constitution. They took over the government in Paris, created their own flag, and organized a militia—the National Guard—led by the recent hero of the American Revolution, the Marquis de Lafayette. As news of the takeover spread,

The Bastille, age-old symbol of royal tyranny, became the object of the people's wrath.

National Guard units began to form all over the country. The King was no longer in control.

Louis XVI

Relaxing at their Versailles palace outside Paris, the king and queen remained oblivious to the significance of the situation. The queen made some disparaging remarks about the "rabble of Paris" and ridiculed the new flag. But then the women of Paris woke up one day to find that there was no bread to be had at any price. Six-thousand strong, gathering some twenty thousand men in their wake as they passed, they marched the twelve miles to Versailles and burst into the palace demanding bread. The peasants seized the royal family and took them back to Paris.

In 1792 the royal family tried to slip out of the country, but they were caught and again taken prisoner. Other countries threatened the Assembly with war if the king and queen were not protected. The Assembly responded by declaring war itself. A coalition of countries including Prussia, England, Austria, Netherlands and Spain invaded France with the intention of putting down the revolution and restoring the French monarchy. The King was charged with treason and beheaded.

Now the revolutionaries began to fight among themselves. An extreme faction, the Committee of Public Safety, emerged at the forefront. Led by Maximilien Robespierre they wanted to "protect France from its enemies inside and outside the nation." They called for the death of all counter-revolutionaries, aristocrats, priests, and suspects. In the name of the glorious revolution, the mobs set up their own courts and began the executions. The Reign of Terror, with Robespierre, Georges Danton, and Jean Marat at its helm, lasted for six months. The crowd cheered as the guillotine blade fell again and again.

Georges Danton

Bloodlust and conflicting ambitions quickly threw the new government into turmoil. Suspicion was everywhere. No one was safe from the executioner. Marat was killed in his tub by Charlotte Corday, a girl from the country who wanted the violence to end. Robespierre succeeded in having Danton executed in the spring, but by summer he too had lost his head. On that day, the Terror was over, and

Marquis de Lafayette

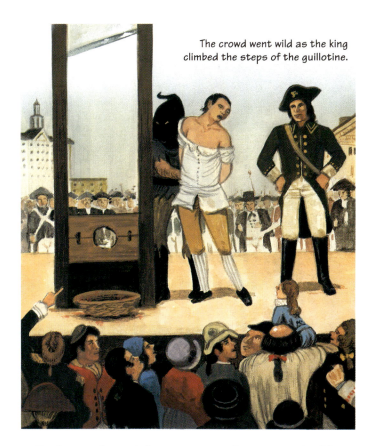
The crowd went wild as the king climbed the steps of the guillotine.

"all of Paris danced for joy." More than 25,000 had lost their lives during this terrible time.

For the next ten years the chaos, terror, and bloodshed of the Revolution continued to shred the fabric of French society. The feudal system collapsed and the power of the Church was broken. The gigantic estates of the aristocrats were fragmented as France became a nation of small landholders. Also eliminated were the rigid price controls enforced by merchants and artisan's guilds. Although not yet a democracy, France was on its way to becoming a modern state. The monarchs of Europe struggled to snuff out the flames of liberty that were breaking out everywhere. One man stepped forward to impose order on a world in chaos. That man was Napoleon Bonaparte.

169

Charlotte Corday murdered Marat in an effort to stop the Terror.

Napoleon became a dictator
in the name of liberty.

Napoleon Bonaparte was born to Italian parents on the French island of Corsica. Educated at a French military school, he was clumsy and never learned to spell or read French very well. But he never doubted his own grand destiny, his "glorious future." In 1796 when he was only 27, he became General of the Army of France. A little over five feet tall, he looked like a boy, but he seemed to have no sense of fear. His soldiers affectionately called him "the little corporal." He promised his men "honor, glory, and riches," and his men followed him without question. He inspired his armies as he overcame stronger forces with his daring tactics. His Grand Army swept through Europe conquering everything in its path.

Napoleon's success hinged upon a whole new way of waging war. He did away with the traditional method of sending soldiers forward in stiff lines and shooting in volleys. Instead he sent out a front line of "skirmishers," soldiers who moved forward, taking cover as they went. They were to shoot only when they had a good target. The main force, formed in massed columns, followed to within charging distance. Artillery was used to blow holes in the enemy lines before a cavalry charge. The Grand Army gained the advantage of speed by forsaking the usual caravan of supply wagons and living off the land whenever they could. Many an opposing army, dragging its wagons through the mud and snow, over mountains and across rivers, found itself overwhelmed by the fleet French troops.

In fourteen months Napoleon conquered northern Italy and forced Austria to settle for peace. When he returned to Paris in 1799 he was a hero. He seized the government and named himself First Consul of France. At first Napoleon ruled with intelligence and enthusiasm. He brought order and peace to the country. He devised a fair tax system and set in place a very fair judicial system called the Napoleonic Code, which is still in use today.

Napoleon's governmental reforms were consistent with the principles of the Revolution, yet his personal ambitions were anything but. In 1804 he declared himself Hereditary Emperor of France. His power was so great that Pope Pius VII could not decline his invitation to preside over the coronation ceremony. But as the Pope approached Napoleon with the crown, Napoleon took the crown from the Pope's hands and placed it on his own head. Then he crowned his wife Josephine as Empress. Once on the throne he forgot all about the ideals of the Revolution. He was as tyrannical as any of the old kings. He executed anyone who opposed him.

By 1812 he had subdued most of Western Europe and destroyed the Holy Roman Empire, either through force of arms or through treaties and alliances. But that summer he set out on a crusade that would prove to be his undoing—the invasion of Russia. He started out with an army of almost 600,000 men. As the French moved eastward, the Russians fell back, refusing to engage in combat after the disastrous Battle of Borodino. When the victorious French entered Moscow they found a city aflame. The Russians had removed everything of value from the city and then set it on fire. Napoleon decided to withdraw his troops, and it was only then that the brilliance of the Russian strategy became clear. The French

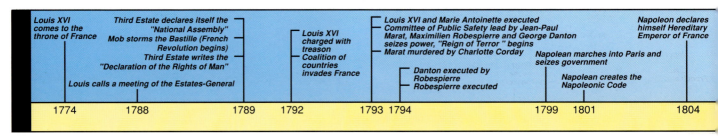

Louis XVI comes to the throne of France	Third Estate declares itself the "National Assembly" — Mob storms the Bastille (French Revolution begins) — Third Estate writes the "Declaration of the Rights of Man" — Louis calls a meeting of the Estates-General			Louis XVI charged with treason — Coalition of countries invades France	Louis XVI and Marie Antoinette executed — Committee of Public Safety lead by Jean-Paul Marat, Maximilien Robespierre and George Danton seizes power, "Reign of Terror" begins — Marat murdered by Charlotte Corday — Danton executed by Robespierre — Robespierre executed		Napoleon marches into Paris and seizes government — Napolean creates the Napoleonic Code	Napoleon declares himself Hereditary Emperor of France	
1774	1788	1789	1792	1793	1794	1799	1801	1804	

Formerly Spanish
Formerly Portuguese
Formerly French

REVOLUTION IN LATIN AMERICA

One of the first official acts of the triumphant revolutionaries in France was to free the slaves in all French colonies. Haiti, on the island of Hispaniola in the West Indies had become one of France's most important colonial holdings. With its thriving sugar, coffee, and cotton plantations, it had proven to be a marvelous source of wealth for France. At the time of the Revolution its population consisted of about 40,000 whites, 22,000 mulattos, and 450,000 black slaves. The conditions for the slaves were terrible. Each year the plantation owners had to buy 40,000 replacements for the slaves who had died as a result of cruelty and overwork. Those who resisted were hanged, burned at the stake, or broken on the wheel.

The plantation owners of Saint-Domingue, as Haiti was then called, tried to keep the declaration of emancipation a secret, but the slaves found out about the decree and demanded their freedom. From the ranks of the rebellious slaves a leader emerged: Toussaint L'Ouverture. In 1791 Toussaint organized a successful slave revolt. The slaves took over the colony and declared Saint-Domingue an independent and sovereign state. The whites fled across the island to sanctuary in the Spanish colony of Dominica. By 1801 Toussaint had reorganized the government, written a constitution, ended customs duties, and abolished slavery. For ten years Toussaint and his forces resisted attempts by the French, Spanish, and British to retake the colony.

By that time, Napoleon had assumed control of the government of France. He had been forced to sell the

had already stolen any food or supplies they could find on the way into the country. Now there was nothing left. Starvation, disease, and the terrible cold of the Russian winter began to do their work. By the end, there was almost no army left. Fewer than 40,000 men got home and, of those, only 10,000 were still able to fight! Napoleon was forced to abdicate and went into exile on the island of Elba.

Once more a monarch assumed the throne of France—Louis XVIII, the brother of Louis XVI. But before long Napoleon had escaped and returned to the mainland with a force of about 1,000 men, to begin a march on Paris. As he traveled, Napoleon was greeted with joy by his old soldiers and soon his army had swollen to 125,000. The nations of Europe were not about to let Napoleon regain his former power. In 1815 the combined armies of England and Belgium led by the Duke of Wellington stood against Napoleon at Waterloo, in Belgium. The defeat of Napoleon's army was complete. This time Napoleon was exiled on the remote island of St. Helena, where he died six years later at the age of fifty-two.

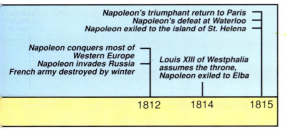

The French resorted to treachery to capture the brilliant Haitian liberator, Toussaint L'Ouverture.

Louisiana Territory, France's vast holdings in North America, to the United States in order to raise money for his European wars. Now he realized how valuable a source of income the Haitian colony had been, and decided to reclaim it and establish it once again as a French possession. A French invasion force of eleven ships carrying 32,000 men landed on the island. After three months of bitter guerrilla warfare Toussaint agreed to surrender, but only on his own terms: that slavery not be re-established, that his officers be given posts in the French army, and that he be permitted to retire peacefully on a plantation of his own. The French accepted his terms, and then, when he turned himself in as promised, they arrested him, put him in irons and shipped him back to France. Once there, he was thrown into a dungeon where he died from cold, hunger, and disease.

One of his officers, Jean-Jacques Dessalines, assumed leadership of the revolutionary army and although vastly outnumbered, they fought on. Help for the revolutionaries arrived in the form of yellow fever, which killed the European soldiers by the thousands. The French, becoming desperate, resorted to torture and savagery in the hope of terrorizing the blacks into submission. But the rebels' outrage only hardened their determination to defeat the invaders at any cost. The French finally gave up and returned to France in 1803, and Dessalines declared himself emperor for life.

172

Simon Bolivar— the Washington of South America

The spark of revolution next leapt across the Gulf of Mexico to the South American mainland. The Spanish colonies there were united in their hatred of Napoleon, who had conquered Spain and installed his brother, Joseph Napoleon, on the Spanish throne. When the news reached Venezuela that a Frenchman had become king of Spain, the colonists deposed their Spanish governor and established a new government based upon the existing *cabildo*, or town council, system. One of the leaders of the cabildo was Simón Bolívar.

Simón José Antonio de la Santissima Trinidad de Bolívar was born in Colombia in 1783. The son of wealthy landowners, he grew up much like any young man of similar circumstance. He was a creole or native-born South American. Creoles, generally a prosperous and refined group, were considered second-class citizens by the Spaniards. When they traveled to Spain, as they often did for business or to attend school, they were snubbed and insulted. Bolívar had visited the United States and Europe, and having studied the writings of Jefferson and Paine, was inspired by their commitment to the ideals of liberty and equality. Embittered by Spain's attitude toward the creole colonists, he dedicated himself to the cause of revolution. "By my honor," he swore, "I will not rest, not in body or soul, until I have broken the chains of Spain."

The Creoles of Venezuela had taken their first shot at independence while Spain was occupied with trying to defend itself against Napoleon's Grand Army. Under the leadership of Francisco de Miranda, the cause had been going well until an earthquake destroyed Caracas in 1812. Because the earthquake occurred on a holy day, the Catholic Church was able to convince the people that they were defying the will of God by rejecting their king. The independence movement was snuffed out, and the royalists regained power. Miranda was captured and died in prison, but Bolívar, considered unimportant, was allowed to leave the country.

Bolívar went into exile in Jamaica and Haiti. In Haiti he requested aid for his cause from Jacques Dessalines, who had only recently led the Haitian revolutionaries to victory. The Haitian president agreed to help Bolívar on the condition that Bolívar free the slaves once independence had been achieved. Using Haiti as his base, Bolívar gathered a small army and returned to South America, where he joined forces with the guerrilla fighter José Antonio Paéz and his band. A group of 6,000 international volunteers—mostly English, Irish, and Scots—also joined Bolívar's army.

Despite heavy casualties and overwhelming odds, Bolívar finally drove the Spanish from New Granada—the area that is now Venezuela, Colombia, and Ecuador. But he could not rest, fearing retaliation from the Spanish forces garrisoned in Peru. So, again in the face of almost impossible odds, he led a daring expedition over the high and forbidding mountains of the Andes. The Spanish outpost was caught completely off guard by the audacious move, and was decisively defeated at the Battle of Boyaca in 1819. Venezuela joined the ranks of the free nations of the New World, and Bolívar was hailed as "The Great Liberator."

Toward the end of his life, Bolívar grew disillusioned when he saw that the new leaders were every bit as selfish, cruel, and tyrannical as the Spanish had been. In despair he wrote, "In gaining our freedom we have lost everything else. There is no good faith in America, nor among the nations of America. Those who have served the revolution have plowed the sea."

Bolívar had a counterpart in the Argentinian creole, José de San Martín. Born in Buenos Aires, San Martín returned to Spain with his family, where at the age of seventeen, he became a lieutenant in the Spanish army. A hardened veteran of the Spanish wars against the Moors and the French, he returned to his homeland in 1812 to join the struggle for independence that was already under way.

With his military knowledge and experience, San Martín proved invaluable to the cause. He quickly transformed a ragged collection of gauchos, slaves, and poor Creoles into a tightly disciplined army and drove the Spanish from Argentina. But, like Bolívar, he knew that the hard-won liberty would never be secure as long as

José de San Martín

there were Spanish troops in South America. As Bolívar made his way toward Peru, San Martín devised a similar plan to cross the Andes into Chile to oust the Spanish troops stationed there. It took him three years to win the support of Argentinian leaders for his daring campaign.

Overcoming the unbelievably harsh conditions in the mountains, San Martín and his 5,000-man army entered Chile, where they were joined by Chilean freedom fighter Bernardo O'Higgins. After several fierce battles the Spanish withdrew, and Chile was a colony no more. O'Higgins stayed on as leader of the new nation, and San Martín worked his way north to join Bolívar in Peru. With independence finally assured, Bolívar and San Martín—the two great liberators—met in Ecuador to decide between them the political future for South America. No one knows exactly what was said but no agreement was reached, and the dream of a united South America remained only a dream.

Devastated by the failure of the negotiations, San Martín returned to his home in Argentina. He found that his beloved wife had died and that everywhere, jealous enemies were plotting against him. He went into voluntary exile in France. Like Simón Bolívar, he died a sad and disillusioned man.

Of all the Spanish colonies in the New World, Mexico—New Spain they called it—was the prize. With its fertile fields, its overflowing silver, gold, and mineral mines, and its large population, it was far and away the most valuable of Spain's colonial possessions. But just as in their other colonies, the Spanish ruled Mexico with an odd combination of cruelty and indifference that was virtually guaranteed to generate bitterness and unrest among both the colonists and the native peoples.

Miguel Hidalgo y Costilla, an intelligent and extremely popular country priest, drew the suspicious eye

173

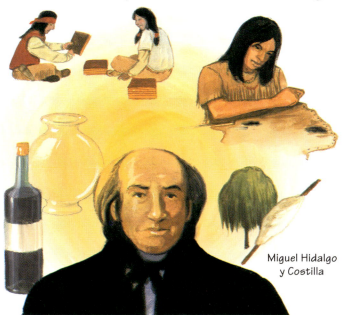

Miguel Hidalgo y Costilla

Mexico endured the
shock waves of
revolution for over
sixty years.

Benito Juarez

Antonio Santa A[...]

174

of the Church with his unorthodox, perhaps even heretical behavior. He read banned books, espoused dangerous ideas, and devoted most of his time to improving the lot of the natives. He tried to give them a future by training them in various trades: tile-making, leatherworking, the production of olive oil and wine. He even planted mulberry trees so that the people might cultivate silkworms and prosper. But the Church and the colonial government had no interest in seeing the condition of the natives improved, and ordered him to cease his dangerous activities.

Hidalgo persisted in his conviction that the way the Indians were being treated was wrong. Ignacio Allende, a creole landholder and close friend agreed, and in 1810 they began to plan an uprising that would free the Mexican people from Spanish domination. It was their intention to proceed slowly and carefully. But somehow word

of their plan got out, and they were forced to act sooner than they would have wished. The Indians, oppressed and exploited for so long, flocked to join the rebellion. On September 16, 1810, Mexican Independence Day, Hidalgo exhorted the gathered multitude to action with a passionate speech that ended with the inspiring words, "Long live America! Long live religion! Down with bad government!" It was the battle cry of the revolution, and it was *el Grito de Dolores*—the Cry of Sorrows.

Hidalgo was named leader of the insurgent forces, and many fellow priests joined the ranks of the revolutionaries. After capturing Guanajuato, the second largest city and a major silver mining site, they marched on toward Mexico City. But in one major battle on the way, Hidalgo lost over 2,000 men. He drew back to Guanajuato and set up a revolutionary government. There he immediately declared the abolition of slavery,

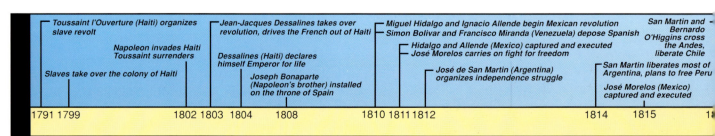

Toussaint l'Ouverture (Haiti) organizes slave revolt	Jean-Jacques Dessalines takes over revolution, drives the French out of Haiti	Miguel Hidalgo and Ignacio Allende begin Mexican revolution	San Martin and Bernardo O'Higgins cross the Andes, liberate Chile
Napoleon invades Haiti Toussaint surrenders		Simon Bolivar and Francisco Miranda (Venezuela) depose Spanish	
	Dessalines (Haiti) declares himself Emperor for life	Hidalgo and Allende (Mexico) captured and executed José Morelos carries on fight for freedom	
Slaves take over the colony of Haiti			San Martin liberates most of Argentina, plans to free Peru
	Joseph Bonaparte (Napoleon's brother) installed on the throne of Spain	José de San Martin (Argentina) organizes independence struggle	
			José Morelos (Mexico) captured and executed

1791 1799   1802 1803 1804   1808   1810 1811 1812   1814   1815 1[...]

the cessation of the payment of tribute to Spain, and the end of Spanish monopoly of the farmlands. Then, hoping for assistance from the United States, Hidalgo and Allende began moving their force to the north. Entrapped and captured, they were executed by firing squad and then decapitated. As a warning to others, their heads were hung in an iron cage in Guanajuato for the next ten years. José María Morelos, another churchman, tried to carry on the fight. He too was captured and executed.

For the next sixty years the struggle continued, again and again betrayed by corruption and villainy. Mexico did achieve its independence from Spain in 1821, but the internal struggles between rich and poor, between republicans and royalists, did not end. For many years, General Antonio Santa Anna ruled the land. A corrupt opportunist, he was now a liberal, now a conservative, with no personal convictions or motives other than a burning desire for power. During those turbulent years, he was in and out of office eleven times. By the 1850s the country was broke, its economy at a standstill, yet Santa Anna spent money like there was no tomorrow—on statues of himself, fancy uniforms, and bribes to hold the army's loyalty. He even taxed the doors and windows in the peasants' homes. Those who could not pay the tax had to brick up their windows and live in the dark.

Benito Juárez, a pure-blooded Indian and a liberal, forced Santa Anna out of office and assumed the presidency in 1855. He tried to equalize land ownership by confiscating Church property and redistributing it to the people, but the Indians were too poor to buy the land at any price. At the request of the conservative element in the Mexican government, France tried briefly to gain control of the country. Maximilian, a Hapsburg archduke, was installed as Emperor of Mexico, but was quickly deposed and executed by Juárez and the liberals. Juárez returned to power and, with the defeat of Maximilian, was finally able to break the conservative grip on the government and the economy of the nation. It was he who finally succeeded in establishing Mexico as a nation among nations, gaining recognition from the United States and from the nations of Europe. His "Laws of the Reform" opened the door to economic equality for the people of Mexico and started the long-suffering country on the road to becoming a modern and progressive republic.

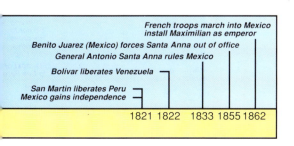

Quiz

1. The King of France at the time of the French Revolution was Louis XVI.

Ⓐ True   Ⓑ False

2. The French people's nickname for Marie Antoinette was

Ⓐ Madame Deficit.   Ⓒ Maria Teresa.

Ⓑ Madame Cake.   Ⓓ The Headless Queen.

3. The storming of the Bastille took place on July 14,

Ⓐ 1776.   Ⓒ 1792.

Ⓑ 1789.   Ⓓ 1795.

4. The leaders of the Reign of Terror were Marat, Robespierre, and Danton.

Ⓐ True   Ⓑ False

5. Napoleon declared himself Emperor of France in

Ⓐ 1799.   Ⓒ 1812.

Ⓑ 1804.   Ⓓ 1815.

6. The man known as the liberator of Haiti was

Ⓐ Bernardo O'Higgins.   Ⓒ Napoleon.

Ⓑ Jean-Jacques Dessaline.   Ⓓ Toussaint L'Ouverture.

7. Simón Bolivar is the national hero of

Ⓐ Venezuela.   Ⓒ Peru.

Ⓑ Argentina.   Ⓓ Chile.

8. José de San Martín fought with Bernardo O'Higgins to free

Ⓐ Ireland.   Ⓒ Brazil.

Ⓑ Saint-Domingue.   Ⓓ Chile.

9. Benito Juarez and his liberal government tried to

Ⓐ equalize land ownership.   Ⓒ conquer the United States.

Ⓑ raise taxes.   Ⓓ conquer France.

10. Maximilian was sent by France to take over the Mexican government because

Ⓐ Santa Anna died.   Ⓒ Hidalgo asked France for help.

Ⓑ Napoleon wanted Mexico.   Ⓓ Conservatives feared Juarez.

Chapter 16
The American Civil War—A House Divided

Less than a hundred years after the United States won its war for independence against England, the young nation was almost torn apart by another fight for freedom—this time a war within. Even though the states were united under one central government, the different regions of the country had grown up under such different economic and social conditions that by the 1850s they were seeing each other as opponents rather than as members of the same Union.

The North had developed an economy primarily based on industry and manufacturing. The whir and clatter of machinery set the tempo for the rhythm of life, as factories large and small churned out goods of every description, from children's shoes to railroad trains. A constant stream of people drawn to the big cities, both from Europe and from the surrounding countryside, provided plenty of labor for the factories. The countryside was spangled with small farms, mostly family-owned and op-

erated, which grew crops to be sold in local markets and nearby cities. The South meanwhile had followed an opposite path. There, factories were few and far between. Cotton and tobacco reigned supreme—crops grown on a grand scale in that ideal climate and sold to eager buyers all over the world. The rhythm of life was set by the droning of insects, the rustling of leaves, and the work songs of slaves in the fields.

From its beginnings in the early 1600s, the use of African slaves as workers on the enormous cotton and

Outbreak of the Civil War, 1861

Union States and Territories

Border States and Territories

Confederate States and Territories

176

The smell of smoke and sweat mingled with the grime of factories in the North's big cities.

Plantation owners in the South depended on slave labor.

tobacco plantations had become the driving force of the South's economy. Only a very small percentage of Southern whites actually were wealthy enough themselves to own slaves, but the wealthier ones often owned a great many. Slavery came to be seen as a natural and indispensable part of the Southern way of life.

Slavery was unpopular with most Northerners. Some found it morally repulsive, a stain on the nation's conscience. Others saw it as a political evil, translating the conflict between agriculture and industry into a conflict between pro- and anti-slavery forces. People who wanted to do away with, or abolish, slavery were called "abolitionists" (or much worse names in the South!). Many Northern states passed laws to limit or abolish slavery.

In 1808, Congress prohibited any further importation of slaves into the United States. Defying the law, smugglers continued to bring men and women bought in the West Indies into Southern ports. Federal authorities trying to stop this illegal traffic received scant cooperation from Southerners. Resentment grew—between North and South, between agriculture and industry, between slave state and free state, between the federal government and the state governments.

As the nation grew westward, it became clear that its ultimate fate depended on whether the new states joining the Union were to permit or prohibit slavery. If the new states were slave states, the South would gain power in Congress, and vice versa for the North. Various attempts were made to solve the issue. The Missouri Compromise

in 1820 set a continent-wide extension of the Mason-Dixon Line, the southern border of the state of Pennsylvania, as the dividing line between slave and free states. But the Compromise of 1850 disregarded the Missouri Compromise and admitted California to the Union as a free state. In 1854 the Kansas-Nebraska Bill admitted Kansas as a state, allowing the people to decide for themselves whether they would or would not have slaves. The new state soon earned the nickname, "Bloody Kansas," as the debate over slavery erupted into violence and hatred.

The slaves knew that to the North lay freedom, and despite the danger and the hardship some escaped, traveling at night with the North Star as their guide. Whites sympathetic to the plight of the slaves helped them by providing safe hiding places and food along the way. The route from one safe haven to the next became known as the Underground Railroad, and many slaves found freedom waiting at the end of the line.

When slave owners tried to recover what they considered to be "lost property," northerners resorted to arms to protect the fugitive slaves from their former masters. In 1850, Congress passed the Fugitive Slave Law, which gave slave owners the right to pursue and recapture runaways. Many Northern states responded by passing Personal Liberty Acts, which guaranteed protection and a fair trial to recaptured slaves. The ultimate affront to abolitionists came in 1857 with the Supreme Court's Dred Scott decision, which declared that slaveholders moving into free states could take their slaves with them without changing the status of the slaves.

In 1858 a series of seven debates took place in Illinois between Stephen A. Douglas, a Democratic senator, and Republican Abraham Lincoln, who was campaigning for Douglas's seat in Congress. Douglas supported the notion of "popular sovereignty"—each new state deciding for its own on the issue of slavery. Lincoln held to the position that all new states must be free, but that slavery could continue in states where it already existed. These debates were closely followed all over the country, and established Lincoln as a politician to be reckoned with.

Abraham Lincoln was born in Kentucky. As a child he moved with his family from Kentucky to Indiana, and from there to Illinois. Well over six feet tall, strong and self-educated, he worked at many jobs as a young man, earning local fame for his honesty and his skill as a rail-splitter. When he was nineteen years old, he made a trip down the Mississippi River on a flatboat and saw the reality of slavery for the first time. He was revolted by the sight and was later quoted as saying, "As I would not be a slave, neither would I be a master." He went on to study law,

entered politics, and in the election of 1860 became the Republican candidate for President of the United States.

In 1859 John Brown, a militant abolitionist from Kansas with financial backing from prominent New England anti-slavery groups, had led a raid against the army arsenal at Harpers Ferry, Virginia. Brown believed that his opening blow would bring slaves flocking to join him in the fight for freedom. But the raid was unsuccessful. The slaves did not rise up. Government forces commanded by Colonel Robert E. Lee quickly apprehended Brown and his men. They were found guilty of treason and hung on December 2, 1859. Many in the South believed that the Republicans had supported Brown and his attack.

As he campaigned, Lincoln denied the charges and reiterated his party's position on slavery: that it should spread no further, but could continue where it was. At the same time he did not conceal his own disapproval of the institution of slavery.

Lincoln was elected President in November of 1860. By the time of his inauguration the nation was already in crisis. Several Southern states had already withdrawn from the Union. In a constitutional convention lasting only three days they had formed a new nation, the Confederate States

178

New advances in communications let the whole country know of Lincoln's success in the Lincoln-Douglas debates.

The North entered the war with confidence. They had all the manpower, resources, and equipment the South lacked.

Jefferson Davis' rebel soldiers fought with the courage of their convictions.

of America. With Jefferson Davis, a former U.S. senator as president, and a constitution that made slavery an inalienable right, the Confederate States moved at once to seize all federal property within their borders. In South Carolina, one of the first states to secede, federal troops under the command of Major Robert Anderson were barricaded in Fort Sumter on a tiny island in Charleston Bay, besieged by rebel forces.

By the time Lincoln took office in March, Fort Sumter was running out of food. The Confederacy declared that any attempt to reinforce or resupply the fort would be considered an act of war. In early April Lincoln advised the governor of South Carolina that he was sending food to the fort. Confederate President Davis responded by ordering a full-scale bombardment of the fort. Major Anderson, out of food and ammunition, surrendered the fort and his troops the next day.

The war had begun. In the North, where it was viewed as an insurrection, or rebellion, it was called the "Civil War." In the South it was called the "War Between the States." In its essence, the Civil War was not about slavery, although the divisive issue had certainly created much enmity between the two sides. The war was fought to test and to set the balance of power between the fed-

eral government and the government of each individual state. How far could any state go in resisting central authority? How far could the federal government go in forcing its will on any state? That was the real issue to Lincoln, anyway. He believed it was his duty to preserve the Union at all costs. At first he referred to the crisis as a rebellion to be quickly put down. But within a month of the fall of Fort Sumter, eleven states had joined the Confederacy, and Lincoln began to prepare for all-out war.

The North entered the war with a confidence bordering on cockiness. It had almost ten million able-bodied men against a little more than one million in the South (not including 500,000 slaves, of course, whom the Southerners were obviously reluctant to arm). The North had nine out of every ten factories in the U.S.—the Confederacy had only two factories capable of producing weapons and munitions. The North had an abundant food supply—most of the land in the South was devoted to cotton and tobacco, which are hardly what anyone would call good eating. Most important, the North had an already functioning government, an army and a navy, systematic taxation, and a stable economy, all of which the newly formed Confederacy had to hammer out from scratch.

But the South had its strong points, too. And by far the

most valuable of its assets was a core group of military leaders made up of the cream of the crop of the former U.S. Army, most of whom hailed from Virginia. Colonel Robert E. Lee, a West Point graduate, was asked by President Lincoln to assume command of the entire Union Army. He chose to serve the South instead.

And too, the men and boys who answered Jefferson Davis' call for 100,000 Confederate soldiers fought with the spirit of rebellion and the passion of defending their homes and their way of life. But at the same time, the men of the North responded with patriotic fervor to President Lincoln's call for 75,000 volunteers.

First to command the North's Army of the Potomac was General George B. McClellan. His abilities as an organizer and as an inspiration to his troops were unequaled. But in the face of battle he proved to be cautious and timid. Even with the sure knowledge that he had more troops and artillery than the enemy, he hesitated to attack Lee's Army of Northern Virginia.

At the first Battle of Bull Run in July, 1861, Union forces, hampered by inexperienced leadership, retreated in panic just when victory was within their grasp. It was the same story at the Battle of Seven Pines and again at the Battle of Seven Days. Early in the war it seemed as if the mighty Union Army did not know how to fight, and the Southerners, under the command of their brilliant military leaders, won more than their share of the early battles. But then the tables turned.

Lee ordered a huge force of 50,000 men to head north, intending to invade Maryland and encircle Washington D.C. But the Confederate troops were met by McClellan's 100,000 man army. They clashed at a place called Antietam Creek. In this one bloody battle, Lee lost more than 20 percent of his soldiers, while the North suffered 10 percent killed or wounded. McClellan still had more than 80,000 troops, vastly outnumbering the fleeing remnants of Lee's army, but instead of pursuing, he rested his troops and allowed Lee's battered army to escape. To Lincoln, who saw Antietam as a missed opportunity to end the war in short order, it was a hollow victory. Exasperated by McClellan's timidity, he turned the army over to the command of General Ambrose E. Burnside.

But the victory at Antietam convinced Lincoln that the time was right for another move he had long considered—the emancipation of the slaves. The already strong Northern moral opposition to slavery, and a growing bitterness over the cost of the war in lives and money, had made emancipation an overwhelmingly popular cause in the North. On January 1, 1863 President Lincoln issued the Emancipation Proclamation, which declared that

The toll in lives lost and limbs shattered was terrible as brother faced brother on the field of battle.

Ulysses S. Grant—his nickname, "Unconditional Surrender," came from his initials. It also accurately described his approach to warfare.

". . . all persons held as slaves within states in rebellion against the United States. . . shall be. . . forever free. . . ." By the end of the war, 180,000 freedmen and free blacks from both the North and the South, had enlisted in the Union Army. They fought for the Union and for freedom too.

In the spring of 1863 Lee led his army on another advance to the North. They met the Union force, under General Meade now, at Gettysburg, Pennsylvania, and a bloody battle ensued. When it was over three days later, again Lee was defeated, and again the Union Army did not push on to total victory. At the same time the Union Army of the West, commanded by a gruff, cigar-chomping general by the name of Ulysses S. Grant, captured Vicksburg, Mississippi, effectively gaining control of the Missisippi River and cutting the South in half. Grant did not rest his troops after the victory at Vicksburg, but instead pushed on without hesitation into

Georgia. At long last, Lincoln had found his general. In the spring of 1864 Lieutenant General U.S. Grant, a West Point graduate and a veteran of the Mexican War, became the Supreme Commander of the Union Armies.

As Grant and his army moved on the Confederate capital at Richmond, Virginia, General William Tecumseh Sherman and his Union troops captured Atlanta, Georgia, and then pressed on to Savannah and the sea. It was Sherman who said that war is hell, and it was Sherman who made it so. His army cut a swath of total destruction sixty miles wide as it moved across Georgia and then up the coast into South and North Carolina.

Civil War doctors did the best they could under the worst of conditions. Amputation, with no sterilization or anesthetic, was often the only way to save a life.

181

Robert E. Lee, one of the greatest leaders in the history of the U.S. military, was offered command of the Union Army. He chose to fight for the South instead.

The defeat of the South brought an end to its slavery-based way of life and left thousands of southerners, black and white, searching desperately for new beginnings.

At Appomattox Courthouse, Grant allowed Confederate soldiers to keep their horses so they could return to working their fields.

Grant's progress toward Richmond was relentless and unstoppable. Day after day his men moved forward; mile by mile, yard by yard, foot by foot, life by life, as the death toll mounted and the goal came nearer.

On April 9, 1865, at Appomattox Courthouse in Virginia, Lee surrendered the Confederate Army of Northern Virginia to Grant, and the war was over. From the Confederate States of America, Grant demanded total and unconditional surrender. But with the men of the Confederate Army he was sympathetic and kind, requiring simply that they surrender their weapons and return to their homes. When Lee explained that some of his men owned their own horses and could use them on their farms, Grant let them ride away.

More than 600,000 men had been killed or wounded, and the South had been devastated. But the Union was whole again and slavery had been abolished forever. President Lincoln accepted the cheers of the crowd gathered on the White House lawn as the peace was announced. Just a few short weeks before he had taken the oath of office for his second term, and in his second Inaugural Address, with the peace well in sight, he'd urged an end to the bitterness of war: "With malice towards none, with charity for all," he said, "let us bind up the nation's wounds. . . ."

But Lincoln never had the chance to lead the nation back to health. On the night of April 14, 1865, while watching a play at Ford's Theater in Washington, he was shot in the head by an actor and Confederate sympathizer named John Wilkes Booth. The next morning he was dead, and the country was plunged into the most intense mourning it had ever known.

John Wilkes Booth did his beloved South no favor when he killed the man who had overseen its defeat. For many in the North were less compassionate than Lincoln, and few were more capable. Without Lincoln's guiding hand, the years following the war became a time of bitter memories and revenge, and the chance to give the freed peoples their rightful place in society was lost.

With the end of the war came the challenge of rebuilding the nation. Would the U.S. be different today if Lincoln had lived?

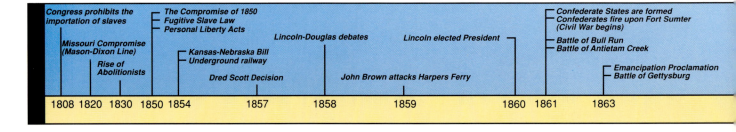

Congress prohibits the importation of slaves	The Compromise of 1850 — Fugitive Slave Law — Personal Liberty Acts				Confederate States are formed — Confederates fire upon Fort Sumter (Civil War begins)
Missouri Compromise (Mason-Dixon Line)		Lincoln-Douglas debates	Lincoln elected President	Battle of Bull Run — Battle of Antietam Creek
Rise of Abolitionists	Kansas-Nebraska Bill — Underground railway			
	Dred Scott Decision	John Brown attacks Harpers Ferry		Emancipation Proclamation — Battle of Gettysburg
1808 1820 1830 1850 1854	1857	1858	1859	1860 1861 1863

Quiz

1. **Before the Civil War, the two main crops in the South were**

   Ⓐ cotton and corn.
   Ⓒ corn and wheat.
   Ⓑ corn and tobacco.
   Ⓓ cotton and tobacco.

2. **Before the war,**

   Ⓐ the North was industrial.
   Ⓒ the South was industrial.
   Ⓑ the South was anti-slavery.
   Ⓓ the North was pro-slavery.

3. **The southern border of the state of Pennsylvania was also called**

   Ⓐ the Missouri Compromise.
   Ⓒ the Underground Railroad.
   Ⓑ the Kansas-Nebraska Line.
   Ⓓ the Mason-Dixon line.

4. **Under popular sovereignty, each new state could choose whether or not to legalize slavery.**

   Ⓐ True
   Ⓑ False

5. **Fort Sumter was in _____, one of the first states to secede from the Union.**

   Ⓐ South Carolina.
   Ⓒ Georgia.
   Ⓑ North Carolina.
   Ⓓ Virginia.

6. **Jefferson Davis was elected president of the Confederate States of America.**

   Ⓐ True
   Ⓑ False

7. **The North won the first Battle of Bull Run.**

   Ⓐ True
   Ⓑ False

8. **The Emancipation Proclamation resulted in many freed slaves joining the Union Army.**

   Ⓐ True
   Ⓑ False

9. **The Union general who accepted Robert E. Lee's surrender was**

   Ⓐ George McClellan.
   Ⓒ U.S. Grant.
   Ⓑ Ambrose E. Burnside.
   Ⓓ William Tecumseh Sherman.

10. **President Lincoln was assassinated by**

    Ⓐ John Wilkes Booth.
    Ⓒ John Brown.
    Ⓑ Robert E. Lee.
    Ⓓ Jefferson Davis.

General U.S. Grant becomes Commander of Union Army
General William Sherman captures Atlanta, Georgia and Savannah

Robert E. Lee surrenders
Civil War ends
Lincoln assassinated by John Wilkes Booth

1864   1865

Gandhi led the people of India to independence without the use of violence. His ideas about civil disobedience inspired other great leaders like Martin Luther King, Jr.

Chapter 17

The Age of Imperialism

184

It is very hot—perhaps 110°— as the procession slowly makes its way through the dusty streets of the village. Villagers hurry out to greet you and offer you water. As you pause to swallow a few mouthfuls of the precious liquid, you notice a knot of British soldiers watching the procession from the shade of a palm tree. Quickly you look away. Although the march has been peaceful so far, their guns make you nervous. More than once, Mahatma's non-violent methods have been met by British steel.

Just as you rejoin the procession, a cry rings out from the front of the line. "The sea! The sea!" The cheering marchers quicken their pace. Soon your feet are bathed by the cool waters of the Indian Ocean. Trailing behind the small, frail figure of Mohandas K. Gandhi, you have marched two hundred miles to collect salt from the ocean rather than pay the unfair British tax.

Some of your friends laughed when you announced your plans to participate in the march. "Your civil disobedience is a waste of time," they said. "The British will never grant India its independence." But you have faith. With Gandhi's leadership, you know that some day India will be free.

It was the Age of Imperialism. Britain, though the leader in the imperial sweepstakes, was by no means the only player. The latter half of the eighteenth century saw land grabs by nearly all the European nations and by latecomer Japan. Conquest and colonization were nothing new, of course; but in the late 1800s two recent developments combined to create an imperial frenzy that left virtually no part of the earth untouched.

The first of these factors was the Industrial Revolution. Machines made it possible to manufacture goods on a scale never before imagined. But with increased production came an increased demand for raw materials, and a need for new markets in which to sell the finished goods. By taking possession of weaker, less developed countries, the industrialized nations could claim their raw materials and markets for themselves.

Equally important to the growth of imperialism was the rise of nationalism. Way back in 1789 the French Revolution had filled people's heads with dreams of national unity and popular rule. Yet, fifty years later, many dreams of nationhood remained unfulfilled. The Italian peninsula, for example, contained about thirty separate states or provinces, many of which were controlled by Austria, France, or Spain. Local kings feared that unification would bring an end to their power and the Roman Catholic Church had no desire to give up control of *its* states in Central Italy. But in spite of these obstacles, the Italian nationalist movement grew. One of the most ardent supportes of unification was Guiseppe Mazzini, often called "the soul of Italian unity." He dreamed of an Italy where democracy and independence would go hand in hand. Mazzini led an ill-fated rebellion among the Italian states—a rebellion that was promptly crushed by French and Austrian forces. But the fires of nationalism were not extinguished. Instead the torch passed to a new kind of nationalist.

That man was Count Camillo di Cavour. A skilled politician, Cavour was prime minister of Sardinia, the only state ruled by an Italian king. Where Mazzini had been an idealist, Cavour was a realist—the so-called brain of Italian unity. The way to unite the country, he believed, was not through a democratic uprising but through political maneuvering, by pitting one ruling power against the other. In 1859 he put his plan into action. After signing a secret alliance with France, Cavour declared war on Austria. With France's help, Austria was defeated and its former provinces in northern Italy were incorporated into the kingdom of Sardinia.

While Cavour was unifying northern Italy, Guiseppe Garibaldi and his red-shirted followers were waging a daring campaign to free the southern island of Sicily. Despite being ill-trained and poorly armed, they seized control of the island in only six weeks—winning for Garibaldi the popular title "the sword of Italian unity." The victorious Garibaldi headed north, intending to liberate Rome and unify all of Italy. But Cavour had no inten-

tion of allowing Garibaldi to complete his mission. The rebels' victory in the south had served Cavour's own purposes, but if Italy were to be united, it would be united under Sardinian rule. So Cavour marched southward with Sardinian troops and met up with Garibaldi just outside of Rome. Cavour was quite prepared to fight but that proved to be unnecessary. When confronted by Cavour, Garibaldi handed over control of his troops and his conquests. Galloping up to Sardinian King Victor Emmanuel, he waved his hat and cried, "I hail the first king of Italy!"

Like Italy, Germany was deeply affected by the revolts that swept Europe in the aftermath of the French Revolution. The Vienna Congress had resulted in thirty-nine separate German states, dominated by Prussia and, to a lesser degree, Austria. The desire for unification had grown, until, by 1848, it had become nearly universal. A National Assembly was elected in that year to write a constitution, but liberals and conservatives differed violently on what form the unified government should take. When fighting broke out between the two camps, the Prussian King Frederick Wilhelm sent in the army and broke up the assembly. The liberals fled, and from that point on, German nationalism took a decidedly undemocratic turn.

In 1862 Otto von Bismarck became prime minister of Prussia. Bismarck was an aristocrat with open contempt for "tedious humanitarian babblers." It was his belief that German unification could only be accomplished "not through speeches and majority decisions...but by blood and iron." Prussia began to militarize. In 1864 Bismarck provoked a conflict with Denmark as an excuse to declare war against that country (a tactic that would later be used by Adolph Hitler). After defeating Denmark, the

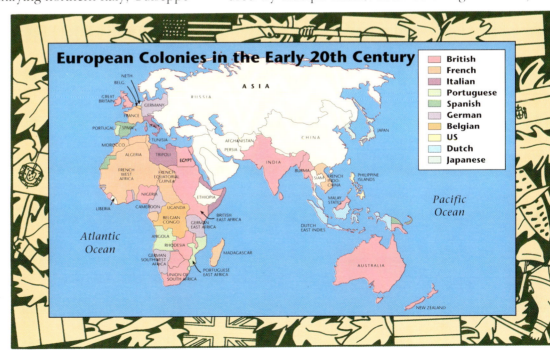

European Colonies in the Early 20th Century

British
French
Italian
Portuguese
Spanish
German
Belgian
US
Dutch
Japanese

Bismarck used blood and iron to forge the modern nation of Germany.

Prussian war machine turned against its rival Austria. The brief but decisive Seven Weeks War resulted in Austria's downfall, whereby Prussia assumed control of all of northern Germany. Another "incident"—this time involving the French ambassador—led to the Franco-Prussian War of 1870. The overconfident French were unprepared for the modern and highly efficient Prussian army. In less than six months France was defeated and forced to surrender the resource-rich border provinces of Alsace and Lorraine. With Prussia's victory over France, the southern German states joined with the north and Germany was united at last. Amid much celebrating, Wilhelm I of Prussia was proclaimed Kaiser of the second German *Reich*. But the new nation bore little resemblance to the democratic state dreamed of by the early nationalists. Democracy and individual rights had been replaced by militarism and autocratic rule. Feelings of national pride had been transformed into a warlike belief in national superiority.

It was this aggressive nationalism, combined with the need for markets and raw materials, that fueled the race for empire in the late 1800s. "Virile peoples establish colonies" was an often repeated sentiment of the times. European leaders applied Darwin's new theory of "survival of the fittest" to the political world, citing it as "scientific" justification for imperialist acts. The powerful nations of the world, they insisted, had the right, if not the duty, to decide the fate of inferior nations.

Imperialism in Asia

The peninsula and islands of Southeast Asia were first visited by Europeans in the 1500s. Portuguese spice traders built trading posts on several islands in the East Indies. The Spanish were the first to reach the Philippines, which they promptly conquered. The Dutch arrived in Southeast Asia in the 1600s, and eventually took control of most of the East Indies where they established a colony called the Dutch East Indies. For many years, European interest in Southeast Asia was limited mainly to the islands. Not until the 1700s did Europeans begin to colonize the Southeast Asian peninsula, which comprises the modern-day nations of Thailand, Malaysia, Vietnam, Laos, and Cambodia. At first the Europeans built plantations on the mainland and raised cash crops such as coffee, tea, and sugar. Then, with the beginning of the industrial revolution, the peninsula became an important source of raw materials. Britain and France, the first countries to industrialize, took the lead in establishing colonies on the peninsula.

Along with the French industrialists who descended on Vietnam came missionaries—mostly Catholic priests—who converted many Vietnamese to Christianity. But the emperor Tu-Duc was resentful of the new religion and vowed to expel Christianity from the land. Thousands of Vietnamese Christians and many French priests were put to death. To protect their remaining missionaries in Vietnam, the French sent troops to the peninsula. Once established, the French military presence in Southeast Asia grew until, by the end of the nineteenth century, the French controlled not only Vietnam, but also Laos and Cambodia. Together, the three countries formed the colony of French Indochina.

As the European nations sought to extend their influence throughout the world, their eyes turned toward China, which had been isolated from foreign contact for centuries. The Manchus, who had conquered China in 1644, had little tolerance for other Chinese and no use whatsoever for European "barbarians." Under the rule of the Manchus' Ch'ing dynasty, Chinese ports were closed to European ships. The one exception was Canton, which was open to British merchants as long as they remained confined to a small district of the city. The British kept pushing for increased trade between the two countries, but although Chinese tea and silk were in great demand in the West, the Chinese had no interest in British goods. They insisted on being paid for their tea and silk in silver. Needless to say, the balance of trade was not in Britain's favor.

Then, in the early 1800s the British found something the Chinese *did* want: opium, which Britain could obtain cheaply and plentifully in India. British merchants began importing the dangerous drug in volume. They found a receptive audience among the Chinese population, who were miserable from 150 years of Manchu rule. As opium addiction began to spread through China, the balance of trade began to shift in favor of Britain. The Chinese government moved quickly to outlaw the opium trade, but British traders continued to smuggle huge quantities of the drug into the country, reaping enormous profits in return.

In 1839 a Manchu official seized and burned 20,000 chests of opium that had been smuggled into Canton aboard a British merchant ship. To preserve the nation's honor—and its lucrative drug trade—Britain sent naval forces to China. Although the Chinese far outnumbered the British, their antiquated navy was no match for British cannons and steam-powered warships. After a series of fierce but one-sided battles known as the Opium War, Britain defeated China and forced it to accept the 1842 Treaty of Nanking—the first of what China called the "Unequal Treaties." Under the terms of the treaty, China had to repay Britain for the destroyed opium as well as for the cost of the war. It was forced to give up the island of Hong Kong and to open four additional mainland ports to British ships. Lastly, British merchants were granted total immunity from Chinese law.

The other nations of Europe began to make their own demands on the weakened Manchu government. China soon found itself divided into "spheres of influence," each controlled by a different foreign power. Russia controlled Manchuria in northern China. Britain, France, Germany, and some of the smaller European countries each held a sphere of influence along the coast. No other nations were allowed to trade in these zones. Japan joined the party in 1894 when it went to war with China over control of Korea, a nation to which both China and Japan had historical ties. Japan won. As a result, Korea gained its "independence" (which in reality meant Japanese control), and Japan gained the island of Taiwan as well as a small sphere of influence on mainland China. The European nations took advantage of China's defeat to tighten their own grips on the country. The humiliated Chinese were displeased by this situation, but they were powerless to change it. The United States was displeased too, but for different reasons. The U.S. feared that China would be divided up into outright colonies. If that were to happen, America would be left without a share of the pie. It was already too late to claim exclusive rights to any part of China, so the Americans tried a different approach. Secretary of State John Hay sent a note to European leaders outlining a plan that came to be known as the Open Door Policy. In his note Hay requested that all nations be allowed to trade freely throughout China. The European nations agreed with the Open Door Policy in theory, since free trade was believed to be in everyone's best interest. However, when it came right down to giving up exclusive control of its sphere of influence, none of the nations was in any hurry to make the first move. Undeterred, Hay promptly notified each power that the others had agreed. Since it was therefore unanimous, he said, the United States would consider the terms of the Open Door Policy "final and definitive." Hay's bluff worked. In time, most of the nations of Europe accepted the Open Door Policy.

The 1894 war between Japan and China marked Japan's entry into the imperialist sweepstakes. Japan's victory in that war was the result of a painful but successful program of modernization that began in the 1850s. For centuries prior to that, Japan had been almost totally isolated from all contact with the West. So extreme was Japanese isolationism that foreign sailors who were shipwrecked on Japanese shores could be arrested or killed.

Japan had received a rude awakening in 1853, when four American warships headed by Commodore Matthew Perry sailed into Tokyo Harbor. Perry bore a message from President Franklin Pierce to the Shogun ruler requesting "friendship, commerce, a supply of coal and provision (for whalers operating in the waters off Japan), and protection for our shipwrecked people." Although the request was stated in the most diplomatic of terms, Perry's warships conveyed a different message! The Japanese government tried to stall, saying it would consider the

The British navy smashed its Chinese opposition in the Opium War of 1839.

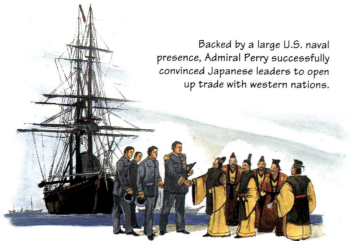

Backed by a large U.S. naval presence, Admiral Perry successfully convinced Japanese leaders to open up trade with western nations.

American request, but a year later Perry returned with an even larger force. In the face of this threat the Shogun had no choice but to open up Japan to U.S. trade. A treaty signed in 1858 granted U.S. merchant ships access to two Japanese ports. The European nations rushed to demand the same trade rights that had been granted to the United States. Within a year Japan had signed treaties with Britain, Russia, France, and the Netherlands.

Reluctantly, Japan began trading with the outside world. Some Japanese, realizing that the days of shoguns and samurai warriors were gone forever, were all in favor of opening the country up to outside influences. Others believed that exposure to Western ideas would only ruin Japanese culture. They wanted to expel the "barbarians" and return Japan to the old ways. The government hoped that foreign trade would bring increased prosperity, but

while some Japanese did get rich, many more found their traditional livelihoods destroyed. Angry mobs began attacking foreigners and Shogun supporters in the streets. For the first time the emperor spoke out against the government, declaring that if the present situation continued "the national glory which has lasted for thousands of years will be utterly tarnished." Japanese citizens rallied behind him. When he issued an imperial edict stating that all foreigners must leave Japan within twenty days, he received so much popular support that the Shogun was afraid to override the emperor's rash pronouncement.

Needless to say, the foreigners had no desire to leave. Too much money was at stake. Instead, in 1865 a combined fleet of British, French, and American warships sailed into Osaka Bay, and the emperor was forced to back down. But although he failed to expel the Westerners from Japan, he succeeded in restoring the power and prestige that had once belonged to the imperial family. Shogun rule was over. In 1868 the 15-year-old Emperor Mutshito assumed the throne, beginning an era in Japanese history known as the Meiji Empire, meiji meaning "enlightened rule."

The new emperor understood that the only way to preserve Japan's independence in the face of European imperialism was to increase his country's strength. It was once believed that modernization would mean the destruction of Japanese heritage.

188

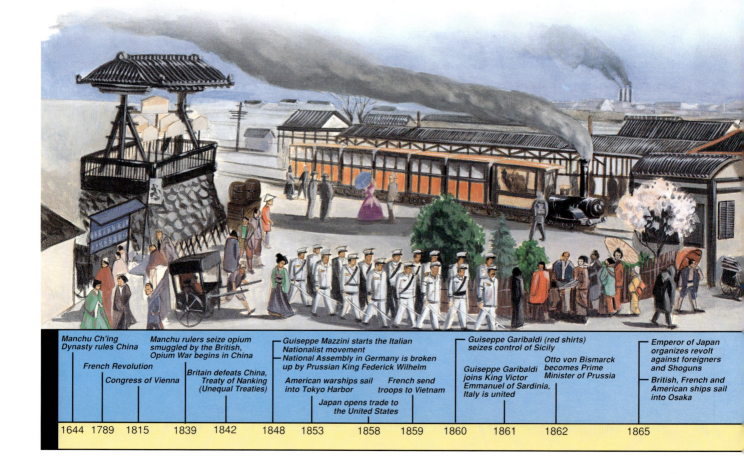

Manchu Ch'ing Dynasty rules China		Manchu rulers seize opium smuggled by the British, Opium War begins in China		Guiseppe Mazzini starts the Italian Nationalist movement			Guiseppe Garibaldi (red shirts) seizes control of Sicily			Emperor of Japan organizes revolt against foreigners and Shoguns
	French Revolution		Britain defeats China, Treaty of Nanking (Unequal Treaties)	National Assembly in Germany is broken up by Prussian King Federick Wilhelm				Otto von Bismarck becomes Prime Minister of Prussia		
		Congress of Vienna		American warships sail into Tokyo Harbor	French send troops to Vietnam		Guiseppe Garibaldi joins King Victor Emmanuel of Sardinia, Italy is united			British, French and American ships sail into Osaka
					Japan opens trade to the United States					
1644	1789	1815	1839	1842	1848	1853	1858	1859	1860	1861	1862	1865

Now the Emperor realized that he could take advantage of Western science and technology in order to make Japan a world power. He began a series of reforms aimed at building Japan's military and industrial might. The Meiji government abolished the old feudal system, replacing clan rulers with government appointees. Local samurai bands gave way to a national imperial army with a three-year military service requirement for all Japanese males. The government proclaimed universal education, causing the literacy rate to explode. But the greatest progress took place in Japanese industry. Steel mills, shipyards, power plants, and other industries essential to military production were the first to grow. Others soon followed, and by 1890 Japan had become the first industrialized nation in Asia.

Like all industrialized nations, Japan needed raw materials for its industries and markets for its manufactured goods. And like the nations of Europe whose imperialism had been driven by nationalism, Japan viewed the establishment of an empire as not just a necessity, but a right. The 1894 conflict with China came first. Japan's easy victory in that war brought it new respect from the European powers. Ten years later Japan clinched its reputation as a new world power by winning a war with Russia.

Like Japan's earlier war with China, the Russo-Japanese War of 1904 was waged over control of Korea, to which Russia had tried to stake a claim. Once again, Japan came out the victor. Russia was forced to turn over to Japan its sphere of influence in Manchuria. Even more important than its territorial gains, Japan's defeat of Russia placed it in a position of power among the nations of the world. For the first time an Asian nation had defeated a European nation. Imperialist Japan was now a force to be reckoned with.

Increased contact with the Western world led to rapid westernization of Japan's ancient culture.

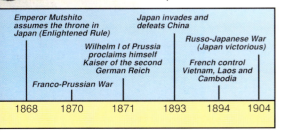

Emperor Mutshito assumes the throne in Japan (Enlightened Rule)

Franco-Prussian War

Wilhelm I of Prussia proclaims himself Kaiser of the second German Reich

Japan invades and defeats China

Russo-Japanese War (Japan victorious)

French control Vietnam, Laos and Cambodia

| 1868 | 1870 | 1871 | 1893 | 1894 | 1904 |

Quiz

1. Which of the following was not a reason why imperialist nations established colonies?

Ⓐ the colonies' technology   Ⓒ the colonies' raw materials
Ⓑ They felt it was their right.   Ⓓ to demonstrate their power

2. The "brain of Italian unity," the man who engineered the country's unification, was named

Ⓐ Giuseppe Garibaldi.   Ⓒ Giuseppe Mazzini.
Ⓑ Benito Mussolini.   Ⓓ Camillo di Cavour.

3. Who was Otto von Bismarck?

Ⓐ first *Kaiser* of Germany   Ⓒ author of German constitution
Ⓑ Prussian who unified Germany   Ⓓ Austrian general

4. British traders went to China seeking

Ⓐ coffee, sugar, and chocolate.   Ⓒ tea and silk.
Ⓑ opium.   Ⓓ manufactured goods.

5. The Open Door Policy

Ⓐ opened American ports.   Ⓒ urged free trade with China.
Ⓑ allowed Chinese immigration.   Ⓓ urged free trade in Europe.

6. In 1894 Japan went to war with

Ⓐ Russia.   Ⓒ Korea.
Ⓑ China.   Ⓓ Prussia.

7. The only Chinese port not open to European ships during the Ch'ing Dynasty was Canton.

Ⓐ True   Ⓑ False

8. Which of the following was not a contributing factor to the downfall of Japan's Shogun government?

Ⓐ defeat in the war against China   Ⓒ an economic crisis
Ⓑ fear of contact with the West   Ⓓ the Emperor's popularity

9. France sent troops to Vietnam

Ⓐ to enforce its trading rights.   Ⓒ to conquer Indochina.
Ⓑ to expel Portuguese traders.   Ⓓ to protect its missionaries.

10. Commodore Perry sailed into Tokyo Harbor to

Ⓐ force free trade with Japan.   Ⓒ defend American merchants.
Ⓑ enforce the Open Door Policy.   Ⓓ overthrow the Shogun.

British insensitivity to Indian culture led to the Sepoy Rebellion, when Hindu and Moslem soldiers refused to "bite the bullet."

The British Raj

"The sun never sets on the British empire." So went the well-known saying, and without exaggeration. So vast and far-flung were Britain's territories in 1900 that before the sun had set on the western edge of the empire it had already risen again in the east. An island nation of only 121,000 square miles, with a population of only 41 million, Britain at the turn of the century ruled an empire of over 11 million square miles and a colonial population of 345 million.

Of all the colonies in the British Empire, the most valuable was India, the "jewel" in the British imperial crown. The British had first established a foothold in India in the early 1600s. From trading posts along the Indian coastline at Calcutta, Bombay, and Madras, the British East India Company conducted a profitable business. However, with the collapse of the ruling Mogul Empire in 1707, India lapsed into a period of anarchy and war that threatened British trade. The British East India Company began to fortify its trading posts. It raised its own army and began taking control of Indian territory, either by conquest or by making deals with local rajahs, or princes. Soon the company's agents were more powerful than the local rulers. As a result, the British East India Company controlled India for nearly a hundred years.

In 1857 a rebellion broke out among the Indian soldiers, called sepoys, who served in the company's army. British insensitivity to Indian culture had long been a source of unhappiness among the native population. The situation exploded when the East India Company demanded that its troops use a new kind of bullet, one that required the soldiers to bite off the ends of the cartridges, which were greased with the fat from cows and pigs. Since the consumption of pork products is forbidden to Moslems, and Hindus are prohibited from eating the meat of cows, the sepoys refused to comply with orders—refused to "bite the bullet," as it were. When British officers insisted, the sepoys rebelled, and the British Parliament was forced to send troops to put down the revolt. Many lives were lost. From then on the British government took over direct control of India. India was made a British colony, and in 1877, amid an elaborate spectacle, Queen Victoria of England was proclaimed Empress of India.

To the British, India was a valuable possession, and they guarded it jealously. So when the French tightened their hold on nearby Indochina in the 1880s, Britain viewed it as a threat. To keep the French from expanding toward India, Britain took over Burma as a buffer zone. Ceylon, Malaya, and Singapore were also added to the British crown. To safeguard India's northwest boundaries against invasion by Russia, Britain seized Afghanistan. Persia, which also lay between Russia and India, was divided into two spheres of influence.

Colonial status was a mixed blessing for India. Although British rule brought improvements such as roads, hospitals, and irrigation canals, it destroyed India's fragile native economy. Valuable raw materials were shipped off to Britain. British manufactured goods flooded Indian markets, putting local industries out of business. Traditional Indian spinners and weavers could not compete with the machine-made cloth which poured in from the textile mills of England. Additionally, the Indian people found themselves treated like second-class citizens in their own land, with little say in how their country was run. Positions of power in government and industry were filled by British citizens who banned Indians from their hotels, restaurants, and clubs. In 1890 only two percent of the officials of the Indian Civil Service were Indian!

Resistance to British rule began to mount. After a series of violent uprisings in the early 1900s, the colonial government began to allow more Indians into the ranks of power, but it was too little, too late. Then, in 1919 an incident took place that damaged British-Indian relations beyond repair. In the town of Amritsar, British troops massacred an unarmed crowd of protesters, killing nearly four hundred Indians and wounding 1,200 others. Horrified Indians everywhere swore to rid themselves of British rule.

In 1920 Mohandas K. Gandhi became leader of the Indian National Congress, an influential group formed in 1885 to win reforms for India. Gandhi brought to the Indian independence movement a revolutionary tactic for overcoming the British: nonviolent resistance. Gandhi knew that an armed uprising against the British could never succeed so he urged his followers to use peaceful methods instead. He instructed Indians to refuse to work in British mines, factories, and shops. He shut down the British rail system by getting thousands of Indian women to lay down on the tracks. When the British put a tax on salt—a necessary commodity in India's searing climate—he marched his followers two hundred miles to the sea to get salt from the ocean.

During India's twenty-year struggle for independence, Gandhi spent seven years in jail as a result of his acts of civil disobedience. Unfortunately, despite Gandhi's nonviolent example, the path to independence was marred by a bloody power struggle between Hindus and Moslems. In an attempt to stop the violence, Gandhi began a fast for peace that nearly cost him his life. But the fighting continued, and as a result the British were forced to divide India into two nations before granting independence in 1947. Part of the country became a Moslem nation called Pakistan. The rest of India remained in Hindu control. Shortly after independence, the man revered by his followers as Mahatma, an Indian word meaning "great soul," was assassinated by a Hindu gunman.

The British in Ireland

Britain's ties to Ireland go back even further than its ties to India. The "Irish problem" had plagued Britain ever since the Norman-English conquest of Ireland in the twelfth century. Ever since, a ruling class of wealthy Protestant Englishmen had controlled the land. The English landowners made life miserable for the poor Catholic peasants. In a common practice called "rack-renting," British absentee landlords charged Irish tenant farmers exhorbitant rents for the right to live on and work their land. So the religious, political, and economic inequalities that troubled Ireland in the late 1800s were nothing new. However, the situation had grown worse during the disastrous potato famine of the 1840s, when blight destroyed the entire potato crop—Ireland's basic food. The British failed to use their new railroads and steamships to provide relief to the starving peasants. The result was a medieval famine right in the heart of modern Europe. Tens of thousands of Irish died. Many others were forced to emigrate, mostly to the United States. Anti-British sentiment smoldered throughout the rest of the century. Several times, sympathetic British politicians introduced bills granting "Home Rule" to Ireland, but the bills were defeated each time by Conservative members of Parliament. In 1912 Home Rule finally passed, but it was immediately protested, not by British conservatives this time, but by Protestants in the Northern Ireland province of Ulster. The Protestants feared that if Ireland became independent, they would be overrun by the Catholics in southern Ireland. As a result they promised armed resistance to Home Rule. So a rider was added to the bill, declaring that Home Rule would not go into effect until the Ulster question was settled. Then the entire issue of Home Rule was interrupted by the outbreak of World War I.

To say that Ireland did not support the British war effort is an understatement. Ireland not only failed to side with Britain against Germany, one Irish faction actually

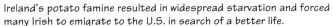
Ireland's potato famine resulted in widespread starvation and forced many Irish to emigrate to the U.S. in search of a better life.

used German arms to stage an anti-British rebellion in Dublin in 1916. By the time the war ended, the Irish Home Rule movement of 1914 had given way to the extremist Sinn Fein (Gaelic for "ourselves alone") for whom nothing but complete independence would do. The years 1919-1921 were filled with violence as Irish rebels waged a campaign of guerrilla warfare that including ambushes, murder, arson, and terror.

In 1921 the Sinn Fein split in two, and the more moderate of the two factions struck a bargain with Britain. As a result Ireland was divided in two. The six mostly-Protestant counties of Ulster maintained their old relationship with Britain and became Northern Ireland. The twenty-six Catholic counties of southern Ireland became a nation called the Irish Free State. The Irish Free State had its own Parliament and armed forces, but was still loosely tied to the British Crown. This arrangement failed to satisfy the Sinn Fein extremists. They began a new round of violence in an attempt to dissolve all ties to England and unite the entire country under Irish Catholic control. The Irish revolution turned into a civil war between supporters of the Free State and supporters of a united Irish republic. Eventually the situation settled down. The extremists, who had boycotted the Free State's government at first, ended up getting themselves elected to Parliament. In 1949, through peaceful means, they achieved their goal of severing all ties to Britain. The former Irish Free State became a totally independent nation called the Republic of Eire. The extremists' second goal, the unification of the entire island, continues to be a source of civil strife in Northern Ireland to this day.

Imperialism in Africa

In India it was the fall of the Mogul Empire that opened the door to European imperialism. In North Africa it was the weakening of the Ottoman Empire. As the Turks lost their hold on North Africa, several territories broke away and proclaimed their independence: first Morocco, then Egypt, Tunis, Tripoli, and Algiers. Without the might of empire to back them up, these new states were easy targets for the imperialist nations of Europe.

France took advantage of North Africa's vulnerability to establish the first French colony in Africa. For many years raiders from Algiers and other North African countries had attacked French ships in the Mediterranean. In 1830 France used these pirate attacks as an excuse to invade North Africa. Algiers became a French colony called Algeria.

In the 1880s France began expanding its North African empire. First it annexed part of Morocco and Tunis—

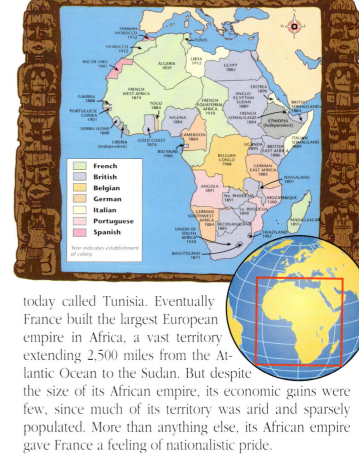

today called Tunisia. Eventually France built the largest European empire in Africa, a vast territory extending 2,500 miles from the Atlantic Ocean to the Sudan. But despite the size of its African empire, its economic gains were few, since much of its territory was arid and sparsely populated. More than anything else, its African empire gave France a feeling of nationalistic pride.

Britain, on the other hand, benefited in many ways from its African empire, which was second in size only to France's. British expansion into Africa was driven by men like Cecil Rhodes, for whom the nation of Rhodesia (now Zimbabwe) was named—a man who declared, "I would annex the planets if I could!" Britain's first African possession was Cape Colony in South Africa, which it acquired from the Dutch in 1814. Strategically located at the southern tip of the continent, Cape Colony had begun in 1652 as a Dutch trading post called Cape Town. Ships traveling around the Cape to Asia stopped at Cape Town to take on fresh water and supplies. Soon Dutch settlers, called Boers, began populating Cape Town, and by 1814 it had grown into a sizable colony.

British control quickly began to pose a threat to the Boers' way of life. First came the adoption of English as the official language. Next came the abolition of slavery throughout the British Empire in 1834. The Boers were fundamentalist Christians who believed that slavery was ordained by God. They had forced large numbers of black Africans to work as slaves on their farms. Now, rather than abide by Britain's anti-slavery law, thousands of Boers left Cape Colony on a huge migration northward called the Great Trek. They set up two new Boer republics, the Transvaal and the Orange Free State, where they were pretty much left alone by the British.

Then, in the 1880s the Boers discovered gold and diamond mines beneath the poor grazing land of the republics. As thousands of British settlers streamed into the Boer republics to seek their fortunes, tensions between the Boers and the British rose to the boiling point, resulting in a series of wars called the Boer Wars.

The Boers were finally defeated, but it was an ugly victory for Britain. British troops devastated Boer farms and fields. They imprisoned thousands of Boer men, women, and children in concentration camps, where 20,000 of them died from starvation and disease. After the war, the former Boer republics were combined with Cape Colony to form a single British colony called the Union of South Africa. As one of the terms of the Boers' surrender the British had promised to allow the colonists (that is, the white male colonists) to elect their own government. Since there were still more Boers than British in South Africa, the Boers gained control of the government. Under Boer leadership, blacks and "coloreds"—peoples of mixed blood—were deprived of nearly all their rights including the right to vote—a situation which persists into modern times.

Britain's imperialist expansion was not limited to the Cape. In 1882 Britain occupied Egypt, which had been under French influence since the days of Napoleon. The object of Britain's land grab was the Suez Canal, a 100-mile-long waterway linking the Mediterranean with the Red Sea. The Suez Canal had been built by a private French company. Its completion in 1869 made it possible for ships to travel from Europe to Asia without having to sail all the way around Africa, thereby cutting the length of the voyage in half.

Needless to say, the canal quickly became very important to Britain, since it provided a lifeline to India and other British colonies in Asia. The British decided to claim the canal for their own. This they did peacefully, thanks to some clever behind-the-scenes negotiating between British Prime Minister Benjamin Disraeli and the Egyptian ruler, the Khedive. The Khedive had been given 176,000 shares of stock by the Suez Canal Company as payment for his cooperation in the building of the canal. However, by 1875 the Khedive owed a great deal of money to European lenders. Desperate to raise some cash, he agreed to sell his shares in the canal to Disraeli at a very good price. Britain became the largest shareholder, thereby gaining control of the canal without firing a shot. A few years later all of Egypt became a British protectorate. As such it remained an independent nation, but its foreign policy was closely controlled by Britain.

For many years after the coastal areas of Africa became known to Europeans, the heart of the continent remained a mystery. Vast deserts and thick jungles made overland travel difficult. Rapids and waterfalls made it equally hard to travel by river. Some of the first explorers to penetrate the interior of the continent were missionaries, who set out to bring Christianity to the natives. The most famous of these nineteenth century missionaries was Dr. David Livingstone of Scotland. Livingstone "discovered" (that is, made known to Europeans) the Zambezi River and the enormous waterfall which he named Victoria Falls after England's Queen Victoria.

In 1865 Livingstone set out to find the source of the Nile. When nothing was heard from him for two years, a reporter named Henry Stanley was sent after him. After 126 days of travel Stanley caught up with his quarry, uttering the now-famous line, "Dr. Livingstone, I presume?" Fascinated by Africa, Stanley became an explorer in his own right. His speeches and writings generated a great deal of interest in Africa. When the Belgian King Leopold II learned about Stanley's exploration of the Congo River, he began to consider the commercial possibilities of the region. Leopold commissioned Stanley to survey the Congo river basin, and to build a chain of forts and trading posts there.

The Suez Canal provided Britain with a lifeline to its eastern colonies.

The Livingston expedition was awestruck by the thundering power of Victoria Falls.

194

Within five years, Leopold had carved out an enormous private colony along the banks of the Congo River—the first European colony in central Africa. The Congo Free State, as it was called, grew into an empire of 90,000 square miles—an area twenty times larger than Belgium itself! King Leopold made a personal fortune of twenty million dollars in African ivory and rubber. Not until 1904 did the Belgian people discover that Leopold's private empire had been built with the blood of African slaves. When the cruel treatment of Africans on the Congo's plantations became known, the Belgian government seized control of the colony, which it renamed the Belgian Congo.

The recently unified nations of Germany and Italy were latecomers to the African continent. However, both countries had a keen interest in joining the imperialist club. Despite its youth, Germany was already a great military and economic power in Europe. It sought an empire in Africa as a way of confirming its status. Italy, on the other hand, was a weak nation which wished to be a great power. The establishment of colonies, it hoped, would give it that status. In 1884 Germany called a meeting in Berlin to discuss the division of "unclaimed" African territories into colonies. (Needless to say, no African representatives were invited!) The Conference of Berlin set ground rules for establishing colonies so that the European nations could expand their empires without risking conflict among themselves.

After the conference, imperialism really took off. "Those who take no part in this great rivalry," declared a German historian, "will play a pitiable part in time to come." Germany lost no time in grabbing a starring role for itself. It quickly took control of a large, though not particularly valuable, African empire. Italy tried, but failed, to conquer Ethiopia; it had better luck with the large but impoverished nation of Tripoli (now Libya) in 1912. Britain kept expanding its African empire gradually until, by 1900 it had added the modern-day nations of the Sudan, Nigeria, Ghana, Kenya, and Uganda to its list of possessions. France increased its holdings by grabbing a huge chunk of land on the African equator, along with the island of Madagascar. Spain and Portugal, which had started the age of exploration, picked up a few possessions of their own. By 1914 there were only two independent nations left on the entire continent: Ethiopia in the northwest, which had valiantly resisted Italy's advances, and Liberia, the tiny west-coast nation founded by liberated slaves from the United States.

African peoples became strangers in their own land under the weight of European domination.

There is no denying that the European nations often brought improvements to their African colonies. They developed industries, improved agriculture, and built roads, hospitals and schools. So why did Africa find itself worse off after the Age of Imperialism than it had been before?

For one thing, African peoples lost control over their own destinies. They had no say in the use of their land and resources. True, their countries were improved in some ways. But the Europeans did not work with the Africans to bring these improvements about. The Europeans treated the Africans, at best, as if they were children. Often, they were treated more like animals, whom the rulers must "tame" with Christianity and European culture. Native African cultures were considered worthless. Traditional religion, art, language, and tribal systems of government were considered "savage" customs to be destroyed in the natives' best interests. The ancient trade routes that had crisscrossed Africa were also destroyed. Where once African nations had traded among themselves as equals, now Africa's economy was tied to the world economy. Unfortunately, Africa was stuck in an inferior role as supplier of raw materials and consumer of European manufactured goods. Furthermore, European nations divided Africa up into colonies with no consideration of ancient tribal divisions. When the former colonies of Africa finally received their independence, age-old tribal hostilities returned. Many African nations are still plagued with instability and civil war, partly as a result of the randomly-drawn national boundaries left over from colonial days.

As for the benefits gained by the European nations, the truth is that in many cases imperialism did not "pay." An economist once reckoned that France's total gain from its African colonies was 16 million francs, while its total expenditure was 174 million. Whether or not these figures are accurate, it is certain that money was not the only motive for European imperialism in Africa. Nationalist pride, the concept of duty (as Rudyard Kipling put it, "the white man's burden"), and the desperate need to "keep up with the Joneses" all played a part in the imperialist scramble for Africa. Was it worth it? To an Englishman of the time, basking in the glory of the British Empire, perhaps it was, but from the modern perspective, the imperialist nations of Europe seem to have won few lasting gains from their adventures in Africa.

The United States as an Imperialist Power

The Monroe Doctrine of 1823 had put limits on European expansion in the Western Hemisphere. But throughout the nineteenth and early twentieth centuries, the United States' own expansion was limited only by the imagination of its leaders. Many Americans believed that the same "manifest destiny" that had led them westward across the continent would eventually bring all of North and South America into the union—along with some strategically-located islands in the Pacific and Caribbean. At the same time, France's bold move in sending an army to Mexico while the United States was knee-deep in civil war convinced Americans that the European nations were not to be trusted. From 1870 to 1930, expansionism and isolationism went hand in hand.

America's mid-century expansion began with the Mexican-American War in 1846. U.S. president James Polk used a longstanding dispute over Texas as an excuse to go to war with Mexico. But his real goal was to get California, which would provide the United States with a "Golden Gate" to the riches of the orient. The war ended in 1848 with the utter defeat of Mexico. Under the terms of the treaty of Guadalupe Hidalgo, Mexico was forced to give the U.S. an immense tract of land including California, Nevada, Utah, Arizona, and parts of New Mexico and Colorado, in return for a payment of fifteen million dollars. But with this new territory came new questions. Would the new territories be slave or free? And who had the right to decide? These inflammatory issues would lead directly to the outbreak of the Civil War in 1861.

After the Civil War, America resumed its expansion drive with the 1867 seizure of the Midway Islands, a chain of "uninhabited flyspecks" in the Pacific. Ignored at the time by just about everyone, the Midway Islands would have the eyes of the entire world focused upon them during World War II, when the United States engaged the Japanese there in one of the major naval battles of the war.

Not all of the United States' growth during the Age of Imperialism took place at gunpoint. In 1867 the American Secretary of State William Seward decided to purchase Alaska from the Russians. With the help of the Russian ambassador, who wined and dined and probably bribed key members of the House of Representatives, Seward barely won enough Congressional votes to approve the Alaskan deal. Detractors called the purchase "Seward's Folly," but for about seven million dollars, or two cents an acre, the United States acquired nearly 600,000 square miles of land that proved to contain rich deposits of gold, copper, oil, and natural gas.

In that same year, Liliuokalani became queen of Hawaii. A fierce patriot, Queen Liliuokalani resented the power of the American landowners on the islands. The Queen swore that she would return Hawaii to the control of Hawaiians. In 1893 she tried to oust the white-dominated Hawaiian legislature by issuing a new constitution that proclaimed her the absolute ruler of the islands. Immediately the American plantation owners organized a revolution. They were backed up by marines from the United States naval base at Pearl Harbor. Faced with the threat of American military might, the queen fled, and the revolutionaries promptly raised the American flag.

For several months the United States debated over what to do with Hawaii. The American landowners who had led the revolution wanted America to annex the islands. But a special commission organized by President Cleveland reported that the islanders did not want to be annexed. So Cleveland proposed returning the islands to the queen instead. Popular opinion supported Cleveland's stance. However, the American revolutionaries refused to comply. If the United States would not annex Hawaii, they declared, then they would form an independent republic. This they did on July 4, 1894. However, when the Spanish-American War broke out a few years later, American opinion changed, and Hawaii was formally annexed by the United States.

In keeping with the Monroe Doctrine, the United States flexed its muscles in Latin America several times in the late 1800s. In Chile in 1892, the United States intervened in a civil war between the congress and the president, unfortunately backing the losing presidential side. A few years later America nearly went to war with Britain over a boundary dispute between Venezuela and British Guyana. In each case, war was narrowly averted. Then, in 1895 trouble developed between Spain and its island of Cuba, situated just off the coast of Florida. This time militarism won out, and in 1898 America found itself engaged in a full-scale war with Spain.

Cuban patriots had launched an unsuccessful revolution against Spain in 1868. In 1895 they began a new guerrilla war and managed to win control of most of the Cuban countryside. To cut off the rebels' food

Queen Liliuokalani of Hawaii

Future president Teddy Roosevelt led his Rough Riders to victory at the battle of San Juan Hill.

"Remember the Maine!"

supply, the Spanish Governor-General began herding Cuban farmers into concentration camps, where 200,000 of them died from starvation and disease. When word of the cruel treatment of the Cuban people reached the United States, anti-Spanish sentiment swiftly began to grow, fanned by propaganda from pro-revolutionary committees called juntas.

In January of 1898 riots broke out in the Cuban capital of Havana. To protect U.S. interests there, President McKinley dispatched the battleship U.S.S. Maine to Havana. On February 15, while anchored in Havana Harbor, the Maine was sunk to the bottom by an enormous explosion. Of the 350 sailors aboard the ship, 266 died. Many Americans assumed that Spain was responsible for the sinking of the Maine and immediately began clamoring for war. In fact, it has never been determined who planted the mine that caused the explosion. It would have made little sense for Spain to commit an act that was almost guaranteed to bring the United States into the war on the rebels' side. More likely is the theory that Cuban revolutionaries sank the ship, knowing that Spain would bear the blame.

Unlike the American masses who quickly adopted "Remember the *Maine!*" as their rallying cry, President McKinley wanted to avoid war with Spain. For several months,

Emilio Aguinaldo—
Filipino patriot

McKinley tried to get the two sides to agree to a truce under which Spain would grant Cuba some democratic reforms, and Cuba would agree to remain a Spanish colony. But in April of 1898, McKinley was forced to inform Congress that he had "exhausted every effort" to work out a settlement. America prepared for war. But first, so that no one could accuse the U.S. of being imperialist, Congress passed the Teller Amendment stating that the U.S. had no intention of claiming Cuba for its own.

Ironically the first major battle in the Spanish-American war was waged not in Cuba, but in the Spanish-held Philippine Islands. When war was declared, Commodore George Dewey rushed his battleships from their base in Hong Kong to Manila Bay in the Philippines. There he destroyed the Spanish fleet in a matter of hours. His victory in Manila made Dewey immensely popular in the States and whetted the American appetite for more action. However, it was several months before the actual war in Cuba got under way. The first hurdle was training and organizing the 200,000 men who had answered McKinley's call for volunteers. The recruitment effort had been aided by Theodore Roosevelt, the Assistant Secretary of the Navy, who had resigned his post in order to become an officer in the First Volunteer Cavalry. Roosevelt assembled a colorful force of fighting men—including cowboys, Indians, policemen and well-known athletes—who became known as the Rough Riders. But the volunteer army that gathered in Tampa, Florida, could not set sail for Cuba until the American navy had located the Spanish fleet in the Atlantic. It was late May before Spanish ships were sighted in the Cuban harbor of Santiago, on the far side of the island. American troops landed nearby and began a difficult advance toward Santiago. On July 1, Roosevelt's Rough Riders and the black soldiers of the Ninth Cavalry stormed the Spanish stronghold at San Juan Hill, allowing the Americans to move their artillery within blasting range of Santiago harbor. The Spanish fleet was forced to put to sea, where it was trapped and destroyed by the American navy. On July 16, Santiago surrendered. A few days later, with the capture of Puerto Rico, the Spanish-American war came to an end.

The war may have been over, but in the United States the battle was just beginning. The original goal of the war had been to win independence for Cuba. But the terms of the treaty drawn up in Paris after the war called for a great deal more than that. In addition to granting Cuba its freedom, Spain was forced to surrender to the United States the islands of Puerto Rico, Guam, and the Philippines. When Spain protested, the United States agreed to pay 20 million dollars for the islands to make the treaty easier to digest. However, it was still not acceptable to anti-imperialists in the United States. They believed that America had no business forming an empire as if it were one of the "corrupt" European nations. When Commodore Dewey had freed the Philippines from Spanish control, the Filipinos had assumed that independence would soon follow. After all, the war had been fought to guarantee independence for Cuba. How could the United States deny the Philippines their right to self-rule?

Many Americans asked themselves the same question. The Senate battle over ratification of the Treaty of Paris was one of the toughest fights in the history of Congress. Eventually it passed—but only by one vote. Even before the treaty was ratified, a bloody revolution broke out in the Philippines. It was led by Emilio Aguinaldo, a Filipino patriot who had received American support during the war against Spain. Angry at the United States' betrayal of his country, he launched a violent guerrilla campaign against his former allies. When it was over, America had its empire but the country's imperialist adventures had left a bad taste in many American mouths.

Nevertheless, the United States continued to expand its influence throughout the world. By proclaiming an Open Door Policy in China, the United States increased its presence in Asia. When the Boxers, a secret society of Chinese nationalists, launched an attack on foreigners in China in 1900, the United States participated in the international army that was sent to put down the revolt.

However, it was in the western hemisphere that America's real interests lay. The Spanish-American War had convinced Theodore Roosevelt, now the President of the United States, that it was of the utmost importance to the United States that a canal be built across Central America. During the war, the battleship USS *Oregon* had to travel 12,000 miles from the West Coast all the way around the tip of South America in

Roosevelt's "gunboat diplomacy" made the Panama Canal a reality.

198

					Britain acquires Cape Colony					Livingstone expedition	Plantation owners overthrow Queen Liliuokalani of Hawaii		Spanish-American War		Boxer revolution in China
	Monroe Doctrine Manifest Destiny		The Great Trek		Potato famine hits Ireland			King Leopold II establishes colonies on the Congo river				Boer Wars breaks out between British and the Boers			
	British East India Company controls India	France invades Algiers, establishes Algeria		Sepoy Rebellion		U.S.Civil War		U.S. occupies Midway Island U.S. purchases Alaska from Russia			India National Congress formed		British seize Ceylon, Malaya, Singapore and Afghanistan	Treaty of Paris	
					Mexican-American War			India becomes a British Colony Britain gains control of Suez canal from France							
1814 1818		1823 1823 1834 1840 1846 1857				1861 1865 1867		1875		1877	1880 1885	1893	1895	1898 1899 1900	

order to reach Cuba—a voyage that took 68 days at top speed. The existence of a canal would reduce the distance by a third.

Several years earlier a French company had obtained rights to build a canal across the isthmus of Panama, which was then controlled by Colombia. The French company had gone bankrupt and was willing to sell its canal rights to the United States for $40 million. President Roosevelt was determined to accept the French offer. But the Panama site was only one of the locations under consideration. A more popular alternative was in Nicaragua, a site which would require a longer canal but would be closer to the United States. In 1902 a long-dormant Nicaraguan volcano exploded, killing 30,000 people. That convinced Congress to approve the Panama site. Roosevelt sent Secretary of State John Hay to Colombia to negotiate a treaty by which the United States would lease a ten-mile-wide canal zone in Panama. However, when the Colombian senate heard the Americans' proposal—$10 million up front and $250,000 rent per year—they promptly rejected the treaty. Why, they asked, should the French company get $40 million from the U.S. for canal rights, which Colombia had granted them in the first place, while Colombia would only get $10 million for the actual land?

But Roosevelt was not to be denied. For several years there had been anti-Colombian uprisings in Panama. No sooner did the Colombian senate reject the U.S. treaty than a new rebellion broke out. It seemed like a lucky turn of events for Roosevelt, but in reality luck had nothing to do with it. The "rebels" were railroad workers and members of the Panama City fire department whose "revolution" was sponsored by the French company that owned the rights to the canal. Of course, Roosevelt lost no time in supporting the so-called revolution. With American assistance, the Republic of Panama was born! Only days later the new government approved the terms of the American treaty.

The canal was completed in 1914. Roosevelt often boasted about having "taken" the Canal Zone while Congress debated. As time went on, however, America came under heavy criticism for its behavior in Panama. In 1921, the United States agreed to pay Colombia $25 million for the loss of Panama. Then, in 1978 the U.S. agreed to return the canal zone, and eventually the canal itself, to Panamanian control.

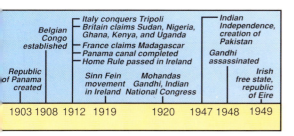

Quiz

1. What was the Home Rule movement?

- Ⓐ law forcing British to stay home
- Ⓒ Indian independence movement
- Ⓑ movement for Irish self-rule
- Ⓓ British anti-foreigner movement

2. As a result of violence between Hindus and Moslems,

- Ⓐ Gandhi was sent to prison.
- Ⓒ Gandhi died from his fast.
- Ⓑ Indian was split into two nations.
- Ⓓ Indian independence was denied.

3. The first French colony in Africa was

- Ⓐ Cape Colony.
- Ⓒ Algeria.
- Ⓑ Ethiopia.
- Ⓓ Egypt.

4. Who were the Boers?

- Ⓐ German imperialists
- Ⓒ Indian soldiers
- Ⓑ French pirates
- Ⓓ Dutch settlers

5. The American declaration limiting European imperialism in the Western Hemisphere was

- Ⓐ the Monroe Doctrine.
- Ⓒ the Treaty of Paris.
- Ⓑ the Open Door Policy.
- Ⓓ Manifest Destiny.

6. Which was not a result of imperialism in Africa?

- Ⓐ African traditions were lost.
- Ⓒ Africa's economy grew.
- Ⓑ Trade routes changed.
- Ⓓ Africa was divided into colonies.

7. What event was nicknamed "Seward's Folly"?

- Ⓐ the U.S. purchase of Alaska
- Ⓒ the Spanish-American War
- Ⓑ the Panama Canal purchase
- Ⓓ the annexation of Hawaii

8. Who was Leopold II?

- Ⓐ a German monarch
- Ⓒ a British ruler
- Ⓑ a Filipino leader
- Ⓓ a Belgian king

9. Because of the Spanish-American War, America gained which of the following?

- Ⓐ Mexico, Cuba, Puerto Rico
- Ⓒ Cuba, Puerto Rico, Philippines
- Ⓑ Puerto Rico, Guam, Philippines
- Ⓓ Midway, Philippines, Hawaii

10. Which event was not a factor in the building of the Panama Canal?

- Ⓐ Nicaraguan volcanic eruption
- Ⓒ a revolution in Panama
- Ⓑ the Boxer Rebellion in China
- Ⓓ bankruptcy of French company

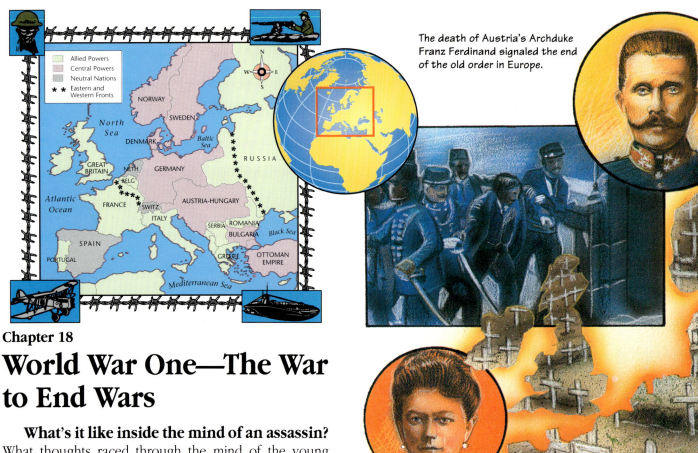

The death of Austria's Archduke Franz Ferdinand signaled the end of the old order in Europe.

Duchess Sophia

Emperor Franz Josef

Chapter 18

World War One—The War to End Wars

What's it like inside the mind of an assassin? What thoughts raced through the mind of the young Serbian, Gavrilo Princip, as the motorcade of the Archduke Franz Ferdinand rolled through the streets of Sarajevo?—"Today, I'll be the one to make the headlines"—"Today, I'll be the one in the spotlight"—as he pushed his way to the front of the crowd and emptied his pistol into the open car—"Today, I'll change the world!"

"Death to the oppressors!" Gavrilo shouted as the police wrestled him to the ground.

Franz Ferdinand was the son of Emperor Franz Josef and heir to the ancient Hapsburg dynasty, which at the dawn of the twentieth century controlled a large area of Europe known as Austria-Hungary. The nations of Europe existed in a precarious state of equilibrium, each one armed to the teeth, either expecting an attack or planning one. By assassinating the Archduke, Gavrilo Princip had hoped to liberate his small country from Austrian domination. Instead Princip sparked the continental tinderbox that blazed into the first "modern" war: a war in which millions of Europe's young men ran headlong into death's embrace and killing machines reached new heights of efficiency and terror. It would prove to be the first war in history to have an impact upon virtually the entire world.

Ever since the time of Napoleon, the great nations of Europe—France, England, Germany, Austria-Hungary, Italy, Russia—had lived in a state of constant tension. Everywhere militarism, nationalistic pride, and patriotic fervor ran high as the marching bands pounded out their cadences, the people waved their flags, and the parading troops filed by in endless rows. Only Great Britain, secure with its world-spanning empire and the mightiest navy in the world, held aloof from the martial enthusiasm of the European mainland, maintaining only a small volunteer army and a cautious diplomacy.

The constant threat of war led to a web of treaties, alliances, and pacts as the nations "took up sides" to try to maintain the balance of power. Austria-Hungary joined with Germany and Italy to form the Triple Alliance. Great Britain, France, and Russia made up the Triple Entente. Protective treaties proliferated as more powerful nations

Map legend:
- Allied Powers
- Central Powers
- Neutral Nations
- ** Eastern and Western Fronts

month Austria-Hungary declared war on Serbia. Russia's Czar Nicholas had promised protection to Serbia, so Russian troops were prepared for battle. Germany had long feared the Russian giant, and as soon as Russia mobilized to support Serbia, Kaiser Wilhelm declared war on Russia—and then on Germany's age-old enemy, France.

German leaders believed they could quickly defeat the French by marching their troops through Belgium, which had declared neutrality, and attacking France from the north. England, honoring its protective treaty with Belgium, was forced to declare war on Germany. A few months later the mighty Ottoman Empire, which dominated the lands east of the Mediterranean, joined Germany and Austria-Hungary to form the Central Powers. Italy, although a member of the Triple Alliance, remained neutral until 1915 when it broke away from the Alliance and came into the war against Austria-Hungary. The battle lines were drawn: Germany, Austria-Hungary, Bulgaria and the Ottoman Empire against France, Russia, Serbia, Great Britain, Belgium, and Italy.

As the first battles of the war were fought, it became apparent that something new and terrible was happening. Well-disciplined French troops in their bright red-and-blue uniforms, marching shoulder to shoulder straight at enemy lines, were mowed down like blades of grass by a new German weapon: the machine-gun. The Germans, in their dull grey uniforms designed to provide camouflage, sat behind their guns and blasted hundreds of bullets a minute at the hapless French.

More than a million soldiers died in the first year of the war that grew to engulf the entire western world.

In the first year of the war more than a million soldiers died as leaders on both sides remained blind to the meaning of the new technology—that the old ways of waging war were useless. Once they understood, the face of the war changed. From a noble and heroic adventure it became a living hell of mud and blood. The troops dug deep trenches fortified with sandbags and tangles of barbed wire. In the trenches, they lived and died as the bullets whistled overhead. The new artillery was far more powerful and accurate than anything known before, and major infantry attacks were preceded by intense barrages of cannon fire that chewed up the men, the ground, and the trenches alike. Heavy rains made the churned earth a muddy quagmire and filled the trenches with water, making the soldiers' misery complete. The Western Front was a double line of opposing trenches that stretched from the English Channel to Switzerland.

The slender strip of barren land between the two barriers was "no-man's-land," where any soldier was a

pledged armed support to smaller but strategically important countries. One such pact, which was to have a major effect on the course of the war, was between Great Britain and Belgium, a small country to the north of France.

On June 28, 1914, when Franz Ferdinand was killed by the wild-eyed Serbian nationalist, the complex diplomatic network came alive, resulting in almost immediate mobilization for war all across the continent. Within a

sitting duck, and which had to be crossed under full fire when advancing against the enemy line. Hundreds of thousands were killed to gain a few hundred yards of muddy ground, which was often lost again in an equally bloody counterattack. At the Battle of the Somme in 1916, the British lost nearly half a million men to advance less than five miles. Within six months the Germans had retaken most of it. With such losses, England's volunteer army was soon decimated, and in 1916 all able-bodied Englishmen became eligible for service.

As the war slogged on, new weapons were introduced by both sides. In early 1915 the Germans unleashed a chlorine-gas attack in the Ypres area of Belgium. Totally unprepared, the Allied troops could only put damp cloths over their faces to protect themselves from the deadly fumes. Soon gas masks were standard issue, even for horses and dogs. By the end of the war, both sides were using a wide variety of deadly gases, but with some caution, since a sudden shift of the wind could often send a cloud of death back upon the ones who had released it.

In 1916, the British introduced an armored tank that moved on endless tracks. Barbed wire, mud, shell holes, nothing could stop it as the treads chewed steadily ahead. Machine-gun fire bounced off the tank's armor plate, and by walking behind the tanks, troops could finally reach enemy lines without being open targets.

For the first time ever, men fought in the sky. The recently invented airplane was used initially only for observation. But soon pilots were firing their pistols and rifles at one another. The Germans were the first to mount a machine gun in front of the pilot, synchronized to fire between the whirring propeller blades. Only the pilot, the "Knight of the Air," retained the patina of the glamorous warrior of old. Alone in the endless blue of the sky he pitted his machine and his skill against the enemy. With five kills to his credit he became an ace. He cut a dashing figure with his leather jacket and white scarf and if he survived the day, he ate and slept in comfort far from the rat-infested trenches. But only one in five combat pilots lasted six months. The most famous ace was Baron Manfred von Richthofen, the "Red Baron," who scored eighty kills before he was shot down in 1918.

The German navy was bottled up in port after their first major sea encounter, the Battle of Jutland. But the German submarines—the U-boats—roamed the Atlantic like sharks, preying mercilessly on Allied ships bearing supplies and food for the war effort. The United States had remained neutral in the war, but many of the ships bearing aid for the Allied cause were American. Subject to the English blockade of Germany, American ships were seized if bound for German-occupied terri-

tory. At the same time they were vulnerable to the U-boats lurking unseen beneath the waves, carrying out Germany's policy of unrestricted submarine warfare.

President Woodrow Wilson adopted a policy of tolerance for British blockade actions against U.S. ships but took a stern position with the German sea raiders. He declared that Germany would be "strictly accountable" for any loss of American life or property as the result of a submarine attack.

On May 1, 1915, the British passenger ship *Lusitania*, fitted out with deck guns, set sail from New York City bound for England with a full complement of passengers and a cargo of war supplies. The German embassy had run a notice in New York newspapers warning passengers of the risk in-

WAKE UP, AMERICA!

CIVILIZATION CALLS EVERY MAN WOMAN OF CHILD

The New York Times.

GERMANY DECLARES WAR ON RUSSIA, FIRST SHOTS ARE FIRED; FRANCE IS MOBILIZING AND MAY BE DRAWN IN TOMORROW;

volved in sailing on any Allied ship into the war zone, but passengers paid little heed. The *Lusitania* had a speed of more than twenty-three knots, and it was believed no submarine could catch her. The nature of the cargo was ignored. On May 7, 1915, at 2:10 p.m., the *Lusitania* was torpedoed off the coast of Ireland by the German submarine U-20. The giant ship sank to the bottom in eighteen minutes, taking 1,198 people including 127 American citizens with it.

President Wilson resisted the urge to retaliate and, after intense and lengthy negotiations, the Germans agreed to cease their attacks on civilian vessels. In 1916 Wilson was re-elected with the slogan "He kept us out of war." Despite the loss of the Lusitania and other ships, the American people still had no wish to become embroiled in Europe's war. But early in 1917 Germany resumed its unrestricted submarine attacks in a desperate attempt to stop the flow of supplies from the U.S. to England. It became clear that neutrality was no longer an option for the United States. On April 2, 1917, President Wilson asked Congress for a declaration of war against Germany.

Like Great Britain prior to the war, the United States maintained only a small standing army made up entirely of volunteers. The strong antiwar sentiment prevalent in the country had prevented any significant military build-up. But the continuing activity of the German U-boats had angered the American people, and when the U.S. finally entered the war, young Americans thronged to enlist in the fight against the hated Kaiser. Despite the large number of volunteers, more soldiers were needed, and in 1917 a draft of all men between the ages of twenty-one and thirty was initiated. The following year the age bracket was expanded to include everyone from age eighteen to age forty-five. All told nearly five million Americans were called to arms. Two million marched aboard ships bound for the killing fields of Europe under the rallying cry, "Lafayette, we are here!" (The help that France had given the young nation during the struggle of the American Revolution had not been forgotten.) The U.S. Navy went hunting for German submarines, and the farms and factories of America shifted into high gear to produce supplies and weapons for the war.

Meanwhile, the Bolshevik revolutionaries in Russia, which was being drained of its resources by the war, deposed the czar and made a separate peace with Germany. This reduced the threat from the east and allowed German planners to devote all their attention and manpower to the fighting on the Western Front. The first Allied Expeditionary Force, under General John J. Pershing, had arrived in France by June, 1917, but it was another six months before the U.S. was ready to engage in combat.

In the spring of 1918 the situation in France was desperate. The outnumbered Allied forces could not stop the German advance. In March, German forces gained thirty miles in a crushing defeat of the British and kept the

127 America passengers aboard the British ship Lusitania were killed in a German U-boat attack.

Woodrow Wilson kept the U.S. out of "Europe's war" for as long as he could.

pressure on until by May they had reached the Marne River on the outskirts of Paris. They were finally stopped in the nick of time by a combination of American and French troops at the Battle of Chateau-Thierry.

In this, its first engagement, the Allied Expeditionary Force had proved its mettle. The presence of the U.S. doughboys on the battlelines rejuvenated the Allied forces, and the tide began to turn. The British and French drove the Germans back at Amiens, while the Americans won at St. Mihiel. Meanwhile, Bulgaria surrendered, the Ottoman Empire signed a peace treaty, and Austria-Hungary was being trounced by Italian forces. The last battle of World War I began on September 26, 1918. Nearly 900,000 American troops joined their British and French comrades in the fighting between the Argonne Forest and the Meuse River. Along the entire Western Front the enemy was in full retreat.

On November 11, 1918, Germany agreed to surrender under any terms dictated by the Allies. Kaiser Wilhelm abdicated and fled to Holland in self-imposed exile. The First World War was over. More than sixty-five million men had been mobilized. Of those, eight and a half million had been killed and twenty-one million wounded. Twenty-four nations around the world had united to vanquish Germany and its allies.

204

Immediately, the victorious leaders of the "Big Four" Allied powers— George Clemenceau of France, Lloyd George of England, Vittorio Orlando of Italy, and Woodrow Wilson of the United States, met at Versailles for the Paris Peace Conference to decide the losers' fate. Woodrow Wilson argued passionately that the end of the hostilities could also be the beginning of a better world. He presented an enlightened settlement plan that included the Fourteen Points—guidelines for the peaceful resolution of conflicts between nations. The fourteenth point was a call for the creation of a League of Nations to guarantee the freedom and independence of all nations, big or small.

But the European victors whose land and people had been ravaged by the war were less concerned with universal peace than with revenge. England and France took Germany's African colonies. Many German territories received their independence, among them Poland and Czechoslovakia. The Austro-Hungarian Empire was abolished and Austria and Hungary became separate countries. And the Central Powers were held responsible for all the costs and losses of all the nations involved in the war. In June 1919 the Treaty of Versailles was signed. It included only one of Wilson's Fourteen Points, but by far the most essential: the League of Nations would become a reality.

Wilson returned from Versailles only to find that his greatest foe was right at home. The Republican-controlled Senate refused to allow U.S. membership in the League— the brainchild of a Democratic government. Wilson was crushed, and the League of Nations was therefore never more than the shadow of what it might have been. This act of small-minded stubbornness, coupled with the harshness of the armistice terms forced upon the proud German nation, directly contributed to the fact that the tension in Europe continued unabated. After all the incredible carnage and waste of the war, the bad feelings would resurface with a vengeance only twenty years later.

With the end of the war Wilson hoped to build a fair and lasting peace. Instead, seeds of resentment were planted which would lead to another confrontation some twenty years later.

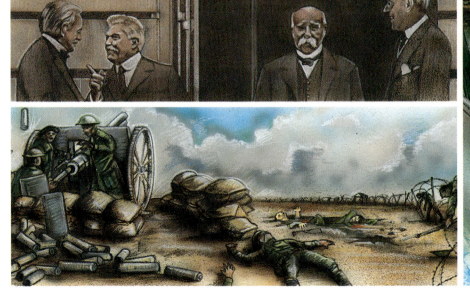

Archduke Franz Ferdinand of Austria-Hungary assassinated

Germany declares war on Serbia, Russia and France
England declares war on Germany

Ottoman Empire joins Germany, Austria-Hungary and Bulgaria to form "Central Powers"
France, Russia, Serbia, Great Britain, Belgium and Italy form "Allied Powers"
Western Front established
Lusitania torpedoed

Chlorine-gas used at Ypres, Belgium

Woodrow Wilson re-elected President of the U.S.
Battle of the Somme
British introduce armored tanks
Airplanes with machine guns introduced by Germans

U.S.A. joins Allied Powers
Draft initiated in U.S.A.
Bolshevik revolution begins, Russia makes separate peace with Germany

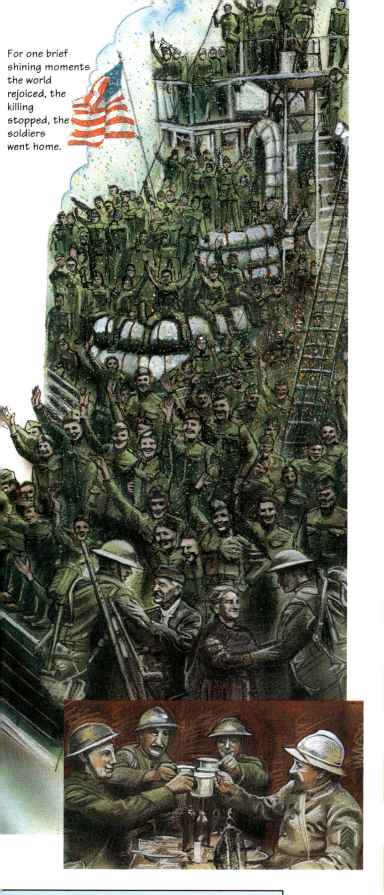

For one brief shining moments the world rejoiced, the killing stopped, the soldiers went home.

- American and French troops stop Germany at Chateau-Thierry
- Last battle at Argonne Forest
- Germany surrenders

Treaty of Versailles signed
League of Nations created

1918   1919

Quiz

1. **By assassinating Archduke Franz Ferdinand, Gavrilo Princip hoped to**

   Ⓐ end World War I.   Ⓒ start World War I.

   Ⓑ liberate his country.   Ⓓ end all monarchy.

2. **The Hapsburg Dynasty controlled an area of Europe called**

   Ⓐ Germany.   Ⓒ Austria-Hungary.

   Ⓑ Sarajevo.   Ⓓ Serbia.

3. **Over _____ soldiers died in the first year of World War I**

   Ⓐ one hundred   Ⓒ one hundred thousand

   Ⓑ one thousand   Ⓓ one million

4. **The Triple Entente was made up of**

   Ⓐ France, Great Britain, and Russia.   Ⓒ Russia, Bosnia, and Serbia.

   Ⓑ Great Britain, Italy, and France.   Ⓓ Italy, France, and Russia.

5. **Which of the following weapons was not first used in World War I?**

   Ⓐ gas   Ⓒ tank

   Ⓑ machine gun   Ⓓ helicopter

6. **English submarines were called U-boats.**

   Ⓐ True   Ⓑ False

7. **The _Lusitania_ was sunk by**

   Ⓐ a bomb planted by a spy.   Ⓒ a German U-boat.

   Ⓑ an iceberg.   Ⓓ a British airplane.

8. **The United States entered World War I in**

   Ⓐ 1914.   Ⓒ 1916.

   Ⓑ 1915.   Ⓓ 1917.

9. **Great Britain surrendered to Germany in 1918.**

   Ⓐ True   Ⓑ False

10. **The peace plan presented by _____ included the "Fourteen Points."**

    Ⓐ Lloyd George of England   Ⓒ Vittorio Orlando of Italy

    Ⓑ George Clemenceau of France   Ⓓ Woodrow Wilson of the U.S.

Chapter 19
The Russian Revolution

The day before he was murdered in 1915, the mysterious monk Rasputin gave this ominous warning to Czar Nicholas II: "If it is one of your relatives who have brought about my death, then not one of your family will remain alive for more than two years." No prophecy could have been truer, for almost exactly two years later the czar, his wife, his son, and his entire family were dead, and—for better or for worse—the Revolution of 1917 had brought forth a new Russia.

In the waning years of the nineteenth century, Russia was an autocratic state ruled by a czar with unlimited authority and unquestioned personal power. From the capital at St. Petersburg, the czar and his nobles ruled a huge nation that, for the most part, they had never even seen. Insulated behind the walls of the royal residence, isolated from the great masses of people, they issued directives regardless of the results. Instead of absorbing the essence of the western European culture to which they had been introduced during the reigns of Peter the Great and the Empress Catherine II, they merely aped the most superficial elements of the lives of their contemporaries to the west. They spent much of their time trying to impress one another at balls, receptions, and other state functions.

206

For the 80 percent of the Russian people who toiled in the fields of the nobles as serfs, life went on pretty much as it had since the Middle Ages. Their existence was completely dominated by the nobles for whom they worked. They were not free to move from place to place. They could be beaten, bought, and sold. They had no choice but to do whatever work the nobles demanded, and they were often cruelly punished for small mistakes. Frequent uprisings and riots led to increased oppression. Talking or writing about government reforms was forbidden. Secret police were everywhere. People who called out for change were executed or sent into exile in a cold and harsh part of Russia called Siberia.

Worst of all was the plight of Russian Jews. Since the seventeenth century, Jews in eastern Europe had been subjected to relentless persecution. Merchants who resented their competition accused them of secret bloodletting ceremonies and all sorts of fictitious atrocities. Jews never knew when they might be physically attacked. As a result, they withdrew more and more into their own communities, reinforcing their faith by devoting much of their time to Talmudic (biblical) studies. At various times, Talmudic academies were so numerous that more than half of all Jewish males were considered Talmudic scholars. They maintained their high moral standards and an unusual degree of respect for the role of women.

The emancipation of Jews in Europe was initiated in France after the French Revolution. But no relief would come for the Russian Jews until the Revolution of 1917. On the contrary, harsher and harsher laws continued to hem them in. They were permitted to live only in certain areas (simultaneously banned from rural areas and from major cities) and prohibited from holding any significant economic positions. Brutal attempts were made to force them to convert to Russian Orthodox Christianity. The czarist government encouraged attacks, beatings, and murder carried out by fierce mounted cossack warriors.

Czar Nicholas with his family, including his wife Alexandra, and his beloved son Alexis.

Bloody Sunday!—the workers fell...

As a result, in the thirty-three years between 1881 and 1914, more than two million Jews left Russia for the United States. In the largest Jewish migration in two thousand years of persecution, Russia lost—and America gained—a tremendously talented cultural asset.

Meanwhile Russia had begun the process of industrialization that had already been under way in the western European nations for a hundred years. Russia caught up quickly. From 1866 to 1876 ten thousand miles of railroad were built. Thousands of peasants left the land to work in the factories of St. Petersburg, Moscow, and Baku. By 1900 several million Russians were working in factories. Slowly, ever so slowly, the standard of living began to improve—but not by much. Too often the peasants found the factory owners as unfair and uncaring as the landowning nobles had been.

This was the situation that faced Nicholas II when he became czar in 1894. By all accounts, Nicholas II was a kindhearted man who sincerely wanted to better the lot of the Russian people. But he was not strong enough to control the forces of change in Russian society, which had now reached the boiling point. He began his reign with hope and ended it in the grave.

In 1904 with no warning or declaration of war, Japanese torpedo boats fired at the Far East Russian fleet. The Russo-Japanese War was the result of a desire by both Japan and Russia to control major interests in Korea and Manchuria. The Russian army was driven out of Korea into Manchuria. Russia was soundly thrashed by the Japanese on land and sea. The peace of 1905 required Russia to evacuate Manchuria and to yield nearby territory to Japan. It was the first time in history that a Western power lost a war to an Asian country.

On January 22, 1905, thousands of workers, including women and children marched peacefully on the czar's palace in St. Petersburg. They were petitioning the czar for better working conditions, more personal freedom, and an elected national assembly. Nicholas's soldiers fired on the crowd from the steps of the palace. Many hundreds of unarmed workers were massacred. The day went down in history as Bloody Sunday.

Bloody Sunday was the end of any peaceful demand for change. Strikes, riots, and revolutionary battles broke out. Bands of peasants, now armed, roamed the countryside attacking the nobles and burning their estates. In order to put a stop to the revolt, Nicholas agreed to set up an elected Duma, or parliament. The Duma would have the power to rule on all proposals for new laws.

207

...as the soldiers fired.

Although some people were satisfied with this change, others felt that the Duma was not enough. As it turned out, they were right.

In their first two meetings, the Duma's liberal policies so frightened the czar that he immediately dismissed them. A third, more conservative assembly rigidly repressed all revolutionary activity. A fourth Duma, convened in 1912, was permitted to continue but was given virtually no power except to advise the czar in matters dealing with foreign affairs.

Rasputin—the "Mad Monk."

Meanwhile, Czarina Alexandra was falling under the spell of the sinister monk named Rasputin. Grigori Yefimovich Rasputin was a Siberian peasant and self-professed holy man who had ingratiated himself with certain members of the nobility, particularly the ladies. Dressed in a long black robe with an ornate crucifix hanging from a heavy gold chain around his neck, he heard their confessions and gave them counsel. Although Rasputin appeared to live simply and rarely accepted money for his services, many Russian nobles were suspicious of him. They heard rumors of wild parties and strange meetings at his house and were repulsed by his rustic manners and infrequently washed clothing.

Rasputin used the Czarina's son, Alexis, to gain Alexandra's undying trust and confidence. Alexis suffered from hemophilia, a disease in which the blood does not coagulate properly, and even a slight wound can lead to death. Rasputin treated Alexis several times with apparently greater success than the court physicians. Alexandra became convinced that Rasputin could heal her son's illness when medical doctors could not. At one point Alexis suffered a wound while on a hunting trip. When three doctors expressed the opinion that the boy would die, Alexandra contacted Rasputin by telegraph. His answer quickly came: "The little one will not die." The bleeding stopped the next day. From then on Rasputin's influence over the royal family was insurmountable.

In 1914 Russia entered World War I on the side of the Allied powers. But the common people of Russia were not interested in fighting Germany, and the war went badly for Russia. Millions of Russian soldiers were killed, wounded, or taken prisoner. The food shortages became more severe than ever. The poor became even poorer. In 1915 Czar Nicholas left Russia to personally direct the Russian troops, leaving Alexandra (and in terms of influence, Rasputin) in control of the government. Alexandra's

dependence upon her ignorant peasant magician infuriated a faction of the nobility that included other members of the royal family. In 1916, convinced that the very survival of the Russian nation was at stake, they hatched a plot to do away with Rasputin.

Rasputin was invited to the home of Prince Felix Yusopov and treated to poisoned wine and cakes. Much to the assassins' surprise, Rasputin seemed unaffected even after consuming copious amounts of wine and desserts. Hoping to finish the job, Yusopov shot him, but Rasputin stubbornly started dragging himself out of the room. It took four more bullets to stop him. Then the conspirators wrapped his body in an old curtain and threw it into the Neva River. Unwittingly, Yusopov and his confederates had brought the first part of Rasputin's dire prediction to pass. With the relentless logic of a Greek tragedy, the prophecy unfolded to its inevitable conclusion.

During the years following the uprising of 1905, the flames of rebellion had become a raging conflagration. The various revolutionary groups could not agree on how change should occur. Some political factions wanted to limit the czar's power and create a constitutional monarchy like Great Britain's. Others believed that Russia's many problems could be solved once and for all by a system of socialism.

Socialism is an economic and political theory based on the belief that the government has the responsibility to see that every citizen has a job and earns a decent living. A true socialist society would have no private ownership of property and no profit system. The most influential of all the early socialists was a German thinker of the 1800s named Karl Marx.

Marx believed he could change history.

Many of the revolutionaries in Russia had studied the works of Marx. He and his friend Freidrich Engels had explained their ideas in the Communist Manifesto which was published in 1848. They believed that the days of capitalism were numbered—that the middle class (the bourgeoisie) would soon be overthrown by the workers (the proletariat). These communist leaders believed it was wrong for the factory owners to make most of the money. They

Sailors mutinied on the battleship *Potemkin*.

crowd, but the soldiers refused to shoot. Without the army behind him the czar was nothing. Powerless and defeated, he abdicated the throne and allowed the revolution to run its course.

The czar and his family were imprisoned, and a provisional government made up of leaders of the Duma took control. The new government promised democracy, but it did not meet the people's demand to pull Russia out of World War I. The people knew that getting rid of the czar was not enough. It was the *war* that was draining supplies, killing the men, and taking the food.

Conditions in the country grew worse. The Russian factories could not produce enough guns and ammunition. There were constant shortages of food, fuel, and other needed supplies. Workers and soldiers formed councils called soviets, and took over local governments in the cities and towns.

As the provisional government struggled to restore order to the nation, a socialist revolutionary group called the Bolsheviks (meaning "members of the majority") was preparing to make its move. The Bolshevik party was not very large, but it was well-organized and effective—it had been preparing for this moment in history for a long time. The Bolshevik slogan of "Peace, Land, and Bread" won the support of many Russian people. Furthermore, the Bolshevik party was the only party willing to stop the war. It also promised the peasants land right away. The Bolsheviks formed a militia called the Red Guard and on November 6, 1917, took over the government by force. The leaders of the provisional government did not resist the takeover, and the Bolsheviks acted quickly to consolidate their control. They placed the provisional leaders under arrest and declared their party, which they called the Communist party, the rulers of the country.

said that the workers should get a significant share of the profits for all of their labor. Marx and Engels encouraged workers everywhere to rise up against the powerful middle class. These revolutionaries pictured a perfect world in which there would be no social classes and where government would be unnecessary. Their ideas would become an important force in twentieth-century history. Some of the anti-capitalists in Russia wanted to see Marx's ideas become a reality in their country.

On the morning of February 25, 1917, the women of St. Petersburg went to market, as they did each day. They were accustomed to the shortages and inconveniences caused by the war, but on this morning even bread could not be had—not anywhere. This was too much. Angry crowds began to gather in the streets. "We want bread! We want bread!" the people shouted. Some carried banners that voiced their rage and frustration: "End the war!" and "Down with the czar!"

At first, the police and the army tried to control the crowds. But soon soldiers began to join the rebellion, marching alongside their friends, wives, and neighbors. Czar Nicholas ordered his troops to open fire on the

Soldiers threw down their guns to
join the revolution.

Lenin returned from exile in Germany to lead the revolution.

The victory of the Bolsheviks was also a personal victory for their leader, a bald man with piercing eyes and a close-trimmed beard who called himself Lenin. The czarist government had killed Lenin's brother and had exiled Lenin as a revolutionary seventeen years before. The Bolshevik takeover marked Lenin's triumphant return to his homeland. Lenin had studied the writings of Karl Marx and considered himself a Communist revolutionary. But he disagreed with Marx's theories on several key points. Karl Marx had pictured an ideal society with no need for government. But Lenin felt that a strict Communist party should be in charge. The country would need a planned economy, and it would be the Communist party that would draw up the plans. The Communists would take over the local soviets. The democratic reforms begun by the provisional government would be stopped. All political parties except the Communist party would be banned. In the first free elections to choose a new assembly following the Bolshevik uprising, the Communists were outvoted two to one. They responded by closing the assembly after only one day.

Lenin and the Communists immediately ended Russian involvement in World War I by signing a separate peace treaty with Germany. They placed all major industries under direct government control. They ordered the land to be equally divided among the peasants. They abolished the age-old Russian class system and confiscated all land owned by the Russian Orthodox church. Their secret police force terrorized and intimidated anyone deemed an enemy of the revolution.

Although the Communists had quickly consolidated their power in the large cities of central Russia, there was much resistance to their rule in other parts of the enormous nation. In 1918 Russia was torn apart by a civil war. The Communists, or Reds, found themselves opposed by a formidable coalition of anti-Bolshevik groups called the Whites, who were determined to regain control of the country. The White army included members of other political parties, national minorities such as Ukranians, Poles, and Finns, and troops sent by more than twenty

countries, including Great Britain, France, Japan, and the United States.

For two years the Whites and the Reds fought for control of the nation. Fifteen million Russian people died of starvation or disease. True to the vengeful prophecy of Rasputin, among those who perished were Czar Nicholas II and his entire family, executed with little ceremony by the Red Army. Finally in 1920, the superior organization and leadership of the Red Army and the support of the majority of the proletariat, or working class, brought victory to the Communist forces. Russia had been transformed into a new nation, but at a terrible cost.

Factories were closed. There was nothing to buy or sell. The economy was at a standstill. Among the

The Red Army crushed all resistance in the giant nation.

millions who had died were the brightest and most skilled people in Russia. The whole point of the Bolshevik revolution, so the people had been told, had been to help the peasants. Now Lenin ordered farmers to turn their crops over to the government. Some farmers rebelled. There was more fighting. Throughout the early 1920s, the Communists struggled to maintain power. In 1922 the Communist government divided the Russian empire into several republics. The republics were then joined to form one huge Communist nation. That nation was called the Union of Soviet Socialist Republics, or USSR.

In 1922 Lenin became too ill to carry on with the work of leading the party. Two high-ranking Communist officials struggled behind the scenes to become his successor. The man that most people expected to become the new party leader was Leon Trotsky. An inspiring writer and speaker, he was the military genius who had led the Red Army to victory in the civil war. He was as well-known as Lenin and extremely popular with the Russian people.

But Trotsky had a deadly rival in the person of a quiet man named Joseph Stalin. Stalin was not a public

Trotsky advocated the worldwide spread of communism.

Stalin was born Joseph Dzhugashvili in 1879, in a region of the Russian empire known as Georgia. At the wish of his mother, he studied to become a priest until, when he was thirteen years old, he read the works of Karl Marx. Marx's ideas changed Stalin's life. One day he announced to his family, "There is no God!" He decided to dedicate himself from that moment on to the Communist revolution.

In 1913, Dzhugashvili changed his name to Stalin, which is Russian for "man of steel." Like steel, Joseph Stalin was strong and cold. Although many of Russia's czars had been cruel dictators, Stalin quickly gained a reputation for being the most tyrannical leader in Russian history. He had statues of himself erected in every city and town—statues that made him look taller and more handsome than he really was. He rewrote Russian history to make it sound as if the Russian people had actually chosen him to be their leader. He believed that the Soviet Union had to be strong to protect itself from foreign enemies. "We are fifty or one hundred years behind the advanced countries," he declared. "We must make up this lag . . . or they will crush us."

To make this goal a reality, Stalin put his Five-Year Plan into action in 1928. Under the Five-Year Plan, almost all of the country's resources would be devoted to building heavy industries like steel mills, cement factories, and power plants. Every sector of the economy would be controlled by the government. The government would tell factories what to produce and how much. It would tell workers where to work and for how long each day.

The cost of the Five-Year Plan was paid by the peasants. The government tried to control agriculture in the same way that it was controlling industry. Huge farm "collectives" requiring hundreds of workers replaced privately owned farms. Stalin insisted that farmers use the new government machines, but he did not provide the training they needed to use the machines effectively. Farm production went down and the food shortages came back.

hero like Trotsky, but he held the important position of General Secretary of the Communist party. He skillfully used his power as party secretary to fill key positions in the government with his friends and followers.

Lenin died in 1924. By 1927 Stalin had taken over the party and the nation. In 1929 Trotsky was expelled from the Communist party and exiled from the USSR. He lived in Mexico until 1940, when he was assassinated by Communist agents.

Joseph Stalin—the "Man of Steel"—ruled with an iron hand.

The Five-Year Plan succeeded in transforming Russia from a backward country into an industrial giant, but at the cost of millions of lives and untold human suffering. By 1938 the USSR was one of the most powerful industrial nations in the world, and one of the most oppressive and rigidly controlled totalitarian states in modern times.

A totalitarian state is a dictatorship in which the government has total control and individuals have no rights. Citizens can only obey without question. People are prisoners in their own countries. An impenetrable "iron curtain" surrounded the USSR, and the nation and its people were isolated from the rest of the world.

Stalin ruled until his death in 1953. In his many years as leader, he changed the Soviet Union in several major ways. On the plus side, education was universally available and the literacy rate in the USSR put other countries,

The object of collectivization was to grow more food using fewer workers. But the peasants who had struggled for years to have the opportunity to own their own land did not take well to having their hard-won farms taken away. Some burned their grain and killed their farm animals rather than turn them over to the government. For their resistance to his plan, Stalin shipped thousands of farmers and their families to the frozen wasteland of Siberia, where historians estimate that between five million and ten million people died.

212

This is the badge of a hero of the Revolution.

Only the best and hardest workers could wear this badge.

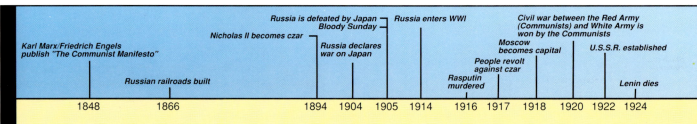

Karl Marx/Friedrich Engels publish "The Communist Manifesto"

Russian railroads built

Nicholas II becomes czar

Russia is defeated by Japan
Bloody Sunday

Russia declares war on Japan

Russia enters WWI

Rasputin murdered

People revolt against czar

Civil war between the Red Army (Communists) and White Army is won by the Communists

Moscow becomes capital

U.S.S.R. established

Lenin dies

1848   1866   1894   1904   1905   1914   1916   1917   1918   1920   1922   1924

including the United States, to shame. Opportunities for women made great leaps forward, again more quickly than in other Western nations. The government provided medical care and health benefits for all citizens. Slowly, the standard of living improved. But the people paid a terrible price. Their lives were more tightly controlled by the government than before the Revolution. Millions were harassed, tortured, and killed by their own government, and overall living conditions remained poor compared to the other nations of the West.

The Five-Year Plan turned Russia into an industrial giant, and one of the most oppressive totalitarian states of modern times.

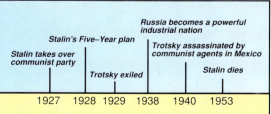

Russia becomes a powerful industrial nation

Stalin's Five–Year plan

Stalin takes over communist party

Trotsky assassinated by communist agents in Mexico

Trotsky exiled

Stalin dies

1927 1928 1929 1938 1940 1953

Quiz

1. By 1900, two million Russians were working in

Ⓐ hospitals. Ⓒ Siberia.

Ⓑ factories. Ⓓ salt mines.

2. Nicholas II became czar in the year

Ⓐ 1904. Ⓒ 1894.

Ⓑ 1940. Ⓓ 1944.

3. Russian peasants who worked on the land for the nobles were called *serfs*.

Ⓐ True Ⓑ False

4. The *Communist Manifesto* was written by

Ⓐ Lenin and Trotsky. Ⓒ Marx and Lenin.

Ⓑ Trotsky and Stalin. Ⓓ Marx and Engels.

5. February 25, 1917, is known as Bloody Sunday.

Ⓐ True Ⓑ False

6. The Russian word that means "member of the majority" is

Ⓐ duma. Ⓒ czar.

Ⓑ bolshevik. Ⓓ soviet.

7. The first leader of the Communist party was

Ⓐ Lenin. Ⓒ Marx.

Ⓑ Trotsky. Ⓓ Stalin.

8. Which of the following nations did not fight on the side of the White Army?

Ⓐ Great Britain Ⓒ France

Ⓑ The United States Ⓓ Italy

9. Stalin's Five-Year Plan resulted in the death of between five and ten million Russian peasants.

Ⓐ True Ⓑ False

10. A dictatorship in which the government has total control is

Ⓐ a democracy. Ⓒ an altered state.

Ⓑ a monarchy. Ⓓ a totalitarian state.

Chapter 20

The Great Depression— Hey Buddy Can You Spare a Dime?

During the years 1917 and 1918 nearly two million young American men went overseas to help fight World War I. Their experience marked the dawn of major social and economic changes in the United States. The American soldiers in Europe had witnessed the power and strength of their country in action. Their victory had given them pride and confidence. The war had shown the American people and the rest of the world that America could accomplish whatever it set out to do.

The dynamic decade following the triumphant return of the doughboys came to be known as the Roaring Twenties. President Warren G. Harding and his administration had absolute faith in the ability of big business to continue the nation's prosperous growth and stood firmly behind the leaders of industry in carrying out their plans. Harding's sudden death in 1923 did nothing to alter the relationship between the government and industry. Vice President Calvin Coolidge assumed the presidency and was elected to another term in 1924. He said things like: "the business of America is business," and "a man who builds a factory builds a temple." The country could not have agreed more.

With no limitations on industrial growth, the nation delighted in flexing its muscles and enjoying its new found strength. By the end of the 1920s Americans were using more electricity than all the rest of the world combined! Radios, telephones, washing machines, and vacuum cleaners were suddenly as common in American homes as the newspaper. The movie industry flourished as people flocked to see the amazing new moving pictures. Automobiles of every shape and color poured off the assembly lines to meet the growing demand. Charles Lindbergh's solo flight across the Atlantic Ocean in his plane, *The Spirit of St. Louis,* cleared the way for the birth of the aviation industry.

But even as the nation soared ever higher on the wings of prosperity, little cracks began to appear in the framework of the economy. With the end of the war, huge shipments of grain to Europe had abruptly ceased, eliminating a vast market for U.S. farm products. The development of synthetic materials like rayon to replace wool and cotton in the manufacture of clothing reduced farm income even more.

Many farmers borrowed heavily, carrying huge mortgages on their land as they tried to stand up under the pressure. The increasing use of oil for heat and power reduced the need for coal, a labor-intensive commodity. Suddenly, large numbers of miners found themselves out of work.

But most Americans still had their jobs, a healthy income, and total faith in America's future. The signs of trouble, the struggling farmers and the laid-off miners, were ignored by the government and by most people. As never before in the United States, people had more money than they needed. They demonstrated their faith in the future by investing in stocks, or shares in businesses. After all, business could only get better. The stock market replaced the farmer's market as the place where people met to buy and sell. Wall Street became a place where anyone could make a fortune overnight. Stock prices climbed higher and higher. It seemed as if there was no limit to America's economic growth. It was in this spirit that Herbert Hoover was elected president in 1928. The Republicans had led the nation in eight years of unprecedented prosperity. No one saw any need to change.

Early in 1929 some major investors began selling their stocks and buying government investment bonds instead. This seemed strange, but the general public did not change their buying habits—they continued to invest more and more. But on October 29, 1929, for reasons no one quite knows, the bottom fell out of the market. It was truly "Black Tuesday." People in panic clamored to sell their stocks as they watched the prices plummet. Many investors, who had borrowed money to buy their stocks in the first place, suffered complete financial ruin. The United States had entered the Great Depression.

Financial panics had happened before in the country. As recently as 1907 Wall Street had been shaken by fears of bank failures. Economists had come to regard these negative economic experiences as part of the normal business cycle. Their research told them that these cycles usually lasted from two to five years. This time it was different, but Herbert Hoover and his administration in Washington held fast to the belief that the market would eventually right itself. Any interference by the federal government, they said, would be an unfair extension of the federal government's power over that of the states, even if the interference consisted of giving help to struggling people.

What the government could do, Hoover believed, was to lower taxes so people could keep more of their money for spending. The government could also create jobs by sponsoring the construction of dams and highways. He encouraged farmers to form cooperatives and raise fewer crops, and he urged banks to lower interest rates. "Prosperity is just around the corner," he said, but it did not appear. All over the country, people lost their life savings as their banks went out of business. Farmers lost their farms when they could not pay the bills.

In the cities, once-prosperous businessmen sold apples on street corners. Breadlines and free soup kitchens served food to lines of hungry people that stretched for blocks. Many who had lost their homes lived in shacks on the outskirts of towns. People began blaming Hoover

Worldwide financial collapse turned prosperous citizens into homeless drifters desperate for work and food.

for the depression and called the shanty towns "Hoovervilles." After World War I Congress had approved a bonus for war veterans to be paid in 1945. In 1932 a group of veterans demonstrated in Washington, demanding that the bonus be paid right away. Hoover ordered troops out to disperse the so-called Bonus Army. Shots were fired. Blood was shed. The bonus was not paid.

FDR's "alphabet soup" of government programs helped get the U.S. back on its feet.

The American people felt that they had been betrayed by their government. The country was not only economically depressed, it was emotionally drained as well.

Now it was time for a change, and in the election of 1932 Franklin Delano Roosevelt, a Democrat, won by a landslide. Roosevelt, soon dubbed FDR by the press, told the country that it had "nothing to fear but fear itself." He called for a "New Deal" for the American people and began taking action. During the next one hundred days major legislation was passed which would have its impact upon the nation's economy for decades to come.

The Federal Deposit Insurance Corporation (FDIC) insured bank accounts so people would know their money was safe. The National Industrial Recovery Act (NRA) created jobs. Minimum wage laws assured workers a decent wage. The Agricultural Industrial Act (AIA) controlled crop prices. The Federal Emergency Relief Administration (FERA) put federal funds in the hands of state agencies to care for the poor. The list grew—the WPA, the TVA, the CCC—until Roosevelt's critics began talking about his "alphabet soup" of government programs.

Stricken with polio, Roosevelt set an example for the nation.

After four years of the New Deal more than ten million Americans were still unemployed. But FDR never seemed to lose his good humor or confidence. His "fireside chats" on the radio kept people informed about what the government was trying to do and why. His high spirits seemed to be infectious. In 1936 he was elected to a second term by an overwhelming majority.

The effects of the Great Depression reached far beyond the borders of the United States. The nations of Europe had not recovered from the devastation of World War I, and hard times caused political unrest in many countries. In Germany the value of the currency dropped so much that people pushed wheelbarrows full of money just to buy food. Adolf Hitler had begun organizing the National Socialist German Worker's (NAZI) Party in the 1920s. He won the devotion of a large group of followers with his fiery speeches and his belief that Germany must avenge the losses it suffered in the Treaty of Versailles.

216

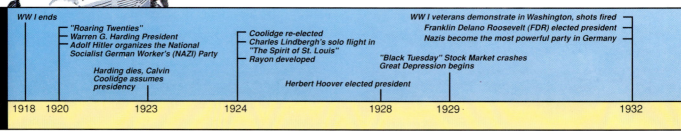

The Nazis became the strongest party in Germany, receiving 32 percent of the vote in the 1932 elections. Although many people disapproved of Hitler, his popularity grew until the German President Von Hindenburg appointed him Chancellor of the Reichstag (Leader of the Parliament) in 1933. In August, 1934, Von Hindenburg died and Hitler proclaimed himself *Führer* ("leader" or "ruler") of all Germany. Hitler pledged to return Germany to the position of power and wealth it had held before the war and received the unqualified support of the majority of the German people.

On September 1, 1939, Hitler attacked Poland, and England and France honored their treaty obligations by supporting the defenseless nation. It was the beginning of World War II, and it would not be long before a new generation of Americans was heading across the Atlantic to test the mettle of the spirit of democracy.

Germany's ruined economy paved the way for Hitler's rise to power.

- New Deal
- Federal Deposit Insurance Corporation (FDIC)
- National Industrial Recovery Act (NRA)
- Agricultural Industrial Act (AIA)
- Federal Emergency Relief Administration
- Hitler becomes Chancellor of the Reichstag

Hitler proclaims himself "Fuhrer" of Germany

FDR re-elected

Hitler attacks Poland

1933   1934   1936   1939

Quiz

1. The decade following World War I is known as

- Ⓐ the Gay Nineties.
- Ⓑ the Roaring Twenties.
- Ⓒ the Great Depression.
- Ⓓ the Roaring Thirties.

2. After Warren G. Harding's death in 1923, _____ became President.

- Ⓐ Calvin Coolidge
- Ⓑ Franklin Delano Roosevelt
- Ⓒ Herbert Hoover
- Ⓓ Theodore Roosevelt

3. Which of the following industries did not grow in the 1920s?

- Ⓐ automotive
- Ⓑ aviation
- Ⓒ movies
- Ⓓ computers

4. The stock market is where people buy and sell shares in businesses.

- Ⓐ True
- Ⓑ False

5. The stock market crash on Tuesday, October 29, 1929, is called

- Ⓐ Blue Wednesday.
- Ⓑ Stormy Monday.
- Ⓒ Black Friday.
- Ⓓ Black Tuesday.

6. The shanty towns jobless people lived in were called "Hoovervilles" for the inventor of the vacuum cleaner.

- Ⓐ True
- Ⓑ False

7. The "Bonus Army" was led by Adolph Hitler.

- Ⓐ True
- Ⓑ False

8. President Roosevelt's plan to end the depression was called

- Ⓐ the New Deal.
- Ⓑ Alphabet Soup.
- Ⓒ the Fireside Chat.
- Ⓓ the Civilian Conservation Corps.

9. In 1934 Adolph Hitler became the leader of

- Ⓐ England.
- Ⓑ France.
- Ⓒ Germany.
- Ⓓ Poland.

10. World War II began in

- Ⓐ 1940.
- Ⓑ 1939.
- Ⓒ 1938.
- Ⓓ 1937.

Chapter 21

World War II—The Big One

The woman crept silently through the darkness. "Hurry," she whispered to the young airman who followed close behind her. "We are almost there." Below them in the distance, a German transport lumbered past. She motioned to him to wait. As he crouched in the shadowy hills, his heart beating wildly, he thought about what an amazing journey this had been.

He was a British Royal Air Force pilot who had been shot down in Belgium behind German lines. Sympathetic townspeople had hidden him in a monastery until members of the Belgian underground could arrange his escape. For three weeks he had awaited the arrival of his guide. But he had not expected anyone like Dédée! Young and slim, her fair hair dyed black to prevent identification, Dédée had personally escorted more than a hundred escapees to safety on thirty-two trips across occupied France and through the rugged Pyrenees. Now she beckoned him forward. "The border is two hundred yards straight ahead," she whispered. "Someone will be waiting for you on the other side. Good luck! *Vive la résistance!*" With that she disappeared into the darkness. Dédée de Jongh, the legendary "Comet," had spirited another Allied soldier to safety.

World War I was to be "the war to end wars." The U.S. had entered the conflict "to make the world safe for democracy." Yet twenty years later, democracy was in greater jeopardy than ever and the world stood poised yet again on the brink of global conflict.

In 1929 the Great Depression rocked the industrialized nations of the world, hitting Germany particularly hard. Still stinging from their defeat in World War I and suffering from unemployment, hunger, and poverty, the German people turned to a leader who promised to restore the Fatherland to its former glory.

Adolph Hitler was the head of the National Socialist, or Nazi, party. Hitler and the Nazis offered a philosophy and a course of action that appealed to the Germans' wounded pride. True Germans, he said, were Aryans, a culturally and physically superior race, whose destiny it was to rule the world. He blamed non-Aryans, particularly Jews, for all of Germany's woes. The Nazi party grew very slowly in its early years, but after 1929, as unemployment mounted, so did the Nazis' support. In 1933 Hitler became Chancellor of Germany. He quickly moved to wipe out all opposition from political parties and unions. In 1935 anti-Jewish laws stripped German Jews of their citizenship rights and for-

bade marriage between Jews and non-Jews. Under Hitler's dictatorial regime the terror continued to escalate. The result was that many Jews and liberal German intellectuals fled to other countries. Woe to those who did not flee. They were destined for barbaric destruction.

A large part of Hitler's appeal was his promise to build a new German empire, the Third Reich. In direct violation of the Treaty of Versailles he began to rebuild Germany's armed forces. Hitler gambled—correctly—that the League of Nations would do nothing to stop him. With guns,

Adolph Hitler rose to power with his promise to restore Germany to its former greatness.

German storm troopers moved through Europe in an attempt at total conquest.

tanks, and weapons rolling off the assembly lines the German economy flourished, while the propaganda machine commanded by Joseph Goebbels sang *der Führer's* praises. The German people admired Hitler as a "man of the people." He was getting things done!

Hitler's rise was not without precedent. In 1922 Benito Mussolini had marched his followers, the Fascists, into Rome and proclaimed himself *Il Duce*, the undisputed ruler of Italy. Mussolini promised to restore the glory of the Roman

Italy's Mussolini and Japan's Tojo were staunch allies of Hitler and the Nazis.

Empire. His totalitarian regime did succeed in improving Italy's economy—unemployment was eliminated by putting the jobless in the army, and new roads and public works were built. But this progress came at the expense of freedom. Mussolini's opponents were jailed or killed. Il Duce's rule was absolute.

While Mussolini and Hitler tightened their holds on Italy and Germany, a military leader named General Hideki Tojo came to power in Japan. The same "isms" that were sweeping Europe—nationalism, militarism, imperialism—were taking hold in Japan. As his first move to create a powerful Japanese empire, Tojo invaded the Chinese province of Manchuria in 1931. The League of Nations protested, but Japan simply withdrew from the League.

Italy moved next. In 1935 with no resistance from the League of Nations, Mussolini's troops invaded the African nation of Ethiopia. The following year Hitler sent troops into the Rhineland, an area of Germany bordering France. The Treaty of Versailles had barred German troops from occupying this buffer zone, but Britain and France made no attempt to enforce the treaty as they were reluctant to take any action that might lead to war. Hitler's next move was to annex Austria in early 1938, saying that all German-speaking peoples belonged to one nation. When the League of Nations again did nothing to stop him he moved on to Czechoslovakia.

France and Britain continued to do nothing. The unprecedented horror of the First World War had persuaded the two nations to pursue "peace at any price." Across the sea, Americans sympathized with the victims of aggression but were reluctant to get involved in another European war. Too many American lives had been lost in World War I. Too many war debts remained unpaid. The U.S. reinforced its policy of isolationism with a series of Neutrality Acts designed to keep America from getting pulled into the coming overseas conflict.

In 1939 in a move that stunned the world, Hitler's Germany and Stalin's Russia signed a pact of friendship. Although Nazism and Communism were staunch enemies, the two nations realized the benefits that each could gain from an alliance. Stalin hoped that this treaty would buy the USSR time to build up its forces in anticipation of a future attack by the power-mad Nazis. In addition, secret clauses in the pact promised that the Soviet Union would gain possession of the Baltic republics of Estonia, Latvia, and Lithuania, as well as a chunk of Poland. Germany for its part could now attack Poland with no fear of counterattack on the Eastern front. And attack it did.

On September 1, 1939, Germany launched a *blitzkrieg*, or "lightning war," against Poland. No longer able to stand idly by, England and France declared war against Germany

Axis nations
Allies and friendly nations
Extent of Axis conquests, 1943
Neutral nations
Free French territories
occupied by Allies
Finland was at war with USSR
in 1944 and with Germany in 1945

and the other "Axis" powers, Italy and Japan. World War II had begun.

The world was shocked by the new kind of warfare that Hitler unleashed. German Stuka planes, equipped with terrifying whistles, bombed Poland's cities, airfields, and railroads relentlessly while wave after wave of tanks mowed down lines of Polish horse cavalry by the thousands. Just as in World War I, new technology produced a revolution in war tactics. Within a month the huge country of Poland was smashed.

220

In another lightning attack German troops invaded Denmark and Norway. Denmark fell in twenty-four hours but the Norwegians resisted. Britain managed to muster up some assistance for beleaguered Norway but it was too little, too late. So sure of success was Hitler that even before Norway was subdued, he launched his third blitzkrieg, this time against Belgium, Luxembourg, and the Netherlands. The Low Countries were quickly overwhelmed. Pushing onward, German tanks bored through the "impenetrable" Ardennes forest and into France, cutting the Allied forces in half. Trapped, the Allies retreated toward the coastal city of Dunkirk with the Germans in hot pursuit. It looked as if the French and British troops would be slaughtered upon the shore, but in one of the most spectacular rescue operations ever, while the valiant pilots of the R.A.F. (English Royal Air Force) held Germany's Luftwaffe at bay, a rag-tag collection of British ships—merchant vessels, yachts, steamships, even fishing boats—ferried over 300,000 men to safety across the English Channel.

The operation at Dunkirk has been called a "miracle," but as one British politician noted dryly, "Wars are not won by masterly withdrawals." After Dunkirk, the disheartened and poorly organized French troops were easily overcome. Paris soon fell and with it fell the French will to resist. As a cruel joke Hitler forced the French to surrender at the exact spot where Germany had surrendered to France at the end

of World War I. The northern part of France became an occupied land. In the city of Vichy in the south, the Germans set up a government run by collaborators who would carry out Hitler's wishes.

It was now the summer of 1940, and Britain stood alone to face the Nazi menace. Although the situation looked grim for the island nation, Britain had several factors in its favor. One was the leadership of Sir Winston Churchill, an inspirational statesman who refused to be intimidated by Hitler's threats. Militarily the formidable presence of the British navy in the English Channel protected the island from an amphibious attack; the British army, though badly damaged at Dunkirk and forced to abandon much of its weapons and supplies on French shores, was beginning to recover its strength (thanks in part to America's Lend-Lease Act, which gave President Franklin D. Roosevelt the authority to sell or lend war supplies to any nation whose defense he deemed essential to American security). However, the R.A.F., Britain's only defense against Germany's deadly Luftwaffe, was outnumbered three to one and suffered from

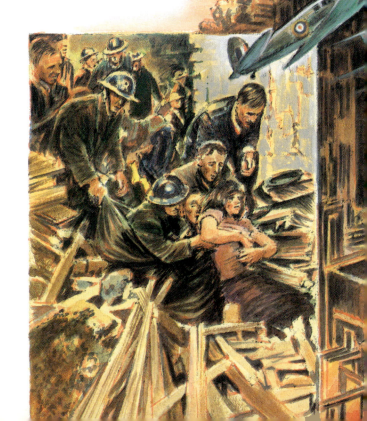

With courage and dignity, the British people withstood nonstop German bomb attacks.

a shortage of pilots. Throughout that summer, the anxious Britons prepared for attack from above. Thousands of women and children were evacuated to the countryside. Elderly men donned Civil Defense uniforms and searched the skies for enemy planes. In mid-August, after Hitler had paused just long enough to reposition his planes on the newly-seized airfields of Western Europe, the onslaught began.

The Battle of Britain raged for ten months. German planes "blitzed" London day and night, wreaking incredible destruction. Some smaller cities and towns were completely destroyed. But Britain refused to give up. Courageous British citizens slept in shelters and subway stations. They organized brigades to put out the fires that ravaged their homes and businesses. They rallied to Churchill's cry, "We shall never surrender!" By the end of 1940, after losing an estimated 2,700 planes to the R.A.F. and to the recently developed radar network that dotted the English coast, Hitler incredibly decided to abandon his plan to conquer Britain.

The Nazi armies moved eastward instead. In rapid succession, the Axis pow-

Only Russia's desperate "scorched earth" defense kept Hitler's blitzkrieg from succeeding.

ers captured Romania, Greece, Hungary, Bulgaria, and Yugoslavia. Now nothing stood between the Führer and his next goal. Despite the 1939 non-aggression pact between the two nations, Hitler was determined to conquer the Soviet Union.

Both Britain and the United States had warned Stalin that Hitler would turn on him, but Stalin dismissed their prediction as Allied propaganda. As a result the Soviet army was completely unprepared for Hitler's "Operation Barbarossa." The attack came on June 22, 1941—the same fateful day in June on which Napoleon had launched his Russian campaign. Spearheaded by 150 divisions and air support, Nazi troops quickly advanced toward the principal cities of Moscow, Stalingrad, and Leningrad, capturing thousands of Soviet soldiers and weapons along the way. Hitler's boast that he would capture the vast Soviet Union in six weeks seemed entirely too likely.

Unfortunately for Hitler, he had once again overestimated his position. For one thing an enormous German occupation force remained in Western Europe and in the recently captured Eastern European nations, so Hitler was unable to unleash against Russia the entire concentrated firepower that had blitzed the West. The three-pronged attack on Russia's major cities meant that invading troops were spread even more thinly. In addition, the Russians adopted a "scorched earth" policy of destroying everything—their crops, livestock, factories, power plants, even houses—to keep them from benefiting the invaders. Together these factors succeeded in slowing down the Germans' progress. After their initial lightning success, Nazi troops became bogged down in a ground war within sight of the domes and spires of Moscow—bogged down long enough for the Russians' secret weapon to wreak havoc on the unprepared attackers. That secret weapon was the same one that had led to Napoleon's downfall a century before: the long, frigid Russian winter.

Hitler had arrogantly anticipated a speedy victory over the Soviets. His troops in their lightweight uniforms suffered miserably as temperatures dropped. Weapons froze and so did flesh. Vehicles would not budge. When it became impossible for rations to reach the front, soldiers ate frozen horse flesh to stay alive. Meanwhile the Russians were preparing for an offense of their own. On December 6, 1941, a huge force of troops and tanks surged forward against the Germans, whose own troops and vehicles were mired in the snow. It was the beginning of the end for Hitler's Russian campaign. But while the Germans and Soviets battled for control of Russia, throughout the conquered lands of Europe the Nazis were conducting another war against the Jews and other "undesirables."

Hitler expressed his hatred for the Jews in *Mein Kampf* ("My Struggle"), which he wrote while he was in jail during the early days of the Nazi movement. As outlined in the book, his plan was to send all Germany's Jews to Madagascar, an island off the coast of Africa. During the war, however, he conceived a much more heinous "final solution"—he would murder all the Jews in Europe! This genocide (extermination of a specific group of people) is now known as the *Holocaust*. Six million Jews—more than two-thirds of Europe's Jewish population—were wiped out in the Holocaust along with millions of Poles, Russians, Gypsies, and other selected targets. Imagine the mighty coordinated effort required to achieve this monstrous goal! Victims were packed like sardines into trains bound for "concentration camps" all over Europe, where they were employed as slave labor. From 1942 to 1945 they were transported in like manner to "death camps" that had been established in Eastern Europe. There they were gassed to death and burned to ashes in huge ovens.

Antisemitism has existed since the Middle Ages, but the world had never seen such a display of horrible cruelty against humanity in modern times. During the course of the war there were two major uprisings against the systematic extermination, both in Warsaw, Poland. An uprising in the Jewish ghetto was crushed after 28 days, and a later uprising by Polish resistance fighters was smashed within two months. The Danes conspired to save the entire Danish Jewish population. Throughout occupied Europe, heroic citizens and armed freedom fighters committed acts of bravery that defied the Nazis' reign of terror. But their efforts were of no more consequence than flea bites to an elephant.

By the time Hitler invaded Russia, the United States Congress had already appropriated 37 billion dollars for rearmament and aid to the Allies. However the U.S. was content with its role as the "arsenal of democracy." Most Americans had no desire to become actively engaged in the war—not until the calm Sunday morning of December 7, 1941, when 353 Japanese bombers suddenly swooped out of the sky over Pearl Harbor, Hawaii. Within minutes half the United States Navy had been destroyed. Within hours America had declared war on

On December 7, 1941, Japanese planes attacked Pearl Harbor, devastating the U.S. Navy. President Roosevelt called it a "day that would live in infamy." He immediately declared war on Japan and its allies.

Dwight Eisenhower, an obscure Lieutenant Colonel in 1941, became supreme commander of the allied expeditionary forces. After the war he was elected 34th president of the U.S.

Japan and the other Axis powers. When most of the countries of Latin America quickly followed suit, World War II truly became a "world" war with a total of 38 nations fighting, only ten of them on the Axis side.

It would be a while before the U.S. Pacific fleet recovered its strength. It would also take time to assemble on European shores enough American men and supplies to launch a full-scale attack against Hitler. Allied leaders decided instead to strike against Hitler's troops in North Africa, the Afrika Korps led by General Erwin Rommel, the "Desert Fox." After months of fierce desert warfare, British General Bernard Montgomery defeated Rommel's troops at El Alamein. This first Allied victory was one of the turning points in the war against Hitler. Shortly thereafter, a joint Allied force led by General Dwight D. Eisenhower succeeded in wiping out the Afrika Corps for good.

A second major blow in the war against Hitler came with the Russian Army's victory against the Germans at Stalingrad in November, 1943. Hitler had been forced to abandon his strike against Moscow the previous winter. But Russia's second-largest city, Leningrad, had been under siege all year. With no food able to reach the surrounded city, nearly one million people had died of starvation. Yet the city had not surrendered. As spring came Hitler decided to attack the southern city of Stalingrad with all the strength his depleted Eastern army could muster. The loss of Stalingrad, he figured, would strike a serious blow to Soviet morale, and it would put the Germans in possession of valuable factories and oil supplies. For four months German tanks and planes strafed Stalingrad, reducing the city to rubble. Defenders fought heroically block by block, street by street against the better-armed invaders. Then, in November the Russians launched a massive and unexpected counterattack. Overwhelmed and quickly surrounded, the Germans once again became bogged down in the harsh Russian winter. As food gave out and the airstrip became inoperable, Hitler's troops were forced to surrender. The Soviets then began to drive the Germans out of the rest of the country.

Beginning with the city of Cologne in 1942, the British and American air forces had unleashed a relentless bombing attack on industrial targets and railroad yards inside Germany. Improved radar devices allowed them to conduct bombing raids regardless of the weather. By 1943 the Allies had perfected the "blockbuster" bomb with which they devastated the German seaport of Hamburg. A daring attack on Germany's much-needed oil fields in Romania destroyed 40 percent of their production capacity. But the climax of the aerial war took place in February and March of 1944, when American fighters shot down eight hundred German planes. From that point on, the Luftwaffe no longer posed a significant threat to the Allies.

With the Luftwaffe out of the way, the Allies were ready for a major land assault against the Germans. While the Russian army slowly pushed the Nazi intruders westward, the Allies began an invasion of Italy. Their first destination, the island of Sicily, fell in a month. As dreams of a new Roman Empire evaporated, the Italians revolted against Mussolini and signed an armistice with the Allies, but the German army took control of the country and continued to fight. The Allies were able to make a successful landing on the Italian mainland. However, conquest

223

Dawn breaks and D-Day begins.

With the final defeat of the German army, the horrors of Nazi prison camps became known to the world.

Pacific Ocean

Areas under Japanese control, 1942
Maximum extent of Japanese control, 1942
Major battles
Allied advances

proved to be a long and costly ordeal. Soldiers on both sides were slaughtered in great numbers in battles at Anzio and Monte Cassino. Rome was not freed until June 4, 1944, and some parts of Italy remained under German control until the spring of 1945.

Only two days after the liberation of Rome, the Allies began their invasion of France. "Operation Overlord" was mind-boggling in scope. Assembled with Allied troops on the shores of southern England were 1,627,000 American soldiers and another 50,000 sailors. Since all of France's materiel was in the hands of the Germans, the Allies had to bring with them everything they would need: tanks, trucks, buses, ambulances, railroad locomotives, bulldozers, entire telephone systems, radio stations, power plants, kitchen facilities and more, not to mention weapons, ammunition, gasoline, food, and clothing.

Throughout the night of June 5, 1944, the Allied invasion force streamed toward the French shores of Normandy. At the first light of dawn on June 6, D-Day began. With battleships, destroyers, and mine sweepers leading the way and thousands of bombers providing cover, the landing forces hit the beaches—only to be riddled with machine-gun fire and toppled into the waist-deep water, where their heavy equipment dragged them down. Slowly, painfully, the landing force inched its way to shore. By the end of the day the Allies had gained a foothold in France. General George S. Patton's tanks immediately swarmed inland with a speed and vengeance that equalled Hitler's blitzkrieg in intensity. A second Allied landing force raced north from French ports on the Mediterranean. Before summer was over France and Belgium were free.

Allied forces were soon poised along the German border from

George Patton was the most flamboyant Allied general. He turned the tables on Hitler with a lightning tank offensive that led directly to Berlin—and victory!

The war in the Pacific continued as Allied troops "island-hopped" ever nearer to the Japanese mainland.

General Douglas MacArthur and Admiral Chester Nimitz led the Allies to victory at Midway, Guadalcanal, and finally, Iwo Jima.

Holland to Switzerland. Hitler decided to launch a surprise last-ditch attack. He would smash through the Ardennes Forest into the center of the Allied line and wipe out the Allies in one stroke. Under cover of darkness, in foul weather that rendered American air defense useless, the Germans attacked with a barrage of artillery fire and twenty-five armored divisions. They broke through the American lines and began racing across Belgium, creating a 50-mile-deep "bulge" in the Allied lines. The Battle of the Bulge raged for a month. While American troops fought tooth and nail to defend the key city of Bastogne, Allied reinforcements raced in from the north and south. Soon the Germans were forced to withdraw.

In February of 1945, the Allies began battling their way to the Rhine. As the Allied troops advanced, the Germans retreated across the river, blowing up bridges behind them. They missed only one, but one bridge was all it took to send eight thousand Americans racing across the Rhine. Despite a heavy air attack from the Luftwaffe's new jet bombers and the recently-developed V-2 rocket, Allied engineers constructed sixty-two temporary bridges across the "impassable" Rhine in just ten days. The Allied army poured across the river and drove deep into the heart of Germany. At the Elbe River, about seventy-five miles south of Berlin, they met up with the Russian army, which had chased the retreating Germans all the way across Eastern Europe. Both armies trained their big guns on Berlin. As the Soviets and the Allies pounded his capital into rubble, Hitler took refuge in an underground bunker where he and several of his top officers committed suicide. Just one week later on May 8, 1945—a day that became known as V-E Day, for "Victory in Europe"—a defeated Germany surrendered.

The war against Hitler had ended, but far away in the Pacific the battle against Japan raged on. The surprise attack on Pearl Harbor had been an enormous victory for Japan. With only one battleship and sixteen bombers remaining, the United States was unable to stop the Japanese from seizing one Pacific nation after another. By the summer of 1941 Japan controlled northern and central China, the Philippines, and most of Southeast Asia, including the Dutch East Indies and French Indochina. Evacuated by submarine from the doomed Philippines, General Douglas MacArthur had vowed, "I shall return." It would take him three years to keep that promise.

Although America's indignation at the Japanese attack spurred the country into action, the anti-Japanese sentiment it aroused led to one of the most shameful incidents

After the death of President Roosevelt, Harry S. Truman was burdened with the decision of whether or not to use the atomic bomb.

deep in the island's jungles and swamps. It took six bloody months but in January of 1943 Guadalcanal was finally in Allied hands. When Australian forces drove back the Japanese from New Guinea just weeks later, it was clear that the Allies had regained control of the seas.

On island after island the Japanese fought ferociously. But by October of 1944 MacArthur had slogged his way to the Philippines. There in Leyte Gulf, he engaged the Japanese in the biggest naval battle in history. In four days of fighting most of Japan's remaining naval strength was destroyed. Still the Japanese did not surrender.

Harry S. Truman, who had become President of the United States upon Roosevelt's death in April of 1945, now faced a gut-wrenching decision. He could order a full-scale invasion of Japan with a possible cost of one million American lives, or he could unleash America's deadly new weapon, the atomic bomb. Throughout the war scientists on both sides had raced to develop a weapon that harnessed the power of the atom. A team of American scientists, working under the code name "Manhattan Project," had completed and tested the bomb in the summer of 1945. It was a weapon whose destructive power was unrivaled by anything else on earth.

After issuing warnings to the proud and stubborn Japanese government, the U.S. plane Enola Gay dropped the first atomic bomb on Hiroshima. Three days later Nagasaki was leveled by a second bomb, and Japan surrendered.

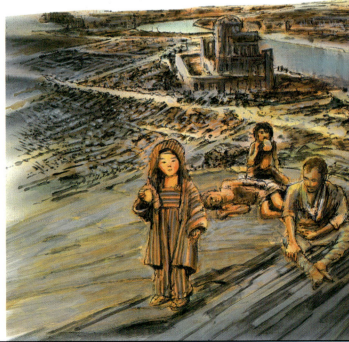

in United States history. On America's West Coast about 112,000 Japanese-Americans were forced to sell their homes and property and move to desolate internment camps for the duration of the war. Although there was no reason to question their loyalty, these victims of blind prejudice spent years behind barbed wire at Manzanar and other dreary camps.

226

America's all-out war effort quickly bore fruit. Within a year of Pearl Harbor the Pacific fleet was back at full strength, ready to turn the tide against empire-hungry Japan. That turning point came in June of 1942 with the fierce air-and-sea battle at Midway Island. Japan's unstoppable drive came to a screeching halt under the relentless assault of dive-bombing American fighters. For the first time Japan was forced to retreat. Eight months later the great American counter-offensive began.

It was to be a two-pronged attack. MacArthur would move through New Guinea and surrounding islands toward the Philippines, while Admiral Chester Nimitz cleaned out the Japanese-held islands in the Central Pacific and moved on toward Japan. By "island hopping"—focusing on strategically important islands and bypassing others—the Allies hoped to save time and lives. The first major engagement of the Allied offensive was waged at Guadalcanal in the Solomon Islands. Nimitz's troops battled the Japanese in the air, at sea, and

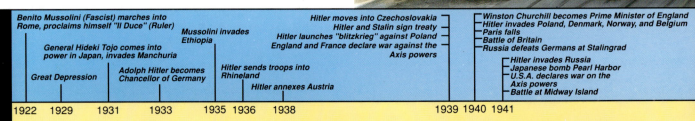

Benito Mussolini (Fascist) marches into Rome, proclaims himself "Il Duce" (Ruler)

General Hideki Tojo comes into power in Japan, invades Manchuria

Great Depression

Adolph Hitler becomes Chancellor of Germany

Mussolini invades Ethiopia

Hitler sends troops into Rhineland

Hitler annexes Austria

Hitler moves into Czechoslovakia
Hitler and Stalin sign treaty
Hitler launches "blitzkrieg" against Poland
England and France declare war against the Axis powers

Winston Churchill becomes Prime Minister of England
Hitler invades Poland, Denmark, Norway, and Belgium
Paris falls
Battle of Britain
Russia defeats Germans at Stalingrad

Hitler invades Russia
Japanese bomb Pearl Harbor
U.S.A. declares war on the Axis powers
Battle at Midway Island

1922   1929   1931   1933   1935 1936   1938   1939 1940 1941

President Truman decided that too many American soldiers had died already. On August 6, 1945, the bomber *Enola Gay* dropped the world's first atomic bomb on the seventh-largest Japanese city, Hiroshima. In a blinding flash of light, an entire city was destroyed and 70,000 people were dead. The U.S. called for surrender but Japan's military leaders refused to admit defeat. Three days later a second atomic bomb was dropped on Nagasaki, resulting in at least another 75,000 deaths. Within five years, deaths resulting from burns and radiation totaled over 300,000.

On August 14, 1945, Japan finally surrendered. After six years and a day of bloodshed and destruction, World War II was over. From its smoldering embers emerged a world in which little remained unchanged. The cost in human lives had been almost unfathomable. Counting both military and civilian losses, 55 million people died worldwide. The bill for arms and war machinery came to more than a *trillion* dollars. Politically and militarily, the United States and the Soviet Union had established themselves as the most powerful nations on earth. And over the entire world now hung the shadow of nuclear destruction.

Allied forces begin invasion of Italy
Italians revolt against Mussolini
Guadalcanal in Allied hands

Rome freed
"D" Day
Battle of the Bulge

Germany surrenders
U.S. drops atomic bomb on Hiroshima and Nagasaki
Japan surrenders
WWII ends

1943   1944   1945

Quiz

1. **Which of the following was not a contributing factor to World War II?**

   Ⓐ militarism Ⓒ fundamentalism
   Ⓑ nationalism Ⓓ imperialism

2. **The name Nazi is another name for which political group?**

   Ⓐ Nazarene Party Ⓒ National Aryan Society
   Ⓑ National Zionist Party Ⓓ National Socialist Party

3. **Who were the three main Axis Powers?**

   Ⓐ Germany, Italy, Japan Ⓒ U.S., France, Britain
   Ⓑ German, Austria, Hungary Ⓓ Italy, Germany, Russia

4. **France and Britain's policy of giving in to Hitler to avoid war was called**

   Ⓐ a pact of friendship. Ⓒ the Neutrality Acts.
   Ⓑ "peace at any price." Ⓓ isolationism.

5. **Over 300,000 trapped Allied troops were rescued from French shores in a daring operation at**

   Ⓐ Vichy. Ⓒ Ardennes.
   Ⓑ Munich. Ⓓ Dunkirk.

6. **What event triggered the United States' entry into World War II?**

   Ⓐ the persecution of the Jews Ⓒ Japan's attack on Pearl Harbor
   Ⓑ Japan's invasion of China Ⓓ Hitler's invasion of France

7. **The Germans' last-ditch effort to plow through the Allied lines resulted in which important battle?**

   Ⓐ Battle of the Bulge Ⓒ Midway
   Ⓑ D-Day Ⓓ Operation Barbarossa

8. **Two important Allied victories took place at**

   Ⓐ Dunkirk and Guadalcanal. Ⓒ Munich and Stalingrad.
   Ⓑ Normandy and Midway. Ⓓ El Alamein and Norway.

9. **Which one of the following was not an important political figure during World War II?**

   Ⓐ Franklin D. Roosevelt Ⓒ Joseph Stalin
   Ⓑ Otto von Bismarck Ⓓ Harry S. Truman

10. **The approximate number of deaths caused by the atomic bombs dropped on Hiroshima and Nagasaki was**

    Ⓐ 70,000. Ⓒ one million.
    Ⓑ 450,000. Ⓓ 300,000.

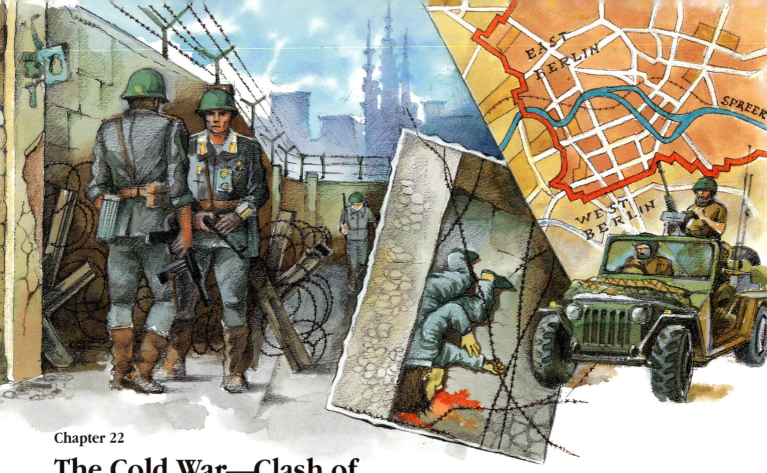

Chapter 22

The Cold War—Clash of the Titans

The Berlin Wall became a symbol of the conflict between democracy and communism.

228

A murmur of excitement raced through the crowd gathered in front of the Brandenburg gate. Candlelight shone on faces flushed with emotion. Suddenly they heard it: a loud crash from the other side of the wall. The crowd began to cheer. One more booming crash and suddenly chunks of stone were flying everywhere. The crowd screamed and rushed forward. Young people on both sides clambered over the breach and embraced atop the ruined wall. Strangers helped each other up and over. Everywhere were shouts of laughter and tears of joy. It was November 1989 and the Berlin Wall, that hated symbol of a divided Germany, lay in rubble.

In February of 1945, as the war in Europe was drawing to a close, the "Big Three" Allied leaders—Franklin D. Roosevelt of the United States, Winston Churchill of Great Britain, and Joseph Stalin of the Soviet Union—gathered at the Russian seaside resort of Yalta. The purpose of their meeting was to decide the fate of post-war Europe. At Yalta the Allies agreed to divide Germany into zones of occupation. Although Berlin, the capital of Germany, fell within the Soviet zone, it was too important to the nation's economy for the Western powers to relinquish, so it too was divided into East and West.

But no agreement could be reached on what to do about the devastated nation of Poland. Roosevelt and Churchill wanted an independent, democratic Poland.

Stalin, however, had a different vision. Hitler's blitzkrieg invasion was not the first time that Russia had been attacked from the west, but Stalin was determined that it would be the last. From now on, he swore, Poland would be part of the buffer zone between the Soviet Union and Western Europe, with a "puppet" government whose strings would be pulled by Stalin himself.

Harry S. Truman, who had assumed the U.S. presidency upon the death of Franklin Roosevelt, viewed these events with dismay but, short of waging war against the Soviet Union there was little he could do. With Russian troops already occupying Poland, it was too late to prevent that country from becoming a communist nation, but Truman vowed to hold the line against any further communist expansion. At that time communist movements were gaining in popularity throughout Europe, as desperate people sought relief from the misery and destruction wrought by the war. Truman realized that if any country was going to check the spread of communism in Europe, it would have to be the United States.

So Truman devised a plan to prevent other countries from falling behind the "Iron Curtain." By pouring economic aid into the war-torn countries of Europe, the United States would ensure the survival of capitalist, pro-American governments. Thus began the struggle between the Soviet Union and the United States—a so-called Cold

War that shaped the course of world events for almost fifty years to come. Not a shot was fired between the two superpowers throughout the course of the Cold War, yet the battle raged on all fronts—military, scientific, economic, and political. Nations all over the world became pawns in the U.S./Soviet power struggle. More than once during the Cold War the entire world found itself poised on the brink of nuclear disaster as the two sides squared off, neither wanting to be the first to back down.

World War I —"the war to end war"— had not lived up to its billing for several reasons, one of them being the failure of the League of Nations. During World War II, Roosevelt and the other Allied leaders became determined to succeed where their predecessors had failed. In July of 1945 fifty-one nations signed the United Nations charter, establishing a new organization dedicated to world peace and international cooperation. Unfortunately, like the League of Nations before it, the United Nations did not have the means to *enforce* its good intentions. As the Cold War escalated and the world became increasingly polarized between the communist nations and the so-called Free World, the United Nations often seemed to be just another battleground in the superpowers' struggle.

United Nations emblem

Berlin, the former capital of Germany, was one of the early battlegrounds. Although it was located in the Soviet-occupied area of Germany, land access had been guaranteed to the West. However, in the spring of 1948, the Soviets began eliminating access, finally blockading all roads and railways. Truman now faced a dilemma: either abandon West Berlin and allow the Communists an important victory, or defy the Soviet roadblock and run the risk of starting a war with the Soviet Union. Truman's solution was clever but expensive. For nearly a full year the United States Air Force *airlifted* supplies into the blockaded German capital. The frustrated Soviets could do nothing to stop the flow of goods to Berlin—except to shoot down American planes, and they were not willing to go that far. Finally, in May of 1949 after some 277,000 American missions, the Soviets ended the land blockade. However, Berlin remained a divided city until 1991.

The nations of Western Europe grew increasingly uneasy about the Soviet threat. In March of 1948, Britain, France, and the Benelux countries signed a fifty-year defense treaty. That alliance soon grew into the North Atlantic Treaty Organization, or NATO, a mutual-defense pact that included the United States, Canada, Denmark, Iceland, Italy, Norway and Portugal, and later Greece and Turkey. The NATO countries viewed their pact as a purely defensive arrangement. To the Soviets, however, it seemed as if all of Europe was ganging up on them. Mistrust and resentment between the two sides continued to grow.

In 1949 the Soviets tested their first atomic bomb. This set off an enormous "Red Scare" in the United States, a mass paranoia that resulted in thousands of ruined lives. The hysteria was fueled by Senator Joseph McCarthy of Wisconsin, who in the early 1950s became one of the most powerful and feared people in America. McCarthy accused rival politicians and other public figures of being "soft on communism." To McCarthy, spies and traitors were responsible for every American "loss" that took place anywhere in the world. One of the biggest of these losses was the communist takeover of China in 1949.

The Manchu Dynasty had ruled the land since 1644, although its power had been on the wane for centuries. By 1900, foreign nations had succeeded in carving China into "spheres of influence." In that year, fanatical nationalists staged an anti-foreigner uprising called the Boxer Rebellion. This mini-war was quickly put down by the Western nations who then demanded even greater concessions from the weakened Chinese government.

In 1911, a republican revolution broke out in China, led by a former peasant named Sun Yat-sen. His party, the Nationalist Party or Kuomintang, promised nationalism, democracy, and a livelihood for all. But even though they succeeded in forcing the Manchu emperor to abdicate the throne, the Kuomintang could not wrest control of the country away from powerful warlords and rival political parties. Sun Yat-sen was defeated and China was torn by civil strife.

The Berlin Airlift defied Soviet roadblocks and provided the people of Berlin with desperately needed food and supplies.

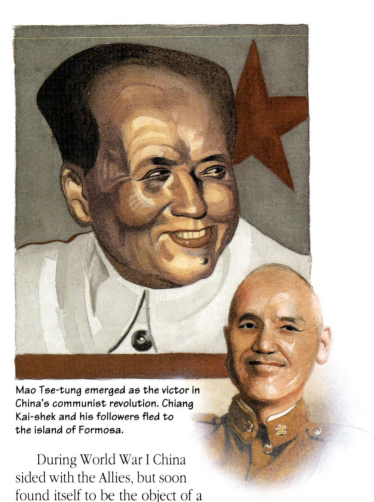

Mao Tse-tung emerged as the victor in China's communist revolution. Chiang Kai-shek and his followers fled to the island of Formosa.

During World War I China sided with the Allies, but soon found itself to be the object of a power struggle between the Western nations and Japan. Tired of foreign control, the Kuomintang turned to Moscow for help. The Soviets were only too happy to help the Chinese throw off the yoke of capitalist exploitation. In 1926, under the leadership of Sun's successor Chiang Kai-shek, the Soviet-trained Kuomintang army took control of the central government. However, Chiang was no communist. He was merely a clever politician who had taken help wherever he could get it. Once in control Chiang promptly purged China not only of foreigners but of communists as well.

Some Chinese communists escaped Chiang Kai-shek's purge and fled to the north of China. There, under the leadership of Chiang's former classmate Mao Tse-tung, they developed a new kind of communism founded on China's hundreds of millions of rural peasants. Mao's Red Army roamed the countryside, making war on landowners and distributing the confiscated land to the peasants. They treated the peasants with respect and allowed them a say in local revolutionary councils. Gradually, not only peasants, but workers and intellectuals—and even many democrats who were fed up with the Kuomintang dictatorship—joined the communist cause.

From the 1920s onward, China was torn by civil war between the Nationalists and the communists. The two sides united to combat the Japanese during World War II,

but after Japan's defeat civil war broke out once again. The Red Army began a long series of victories over the ill-trained and disorganized Kuomintang. Finally, in 1949, Chiang Kai-shek's two remaining strongholds fell. The dictator was forced to flee to the island of Formosa (now called Taiwan) with his Nationalist followers. The mainland became a communist country called the People's Republic of China.

In 1950 the world's attention again turned to Asia—this time to the nation of Korea. During World War II Korea had been liberated from Japanese occupation by a joint Soviet-United States invasion force. The Soviets controlled the northern half of the Korean peninsula, while the United States held the area south of the 38th parallel. When the war ended neither superpower would let go of its half, so Korea ended up being split in two.

In June of 1950 North Korean troops crossed the 38th parallel and invaded South Korea. The U.N. voted to launch a "police action" against the communist aggressors. Under the leadership of American General Douglas MacArthur, an expeditionary force reached Korea just in time to prevent an all-out North Korean victory. In a brilliant counterattack, MacArthur pushed the communists back well north of the 38th parallel, almost to the Chinese border. In response the Chinese sent a huge army into North Korea. The UN troops were driven back. By 1951, the battle line had stabilized roughly along the old boundary between North and South. After two years of peace talks, an armistice was finally reached in 1953. The Korean War had lasted three years and taken a toll of one million lives, but communist aggression had been checked and a third world war averted.

The hot spot soon shifted back to Europe when anti-communist revolts broke out in East Germany in 1953 and Hungary and Poland in 1956. The Hungarian people took to the streets in armed rebellion, denouncing communism and the Soviet Union. Sympathizers throughout the Western world watched in despair as Soviet tanks rolled into Budapest to crush the revolt. Yet the West dared not risk nuclear war by getting involved in Eastern Bloc affairs.

A new hot spot—the Middle East— erupted in 1956, when Egyptian President Gamal Abdul Nasser seized control of the British-owned Suez Canal. Nasser also stepped up his attacks upon the neighboring state of Israel. Israel had been created by the United Nations in 1948 on land which had formerly been part of the British-held territory of Palestine. It was to be a homeland for the Jewish people.

However, the birth of the Jewish state had been immediately followed by an attack from the surrounding Arab countries. Israel had defeated its enemies, but the

On the map:

U.S.S.R.

CHINA

Chinese Intervention
October 1950

UN maximum
advance
Nov. 24, 1950

**North
Korea**

Unsan

Hungnam

Sea of
Japan

Yellow
Sea

Wonsan

⊕ P'yongyang

Armistice Line
1951-53

38th Parallel

Panmunjom

UN retreat
Jan. 1951

⊙ Seoul

Inchon

US Marines
Sept. 1950

**South
Korea**

Area held by
UN Sept. 1950

Pusan

truce that followed the war was an uneasy one. Now Nasser's increased attacks provoked the Israelis to invade Egypt. At the same time, Britain and France began to land troops in the canal zone. Immediately the Soviets threatened to send "volunteers" to defend Egypt. This explosive situation was defused when the UN convinced the invaders to pull out and sent an Emergency Force to the area to maintain the peace. Egypt wound up in control of the Suez Canal, but tensions between Israel and its Arab neighbors would erupt into full-scale warfare several times over the next two decades.

In 1961, the disastrous Bay of Pigs incident brought the Cold War into America's backyard for the first time. The story behind the Bay of Pigs begins in 1959, when a popular revolution on the tiny island of Cuba resulted in the ousting of the dictator Batista and the flight of 100,000 of his supporters to the United States. The new Cuban leader, Fidel Castro, began to nationalize foreign-owned industries and plantations, many of which belonged to American companies. The United States immediately cut off all trade with Cuba. At the same time the U.S. Central Intelligence Agency began

training a group of Batista supporters for an armed invasion of the island.

On April 17, 1961, the band of CIA-trained Cuban exiles landed on the southern coast of Cuba at the Bahia de Cochinos, or Bay of Pigs. These anti-Communists expected to be hailed as liberators by the local peasants. Instead they were greeted by Castro's forces. All were captured or killed.

Not only was the Bay of Pigs a major embarrassment for the U.S., but it also sowed the seeds for a frightening confrontation known as the Cuban Missile Crisis. As a result of the invasion, Cuba allowed the Soviets to install long-range nuclear missiles on the island as protection against any future U.S. attacks. In October of 1962, the Russian missiles were detected by an American U-2 spy plane. President Kennedy demanded that the missiles be removed. The Soviets insisted that the missiles were for defensive purposes only, and refused to remove them. For three days the world stood poised on the brink of nuclear confrontation. Then Soviet Premier Nikita Krushchev relented. The Soviets agreed to dismantle their Cuban missile bases. In exchange, the U.S. dismantled some of its missiles in Turkey that were aimed at key locations in the U.S.S.R.

The Cuban missile crisis—when the U.S. and the Soviet Union came close to outright war.

"I have been to the edge of the abyss and looked over," said Kennedy. During the Missile Crisis, the world had come dangerously close to nuclear war. After the crisis, both the U.S. and the U.S.S.R. agreed to take steps to avoid another such incident. In June of 1963, a "hot line" was installed between the White House and the Kremlin. From now on, the two leaders could discuss their differences rather than react blindly to events. The Cold War entered a new phase, called *detente*. Detente improved relations between the superpowers, but it did not bring an end to the Cold War. Rather, the battlefield shifted once again, this time to Southeast Asia.

The Vietnam War became one of the most divisive events in U.S. history. Thousands of U.S. soldiers lost their lives as U.S. citizens demanded an end to the conflict.

There, the divided nation of Vietnam was engulfed in civil war between the communist North Vietnamese (called the Viet Cong) and the U.S.-supported South. South Vietnam was considered a "domino," which if toppled, might cause neighboring countries to fall to the communists as well. To prevent this from happening, America had sent military advisors to South Vietnam immediately after the nation was divided in 1954. The U.S. had also given the South Vietnamese substantial economic aid and military supplies over the years.

President Lyndon Johnson vowed that he would never send American troops to fight in Vietnam. In the early 60s, the U.S. Air Force was bombing selected targets in North Vietnam. Then came the deployment of Marines to pro-

tect the Air Force bases. More troops were sent to protect the Marines. By 1968 there were 540,000 American troops in Vietnam. Many Americans came to believe that the U.S. was wantonly killing thousands of Asians—that anti-Communism had gone too far. Demonstrations and strikes erupted on college campuses across the country. At Kent State in Ohio and Jackson State in Mississippi, several students were killed by troops which had been sent in to maintain order. The nation was outraged. Yet the war in Vietnam dragged on until 1973, when the last American troops were finally withdrawn. The North Vietnamese soon overran the South, and Vietnam became a communist country. The U.S. effort to contain communism in Vietnam had been a 19-year, $100 billion failure.

232

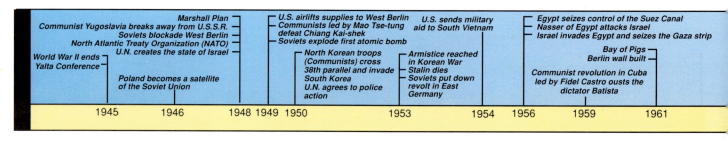

1945	1946	1948	1949	1950	1953	1954	1956	1959	1961

World War II ends
Yalta Conference

Communist Yugoslavia breaks away from U.S.S.R.
Soviets blockade West Berlin
North Atlantic Treaty Organization (NATO)
U.N. creates the state of Israel

Marshall Plan

Poland becomes a satellite of the Soviet Union

U.S. airlifts supplies to West Berlin
Communists led by Mao Tse-tung defeat Chiang Kai-shek
Soviets explode first atomic bomb

North Korean troops (Communists) cross 38th parallel and invade South Korea
U.N. agrees to police action

U.S. sends military aid to South Vietnam

Armistice reached in Korean War
Stalin dies
Soviets put down revolt in East Germany

Egypt seizes control of the Suez Canal
Nasser of Egypt attacks Israel
Israel invades Egypt and seizes the Gaza strip

Bay of Pigs
Berlin wall built

Communist revolution in Cuba led by Fidel Castro ousts the dictator Batista

At the same time the U.S. was struggling with the conflict in Southeast Asia, the U.S.S.R. began to experience serious reaction to its oppressive policies. In 1968, the Eastern European nation of Czechoslovakia took a few tentative steps toward independence. The hard-line communist leader was replaced by Alexander Dubcek who promised "socialism with a human face." Dubcek immediately began to loosen state control over the economy. He also did away with censorship and opened contact with the West. The Soviets did not want Czechoslovakia's new brand of socialism to spread to other Eastern Bloc countries. Nor did they want Czechoslovakia to establish any ties with Western Europe. If that happened, it could be the first crack in the Iron Curtain.

Intoxicated by their new-found sense of freedom, the Czechs were unprepared for the Soviet tanks which rolled into Prague in August of 1968. In a bloody show of force the Soviets removed Dubcek from office and installed a pro-Moscow puppet in his place. They did so without any interference from the West. The superpowers had come to accept each other's European boundaries. Neither wished to risk a world war by meddling in the other's "sphere."

When the Moslem fundamentalism that was sweeping the Middle East began to spread to Afghanistan in 1979, the Soviets became alarmed. Afghanistan bordered the southern Soviet Republics. If the Islamic revolution spread to the Moslem populations there, the people might revolt against communist rule. On the other hand, if the Soviets acted quickly to halt fundamentalism in Afghanistan, they could use that nation as a stepping stone toward a long-desired port on the Persian Gulf.

On Christmas night 1979 the Soviets invaded Afghanistan, killing the president and installing a Soviet protégé. But the Soviets soon became bogged down in a bitter, drawn-out war with Moslem guerillas called *mujaheddin* ("holy warriors"). Despite "sweep and destroy" missions and the reported use of chemical weapons, the Soviets were unable to establish communist control. In 1989, after a futile nine-year war that is sometimes called the "Soviet Vietnam," the Soviets finally withdrew their last troops from Afghanistan. The unpopularity of the war and the harsh toll it took on the Soviet economy proved to be important factors in the collapse of the communist regime—so strikingly symbolized by the fall of the Berlin Wall on that candle-lit November night in 1989.

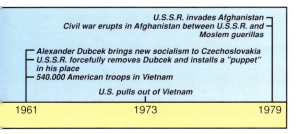

Quiz

1. At the Yalta Conference, the Allied leaders
Ⓐ made peace with Hitler.
Ⓑ planned to attack the U.S.S.R.
Ⓒ divided Germany into zones.
Ⓓ declared war on Japan.

2. The power struggle between the U.S. and U.S.S.R. was called
Ⓐ the war to end war.
Ⓑ the domino effect.
Ⓒ the Red Scare.
Ⓓ the Cold War.

3. Who won control of China in 1949?
Ⓐ Mao Tse-tung
Ⓑ Chiang Kai-shek
Ⓒ Sun Yat-sen
Ⓓ President Diem

4. The Korean War ended when North Koreans crossed the 38th Parallel.
Ⓐ True
Ⓑ False

5. The invasion of Cuba occurred
Ⓐ in the Gulf of Tonkin.
Ⓑ in the Suez Canal.
Ⓒ during the Cuban Missile Crisis.
Ⓓ in the Bay of Pigs.

6. The first of many Arab-Israeli wars occurred between Israel and
Ⓐ Iraq.
Ⓑ Palestine.
Ⓒ Egypt.
Ⓓ Saudi Arabia.

7. Soviet tanks invaded Czechoslovakia in 1968 because of
Ⓐ a liberal Czech government.
Ⓑ Czech nuclear missiles.
Ⓒ a Czech defense pact with U.S.
Ⓓ a Czech invasion of Poland.

8. The Cuban Missile Crisis involved which two world leaders?
Ⓐ Stalin and Kennedy
Ⓑ Krushchev and Kennedy
Ⓒ Breshnev and Johnson
Ⓓ Krushchev and Johnson

9. What was the reason for the Berlin Airlift?
Ⓐ to start a new air route
Ⓑ to defy Soviet roadblocks
Ⓒ to evacuate Americans
Ⓓ to liberate Berlin

10. The mutual defense pact between the U.S. and Europe is called
Ⓐ the Iron Curtain.
Ⓑ detente.
Ⓒ the Treaty of Yalta.
Ⓓ NATO.

Chapter 23

Our Changing World

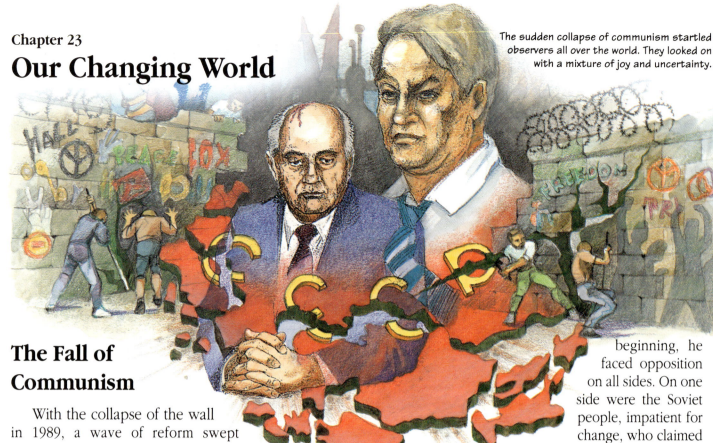

The sudden collapse of communism startled observers all over the world. They looked on with a mixture of joy and uncertainty.

The Fall of Communism

With the collapse of the wall in 1989, a wave of reform swept through the Communist nations of Europe. In the past, the Soviets had crushed any challenge to Communist authority in the Eastern bloc. But now, with their economy in ruins and growing dissatisfaction among their own people, they were powerless to stop the flow of events.

With the end of communist control in the East, East and West Germany began to plan their long-awaited reunification. In only a matter of months, the two nations joined together to form the Federal Republic of Germany. Despite the many challenges facing the nation—such as the economic gap between East and West, and an increase in neo-nazi violence—the new Germany quickly became one of the leading members of the European Community.

Germany was not the only nation to embrace democracy in the late 1980s. The wave of reform struck Romania in 1989, bringing the downfall of long-time dictator Nicolae Ceausescu. In nearby Czechoslovakia, Alexander Dubcek made his first public speech since the Soviet invasion of 1968 and was later elected chairman of the Czechoslovakian parliament. Hungary proclaimed a new democratic constitution. Solidarity Party leader Lech Walesa was elected President of Poland. But the most earthshaking changes of all took place in the Soviet Union.

The story begins back in 1985, when Mikhail Gorbachev became leader of the Soviet Union. Gorbachev promised two types of reform: *glasnost* (openness) and *perestroika* (restructuring). However, from the beginning, he faced opposition on all sides. On one side were the Soviet people, impatient for change, who claimed that Gorbachev was doing too little, too slowly. On the other side were Communist Party hard-liners, who feared that glasnost and perestroika would bring chaos and the destruction of the central government. And throughout the republics of the Soviet Union there was a growing sense of nationalism. Once-independent countries that had been forcibly turned into Soviet republics were beginning to clamor for independence.

In August of 1991, an Emergency Committee made up of high-ranking Communist Party members attempted a coup against Gorbachev. But Boris Yeltsin, the recently elected President of the Russian Republic, announced that Russia was now an independent state, immune to orders from the communist government. The plotters of the coup were arrested, and Gorbachev was restored to office. Gorbachev still believed that the Soviet Union could be preserved, but it was too late to patch things up. Under Yeltsin's leadership, Russia had already broken from the Soviet Union. The other republics soon declared *their* independence. In no time, Gorbachev became a leader without a country. On December 25, 1991, he announced his resignation. The Soviet Union was no more.

Boris Yeltsin became the leader of the new Russia. He promptly outlawed the Communist Party and began measures to introduce capitalism to Russia. But rebuilding the Russian economy was and is not an easy task. Nor is it the only problem facing the former Soviet republics. Early in the twentieth century, the end of imperialism had brought a renewal of ancient conflicts among former colonies. In the same way, the fall of communism brought a wave of ugly ethnic violence to the former Soviet Union and its satellites. The seven Yugoslavian republics also decided to end their union. Violent boundary disputes broke out immediately as Croats fought with Serbs, and Serbs were accused of "ethnic cleansing" against the Moslems in Bosnia-Herzegovina.

Turmoil in Latin America

The post-war history of Latin America features a long parade of military dictators such as Juan Péron of Argentina and François Duvalier of Haiti. These Latin American strongmen had little interest in the welfare of most of their citizens. They represented the ruling class—the landowners and industrialists—who counted on them to keep wages low and the population under control, even if they had to resort to terror and intimidation to do so. They also enjoyed the full support of the United States, which was willing to overlook their undemocratic practices as long as they kept the country out of communist hands.

Throughout Latin America, people began clamoring for governments that would address the growing prob-

The people of Latin America continued to fight for democracy in the face of stiff opposition from both the left and the right.

lems of poverty, illiteracy, and overpopulation. But the movement for democracy was met by opposition from both the left and the right. On the right, of course, were the ruling classes, who opposed any change in the status quo. On the left were the communists, who believed that the only way to bring change to Latin America was through violent revolution. By 1970, in the nations of South America in particular, kidnappings, assassinations, and terrorism had become commonplace. In Argentina and Bolivia, elected presidents were ousted by the military. In Chile, the military (with U.S. help and backing) overthrew President Salvador Allende, the first popularly elected Marxist in Latin America.

In Nicaragua in 1979, the revolutionary Sandinista National Liberation Front expelled the dictator Somoza from

235

the country and established a popular government. However, because the Sandinistas favored many socialist policies, such as redistributing land to the peasants and nationalizing key industries, the United States soon denounced them and cut off all aid. The Sandinistas made some strides in improving life for the peasants—building clinics, establishing a literacy program—but they were hampered by the damaged economy. Rebels opposed to the Sandinista regime, the *contras*, quickly won the support of the United States. Fighting between the U.S.-armed-and-trained contras and government troops grew worse throughout the 1980s. Finally, the American Congress voted to end contra aid but some U.S. government officials continued to aid the contras secretly. When this became public knowledge, the Congress was furious and attempted to jail the participants. In 1990, elections were held and Violetta Chamorro, an anti-Sandinista candidate, was elected president. The contra groups disbanded, and Chamorro set about the task of rebuilding her war-torn country.

Asian Giants

China made great strides under the leadership of Mao Tse-tung. By the mid-1960s, agricultural production had improved to the point where China could feed most of its enormous population. The nation became a nuclear power in 1967 with its testing of its first hydrogen bomb. But the 1960s were also a time of turmoil in China. In 1965, believing that the Communist Party had lost sight of its goals, Mao launched a "Cultural Revolution," during which many long-time party officials, intellectuals, and other influential people were removed from their posts. Some were killed by Mao's youthful Red Guard. Others were banished to distant agricultural communes. By the time the Cultural Revolution ended in 1968, the nation was close to chaos, and much of the progress that China had made since 1949 had been undone.

In the early 1970s, China took strong measures to rebuild its economy. It also ended two decades of isolation from the West—partly because of its growing hostility toward the Soviet Union, with whom it had had a series of border disputes. In 1971 the People's Republic of China was finally admitted to the United Nations. However, over time, many Chinese became unhappy with the government's modernization plan. They felt the plan was moving too slowly and did not include enough democratic reforms. In the spring of 1989, a huge group of students gathered in Tiananmen Square in downtown Beijing, demanding greater democracy for China. The hard-line Communist government sent tanks to end the demonstration. In the massacre that followed, an estimated five thousand students were killed. Nevertheless,

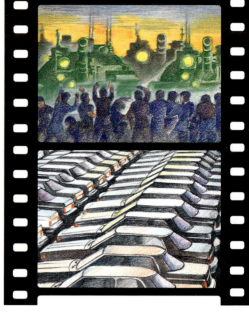

In Tiananmen Square a pro-democracy student demonstration was brutally put down by the communist Chinese government.

Japan transformed itself into an economic giant practically over night.

in the early 1990s China accelerated experiments with capitalism and amazed the rest of the world with its rapid growth. How long can China hold on to communism as the pressure for democracy builds within?

One of the most amazing stories of modernization and economic growth took place in Japan. At the end of World War II Japan was under the control of a U.S. occupation force. The occupation government drafted a new constitution for Japan, transferring all power from the emperor to the Japanese people. It abolished the army and navy and dismissed over five million troops. It also put in place some economic reforms, such as allowing farmers to own their land for the first time. The military occupation of Japan ended in 1952, and by the mid-1950s Japanese industrial production had returned to pre-war levels. From 1960 to 1970, the economy continued to grow at the amazing rate of ten percent a year.

Economic growth brought many social changes to Japan. The Japanese now enjoy one of the world's highest standards of living. But some citizens claim that their country has become too materialistic and that the pressure to succeed has become too intense. On the international front, Japan's trading partners have criticized its trade policies. They resent the existence of trade restrictions that make it difficult to sell foreign goods in Japan, when Japanese goods have flooded western marketplaces for decades. They also insist that Japan should shoulder more of the burden of aid to developing countries. Various internal and external problems led, in the early 1990s, to Japan's first post-war recession. But even with the slackening of the Japanese economy, the island nation continues to be the second most powerful industrial nation in the world after the United States and maintains one of the world's highest standards of living.

Independence in Asia

Despite the problems of underdevelopment and overpopulation, India has managed to remain a democracy. After Gandhi's assassination, Jawaharlal Nehru stepped in to lead the country. Nehru began a series of government projects to build irrigation and flood control systems and to improve transportation and communication. Nehru was succeeded by his daughter, Mrs. Indira Gandhi. In the early 70s, India achieved a controlled nuclear explosion, establishing itself as an important international power. But three wars with Pakistan had damaged the economy and brought progress in the war on poverty to a standstill. As she lost support, Mrs. Gandhi seized more and more power for herself. When her opponents called for her resignation, she declared a state of emergency, complete with censorship and widespread arrests. In 1984, Mrs. Gandhi sent in the army to put down a revolt by a religious group called the Sikhs. Hundreds of Sikhs were killed. In retaliation, on October 31, 1984, Mrs. Gandhi was assassinated by Sikh members of the Presidential Guard. Internal conflict is bound to continue because of the deep hatreds between the various religious factions. However, one important problem has been solved in recent years. With the help of modern technology, India has experienced a "green revolution."

Nehru's daughter, Mrs. Indira Gandhi, led India into modern times.

Nelson Mandela became a symbol of the shackles of apartheid in South Africa.

As a result, this very poor nation is now able to grow enough food to feed its almost one billion citizens.

Neighboring Pakistan had its own set of problems. The first democratic government was unable to cope with the country's problems and was ousted in 1958 in a military *coup d'état*. But the change in government did little to help the country. Most of the population remained illiterate, dependent upon foreign wheat for their survival. To make matters worse, East Pakistan felt ignored by the government, which was located a thousand miles away in West Pakistan.

In 1970, tidal waves swept over East Pakistan's coast and offshore islands. Nearly 500,000 people died in the storm, and countless more fell prey to the disease and starvation that followed. When the government failed to respond quickly to the tragedy, the angry East Pakistanis rebelled. This time, West Pakistan's response was swift. The government sent 80,000 troops to restore order to the ravaged land. In the civil war that followed, thousands of East Pakistani leaders were executed and ten million refugees flooded into neighboring India. But India did not want them and could not afford to feed them. To stop the flow of refugees, India declared war on West Pakistan. More than a million people died in the fighting.

In only two weeks, West Pakistan was crushed, and East Pakistan became a free nation known as Bangladesh. West Pakistan became simply Pakistan, and Zulfikar Ali Bhutto, head of the Pakistan People's Party, became the nation's new leader. Bhutto restored constitutional government to Pakistan and announced economic and educational reforms. He also met with Mrs. Gandhi to work out an agreement between the two nations. But in 1977, Bhutto was removed from office by a military coup. He was executed two years later. A new parliament was elected in 1985, but the military dismissed it. Elections were held again in 1988, resulting in the election of Bhutto's daughter Benazir, the first woman ever to head an elected government in a Moslem nation. However, she too was removed from office by the military.

Tradition and Change in Africa

The independence movement swept across the continent of Africa with amazing speed. The Gold Coast, the first African colony to gain its freedom, became the independent nation of Ghana in 1957. Within a decade, Belgium, England, and France had freed their African colonies. In most of Africa the transition to self-rule went smoothly. However, in Algeria it took seven years of civil conflict before France finally granted the colony independence in 1962. In the Belgian Congo, the end of colonial rule brought immediate chaos. UN troops had to be sent there in 1960 to end the tribal warfare and political assassinations that were ravaging the country.

It was in southern Africa that the independence movement met with the greatest resistance. Angola and Mozambique battled fiercely with Portugal before finally winning their freedom in 1975. In Rhodesia and the Union of South Africa, the white colonists who ruled the country refused to yield control to the much larger native African populations. In Rhodesia, it took a long guerrilla war and a great deal of international pressure before the whites finally agreed to a general election. A Black government was voted into office, and shortly thereafter, in 1980, Rhodesia was reborn as the African nation of Zimbabwe. South Africa proved to be even more stubborn. Its segregation laws, called apartheid, still existed in 1993. Under apartheid, Blacks were forced to live in bleak wastelands called townships. Many Black leaders were killed in prison. Official reports referred to the deaths as caused by "falling out window," "hung himself," and a suspiciously large number of epileptic fits and other illnesses. For many years the leading Black organization, the African National Congress, was banned, and its leader, Nelson Mandela, confined to prison. Finally, in 1989 increasing racial violence forced some changes to South Africa's apartheid rules. The ban on the ANC was lifted, and Mandela was freed from prison after 27 years. Yet even as the struggle for Black rights in South Africa continues the nation is plagued by power struggles based on ancient tribal enmities.

Cooperation in Europe

In the years following World War II, Western Europe began a journey toward unity. In 1957 Italy, France, West Germany, the Netherlands, Belgium, and Luxembourg agreed to establish the European Economic Community, or EEC—familiarly known as the "Common Market." The EEC abolished all tariffs between members, and ensured the free flow of capital, labor, and goods. At first Britain refused to participate in the Common Market, but it joined in 1973, as did Ireland and Denmark. Greece was admitted in 1981, and Spain and Portugal in 1986. Known today as the "European Community," or EC, the organization has become one of the world's economic giants. A common currency and a greater degree of political integration are planned for the future.

Unfortunately, Europe's peace and prosperity do not extend to Northern Ireland, which has been ravaged for decades by civil war between the country's Catholics and Protestants. Northern Ireland had been governed by an elected Assembly for fifty years. But in 1972, in the face of mounting unrest and violence, Britain disbanded the Irish Assembly and began ruling the country directly.

A variety of political groups claim to represent Ireland's Catholics and Protestants. Unfortunately, many people who are eager for change put their faith in the underground military organizations, which are respon-

sible for much of the violence in Northern Ireland. Extremist Protestant groups like the Protestant Ulster Defence Association seek to preserve the union with Great Britain at any cost. Their main opposition is the Catholic Irish Republican Army, or IRA, which is dedicated to freeing the country from British control and uniting it with the Republic of Ireland (Eire) to the south. These military organizations engage in violence against each other, the British army, (which has many troops in Northern Ireland), and the hapless population. Between 1969 and 1986, 2,500 civilians died in Ireland's civil strife. The ongoing violence has also created a hostile climate for industry and investment. As a result, many manufacturing plants have shut down and new businesses are reluctant to invest there. Budget cuts under British Prime Minister Margaret Thatcher in the 1980s further contributed to Northern Ireland's economic decline. It is now one of the poorest countries in Western Europe, with no end in sight to the violence and poverty.

Conflict in the Middle East

The Middle East "flashpoint" ignited twice in brief but destructive wars between Israel and the Arab countries. The Six Day War of 1967 broke out after a long series of border incidents. When Israeli Intelligence learned that Egypt was planning a full-scale attack, Israel struck first. In a lightning victory, the Israelis captured many key areas, including the West Bank (giving Israel control of all of Jerusalem), the Gaza Strip, and the Sinai Peninsula. But after the war, Israel refused to return these Occupied Territories, claiming that they were vital to its security. The Occupied Territories became a new source of conflict between Israel and its neighbors.

On October 6, 1973, during the Jewish High Holiday fast of Yom Kippur, Egypt and Syria attacked Israel on two fronts. Though caught by surprise, Israel mobilized quickly, and the Arab "blitzkrieg" was pushed back. In little more than two weeks, both sides agreed to a truce. But although the war itself was brief, it had long-term effects on Israel and its allies. Meanwhile, the Arab states began an oil embargo, causing an energy crisis throughout much of the world. At the same time, they sharply increased prices, so that the industrialized nations ran up huge debts to pay for their oil. In 1977, in an attempt to resolve the situation, American President Jimmy Carter arranged peace talks between Israeli Prime Minister Menachem Begin and President Anwar Sadat of Egypt. Their historic agreement, called the Camp David Accords, marked the first time that an Arab leader recognized Israel's right to exist. Sadly, Sadat was gunned down shortly after the Accords.

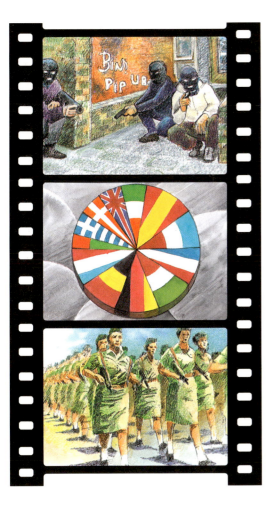

Age-old religious conflicts led to continued violence and suffering in Ireland.

The nations of western Europe forged an economic alliance to compete with Japan and the U.S.

Israeli women showed that combat was not just for men.

the balance of power toward the Moslems. The two sides began a destructive battle for control of the country, with the PLO (Palestinian Liberation Organization) joining the fight on the Moslem side. Israel joined the fray in 1982, when it launched a full-scale invasion of southern Lebanon in an effort to drive out the PLO. Under Israeli supervision, a Christian president was elected. But when he was assassinated a short time later, the Christian militia retaliated by slaughtering hundreds of Palestinian civilians living in the refugee camps. The U.N. sent peacekeeping troops to Lebanon in the mid-1980s. Despite sporadic fighting and outbursts of terrorism, the country began edging toward peace. By mid-1991, most of the militias had disbanded and the remaining PLO troops had been disarmed. In bombed-out Beirut, the streets were quiet for the first time in over fifteen years. Lebanon is now effectively controlled by the Syrian government.

Since 1953, Iran had been ruled by Shah Muhammed Reza Pahlavi. The Shah had the support of the United States and a small group of powerful ruling families, but he was despised by the majority of the people. In 1978 half a million Iranians from all walks of life held a demonstration against the Shah in the capital city of Teheran. The Shah's response to this widespread call for change was to declare martial law. Troops began firing on demonstrators, but the protest movement kept growing, until in 1979, the Shah was forced to flee the country.

After his departure, the fundamentalist Islamic Republican Party, led by Ayatollah Ruhollah Khomeini, assumed control of the country. Fundamentalists blamed their countries' problems on the adoption of Western ways and called for a return to the traditional ways of Islam. Khomeini set up a government based on Islamic law. He shut down newspapers and magazines, banned political parties, and closed universities. Because the United States had supported the Shah, it was singled out as "the Great Satan." In 1979 Iranian terrorists seized the United States Embassy in Teheran and held a group of Americans hostage for two years. In 1980 Iran began a costly war with neighboring Iraq. The eight years of fighting had a disastrous effect on Iran's already faltering economy, as did a devastating 1990 earthquake in which an estimated 400,000 people were killed. Yet even after Khomeini's death in 1989, the fundamentalists retained their hold on Iran. The Shah's ouster had been costly for the United States. A great deal of American capital and many years of economic and military support had gone down the drain.

In early 1991, the Persian Gulf was the site of a new war, this time between the nation of Iraq and a combined United Nations force of thirty-nine countries, led by the United States. The war was sparked by Iraq's invasion of its oil-rich neighbor, Kuwait. Iraqi leader Saddam

239

The two million Palestinians living in refugee camps in Syria, Jordan, Lebanon, and under Israeli rule in the West Bank and Gaza remain a major source of conflict in the Middle East. Some families have lived in the United Nations-supported camps for three generations, ever since their ancestors fled there from the newly created nation of Israel in 1948. When will the Palestinians find a homeland? Where will it be? The answers to these questions are still being disputed by Israel and the Arab nations.

In the late 1980s, more and more Israelis began to settle in the occupied territories. By their presence, they hoped to establish a permanent claim to the occupied lands. Palestinians on the West Bank reacted by waging an *intifada*, or uprising, against the Israeli newcomers. The intifada brought an escalation in violence between Arab and Jew. In the past, terrorist attacks had been occasional events, but during the intifada, they became everyday occurrences in which civilians on both sides continue to suffer heavy losses.

The once-beautiful city of Beirut was reduced to rubble during a civil war that erupted in Lebanon in 1975. For decades, the country had been ruled by a Christian sect called the Maronites, but the presence of more than three hundred thousand Palestinian refugees helped tilt

Hussein had built a huge military machine with the aim of becoming the dominant power in the Arab world. He also wanted to wipe out his country's huge debt to Kuwait and gain access to Kuwait's oil and Persian Gulf coastline. On August 2, 1990, Iraqi troops swarmed across the Kuwaiti border. Within twenty-four hours, Saddam Hussein had conquered and annexed Kuwait.

On January 17, after a worldwide trade embargo failed to persuade Saddam to withdraw from Kuwait, coalition planes began bombing targets in Iraq. Two weeks later, the UN forces launched a massive ground assault. In just one month, with very few casualties on the coalition side, the war was over, and Hussein had been forced to withdraw from Kuwait. For Iraq and Kuwait, however, the war's costs had been steep. Iraq had lost 100,000 troops. Many civilians had also died in both countries. Furthermore, Iraqi troops had set fire to Kuwait's oil wells and dumped 250 million gallons of oil into the Gulf, seriously harming the environment. But despite the destruction, the war had one very positive result: the United Nations had proven that it could be an effective international peacekeeping force.

Of course, humans have been squabbling for centuries over ethnic, religious, and political differences. But today the stakes are higher than they've ever been before. Nuclear proliferation—the spread of nuclear weapons to more and more countries—has greatly increased the chances of worldwide destruction. More than twenty nations either possess, or are on the brink of developing, nuclear weapons, including countries like Israel and India, which have a history of trouble with their neighbors. With so many fingers on the button, what's to prevent a minor border conflict from turning into a nuclear war?

There's yet another problem threatening the world's survival—the problem of environmental pollution. Ever since the Industrial Revolution, air and water pollution have grown steadily worse. Today, we also have to contend with loss of topsoil, acid rain, endangered species, destruction of the rain forest, and holes in the ozone layer, which protects the earth from the sun's ultraviolet rays. Will the nations of the world be able to balance the need for economic growth with the need to protect the earth and its resources?

These are just some of the questions the world will have to address in the twenty-first century. The road

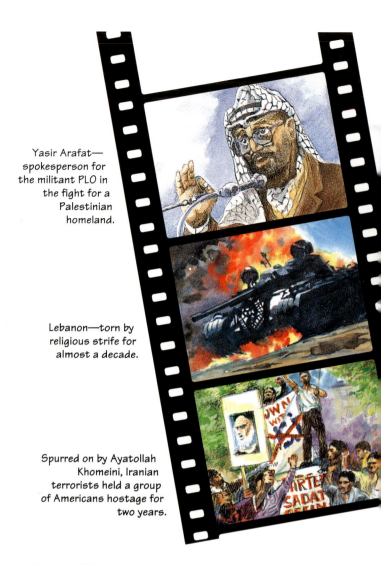

Yasir Arafat—spokesperson for the militant PLO in the fight for a Palestinian homeland.

Lebanon—torn by religious strife for almost a decade.

Spurred on by Ayatollah Khomeini, Iranian terrorists held a group of Americans hostage for two years.

ahead will be a tough one, to be sure, but there are many signs of hope on the horizon. Not too long ago, the idea of a European Community was unthinkable. Only yesterday, there was no end in sight to the Cold War, and if you had told someone in 1987 that in five years the Soviet Union would no longer exist, you would have been greeted by laughter. Yet these things have come to pass. Furthermore, the United Nations, at one time just a stage for Cold War one-upmanship, is on the way to becoming a respected and effective organization. And in 1992, representatives of many nations gathered in Rio de Janeiro for the world's first-ever Environmental Summit, to discuss the preservation of the earth for future generations.

Our earth started with a big bang billions of years ago. Over the centuries, it has seen empires rise and fall. It has seen progress and achievement as well as war and misery. But never before has it seen the potential for self-

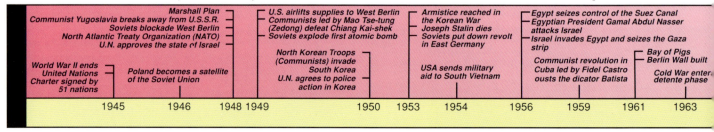

	Communist Yugoslavia breaks away from U.S.S.R. Soviets blockade West Berlin North Atlantic Treaty Organization (NATO) U.N. approves the state of Israel	Marshall Plan	U.S. airlifts supplies to West Berlin Communists led by Mao Tse-tung (Zedong) defeat Chiang Kai-shek Soviets explode first atomic bomb		Armistice reached in the Korean War Joseph Stalin dies Soviets put down revolt in East Germany		Egypt seizes control of the Suez Canal Egyptian President Gamal Abdul Nasser attacks Israel Israel invades Egypt and seizes the Gaza strip		
	World War II ends United Nations Charter signed by 51 nations	Poland becomes a satellite of the Soviet Union	North Korean Troops (Communists) invade South Korea U.N. agrees to police action in Korea		USA sends military aid to South Vietnam		Communist revolution in Cuba led by Fidel Castro ousts the dicator Batista	Bay of Pigs Berlin Wall built Cold War enter detente phase	
	1945	1946	1948 1949	1950	1953	1954	1956	1959	1961	1963

240

destruction that we possess today. Only with increased cooperation and tolerance among all the nations of the world can we ensure that our earth will be around for many centuries to come.

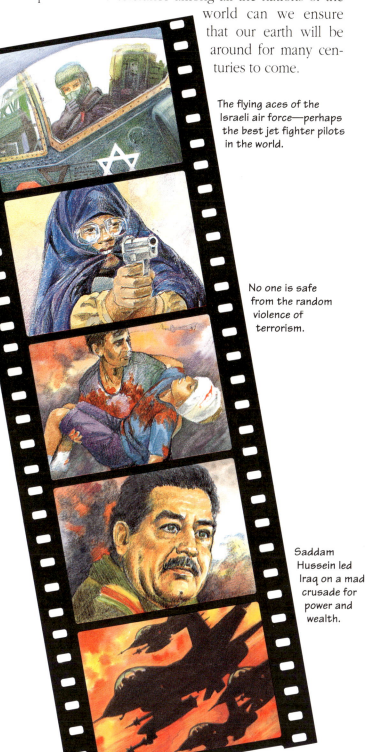

The flying aces of the Israeli air force—perhaps the best jet fighter pilots in the world.

No one is safe from the random violence of terrorism.

Saddam Hussein led Iraq on a mad crusade for power and wealth.

A massive assault by U.N. forces drove the Iraqi army out of Kuwait.

U.S.S.R. invades Afghanistan
Civil war erupts in Afghanistan between U.S.S.R. and Moslem guerillas

Alexander Dubcek brings new socialism to Czechoslovakia
U.S.S.R. forcefully removes Dubcek and installs a "puppet" in his place
540,000 Americans troops in Vietnam

America pulls out of Vietnam

1968   1973   1979

Quiz

1. East Pakistan rebelled and became a nation called

Ⓐ Bangladesh. Ⓒ Afghanistan.

Ⓑ Biafra. Ⓓ Iraq.

2. Algeria finally achieved independence from _____ in 1962.

Ⓐ England Ⓒ Spain

Ⓑ France Ⓓ Italy

3. The _intifada_ is the

Ⓐ religious leader of Iran. Ⓒ Palestinian uprising in Israel

Ⓑ "holy war" in Afghanistan. Ⓓ Christian militia in Lebanon.

4. The civil war in Lebanon began as a power struggle between

Ⓐ The United States and France. Ⓒ Israel and Egypt.

Ⓑ Iraq and Iran. Ⓓ Moslems and Maronite Christians.

5. South Africa's segregation laws are called

Ⓐ intifada. Ⓒ apartheid.

Ⓑ mujaheddin. Ⓓ glasnost.

6. The Persian Gulf War was fought between

Ⓐ Iran and Iraq. Ⓒ Israel and the Arab states.

Ⓑ Iraq and a U.N. coalition. Ⓓ Kuwait and a U.N. coalition.

7. This was one result of China's Cultural Revolution.

Ⓐ loss of jobs by Party leaders Ⓒ progress in art and science

Ⓑ Tiananmen Square massacre Ⓓ better relations with the West

8. Glasnost means

Ⓐ restructuring. Ⓒ closed borders.

Ⓑ joining the Communist Party. Ⓓ openness.

9. Which country was an original member of the European Community?

Ⓐ Britain Ⓒ Greece

Ⓑ Spain Ⓓ West Germany

10. Which has _not_ been a result of the fall of communism?

Ⓐ the unification of Germany Ⓒ the creation of new states

Ⓑ an end to ethnic violence Ⓓ the end of the Cold War

Chapter 24

Perspectives on History

We've come to the end of our "history safari"—a journey through time from the inception of the universe to the end of the twentieth century. Now, in a few short pages, it's appropriate to summarize and put into perspective some of history's larger themes. It's important to realize that history is not merely a telling of our many wars. Rather, it is a chronicle of *all* things humankind has done, of our achievements (and our failures) in art, literature, philosophy, psychology, science, government. So now let us look back briefly at what we've learned, and raise some questions about what we have yet to learn.

These timelines emphasize the point that mankind has been on Earth for a mere eye-blink of time. Three million years of humankind represent about one one-thousandth of the time covered by the top timeline! During those three million years man learned to make tools, control fire, and developed speech patterns that were to propel the human race into today's sophisticated communication. The world has been host to *Homo sapiens sapiens* for less than 30,000 years (less than one hundred-thousandth of the top timeline!). For most of the time that man has been around, things happened very slowly. Then came the Agricultural Revolution less than 10,000 years ago. Things began to move along at a faster clip. But relative to today's continually accelerating conditions, it was still a snail's pace. The last fifty years have brought the world more knowledge—and more ferment—than all prior years of man's history combined together!

The Ages of Man

The Old Stone Age, or Paleolithic Age, extends from about 2.5 million years ago to about 10,000 years ago. This was the hunter-gatherer epoch, and chipped stone was the material used for tools and weapons. Somewhere in those early times—we don't know exactly when—man learned to make and control fire. The New Stone Age, or Neolithic

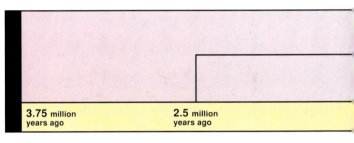

Age, began at about the time of the Agricultural Revolution. Men and women began to domesticate animals, to attempt their own food production, to make pottery from clay, and to finely grind and polish their stone implements.

Very quickly, but at different times in different areas of the world, came the use of copper, bronze, and iron for tools, weapons, and ornaments. Metallurgy was in use in some small farming communities as early as 7,000 B.C.E. The earliest examples of complete copper and bronze artifacts date to about 3,800 and 3,000 B.C.E., respectively. By about 1,800 B.C.E. the Bronze Age had spread throughout Europe. The Iron Age began in the Near East around 1,200 B.C.E. In the British Isles and in China, people made a direct hop to the use of bronze without passing through a copper phase.

The Progress of Civilization

Historians do not agree as to what to call various eras or when to date major periods of civilization. The question is one of reference—you get very different timelines depending upon whether the reference is Europe, the Middle East, Asia, Africa, or North or South America. Even within these geographical areas there are vast differences in "coming out" times for various societies. Nevertheless, there is obvious value in establishing some broad picture of the progress of civilization.

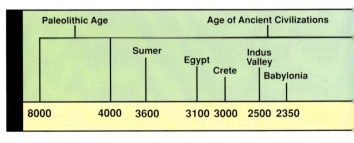

It is worthwhile remembering that the first large towns began in the Middle East, while some areas of the globe did not arrive at this state for another four or five thousand years. It is to be noted that the first complex societies (which we choose to characterize as "civilizations") occurred in the fourth millenium in the Middle East and nearby Egypt, yet other peoples did not reach this state until one, two, or three thousand years later. Of special note is the approximately 1100 years of the Classical Age, during which the Greek city-states and Rome surged forward with philosophy, the arts,

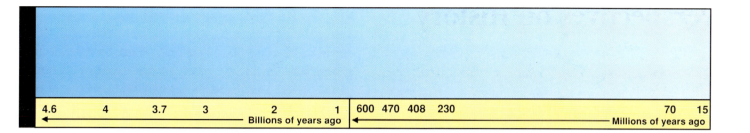

4.6	4	3.7	3	2	1	600	470	408	230		70	15

← Billions of years ago   ← Millions of years ago

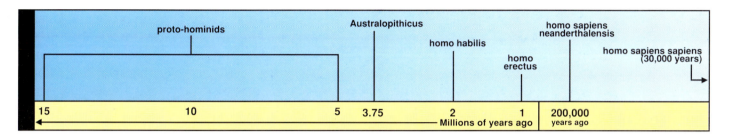

proto-hominids · Australopithicus · homo habilis · homo erectus · homo sapiens neanderthalensis · homo sapiens sapiens (30,000 years)

15	10	5	3.75	2	1	200,000 years ago

← Millions of years ago

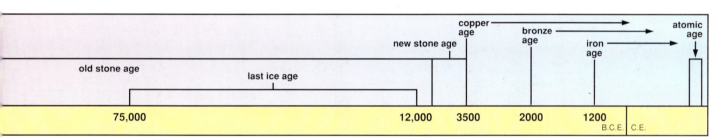

old stone age · last ice age · new stone age · copper age · bronze age · iron age · atomic age

75,000		12,000	3500	2000	1200	

B.C.E. | C.E.

243

Some African cultures made a direct leap from stone to iron. And some Western Hemisphere cultures did not use any of these metals until the Common Era.

Today we live in a "Technological Age," where the most important item being removed from the ground is *oil* rather than metal. And within the past decade, new *laboratory-derived* concoctions are beginning to provide us with the ability to control our lives, our health, and our surroundings.

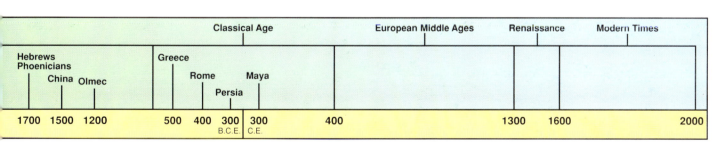

Hebrews Phoenicians · China · Olmec · Greece · Rome · Persia · Maya · Classical Age · European Middle Ages · Renaissance · Modern Times

1700	1500	1200	500	400	300	300	400	1300	1600	2000

B.C.E. | C.E.

government, and an advanced system of laws.

The Middle Ages was a time of slow progress from the fall of Rome to the Renaissance, the great awakening. We've termed the last four hundred years "Modern Times." During this time we've witnessed a major change in our culture as the Industrial Revolution began in England in 1750, setting the stage for the accelerating society of today.

Ancient Civilizations

We noted early in the book that what makes a civilization is not at all obvious. And so we defined it in essence as a culture that has grown beyond simple qualities to exhibit variety, breadth, and growth.

One conclusion that could quickly have been reached as we studied the early great civilizations, is that in order to become a great civilization, a society must be situated near a river system. But is this conclusion correct? In the early days of civilization, mighty rivers did nourish the first great cultures. But as trade became more important, civilizations like the Cretans and the Phoenicians flourished without access to a major river system. Today, Japan, occupying a small rocky island with no important rivers, has the highest income per person in the world. It is plain that as the world develops different forces come into play, and what is certain at one time may not be certain at another. Things change. Different parameters become important. *Different interpretations of history may be required.*

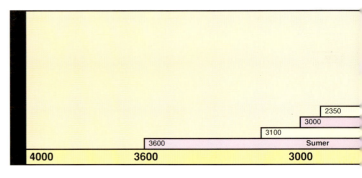

Modern Empires

After the fall of Rome in 476, time stood still in the West during the "Middle Ages." It was once fashionable for historians to call this period the Dark Ages. But this term doesn't take into account the rich Islamic heritage of the Moors in Spain from 711 to 1100, or the equally wonderful Islamic seat of power in Baghdad. And Chinese culture was able to tame the Mongols during the twelfth to fourteenth centuries to create a great society during those same Dark, or Middle Ages.

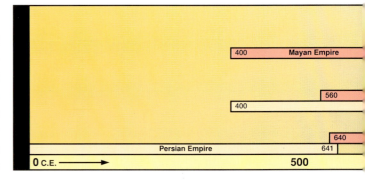

One of the outstanding events in the history of western Europe, and for people everywhere, was the Renaissance, a time of reacquisition of much that had been accomplished by the wondrous Greeks and Romans. During the Renaissance came the most important technological advancement of all time: the invention of the printing press in 1454. And in 1750 came the beginning of the Industrial Revolution, which directly led to today's complex capitalist societies. Since that time our modern era has been a time that differed little from the past in one sense: almost constant warfare somewhere on Earth.

Wars, Warriors and Weapons

For all of civilized time men have fought wars in a constant desire to be "king of the mountain." In earlier times the great people were often the successful warriors, or they achieved their prominence because they were the sons of great warriors. Military prowess made heroes of Alexander the Great, Julius Caesar, Napoleon Bonaparte, and Lord Horatio Nelson. We still fight wars, but today the victor is not determined primarily by great tactics or by numbers of armed forces. The victor today is more often than not the side with the most advanced technology. The winner will often be the side that controls the skies. And that is the side whose planes are the most sophisticated, or whose air-to-air missiles can evade electronic counter-measures. Fortunately, as of 1993 the world has not seen the use of atomic

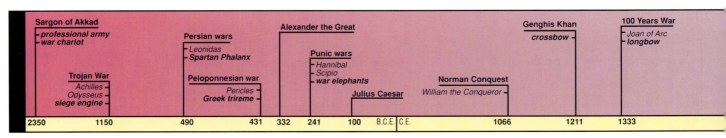

244

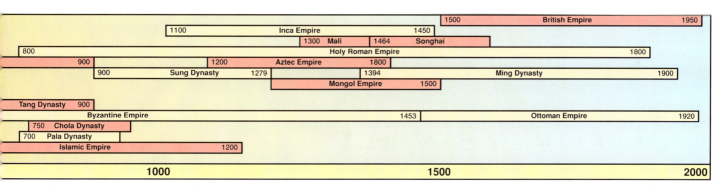

Another thing we've observed is that civilizations tend to rise and fall. We looked at the rise and fall of the Sumerians, Egyptians, Babylonians, Cretans, Indians, Chinese, Greeks, Romans, Ottomans, and the British Empire among many others. Now in the last decade of the twentieth century, the United States and Japan are the most prosperous of nations. Are they, too, doomed to peak and topple over? Most observers say the United States is already on the downward slope. Is a fall inevitable? Does the "rise and fall" pattern of history apply to us? What do *you* think?

The two major empires of the modern era were the Ottoman Empire and the British Empire. The Ottoman Empire was centered at Istanbul, the former Constantinople, which fell to the Turks in 1453. This Moslem state extended along the coast of North Africa, Egypt and the Middle East, and well into eastern Europe. Although it began to decline in the late sixteenth century, it was still a power into the early twentieth century. In the eighteenth and nineteenth centuries the British led the stampede for unbridled empire-building which resulted in the carving up of much of Africa and Asia. But it was only a ripple in the big pond of history. In the twentieth century it all quickly unraveled, and today we have over 180 countries represented in the United Nations.

245

weapons beyond the two bombs used against Japan, which ended World War II on a terrible, fearful note.

Can we visualize a day when war is a thing of the past? One bright note is that Japan, the economic envy of the world, does not depend on armed forces. The Japanese constitution forbids sending military contingents outside their country. Today the king of the mountain is not the nation with the biggest army, but the nation with the best scientific and engineering minds which can build the healthiest economy. Will this trend continue, or will the countries with the largest military machines reign supreme again in the future? What do *you* think?

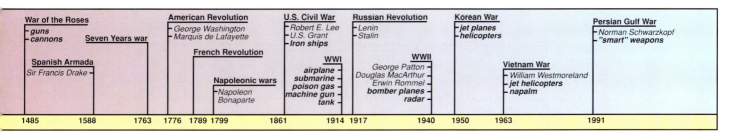

Government, the Law, and Economics

As mankind grew into more highly evolved societies, the profit motive soon became a major driving force. And from this came the institution of slavery. It has taken some 5,000 years for man to overcome his base instincts and to outlaw slavery. Only within the past two centuries has most of the world abolished it, although in some countries slavery in the fullest sense still exists today.

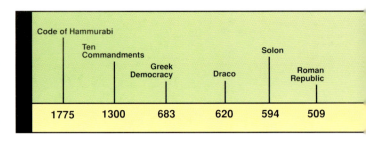

The success of the humanitarian struggle against slavery is symptomatic of a worldwide trend toward humanism over the past five hundred years. Change comes about because of new ideas continually being proposed by the enlightened members of the global community. It took us thousands of years to progress beyond monarchical government—the tyranny of kings—yet it was a phase that mankind had to go through in order to progress. Other systems were tried along the way, but usually with little success. The Greeks introduced oligarchy, but it didn't work very well. Early attempts at democracy in the Greek city-states and the Roman Republic were successful but limited; in both cases only a small fraction of the populace could vote. Modern democracy dates from the American and French Revolutions in the late 1700s, and is still being refined and perfected. In the United States women were not given the right to vote until the twentieth century, and the struggle for true equality for African-Americans and other minorities is still going on. And democracy, the most successful governmental system yet devised, is still just a dream for almost half the world's population. But at least in western societies democracy has succeeded in one major respect—the freedom to think, to say, to vote.

The other great goal is for us all to achieve the maximum development of human potential. Since the Industrial Revolution people have been striving to increase personal liberty and humanism in government, as a reaction to the excesses of the greed that characterized early capitalism. Banding together in common cause, people have managed to improve their lot slowly and painfully, with labor unions at the forefront.

246

Philosophy, Psychology, and Religion

Why is it that people strive to achieve and develop? Do we have to have a society where it's necessary to be "on top?" If you're not on top does that mean you're doomed to live an unhappy life? One of the things that humankind is learning is that we have at best a hazy understanding of what makes us tick. The early Greek philosophers started

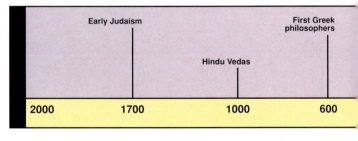

us out on the task of asking questions about the meaning of life, and why we act the way we do. And from their time to the present there has been a steady stream of philosophers pondering the ways of morality, of sin, of religion. And with every answer come ten more questions.

The Age of Reason, also known as the Enlightenment, was a period of great intellectual activity in the seventeenth and eighteenth centuries. Philosophers of the Age of Reason like Descartes, Locke, Voltaire, and Rousseau stressed the use of reason, as opposed to reliance on authority, in finding the truth. Late in the 1700s, the great German philosopher Immanuel Kant developed his concept of transcendental philosophy, in which he proposed that we can never know things as they really are, but only as they appear to us. Kant's ideas have had great impact on the development of philosophic thought since that time.

One of the great modern questioners was Sigmund Freud (1856-1939). He was the first to scientifically investigate the subconscious mind. By psychoanalysis—the studied interpretation of patients' freely associated thoughts—he drew the conclusion that a person's actions are directly related to subconscious memories of childhood experiences and/or repressed sexual fantasies. This startled the medical and scientific community of the times, yet in a few short generations, Freudian concepts of the influence of the subconscious mind on conscious thought have become an integral part of our culture.

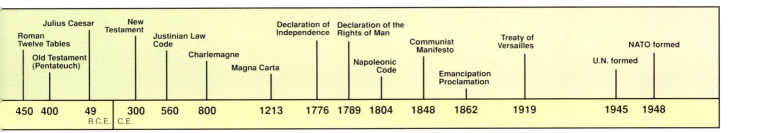

| 450 | 400 | 49 | 300 | 560 | 800 | 1213 | 1776 | 1789 | 1804 | 1848 | 1862 | 1919 | 1945 | 1948 |

One alternative to the brutality of unfettered capitalism is socialism. We've seen that a potentially more humane society was postulated by Karl Marx, who envisioned a "dictatorship of the proletariat." But many experiments with socialism have been tried since Marx developed his theories, with mixed results at best. The big socialist-communist experiments in eastern Europe and Asia during the twentieth century resulted in a stifling of freedom as the price for an economic safety net—not a price that people were willing to pay.

Between the two extremes of rampant capitalism and Marxism, there has been a gradual movement toward democratic socialism, in which capitalism's inherent disregard for the well-being of workers is countered by social safety nets such as unemployment compensation, health care insurance, and retirement programs. The Scandinavians, who have a very positive attitude toward their unions, have developed the most caring social democratic governments. They begin with an objective of everybody participating in the good life, and the government is charged with the responsibility of achieving that end. In the U.S. the attitude is to try to give people a minimum safety net, and then get government out of the way. How to achieve a truly humane society will be a continuing central theme of people and government in the near future. Will a worldwide capitalist society eventually be able to satisfy the needs of the poorest segments of the world? Can we build a society where everybody shares in at least a marginally comfortable level of existence? What do *you* think?

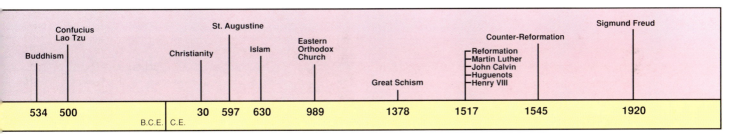

| 534 | 500 | 30 | 597 | 630 | 989 | 1378 | 1517 | 1545 | 1920 |

Another great questioner appeared on the scientific scene in the latter part of the nineteenth century. Charles Darwin was a British naturalist who studied living species and came to some conclusions which are still generating heated debate more than a hundred years after his death. Darwin's theory of evolution holds that all living and past species have evolved over time as a result of a process called natural selection. His theory contradicted scientific beliefs held strongly for thousands of years. Worst of all, it contradicted western religious belief based on the Bible. If human beings are descended from more primitive life forms, what of the story of Adam and Eve? How could people accept this theory and still stay true to their religious beliefs? Yet today, with almost no exception, Darwin's theory of evolution is accepted as fact by the scientific community, and most of the non-scientific world as well. The lesson is that we must be open to new theories, because new theories may prove to be new facts. Firmly and widely held views—even those of historians—are and must be subject to constant reevaluation.

The Arts

Early humans left us the first recorded history in their cave art, which dates from 15,000 to 10,000 B.C.E. Since that time people have continued to express themselves in many ways. In preliterate cultures, the poet preserved and transmitted the beliefs and traditions that gave the culture its sense of identity and purpose. The homeric epics of ancient Greece were probably developed in this way over many generations until they were finally written down. It is no accident that the Greeks represented Homer as being blind, thereby symbolizing not only the poet's inward-directed vision, but also his separation from ordinary men. The Greeks of the Golden Age and continuing in the Hellenic Age cultivated an art form with the objective of showing natural form. In ancient Rome, artists served the state and enjoyed a favored status by glorifying their leaders in poetry, drama and sculpture.

Art	First Cave Paintings	Cretan frescoes			Greek sculpture Gupta art
Literature		Egyptian Hieroglyphics	Epic of Gilgamesh	Homer's Iliad and the Odyssey	Greek Drama Sophocles / Aristophanes
Music				development of early instruments	
	8000	3000	2000	700	300

Much is known about the music of antiquity, although practically none of the music itself has survived. We know that, beginning with the earliest tribal songs and chants, the ancients considered music to be among the highest forms of human endeavor. In fact, music and its emotive power were often considered to be of divine origin. Musical theory, with its close relationship to mathematics, was regarded by the Greeks as a branch of philosophy.

From the beginning of the Middle Ages to the reign of Charlemagne in the 800s, the artistic achievements of classical Greece and Rome were for the most part lost or forgotten in Western Europe. The practice of the arts was kept alive mainly through the efforts of churchmen and Christian scholars. Thus, the arts during this time were primarily concerned with religious themes and motifs.

With the Renaissance came an enormous resurgence of progress in the arts and in the prestige of the artist. Renaissance painters discovered one technical advance after another as they widened the scope of their work to

248

Science and Technology

We have learned in this book about important people and events of the past. But who will be the important people, what will be the major trends of the future? Although we can't predict things to come, we can say with some degree of certainty that instead of generals and warriors, the heroes of the future will be the scientists and engineers who will improve our lives in hundreds of areas, from health to communications.

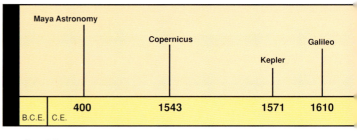

In the sixteenth and seventeenth centuries, Copernicus, Kepler and Galileo shook the establishment by asserting that the universe did not revolve around the earth. This so threatened the religious authorities of the time that Galileo was placed under arrest and forced to publicly retract his claims. But soon the Church found that biblical interpretation could be adapted to incorporate a solar-centered universe, and today it is accepted as fact. What does this say about firmly held views? Clearly as new data comes to light, we must have open minds to weigh against "historical fact" or historical practice. In the modern era, we've actually come to champion those who question traditional thought.

Science really came into its own in the 1700s when it became standard policy for scientists to write and publish papers setting forth their findings. Prestigious scientific societies were established in England and France as forums to discuss the scientific method: the concept that nature follows consistent laws, and that these laws could be determined and tested. This was a major departure from the miracle-oriented views of the medieval world. To Isaac Newton in 1687 goes the distinction of being the first to put together a major *unified* theory. In his *Principia*, surely one of the greatest works of modern science, he explained the laws of motion and gravity. For the most part his theories have stood the test of time.

Perhaps the only giant of the twentieth century to compare with Newton was Albert Einstein, one of the most brilliant and original thinkers of all time. Einstein's scientific reputation was established in 1905, when he published papers on the special theory of relativity, the photoelectric effect, and the theory of Brownian motion (the movement

			Giotto	Da Vinci Michelangelo Raphael	El Greco Caravaggio	Rembrandt	Goya	Monet Van Gogh Manet	Picasso
Roman Poets Horace Virgil	Omar Kayyam "Beowulf"		Dante Boccaccio	Petrarch Chaucer Rabelais	Erasmus Shakespeare Cervantes	Milton	Voltaire Pope Swift	Poe Melville Goethe	Joyce Eliot Hemingway
						Scarlatti Vivaldi	Mozart Bach	Beethoven Wagner	Stravinsky Beatles Jazz
100 B.C.E.	C.E. 1000	1200	1300	1400	1500	1600	1700	1800	1900

include portraiture and landscape painting. The poet Petrarch was crowned with a laurel wreath at a ceremony in Rome, in 1341, thus symbolizing the return to the artistic heights attained by the ancients. Dante's *Divine Comedy* in 1472 was the first work of literature in hundreds of years to be accorded the same degree of honor and respect given to the works of the Classical Age. Today we generally consider the Elizabethan playwright William Shakespeare to be the greatest literary genius of all time.

The immense social upheavals of the late eighteenth century had a tremendous effect on the arts. Symphonic music developed from the small and medium-sized chamber orchestras of the seventeenth century to the huge symphony orchestras we know today. The emphasis on personal freedom and the desire to break free from all limitation gave birth to the Romantic movement, which dominated the arts for almost a hundred years, and led directly to the birth of modern art. Out of the Romantic movement sprang impressionism, expressionism, surrealism, and most of the trends in contemporary art.

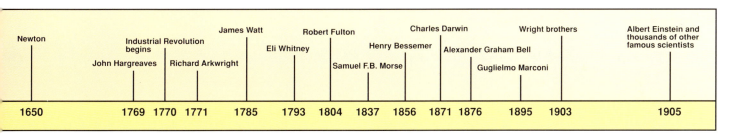

of microscopic particles). His special theory of relativity revolutionized scientific thought by denying the existence of absolute time! It led, along with theoretical and experimental contributions from many other scientists, to the Big Bang Theory. At the time of its publication, many detractors considered the theory of relativity too abstract to be of any practical use. However, the basic premise of Einstein's theory set the stage for the conversion of matter into energy. The first result, unfortunately, was the atomic bomb. More hopeful has been the subsequent use of atomic energy as a source of power. Many in the scientific community expect that safe atomic power will become the major energy source of the future.

Truly, humans have made great progress in fields such as communications, energy, medicine, and space exploration. But science and technology also contribute many new problems for humanity. Social, economic, and political conditions prevent humanity from sharing equally in the benefits of science and technology. Today the technology exists to feed the world, yet many people are still starving. Doctors can save the life of premature babies weighing less than a pound, yet thousands of third-world children die every day from diseases long eliminated in the developed world. We expand our understanding of other planets, but continue damaging our own.

The future of science and technology holds as many questions as it does answers. Perhaps the biggest question of all, one that we must all ponder as we read and watch today's and tomorrow's history unfold, is this: How can we use our knowledge—about history and all other things—to reshape our society so that tomorrow's history is more about human advancement, and less about destruction and war? To that goal we dedicate this book.

Index